Down the Asphalt Path

The Automobile and the American City

Columbia History of Urban Life
Kenneth T. Jackson, GENERAL EDITOR

COLUMBIA HISTORY OF URBAN LIFE

Kenneth T. Jackson, GENERAL EDITOR

DOWN THE ASPHALT PATH

▼ ▼ ▼

The Automobile and the American City

▼ ▼

Clay McShane

▼

NEW YORK
COLUMBIA UNIVERSITY PRESS

Thanks to the *Journal of Urban History* for permission to reprint portions of the author's May 1979 essay, "Transforming the Use of Urban Space: A Look at the Revolution in Street Pavements, 1880–1924."

Columbia University Press
New York   Chichester, West Sussex
Copyright © 1994 Columbia University Press
All rights reserved

Library of Congress Cataloging-in-Publication Data

McShane, Clay.
   Down the asphalt path : American cities and the coming of the
   automobile / Clay McShane.
      p.   cm.—(Columbia history of urban life)
   Inludes index.
ISBN 0–231–08390–4   ISBN 0–231–08391–2 (pbk.)
      1. Automobiles—Social aspects—United States.   2. City and town
life—United States.   3. Sociology, Urban—United States.
I. Title.   II. Series.
HE5623.M35   1994
307.76'0973—dc20   93–17219
                                                        CIP

∞

Printed in the United States of America
c   10   9   8   7   6   5   4   3   2   1
p   10   9   8   7   6   5   4   3   2

For Carolyn

CONTENTS

PREFACE

MY INTEREST IN this topic derives from my earlier book on the suburbanization process in late-nineteenth-century Milwaukee.[1] In my research I came across two items that piqued my interest. In 1878 the State of Wisconsin sponsored a race for primitive steam-powered vehicles on the public roads between Green Bay and Madison, cities about 150 miles apart. Two vehicles finished the race, the winner averaging about 5 miles an hour. Nothing came of this early automobile experiment. Poor rural roads in the U.S. effectively guaranteed that any prototype road-running vehicles would emerge in large cities because their smooth pavements provided the only viable operating surface.

Secondly, a suburban real estate developer in Milwaukee tried to use a small steam engine to replace horses on a street railway line serving his subdivision in 1881. Although a few trial runs proved the economic and mechanical feasibility of the new technology to the new owner's satisfaction, the Milwaukee City Council banned the steam vehicle. It seemed startling that in the 1880s a supposedly technology loving society was willing to ban a new technology for neighborhood interests. Suburban realtors had great influence on the city government, especially because suburbanization was a widely favored public policy. To help the city's expansion Milwaukee's Common Council had granted franchises for street utilities (transportation, electricity, gas, and telephones) readily. Residents of streets on the steamer's route feared high-speed transportation because they worried about both street accidents and the smoke pollution associated with steam power. The City Council followed the wishes of its constituents, rather than the entrepreneurs. Milwaukeeans evidently preferred safe streets to suburbanization.

With a historian's hindsight, these events looked especially odd because both trolley cars and automobiles were waiting around the corner. Were other U.S. cities like Milwaukee in seeking to protect their street environments? Were steam carriages feasible for at least some transportation uses in the 1870s? Could automotive technology have emerged twenty or thirty years before it did in the late 1890s? Did urbanites have the will and power to ban new technologies? Preliminary research suggested that the answer to these questions was yes. American cities, which had the only feasible operating surface for early autos, had long histories of banning their steam-driven predecessors. They allowed only slow, somewhat nonpolluting trolleys and, in a few cities with especially congested populations, elevated railroads. Free-running vehicles on the street, especially if steam-powered, were banned. The bans themselves suggested the feasibility of the technology. Why prohibit something if it doesn't work?

This led to a thesis. Automobile technology emerged in the U.S., not just because of the refinement of internal combustion engines in the late 1890s, but because American urban culture changed. City residents perceived their streets in a different way, thinking of them more as trafficways than open public spaces. The automobile triumphed because it was more than just a form of travel. Rapid acceptance grew, not just out of mechanical superiority, but the motor car's application as a status object and symbol of liberation. The new machines cannot be evaluated just as a technology or another new transportation mode. This work explores not just technology and not just culture, but the two interactively. The technology, as implemented, was largely a social construct.

On the model of Marx's dictum that the windmill produces feudalism and the steam engine produces capitalism, most historians, like most Americans, have tended to view technology as a *deus ex machina*, an inexplicable force appearing from nowhere to work vast changes in a society. For example, since Sam Bass Warner, Jr.'s

Streetcar Suburbs,[2] urban historians have emphasized the impact of technological change on cities. Lately, this simplistic form of technological determinism has come under severe attack from two sources. Present day environmentalists have tended to view technology suspiciously, believing it to be the conscious design of some people or organizations who wish to keep the society from thinking about the long-run impact of innovation. Additionally, economic historians, concerned with the process of economic development, have been unable to explain why some societies are more prone to accept and encourage innovation than others. Other examples of resistance to technology are better known, most notably Japan's prohibition on guns, which lasted more than three hundred years.[3]

A survey of the standard literature on the evolution of the automobile showed the standard form of determinism. To authors such as John B. Rae and James J. Flink, the automobile progressed logically and almost inevitably from the invention of the internal combustion engine.[4] These historians seem to have adopted this simplistic approach from their sources, largely automotive trade journals, which were anxious to claim priority and sagacity for the founders of the industry. The auto innovators, with one notable exception, also did this, at first to protect patent claims, later to stake out a place in history. But, of course, the mere invention of one type of engine did not guarantee the auto's inevitable acceptance as a private carrier. Many other social factors had to coalesce to create the demand for such a vehicle. This work seeks to discuss and evaluate these other factors.

Of necessity, the work is set in large cities. Experts in the somewhat diffuse technical areas that contributed to the innovation of the auto were far more likely to come into contact with one another in large cities. In general, nineteenth-century innovation did tend to take place in cities where such access to technical information was at hand. The early automobile was a luxury item and wealthy Americans tended to live in or near major cities. And, of course, only cities had the smooth pavements and limited access parkways vital to the development and use of frail, prototype vehicles. While autos were developed in some smaller cities, no city with a population under 250,000 lasted very long as an auto producer in the early years of the industry.

Urban transportation policy in the nineteenth century provided regulatory precedents for the motor car. Legal shifts for a kindred transportation mode, the bicycle, proved crucial. Persistent conflict over the transportation uses of streets in nineteenth-century cities had important ramifications for the acceptance of the automobile. John B. Rae's work, *The Road and Car in American Life*,[5] with which I disagree in several places, nonetheless convinced me of another relationship that I had already begun to dabble with. Rae pointed out that road and vehicle transportation technology have always been inextricably intertwined. Improvements in one almost invariably follow closely on the heels of improvements in the other. Extensive use of carriages and wagons required stone pavements: the steam engine was around for a long time before the development of iron rails allowed the creation of railroads; the automobile required smooth pavements. Rae argued that decisions made about roads and streets were the key elements of public policy toward the automobile. The decision of American municipalities in the closing decades of the nineteenth century to adopt asphalt and brick pavements played vital roles in the emergence of the auto. Policy conflict over the regulation of vehicles and the provision of smooth pavements provides the crucial background for automobilization.

The sources and contents of this work follow largely from these ideas. Primarily, I have used engineering periodicals and municipal legal treatises that contained information about street paving and vehicle regulation. John Dillon's *Treatise on the Law of Municipal Corporations* went through five editions before 1920, covering changes in almost every state. The trade periodicals in engineering and related professions contained articles from almost all large cities. Almost every municipal engineer who found himself involved in an important public works project or an unusual administrative set-up, wrote about it for the engineering press. *The Engineering Index,* which I used to lead me to individual articles, included references from local and state engineering periodicals. These periodicals had a national circulation, so smaller, more isolated cities could and did follow the example of their larger competitors, usually with some time lag. Both municipal engineers and city attorneys belonged to networks which wrote for and read these works. My work on Milwaukee, newspaper analysis of New York City, and case studies by other scholars suggest the adequacy of these sources to generalize about urban policy in all cities.[6] The routes taken by large cities "down the asphalt path," explained the automobilizing experience of late-nineteenth and early-twentieth-century America.

The cultural analysis that forms the second half of this work is based largely on New York City and on the *New York Times*. While one should be cautious when basing historical research on New York, and especially on the *Times*, I do not believe that this methodology distorts reality too much when approaching this topic. The prestige connotations of the auto derive from its use by high society in Manhattan. Other Americans followed the automobilization of New York fashionable society in popular periodicals. For example, in 1906 the nationally circulated *Harpers Weekly* enviously noted that 200 New Yorkers owned five or more cars with John Jacob Astor leading the pack with 32.[7] Other New York-based general magazines with national circulations, like *Scribner's*, *Ladies Home Journal*, and *Outing* also followed the doings of the city's motorists. The city's fashionable magazines (e.g., *Town and Country*, *Cosmopolitan*, and *Harpers Bazaar*) helped spread the elite's automobiling style throughout the country. Many early American motorists read *Horseless Age* (later *Motor Age*), also published in New York. *Scientific American*, another prominent New York-based publication, had covered autos since the European experiments of the 1880s.

The auto industry recognized the primacy of the New York market by choosing to introduce new models at the New York auto show, usually held just before the spring buying season. Both *Scientific American* (starting in 1901) and the *Times* (after 1904) published special annual sections covering this show. Industrialists also focussed the long distance trips and tours designed to promote the new technology on New York, the major American media center. European manufacturers, when they investigated the American market, always sent their salespersons to New York City. New York's pattern precedes and resembles those described in case studies of Chicago, Los Angeles, and Atlanta.[8]

The metropolis held the nation's largest concentration of cars, and the *Times* claimed that residents of the Greater New York area owned nearly half the cars registered in the U.S. as late as 1905. It was the site of the first motor vehicle accidents, pedestrian-auto conflicts, and traffic jams. New York built the first limited access suburban roads in the world. As late as 1928, when highway engineers built the world's first cloverleaf intersection in suburban New

Jersey, New York area highway engineers led developments in that discipline. Traffic police, one-way streets, and traffic lights all appeared first in Gotham. The city's dominance of innovation in traffic engineering did not end until the early 1920s. The city's engineering and regulatory style spread across the country through the well known networks of municipal engineers, city planners, and urban reformers.

Using the *Times,* for many purposes an unrepresentative source, does not distort much for this topic. Its coverage of automobility does not seem very different from newspapers elsewhere. New York high society, prominent in the early car culture, used it to record its activities. Nor does the *Times* seem an overwhelmingly pro-auto source. Auto advocates complained that the *Times* opposed automobility because it favored speed limits.[9] Its publishers never encouraged car racing like some of its competitors. Yet the paper still covered races and usually praised the new technology. Basing the analysis on the *Times* allows the use of its uniquely comprehensive index. It is very important to survey at least one daily newspaper in detail, since I would argue that newspapers were the most important printed means of transmitting culture in this society.

I chose 1917 as a cut-off date for somewhat arbitrary reasons. One must stop somewhere. American automobility changed after World War I. The chassis developed for the Liberty truck during the war led to the huge expansion of two complex elements of urban traffic: buses and trolleys. For passenger cars, the battles between Fordism and Sloanism have received adequate coverage elsewhere. To me Sloanist marketing looks like the completion of a process well under way before the war. Technically 1920s engineering refinements like leaded gasoline, four-wheel brakes, safety glass, and all-steel bodies, seem more incremental than fundamental. Another level of government became heavily involved with automobility after the War as most states began road building programs, created the own police, and began to license drivers. I have followed a few issues past 1917 because I did not want to leave readers hanging on such topics as the evolution of traffic signals and emergence of the urban parkway.

ACKNOWLEDGMENTS

ANY AUTHOR ACCUMULATES vast amounts of intellectual, social, and financial debts along the way. I am no exception. Perhaps my most important debt in all three
areas is to my friend and mentor, Professor Stanley
K. Schultz of the University of Wisconsin-Madison.
He had provided me with warm support and the
harsh skepticism the circumstances merited. I was in
such close contact with him while drafting the dissertation on which this book is based that it is often
hard to tell where his ideas leave off and mine begin.
His comments (maledictions?) on my prose have
been of especial value. I was the richer for his ability
to hustle graduate assistantships on my behalf. Professor Joel Tarr of Carnegie-Mellon University, another good friend and *the* guru for studies of urban
technology, has also made a major contribution to
my intellectual development. My colleague at Northeastern, Professor Gerald Herman, has team taught
a course with me on the history of the automobile
for a dozen years. His enormous breadth of vision has
helped transform this work from a narrow urban policy study to a much wider context.

Other scholars have shared their comments on
the manuscript with me, notably Alan Levy of Slippery Rock State University, Robert Fogelson of MIT,
and Coleen Donleavy of the University of Wisconsin-
Madison. Stanley Kutler, also at Wisconsin-Madison, taught me the value of legal sources and how to

use them. Ballard Campbell, Laura Frader, Harvey Green, Donald M. Jacobs, Pat Manning, and Anthony Penna, Northeastern colleagues have given me the benefit of their comments on chapters close to their expertise. I have also learned from comments by students in Pat Manning's methodology course and in my urban history seminar, especially Mark Szmigel. My graduate assistants Bret Abrams, Meg Gourley, and Chris Roberts deserve special thanks, as does my photographer, Tara Herman. All Northeastern historians owe a special debt to Nancy Borromey, who manages the Department so efficiently.

My fellow graduate students at Wisconsin also made a large contribution. Donald Marks listened patiently over many a glass of beer while I spelled out my ideas, rejected the bad ones and helped to refine the good ones. Susan Grigg shared her wit and insight in her comments on several chapters. Andrew J. King offered legal counsel. Margaret Thompson, Edward Hellegers, Douglas Hough, Judy Leavitt, Michael Levine, Joseph Lukonic, Vicki Metzel, Ed Celnicker, Richard Roe, and James B. Smith all made valuable suggestions.

The bulk of the research for this work was done at the State Historical Society of Wisconsin in Madison, at the Library of Congress, and at Northeastern's wonderful new Snell Library, whose interlibrary loan specialists, Yves Yacinthe and John S. McCright, were especially helpful. Other Boston area libraries used include Boston Public Library, the Massachusetts State Library, the MIT Library, Robbins Library in Arlington, and Loeb Library at the Harvard School of Design. Ms. Mary Ellen McCarthy, my mole at Littauer Library, helped me track down some invaluable state government publications. I also used the University of Wisconsin Library, the Carnegie-Mellon Library, the Carnegie Library in Pittsburgh, New York Public Library, the University of Maryland Library, and the Maryland State Archives.

It is customary to praise libraries in the introductions and this work would not have been possible without the collections of these great libraries. I am very concerned that some of them have deteriorated markedly over the last twenty years. The Public Libraries in both Boston and New York are sorely underfunded, hence hard to use. Both are clearly the victims of public policy decisions at the federal level that have left big cities with few choices but to cut budgets. Much harder to explain is the extreme difficulty of using the Library of Congress. In my last two visits in 1991 and 1992, that Library's staff returned more than 40 percent of my book requests stamped "not on shelf." This is a national embarrassment.

Funding for my graduate studies came from the New York State Regents and the Ford Foundation. A pre-doctoral fellowship from the Smithsonian's National Museum of American History allowed me to spend a year doing research in Washington. Other substantial funding, at an especially indigent moment, came from a winning raffle ticket that my mother purchased from the Our Lady of Mt. Carmel Parish (Bronx, N.Y.) Missionary Guild. I revised and expanded this work during my sabbatical leaves at Northeastern and a semester off funded by Northeastern's Research and Scholarship Development Fund.

My family has been unusually supportive, in every sense of the word. Edward F. McShane, my father, communicated some comprehension of urban legal institutions to a non-lawyer son. More important, I acquired a sense of how to live in a city from him. His recurrent attempts to keep the street in front of our home ill-paved during my childhood gave me an important perception of the functions of streets. My brother Peter L. McShane did some research for me in New York City. James A. McShane, another brother and Professor of English at the University of Nebraska, provided an extended and valuable critique. His son Shum spent many hours photocopying early-twentieth-century driver's licenses for me at the Maryland State Archives. My sister-in-law Peggy McShane and my niece Eileen were gracious hosts during research forays to Washington, as was my brother Michael in New York. All three of my children, Kevin, Susan, and Sharon have read drafts, fetched books from libraries, and asked useful questions, including the big one: "Daddy, why do you know all this useless stuff?"

This work is dedicated to my wife, Carolyn, as a token for her love and patience through the last twenty-seven years. This work would not have been possible without her encouragement.

Down the Asphalt Path

The Automobile and the American City

1

URBAN TRAVEL
BEFORE THE TROLLEY

ON MARCH 12, 1840, residents of the Kensington district of
Philadelphia rioted against an attempt to construct a
steam railroad on streets in their neighborhood. The
mob stoned railroad workers (undoubtedly with the
very paving blocks they had been removing), drove
away the city police, tore up the rails and cross ties,
filled in the openings in the street, and replaced the
paving blocks. Contemporary newspapers complained that the rioters were mainly women and children, uncommon participants in Philadelphia's all
too common riots. The press seemed unable to com-
prehend the cause of the riots. After all, railroads
were a symbol of progress and prosperity, vital to the
economic growth of the city.[1]

The railroad might have meant prosperity elsewhere in the city, but it only offered Kensington residents accidents and smoke pollution. The residents
displayed a strong awareness of the reasons behind
American urban planning in the preceding two centuries when they rioted against the destruction of
their street environment. In a sense, they knew William Penn had laid out Philadelphia's broad, gridiron
streets to provide open space for dwellers in densely
built row houses. He planned them to give residents

of his model city ample breathing spaces, playgrounds, and market-places. Railroad rights of way could never be playgrounds or meeting places, so the construction could only make life miserable for Kensington residents and lower the value of their homes. Soot from bituminous coal would make homes and clothing perpetually filthy. Sparks from primitive locomotives posed serious fire hazards in a neighborhood largely constructed from wood.[2]

European town design at the time of the earliest settlements in America had developed from technical and social imperatives of the Middle Ages. Because wars, with their sieges, were recurring events, cities surrounded themselves with high walls. They discouraged or prohibited settlement in suburbs (literally homes under the city wall), which might have offered shelter to an attacking army. As a result, urban land within the walls was at a premium. Cities possessed few open spaces or wide streets, which wasted land more needed for housing. Streets were narrow, wandering, and unpaved. The primitive modes of transportation available did not require a better system. Traffic consisted of foot travel, two-wheeled carts, or pack horses, none of which required wide spaces for passing or turning. Since traffic was light, streets were also used for socializing or markets. The meandering streets of downtown New York and Boston, the two oldest colonial cities, reflect these design considerations.[3]

Preindustrial cities had a different spatial organization from modern cities. Many of them had a large central square fronting on the cathedral or palace of the local prince, as one finds in the Piazza San Marco in Venice. These squares, embryonic versions of the modern central business district, served as open air markets, sites for religious and other meetings, and parade grounds or mustering places for troops. They might also contain administrative offices for the local government. Otherwise, there was little separation of work and residence. Workplaces developed in various sections of the city, and different quarters developed specialized occupational structures.

There was little segregation of poor and rich in preindustrial cities, either. Primitive transportation required all people to live close to their work, so, to the extent that some social segregation existed, it was the reverse of today's pattern. To reduce walking distance to work, residences in the center of the city commanded higher prices, so there might be a concentration of wealthy residents near the central square. Relatively poorer people tended to reside on the outskirts in homes on cheaper land remote from workplaces. One exception to this pattern existed; very wealthy urbanites might maintain weekend or summer residences in the adjoining countryside, especially if travel by water was possible. Such residences enabled the elite to flee the calamitous epidemics which almost invariably attacked overcrowded, unsanitary cities during the summer.

As horse-pulled carriages and wagons improved in the seventeenth and early eighteenth centuries, this pattern began to change. The first enclosed carriage in England appeared in London in approximately 1600, but the development of such vehicles after that date was extremely slow. In the mid-eighteenth century, London attempted to ban carriages in favor of the sedan chair, since carriages presented serious safety problems on the old style streets. Of course, sedan chairs also presented fewer pollution problems. Carters resented the new vehicles. Regulations imposed a stiff annual carriage tax and limited the number of vehicles allowed within the city. Despite this hostile early reaction, carriage and wagon ownership increased. European cities began to protect pedestrians by building raised sidewalks and banning carriages from them. Baroque city planners encouraged carriages. They laid out broad, sweeping boulevards designed to allow greater speed, to facilitate class segregation by isolating neighborhoods, and to make military defense against external or internal opposition easier. Colonists were likely to be familiar with the baroque city plan that Sir Christopher Wren had proposed for London after the great fire of 1666.[4]

There are some indications of increasing traffic. In 1665, Boston widened some of its streets, the beginning of a process still underway. By 1700, Boston and New York had constructed some cobblestone pavements (small rounded stones, about five inches by two inches set end up in a sand base). Pavers found such stones at the bottoms of rivers during the dry summer months. These cities and others also laid gravel pavements, if there was a supply nearby. Charleston and New Orleans paved with crushed seashells. Recurrent bans on encroachments by market stalls reflected some concern with traffic.[5]

Planners designed colonial streets primarily to provide open space, since the only traffic was pedestrians, horseback riders, a few wagons, and carts. In 1674, there was only one carriage in all of New York City and as late as 1761 only eighteen families in Pennsylvania owned carriages. Many municipal ordinances in the late seventeenth and early eighteenth centuries prohibited the galloping of horses, a sign that the number of animals was increasing. These laws required carters and teamsters to walk alongside their horses, rather than drive them in congested areas of cities. The word "teamster," meaning someone who drove a team of horses, first appeared in the English language as a 1777 American usage, according to the *Oxford English Dictionary*, suggesting that heavier wagons were becoming more commonplace. Cities also banned very narrow wheels and heavy loads, both of which destroyed their new street surfaces.[6]

As with all transportation innovations, this increase in the number of vehicles was attributable to improvements in both operating surfaces and the vehicle itself. Lower prices and qualitative improvements in iron allowed cheaper, sturdier vehicles. Wagon manufacturers began to place springs between the axles and body of the carriage, a necessity for a smooth ride. Iron rims on wheels made for greater durability. Englishman Obadiah Elliott patented elliptical springs in 1805, a major design improvement.[7] A number of changes which increased the supply of good streets proceeded hand in hand with these changes in carriage design and were perhaps more important. Americans continued to lay out their cities with broad streets on a gridiron plan suited to carriages. New plans in the late eighteenth and early nineteenth centuries almost invariably adopted this pattern. New York proposed a system of gridiron streets for the unsettled parts of Manhattan. The original street plans for the new cities of the time, Washington, Buffalo, Pittsburgh, and St. Louis, followed a basic gridiron pattern. In many cities, planners built around existing rural roads, which became diagonal, radial roads through the gridiron. Often these radial streets focussed the road system of an entire region. Detroit's 1790 plan had five major radial streets. By 1930 90 percent of Michigan's population lived in towns along these rural feeders. A French civil engineer, Major Pierre Charles L'Enfant, plotted Washington's radial avenues, which he modeled after the latest in Parisian urban design, rather than having them serve as feeders from the countryside. Cities designed later in the nineteenth century, after the coming of the railroad, like Chicago, Milwaukee, or San Francisco, had fewer radial streets.[8]

State governments began to authorize privately owned turnpikes to feed rural traffic into these urban radials in the 1790s, after the Philadelphia-Lancaster Turnpike, chartered in 1792, proved successful. The name derived from British private highways that stretched a spiked spear (or "pike") across their roads on a pivot, so that it could be swung open for tollpayers. The turnpike movement reached its peak in the late 1820s, coincident with the development of the earliest railroads. Private ownership of roads allowed financially weak American states to provide intercity highways. Legislatures granted corporations the right to charge a toll, or user's fee in modern tax jargon, in exchange for construction and maintenance. Graded, paved turnpikes lowered transportation costs by up to 50 percent, creating traffic that the steam railroads would later take over.[9]

The turnpikes and the financial arrangements for their construction had a significant impact on cities, beyond the greater size that increased trade with a hinterland might create. Turnpikes allowed wealthy urbanites to travel more easily to suburban resorts. Indeed, after the coming of the railroad, the only portions of these turnpikes that survived the competition were short suburban sections close to major cities. Some of these turnpikes persisted until the 1890s, levying charges on all suburban traffic along their routes. Municipalities then viewed turnpikes as impediments to development and sought to eliminate them by a variety of stratagems. State legislatures or courts voided their charters on several grounds, especially nonuse. Some cities also adopted the private corporation device to finance ferries, bridge construction, or other public improvements. In 1837 the U.S. Supreme Court sought to limit attempts by private corporations to dominate exclusively these important municipal functions. The Charles River Bridge Case specified a narrow interpretation of their charters. Companies could no longer argue that vaguely worded legislative grants allowed existing firms to block parallel roads or bridges, nor could they claim condemnation damages because new routes damaged their businesses. States would revive the device of independent corporations in the mid twentieth century to build parkways in metropolitan areas.[10]

Just as states sought to improve communications by authorizing gravelled turnpikes, cities sought to improve internal transportation by paving more of their streets—a necessity if cities were to service the growing carriage and wagon trade. Cities began to provide for street cleaning in the late eighteenth century, a sure sign of the presence of both pavements and horses. Since the street sweepings could be sold to farmers for fertilizer, this likely provided a profit for the city. As the wagon and the carriage became more common after 1760, cities also began to realize paving was a necessity for public health, since they could more easily clean horse droppings off paved streets. Accordingly, many cities began major paving programs in the late eighteenth century. By 1800, real estate developers were constructing planned, paved streets in new subdivisions and dedicating them to the public. Cities would later formalize this practice and make the provision of streets a precondition for the official acceptance of any new subdivision.[11]

Like state governments, municipalities lacked the financial resources for an extensive public works program. European cities apparently paid for paving out of the general tax fund, but American cities rarely imposed property taxes before the 1830s. The continental cities also collected very steep vehicle taxes, in order to keep traffic off their narrow, old pedestrian streets. American cities had more adequate street plans and a greater desire to encourage growth; consequently, they charged lower vehicle taxes. Municipalities did place higher taxes on very heavy wagons, and on those with excessively narrow wheels, to preserve pavements, not to limit traffic.

To overcome their fiscal weaknesses, American cities developed a system of special assessments or one-time charges on abutters (those whose property bordered on the street) for improvements. The City of London provided the precedent for this common American practice. After the Great Fire of 1866, it had imposed special assessments on property holders to rebuild the city's drains and pavements. Each abutter paid for the reconstruction of the street in front of his property. New York collected special assessments first, in 1691, when it began a street paving program. It seemed a logical extension of the former policy, which required residents to work on the streets for several days each year. Abutters paid the cost of a street in proportion to their frontage on it. In return, the City usually gave them control over the construction. The City only paved streets after a petition from the holders of a majority of the property front-age, and a majority of all property holders on the street. This created a highly decentralized decision-making system.[12]

The system spread to other cities beginning in the 1760s, coincident with the increase in carriages and the demand for more paving. By the mid-nineteenth century, special assessments had become the prevalent method of paying for streets in all American cities. The exact method varied from place to place. In some cities, abutters only paid two-thirds of the cost, and the city's general fund paid the balance. With few exceptions, the government, rather than abutters, paid for maintenance. The system made large-scale paving programs possible, but special assessments often led to inferior paving. Abutters, while generally concerned with improving transportation and with the lower mortality rate associated with the better drainage and easier cleaning of paved streets, had a variety of other interests at stake. They feared that too much traffic could lower property values. They often sought cheap pavements, regardless of quality, since the city governments, which assumed maintenance costs, would have to pay for repaving. Abutters might also seek very light, flawed pavements to keep heavy traffic off their streets, so they could have the neighborly enjoyment of streets. Such physical impediments were necessary since effective regulation of carriages was nonexistent.[13]

It was on these newly paved streets that the first common carriers for intracity passenger transportation began to appear shortly after 1800. Initially these taxi-like common carriers were hackney coaches (hacks) or the newly developed cabriolet and hansom carriages (cabs). They plied for hire along city streets or stood in wait for customers at public places like docks or inns. Their designers patterned them after private carriages and stagecoaches. High fares limited ridership and the number of vehicles. Customers had to haggle over fares, which typically came to about twenty-five cents a mile. Wealthy urbanites, who desired higher speeds or privacy in their travel, continued to ride hacks throughout the nineteenth century.[14]

In 1826 a French resort operator outside Nantes found that he was deriving more revenue from short-haul passengers on his stagecoaches than from customers riding to his spa. He had serendipitously discovered a new travel mode, the omnibus. The idea spread rapidly to the new world, where Abraham Brower's horses pulled the first omnibus on Broadway, New York City in 1829. Entrepreneurs opened services in most large cities shortly thereafter, mostly the outgrowth of early hackney coach and intercity stagecoach businesses. These twenty-seat vehicles operated on fixed routes at scheduled intervals, picking up anyone who flagged them down and dropping off passengers where they chose. Their drivers typically charged a rider four or five bits (a bit was a 12.5 cent coin), although fares might range from as high as a quarter, to as low as three cents during sporadic price wars. Where hills, heavy ridership, or poor pavements demanded an extra horse to power the 'bus, fares were higher. New York had only 70 omnibuses in 1830, although the number swelled to 350 by 1849, and a peak of 683 in 1854. They carried up to 120,000 passengers daily. By 1858, Philadelphia had 322 omnibuses, descendants of the hourly service from Kensington to the Navy Yard opened in 1833. In 1859, St. Louis had ten different bus routes with headways as low as ten minutes. There were fewer buses in smaller, western cities. Milwaukee, for example, had only four short routes before the Civil War.[15]

The omnibus had severe limits as a transit mode. The rough cobblestone streets of the time limited their speed to five or six miles an hour, not much faster than walking. Thus, they barely expanded the commuting radius. They operated sporadically during the winter since cities did not remove snow from the streets. A few owners substituted sleighs. For most city dwellers, fares were prohibitively high. Riders complained about a lack of comfort. Also, omnibuses always posed a danger. Horses often panicked in traffic, then bit or kicked people. Omnibuses followed a wandering course in the street. Their drivers could not control their horses easily or rapidly brake the top-heavy vehicles on a rough surface, especially when competitors raced each other to pick up a passenger. The omnibus was already on the decline in New York by 1865, but still caused fatal accidents, mostly to pedestrians, at six times the rate per vehicle as the new street railways. There is little indication that these cumbersome vehicles led to any significant changes in urban residential patterns, although a few wealthy individuals did commute on them.

In the absence of adequate ground transportation, ferryboats played an important role in urban travel. In New York, franchises to operate ferries provided a significant part of the municipality's revenues in the colonial period. Philadelphia depended on them exclusively for transportation to its hinterland until the first permanent bridge across the Schuylkill in 1800. Ferries provided the primary means of communication with Camden, N.J. until this century. The development of steam ferry boats explains the rapid growth of Brooklyn and nearby Long Island in the 1820s and 1830s. In 1860, New York had 23 regularly scheduled ferry routes, some on five minute headways. Cornelius Vanderbilt, who later owned the New York Central Railroad, started in the transportation business by operating a sailboat ferry between Staten Island and the Battery. By the 1860s many wealthy business leaders were traveling to their suburban homes on weekends, and especially during the summer, by both steamboat and carriage. This pattern whetted the appetite for a faster means of ground transportation to make healthier, status fulfilling suburban living more available.[16]

Municipal engineers experimented with paving materials in order to improve ground transportation. In the mid-nineteenth century, some vehicle operators suggested iron pavements, but they were too costly and slippery. Hydraulic cement, which American engineers had used extensively in canal building, produced the most interesting of these early experiments. Concrete pavements were smooth and easily drained, but did not provide a good foothold for horses. Moreover, concrete deteriorated rapidly under repeated shocks from iron horseshoes. Concrete might have provided a strong foundation for cobblestone pavements, but once cities had laid utilities like water and sewer pipes under the street, concrete could not be applied. It was very difficult to drill through it to replace substreet utilities until the development of pneumatic drills in the 1880s. There was some antebellum asphalt paving in Europe, but it took American engineers a while to figure out how to make it survive the greater extremes of heat and cold here. Cobblestones and gravel would remain the primary paving materials until the 1890s and cities left most streets unpaved, especially on their outskirts.[17]

One acceptable new form of paving did appear before the Civil War, granite blocks. Cities laid them sparingly because American labor costs made them too expensive to quarry and cut to the proper shape. Only seaports, where ships imported European cut stones as ballast, adopted granite blocks. Thus, New Yorkers called them Belgian blocks. Cost restricted the blocks to the most heavily traveled streets. Granite blocks provided a smoother, more durable operating surface than small, rounded cobblestones. They allowed larger and heavier wagons, but, in the absence of concrete foundations, they were still too rough to allow increased speeds for carriages and omnibuses. Despite municipal limits on weight and tire size, teamsters soon began to buy wagons heavier than even these blocks could bear, lessening their effectiveness and increasing their cost as frequent maintenance became a necessity.

Steam engines provided new forms of urban transit. The earliest railroads operated in Wales in the sixteenth century. They were little more than wooden tracks to provide a smooth surface for the operation of heavy coal wagons. In 1776, they began to replace wood tracks with iron. Before 1825, British engineers constructed several horse-pulled railroads for intercity traffic, more or less a variation on the turnpike boom of the time. Promoters thought steam engines would be too heavy to obtain traction on smooth iron tracks, especially on hills. To the extent that they considered mechanical propulsion, innovators felt that cable or rope pulls on hills, which several of the collieries adopted, might reduce the need for horses. American development was similar. Although there were a few wooden-railed, animal-pulled experimental railways in big cities before 1820, the earliest permanent railways in this country emerged from mining operations in Pennsylvania and Massachusetts in the early 1820s. The mine operators built them to cover short hilly stretches between their diggings and the nearest usable waterway. Horse-powered railways provided relatively easy short-haul travel for bulky products.[18]

Intercity railroads emerged during the turnpike boom of the late 1820s. Projectors realized that two narrow strips of iron would be cheaper to lay than the high-quality gravel roads first developed by the great Scottish road engineer, John MacAdam, or the American designed plank roads. Both required frequent maintenance and replacement. In 1825 the U.S. Congress debated the relative merits of canals, turnpikes, and railroads, all with horses as their primary motive power. Several governmental bodies, including a congressional committee, sought reports on the English experience. Railroads triumphed. In 1827 both the Charleston Railroad and Canal Co. and the Baltimore and Ohio Railroad received charters. Four years later, New York chartered the New York and Harlem River Railroad. These roads were entirely horse-operated at the start and their charters specified a gauge close to the width of most carriage wheels. Legislators apparently anticipated that the rails would serve as a public highway.

Both the Baltimore and the New York railroads entered downtown areas on public streets. Their urban lines reflected an expectation for local ridership. The New York road built its urban section, not on rails, but rather in the form of a stone wheelway with a groove for the railroad wheels. Private carriages of the appropriate width could drive on the flat part of the wheelway. Nineteenth-century street paving manuals drew on this idea of rails for public use. Many of them suggested that cities save money by constructing wide iron or stone wheelways on inexpensive cobble, or gravel streets. However, cities built very few streets in this pattern because of numerous technical problems in their construction. (see illustration 1.1).[19]

European and American railroads soon moved away from this pattern. They discovered that profits were more secure, and operations more efficient, if they became common carriers in the modern sense of the term. They sought to eliminate private traffic from their tracks. First, they adopted construction methods that rendered the tracks useless to all but their own vehicles. They raised and narrowed their tracks and put projecting flanges on the wheels of their own vehicles so that only their carriages could hold to the track. This monopoly was undoubtedly vital in attracting capital for the early railroads. As state governments had turned operating surfaces over to private entrepreneurs in the form of turnpikes, they now turned over control of transportation operation itself, as well as the surface, to private entrepreneurs. The states hoped that a grant of monopoly would hasten completion, accelerating economic development. The adoption of locomotives reinforced the common carrier pattern of railroads. Early steam engines enormously reduced costs per ton-mile, but reached maximum efficiency only if they pulled heavy, long trains, rather than individual vehicles.

Since there was no open land within older cities, early railroads sought downtown access on public streets. Here, they were unable to monopolize traffic. Cities required that they lay tracks flush with the street surface, so that local vehicles, both wagons and omnibuses, could get some of the advantage of running on rails Raised tracks would also block crossing traffic. Undoubtedly flanged wheels on the cars of the railroad company allowed it higher speeds. To limit this competition, railroads (first in New York and New Orleans in the mid 1830s) began to offer local passenger service within cities at low prices, with stops at every corner. Street railways later emerged from these operations.[20]

By 1835, American railroads had switched to steam power, but the very largest cities prohibited them from using steam on downtown streets. Attempts by some of the railroads to run steam engines resulted in riots by residents of the streets on which they ran, notably in New York in 1839, and in the Kensington riots described earlier. City residents objected to steam, both because high speed locomotives made streets dangerous for ordinary purposes, and because they feared boiler explosions, in that day an altogether too common event. Major eastern cities banned locomotives on downtown streets, restricting railroads to horse power. As New York City expanded its frontier of settlement north, it also moved the limit on steam power further and further north, from Fourteenth Street, to Twenty-Sixth Street, then to Forty-Second Street. In the 1870s, the New York Central, fearing another advancement of the line south of which steam was illegal, built a trench in the middle of Park Avenue for its tracks, bridging over every cross street, to guarantee an entrance into the city for its steam locomotives.[21]

The railroads contested such bans on steam power in the courts, claiming that they represented an abuse of municipal police powers. The railroads believed that their state-granted charters and municipal franchises, which did not mention motive power, exempted them from local regulation. However, judges also feared steam power. In 1843, the New York State Supreme Court ruled against the railroads in the most important court test of these bans. The Court opined: "We need no other proof of the fact than what may be derived from our own observation and the experience of the times, that a train of cars impelled by force of steam power through a populous city, may expose the inhabitants, and all who resort there for business or pleasure, to unreasonable perils; so much so that unless conducted with more than human watchfulness, the running of the cars may be regarded as a public nuisance."[22]

Newer cities, obsessed with economic growth, like Atlanta or Chicago, more readily allowed railroads downtown, but eventually forced them onto separate rights of way. Working-class abutters provided the only political opposition to railroads operating in Chicago's streets. Even New York allowed railroads to take over Tenth Avenue for freight traffic, but that was primarily a manufacturing street. Residents referred to the street as "Death Ave." because of its high accident rate. Congress initially allowed tracks and a station on the Mall in Washington D.C., but this line did not run in a residential neighborhood. Ultimately the government forced the railroad to remove its tracks.

The railroads spurred further suburbanization of the upper class. Daily commutation from estates outside the city became possible, because trains traveled faster than omnibuses or stage coaches. The New York and Harlem Railroad offered commuter rail service as early as 1832. Boston probably had more than 2,000 daily rail commuters by 1850. Railroads perceived these daily riders as profitable short-haul business and abetted the habit by offering them low monthly rates, a practice known as *commuting* part of the fare. This, of course, gave rise to the word "commuter." In Massachusetts, the state government encouraged this trend by mandating rebates for such commuters. The rebate was a social welfare measure based on English precedents, which, its proponents believed, would relieve urban housing congestion.

Suburban homes began to spring up within walking distance of railroad stations that were within commuting radius of cities. This trend produced the Main Line suburbs near Philadelphia, so called because they were on the main line of the Pennsylvania Railroad, and other prototypical suburbs like Garden City, New York and Brookline, Massachusetts. Central cities could not annex such discontinuous territory, so the new railroad suburbs established the pattern of suburban political autonomy that became a hallmark of American urbanism.[23] The number of people commuting on these railroads was relatively small. Fares were far too high for most city dwellers, even after commutation. Historian Henry Binford estimates that about 6 percent of the individuals listed in the Boston City Directory commuted from Boston's suburbs in 1850, of whom about one third traveled by railway. Others who desired the new suburban residential style were willing to walk long distances, some more than four miles a day.[24]

Probably the best known suburbanite to take advantage of the new facilities was Henry Thoreau. The transcendentalist picked a site for his mystical ruminations on nature at Walden Pond, a half hour by train from Boston. He built his hut less than 200 yards from the railroad within a short walk of the suburban homes of his commuting literary friends in Concord. Thoreau might complain about modern technology, but he also wanted proximity to Boston's urban amenities.

It was not until the 1850s that municipalities and private entrepreneurs, imitating the successful intraurban traffic on sections of the railroads where cities demanded horse operation, conceived the idea of independent street railways, unrelated to any steam railroad operation. This innovation grew out of a search for faster, cheaper ways to fulfill the new taste for suburban homes. The culture of suburbanization produced the technology, not vice versa. The key technical innovation was the development of grooved rails by Alphonse Loubat in 1852, which allowed rails that were truly flush with the surface of the street. Before then cities had limited rails in streets. While cities would not take advantage of the steam engine, the predominant energy source of the times, and restricted themselves to horse power for local travel needs, the rails did allow them to take advantage of the new iron-based technology to ease transportation. A horse could pull a vehicle at 30 percent higher speed on rails than on the rough pavements of the time and haul twice as many passengers. The superiority of horsecars over omnibuses created a revolution, not only in the traveling patterns, but also in the residential structures of American cities.[25] New York's mayor described the new service as "the greatest invention in the history of man."[26]

New York chartered the first horsecar lines independent of steam railroad connection in 1852. By 1860, New York and Brooklyn already had franchised 143 miles of horsecar lines. Omnibus ridership in New York declined after 1853. It was only after the successful op-

eration of a Boston-Cambridge street railway in 1856 that other urban areas began to adopt the system. Most major cities chartered
their first lines in the late 1850s, and by the time of the Civil War,
the idea had spread as far west as St. Louis and Milwaukee and as
far south as New Orleans.

By 1870, with some minor exceptions, horsecars had completely
driven the omnibus from American cities, notwithstanding the objections by omnibus owners, who unlike their counterparts in some
European cities, had failed to delay the horsecars' introduction.
Some cities did, however, yield to omnibus owners to the extent of
requiring the new street railway companies to buy the old omnibus
horses. Iron rails increased the possible half-hour commuting distance on city streets from about two miles to three miles. Accordingly, horsecars expanded the potential residential area of a city from
12.6 to 28.3 square miles, under ideal geographic conditions. In Boston the proportion of people who commuted from outside the city,
as listed in the City Directory, increased from 6 percent in 1850 to
18 percent in 1860. Horse railways also made downtown more accessible to suburban women, who had been reluctant to walk long
distances on public streets.[27]

Although changes in housing costs and tastes, working hours,
and incomes may have been equally responsible, historians have
credited the horsecar (or, more precisely, iron rails as substitutes for
paving) with creating the first major wave of middle-class suburbanization in American cities. The street railway was a necessary, but
not sufficient, cause of the change. Entrepreneurs only built lines
when they perceived the change in housing taste. Horsecars allowed
the growing number of urbanites, who had the regular hours, steady
employment, and incomes high enough to afford the new style detached houses with yards, to move away from the center of cities.
They moved to the city fringe, thereby accepting a longer commuting
distance to attain better housing. Laborers, who formerly might have
resided in cheap housing at a city's outskirts, a long walk from work,
now tended to live in cheap, densely crowded housing close to the
employment opportunities of the central business district. Often
they took over housing abandoned by the new commuters.[28]

Philadelphia's City Surveyor noted the transition in 1866. While
he still thought of "mechanics and laborers" as living in the suburbs,

he mostly described street railway riders who were wealthier people taking advantage of the residential land now being " . . . brought into the market." He made especial reference to women wealthy enough for horsecars to liberate them for participation in the emerging consumer culture. His remarks justified the easy regulation by which municipal governments encouraged the development of street railway systems:

> Our ladies attended to their shopping and visiting by the cars; the merchant and professional man reach their place of business without fatigue; while the mechanic and labourer, residing at great distances from their work in the suburbs, enjoy the advantages of low rents and free air for their families. The physician, in many cases, has abandoned his own carriage, and with more economy, greater regard for his own health, and with sufficient expedition, now uses the cars for his professional visitations. The capitalist has felt the advantage of railroad routes, in having property, probably long laying idle in the outskirts of the city, brought into the market at remunerative prices.[29]

Municipalities, frequently under pressure from suburban land developers, rapidly franchised the popular new street railway companies. The number of horsecar riders in New York City (and probably elsewhere) tripled in the 1860s. By 1870 New Yorkers took, on the average, 100 rides a year, a measure of the innovation's popularity. Many of the city's more affluent citizens were probably commuting daily and others were making frequent shopping trips, although most residents could not afford to ride, except on special occasions. Lower East Side residents, for example, might take a Sunday outing to distant Central Park. Urbanites saw this technological innovation, rather than better land use policy or housing regulation, as the best solution to the problem of overcrowding. As with the other transportation advances of the nineteenth century, like turnpikes, bridges, or steam railroads, governments left control of a socially desirable innovation almost entirely in private hands. Most Americans believed this would facilitate its most rapid adoption, with a minimum of governmental expenditure and risk. Since municipalities owned streets, their consent was necessary to operate horsecars. Cities applied this power to ensure a rapid development of the suburbs. They imposed only minimal taxation on street railways.

Customarily, a franchise went to a group of suburban realtors who wished to develop their own property. A number of small developer-controlled companies existed in each city, each dominating the routes that led toward its subdivisions. This led to the creation of overly long routes, since promoters might operate horsecar lines at a loss in order to sell their suburban property. Franchises set the fare at five cents, typically half or less than the omnibus fare. Fares did not vary with the distance traveled. Since short-haul inner city travelers paid the same price as longer distance commuters, this fare structure represented a subsidy to the new suburbanites.[30]

Their franchises prohibited horsecar companies from carrying freight, sharing tracks with steam railroads, or switching to steam engines. At the same time, the franchises sought to aid wagon traffic and private carriages by requiring companies to lay their tracks as far apart as the wheels on an ordinary wagon, and to pave the streets on which they ran. The rails had to be laid flush with the street. It was not uncommon in the nineteenth century to see long lines of wagons operating on the railed portions of streets, probably the best paved areas of each city (illustration 1.2). Franchises also obliged horsecar companies to pave the area within their rails and for two or three feet outside them.[31]

In effect, cities granted horsecar companies a monopoly of passenger traffic along certain streets in exchange for the provision of better paving. While the pavements might encourage other traffic, the street railways limited freeloaders on their rails. They devised tracks that technically complied with the law, but discouraged other carriers. The monopoly inherent in having exclusive use of the rails encouraged the spread of horsecars, perhaps as much as their speed advantage over omnibuses. Any carriage owner could enter the omnibus business, so that mode of transportation incurred cutthroat competition and frequent price wars, but street railways promised a secure return for capital. While street railway investments were not absolutely secure, since city councils could franchise competitors on parallel streets, the additional protection that the exclusive right to one street promised undoubtedly explained some of the rapidity with which street railway networks grew across the country.[32]

The street railway did not solve other urban transportation problems. It offered no real improvement moving freight around cities, and even in passenger movement it could serve only a limited part of the demand. Both because abutters on residential streets opposed horsecars and because such streets offered few customers, the street railway operated only on the major radial business streets in each city. While this served and, indeed helped create, the pattern of suburb-central business district travel, it did not serve other needs, notably passengers going crosstown or carrying luggage.

As a common carrier, horsecars also suffered from a lack of privacy. There were frequent complaints about overcrowding and rude behavior by both conductors and passengers. As early as 1870, the novelist William Dean Howells complained about a belligerent Irish drunk on a Boston-Cambridge horsecar. For very wealthy people, carriages and hacks, although slower, remained the preferred modes of travel because of their greater comfort. The great mass of working urbanites could not afford even a five cent fare. For them, walking still remained the major form of transportation.[33]

The horses or mules that powered the new transit system probably provided the greatest limitation to the new technology. Animals were hard to control and caused frequent accidents. The pulling power of a horse was limited, and so was its lifespan. On the average, street railways had to replace horses every four years. In the summer, they rotated teams frequently, since overworked horses often dropped from heat stroke. Street railway companies stationed extra teams of horses at steep hills to help pull the cars up. Horses often died or collapsed en route, delaying both the cars they pulled and those on line behind them. Such delays became a favorite excuse of nineteenth-century schoolchildren to explain lateness. Equine epidemics were a recurring nightmare for street railway owners.

More important, horse transportation had already reached its limits in Manhattan by 1870. Other large cities shortly thereafter expanded to the half-hour commuting limit allowed by horsecars. There was no way to increase the carrying capabilities of cars, since the limiting factor was the strength of horses. Nor could speed be increased. Traffic in rush hours on major streets exceeded capacity in some cities, and more cars could not be added because of the inherent limits of horse speed and power. Pollution was another drawback of horses. Some companies attempted to train their animals to defecate only in their stables since manure could be sold for fertilizer, but most droppings fell in the street where they posed a continual public health problem.[34]

Horsecar-era Americans remained somewhat skeptical of the ability of technology to improve urban environments. Steam power still seemed threatening and improved pavements often had proved a failure. Nevertheless, street railways had provided a faster form of passenger transportation and granite blocks seemed likely to ease freight haulage. Perhaps more important, cities had devised institutional mechanisms to build and operate transportation improvements. In an age that distrusted strong municipal governments, turning internal transportation over to private corporations regulated by franchise grants or charters seemed an ideal way to handle transportation. Paying for pavements by the decentralized process of special assessment probably resulted in the construction of more pavement, but worse ones than even the most corrupt municipal government might have built. It did avoid the specter of strong, centralized municipal governments. American urbanites had already begun the process of seeking technical solutions, privately administered, for the social problems associated with growth and development.

2

THE SEARCH FOR OPEN SPACE: TROLLEYS, PARKS, AND PARKWAYS

CHANGES IN THE spatial patterns of American cities accelerated in the thirty years between 1870 and 1900. Under
the pressure of industrialization American cities grew
incredibly rapidly. The ten largest cities doubled their
population during the thirty years (see table 2.1).
Commerce continued to concentrate in central business districts downtown, as did the new industrial
plants of the era. Thus, downtown sections became
much more crowded and polluted. Population
growth alone would have demanded expansion of residential areas of large cities during this period, but
changes in housing tastes greatly increased expan-
sionist pressures.

In a reaction to industrial growth, middle class
Americans continued to move away from downtown
areas. The increase in heavy industry created environmental problems of air, water, and noise pollution
in central business districts and the nearby residential zone. Industrial growth also created social problems, as waves of alien immigrants arrived in American cities to work in the new factories. Immigrants

tended to live in overcrowded, unhealthy tenements close to down-town employment opportunities. Often, they spoke a foreign tongue. They introduced alien religions and a supposedly alien governmental institution, the political machine. The cultural shocks of migration, discrimination, and poverty tended to create high crime rates in the new ghettos, and a hostility toward outsiders. The middle class fled from these social conditions, as well as the physical problems of pollution and congestion.

Moving to the suburbs represented more than just a flight from the crisis downtown. Industrialism created a new middle class of bureaucrats—a group that had great anxiety about its status and position in society. In a period of great fluidity in society, they de-sired status symbols to differentiate themselves from the working class. To a large extent this new middle class did not earn income from property, as the pre-industrial elite did. They might be profes-sionals, selling skilled personal services, or corporate employees. The status of employees was especially ambiguous since working for someone else had historically implied lower social status. Since the new middle class accepted many of the values of a pre-industrial society, it sought to own homes as a way to show its status. Relatively prestigious, class-segregated neighborhoods presented another way to measure status.

Table 2.1 **POPULATION GROWTH RATES FOR THE TEN LARGEST CITIES, 1870–1900**

City	1870–1880	1880–1890	1890–1900	1870–1900
New York*	31.7%	31.2%	37.1%	156.8%
Chicago	68.3%	118.6%	54.4%	434.8%
Philadelphia	25.7%	23.6%	23.6%	93.1%
St. Louis	12.8%	28.9%	27.3%	84.8%
Boston	30.0%	23.6%	25.1%	123.5%
Baltimore	34.1%	30.7%	17.2%	94.3%
Pittsburgh	68.8%	119.9%	34.8%	274.4%
Buffalo	31.8%	64.8%	37.8%	198.3%
San Francisco	56.3%	27.8%	14.6%	96.6%
Cincinnati	18.0%	16.4%	9.8%	50.9%
Average Growth	37.8%	53.8%	29.0%	106.1%

*Includes Brooklyn.
SOURCE: *U.S. Census.*

Shifting family values also explain part of the change. Historian Robert Fishman finds the root of the suburban ideal in changing family values among London merchants belonging to the expanding evangelical Christian sects of the late eighteenth century. These men aspired to own country estates like the landed gentry. Because of their religious beliefs, they also sought to isolate their wives and children from the evils they associated with urban life. In effect, they tried to keep them captive in a supposedly morally superior country environment. This evangelical double standard gave great moral force to the suburban ideal. It spread rapidly across the Atlantic, where, for a variety of economic and ideological reasons, it had greater impact.[1]

Population growth and this demand for class-segregated suburbs explain only part of the pressure on cities to expand their territory. Traditional row housing might have met the social demands for segregated middle class neighborhoods. Such was the case in continental Europe, where cities grew by adding new rows of homes on their outskirts and the middle class did not cluster exclusively at the edges of cities. Presumably the new American middle class could have opted for this pattern also. Instead their housing taste ran to detached homes on large lots. Many historians have attributed the different housing taste to the rural ethos held by most Americans. Americans believed that social virtue laid in land ownership, with each family secure in its own home, isolated from outsiders. Usually historians trace these cultural values to the eighteenth-century influence of Hector St. John Crevecouer, Thomas Jefferson, and similar thinkers. This reasoning seems hard to accept. If these notions were current in American thought in the eighteenth century, why wasn't their influence felt on housing tastes earlier?

It seems probable that the key reason for the shift to evangelical values in housing tastes came from a series of widely held ideas about health which were peculiar to the United States. Benjamin Rush, the prominent Philadelphia physician of the late eighteenth century, had argued that miasma, a vapor given off by decaying organic material, caused most diseases. Rush based his idea on the distribution of cases during Yellow Fever epidemics. People who lived near swamps or badly drained urban areas were more likely to contract the disease. For example, Philadelphia never had a major Yellow Fever epidemic after it drained nearby swamps. In choosing homes, eighteenth-century urban Americans made the inferences logically drawn from the miasma theory—homes packed closely together with little ventilation and far from vegetation would minimize the danger of miasma entering the home. Some cities even cut down trees within their limits, fearing that they might be giving off miasmatic vapors.[2]

American health theorists of the post Civil War period refined these ideas considerably. Like Rush, they based their notions of causation on observed patterns of disease, but sought more specific causes than Rush's vaguely defined miasma. Discovering that deaths were more likely in densely congested housing and in areas with inadequate sewers, the theorists seized on their knowledge of the respiratory process. They placed the blame on exhaled carbon dioxide in unventilated rooms and sewer gas, an often colorless, odorless gas given off by inadequately flushed plumbing or poorly cleaned privies. Newly discovered antiseptic techniques also suggested a different environmental remedy; light and air could destroy bacteria carried by the carbon dioxide or sewer gas. Therefore, proper ventilation would dilute and remove these disease-causing gases.[3]

Since they believed that the causes of disease were environmental, late-nineteenth-century public health professionals argued that changing the urban environment was the key to lowering the high disease rates of American cities. Physicians and public health departments were among the earliest and staunchest advocates of housing regulation in American cities. Their ideas about health also received wide publicity in the popular press. George Waring, an engineer and perhaps the foremost advocate of sewer gas as a cause of disease, wrote frequently about the evils of bad plumbing and inadequate ventilation in popular, middle-class magazines like the *Atlantic Monthly*. These ideas never received wide currency in Europe, where the medical profession had become more scientifically oriented. It sought biological explanations for disease, rather than the older environmental explanations emphasized in America.[4]

The ramifications of these ideas for housing tastes were obvious. By 1870 Americans perceived crowded, ill-ventilated row houses as a morally, physically, and socially unhealthy environment. The detached lot home answered many health problems. Ventilation from all sides of the house was possible, the better to carry away noxious carbon dioxide or sewer gas odors.[5] It was easier to admit disease-killing light and air into detached-lot homes. Greenery was also vital. Dr. Stephen Smith, New York City's first health commissioner wrote: "The power of trees, when in leaf, to render harmless emanations from the earth has long been an established fact."[6] The yards of the new style homes allowed trees and grass to convert unhealthy carbon dioxide into oxygen. Only after the appearance of these ideas did urban Americans allow the rural ethos and evangelical values to take full hold so that suburban dwellings became the preferred taste in housing.

Prevailing political beliefs prevented nineteenth-century municipalities from directly encouraging the move to the suburbs by anything resembling modern housing policy. Municipally constructed housing was totally out of the question. Nor could cities regulate housing construction to ensure the preservation of open space around new homes. Instead, municipalities moved in two directions in their efforts to develop more open space. First, by an easy franchise policy, they encouraged street railway companies to look for a faster means of propulsion. An increase in transit speeds would throw large amounts of suburban land on the market. Given prevailing housing tastes, subdividers would likely cut this up in a way that provided adequate open space around each home. Secondly, cities began to develop suburban park systems, based on the familiar notion that parks were "the lungs" of the city. Often this process involved donations of land by wealthy suburban real estate speculators, anxious to increase the value of nearby property. Parks, with the green open spaces they provided, gave value to high-density neighborhoods, in a sense substituting for yards around homes. Drives connecting parks also provided high-speed travel arteries for the light carriages owned by some wealthy new suburbanites. This, too, encouraged deconcentration.

Cities looked first for a way to increase transit speeds. The search turned first to steam engines, a familiar power source, and to rails, a familiar operating surface. New York, where population mounted rapidly on narrow Manhattan Island after the Civil War, led the search. City officials believed an elevated railroad provided some advantage over the street-level steam railroads that they had banned previously. Railroads on elevated structures posed no danger to street-level pedestrians, although the smoke and noise problems inherent in steam power remained.

The *Nation* and the *New York Times,* organs that reflected the new middle-class, pro-suburban viewpoint, agitated for technology that could increase travel speeds to the suburbs. Both ignored the adverse environmental impact of steam transit on crowded city streets and pressed strongly for the opening of more suburban land for settlement. Experimentation with the elevateds, popularly called "els," began in the late 1860s. New York City authorized construction of an elaborate system under private auspices in the 1870s. Pressure for their construction also came from real estate interests holding land in upper Manhattan. Suburban real estate groups sponsored the construction of a similar system in Brooklyn in the 1880s, much of it extending to undeveloped land. Residents of streets selected for el construction sought to block them, but initially population pressure was too severe to overcome the lobbying of suburban developers. Middle-class groups and suburban land speculators in other cities, notably Philadelphia, St. Louis, and New Orleans, also proposed els as a solution to overcrowding. Congestion in those cities never reached the crisis dimensions it had attained in New York, so they never granted franchises for these environmental monstrosities. Later, when relatively nonpolluting electric power became possible, Boston, Chicago, and Philadelphia did allow els.[7]

Experiments with light steam engines on street rails also marked the 1880s. Their inventors sought to overcome the fears associated with steam by covering their locomotives with a frame designed to look like an ordinary horsecar, therefore their popular name "dummy engines." They designed the dummies to consume their own smoke or, later, after these proved costly failures, to use relatively clean-burning coke as fuel. These promoters tried to emphasize the safety of the light dummy engines, one even placing a stuffed horse in traces on front of his vehicle to make it further resemble an ordinary horsecar. Once again, the earliest experiments were in New York in the 1860s, but the city banned them after elevated railroads proved a more satisfactory solution to its unique transit problem.[8]

Suburban real estate speculators built dummy lines elsewhere, but, where allowed, the dummies proved expensive to operate. Since cities did restrict them to lightly traveled roads, it is unclear whether they might have proven economically feasible in populated sections of cities. No city allowed them for a long period on the more heavily traveled downtown streets, because of the fear of both accidents and pollution. The relatively densely populated cities of the 1860s and 1870s, with little tradition of suburban living, still placed the values of inner city residents ahead of suburban development.[9]

In 1872 engineer Alexander Halladie found a solution to harnessing steam power on city streets: cable cars. These vehicles operated by gripping an endless cable which a centrally located steam engine pulled through conduits under city streets. This avoided, or rather concentrated, the problem of smoke pollution. The cable also reduced safety hazards. There was no possibility of a boiler explosion on the street and cable car speeds remained relatively low. The speed of the cable limited the maximum speed for any car. Since up to 80 percent of the power of the steam engine was necessary to pull the cable alone, this maximum speed was low. San Francisco limited the first cable cars to ten miles an hour and that became the customary speed in most cities.

Suburban realtors financed most cable car installations. Property holders on San Francisco's hilly Clay Street had subsidized Hallidie's first installation. They sought to increase the value of their land by improving its access to the central part of the city. When developers built the first large-scale system in Chicago in 1883, reports in the street railway trade press emphasized the suburban real estate boom caused by the higher speeds of cable cars.[10]

While the cable car never ran into the legal opposition encountered by elevated railroads, certain limitations of the technology greatly hampered its adoption. Cable installations cost about $100,000 a mile, 40 percent of el costs, but more than ten times as much as horsecars. This limited them to cities which promised very heavy traffic, either because of great population density, or because steep hills hampered walking people and horses. Chicago, with its dense, rapidly growing population, was the main center of cable traction. San Francisco, the other major location for cable cars, also provided dense populations because of its constricted location on a peninsula. Beside, San Francisco's hills were so steep as to be impassable by two horse teams pulling heavy loads. The local horsecar company had stationed extra teams at the foot of hills to help with the ascent, an expensive process. Cable installations in cities that did not meet these prerequisites often resulted in bankruptcy for their promoters.[11]

Trolley cars provided the first commercially and legally feasible solution to the limits that slow horsecar speeds imposed on residential sprawl. The technology of trolleys developed gradually during the 1880s. Frank Julian Sprague installed a system in Richmond in 1887 that was an immediate technical success. Its commercial viability became established a year later. Henry Whitney, a Boston land speculator, and Charles Francis Adams, Jr. (scion of *the* Adams family) built a trolley line to connect their massive suburban landholdings in Brookline with downtown Boston. Reports on the windfall profits Whitney made on his property (he announced in 1891 that the value of Brookline real estate had increased by $17 to $20 million over the previous five years) led to the rapid adoption of trolleys in other cities. Typically, real estate interests led the pressure for their introduction: Trolley cars threw vast additional amounts of land around cities on the market (table 2.2). The first trolleys could speed at twelve miles an hour on city streets. They offered many other advantages over cable cars. Construction costs per mile were one third as much. Power costs were lower, since pushing electricity through a wire required less power than pulling a cable. At their introduction, street railway owners expected that electric operation would cost less than even horse operation.[12]

Electric street railways also overcame the objections that had blocked steam dummies. As with cable cars, electric power confined

Table 2.2 **TRANSIT SPEED AND AVAILABILITY OF SUBURBAN LAND**

Mode	Avg. Speed (mph)	½ hr. Radius (miles)	Land Accessible For Settlement (sq. miles)
Walking	2	1	7.07
Omnibus	4	2	12.26
Horsecar	6	3	28.26
Cable	10	5	78.50
Trolley	12	6	113.86

NOTE: "Land Accessible for Settlement" assumes that there were no geographic obstacles, like hills, rivers and mountains inside the commuting radius. For example, almost half the land within Milwaukee's commuting radius is under Lake Michigan. Trolley speeds more than double above this level in the late 1890s.

SOURCE: Sam Bass Warner, Jr., *Streetcar Suburbs: The Process of Growth in Boston, 1870–1900* (New York: Atheneum, 1973), 17.

pollution to a single power plant and there was no fear that the vehicle itself would explode. Early proponents had feared that cities would ban the overhead wires as potentially dangerous and visually polluting. In practice only New York City and Washington D.C. prohibited them and then only on a few of their downtown streets. The danger of a relatively fast mode of transit on city streets appeared less than in the past. Street railways confined their first electric operations to commercial streets, which already had heavy traffic. The speeds of the early trolley cars seemed safely low, although one racist southerner complained after their introduction in New Orleans: "A great many horses and darkies had panics of fright on the avenue."[13]

Franchises for trolley lines reflected the new municipal priorities that ignored the old environmental constraints to favor the goal of suburbanization. In most cases, the only restrictive clauses in the franchises provided forfeiture of the routes if companies did not complete them within a short time. The franchises also retained the flat five cent fare of the horsecar era. Since trolley cars traveled on far longer routes, this represented an even greater subsidy from short-haul, inner-city riders to longer haul, suburban commuters. The new middle class deemed suburbanization vital; therefore the trolley was "a civilizing influence of great significance."[14]

Street railway policy became a major focus of progressive reformers. Mayors like Hazen Pingree in Detroit, Tom Johnson in Cleveland, and Samuel "Golden Rule" Jones in Toledo, placed low-cost street railways at the heart of their programs for improving cities. They dreamed that lowering fares would end the slums by making suburban living available to all. Johnson felt the social benefits of street railways were so great that they justified fare-free municipal ownership. He described the suburbanizing effects of faster transit speeds: "There was an end of space; an end of the tenement and the slum."[15]

By allowing progressively faster forms of transit to aid decentralization, municipalities had changed the perceptions of many of their citizens about the functions of streets. The now dominant suburbanites lived in detached homes, each on its own lot. They did not perceive the traditional functions of streets as social, economic, and recreational gathering places. Instead, they saw them almost exclusively as thoroughfares whose primary value was for transport. Dangerously high speeds or blighting overhead wires were not a sufficient reason to delay the suburbanite's homeward commute.

Even the higher speed trolley car was unable to serve the many new travel needs of nineteenth-century cities. Franchises almost always prohibited trolley companies from carrying freight, because cities feared that steam railroads might then try to move freight trains through cities on public streets. Even without such a prohibition, any railed system would have been inadequate for urban needs. Heavy freight requires door to door delivery, and there was no way rails could be built to the entrance of every home, business, or factory in a city at a reasonable cost. Also, the farther one went from the downtown area of a city the farther apart the radiating spokes of a street railway system were. As a city expanded, those on the periphery found themselves a longer and longer walk from the nearest trolley line. Few trolley companies offered much crosstown service. Travelers going from downtown terminal to hotel or from terminal to terminal also found it difficult to make appropriate trolley connections, or, where such connections existed, trolleys lacked accommodations to carry luggage. Finally, the trolley offered little privacy or luxury. Horse pulled vehicles or walking still had to satisfy all these other transportation needs.

Cities also encouraged suburban development by engaging in major park acquisition programs during the late nineteenth century. Customarily this involved the development of a large suburban park system with the largest individual park typically around 1,000 acres and five miles from downtown (table 2.2). Planners linked different parks with a series of parkways. Municipalities wanted to be sure that newly developed territory would always have the health-giving, green, open spaces that older sections of the city lacked. Of course these parks also served recreational needs for the new suburbanites, and for inner-city residents who could reach them by private carriage or street railway.

The parks also served a status-fulfilling role. Properly appointed horses and carriages became an increasingly important recreational form for upper-class Americans during the post-Civil War decades. Driving and riding was fun. It also connoted status. Men could display their wealth with expensive carriages and horses. Liveried coachmen and even footmen could take their employers' wives for drives on elite streets or the new park roads. According to nineteenth-century social critic Thorstein Veblen, displaying leisurely wives was an important status symbol in its own right. Like the new suburban homes, carriages enabled wealthy urbanites to imitate rural lifestyles. Carriages especially appealed to the *nouveaux riches,* because they substituted a consumer good for such traditional sources of status as family name or club membership. Thus, Josie Woods, owner of Manhattan's fanciest brothel, owned an expensive customized Victoria with a prize team of matched horses. Her liveried coachman and footmen took her for daily rides on Manhattan's most fashionable drives. Other newly made captains of industry or finance imitated Woods. Recreation historian Foster Rhea Dulles has noted: "Horses were expensive enough to be proof against any alarming tendency towards democratization."[16]

Drives on which the wealthy could promenade their outfits were important parts of the large new parks. By 1890 the largest cities in the U.S. had built, on the average, twenty miles of park drives (table 2.2). Leisurely rides on evenings or weekends became an important part of life for the growing carriage set. Such carriage display also fit into the new class structure of industrial America. These park drives sometimes created routes downtown for the new suburbanites, or high-speed travel between different suburbs. Access to carriage drives became an important promotional device in developing the more fashionable of the new suburbs.[17]

The park movement grew out of the same esthetic tradition of idealizing a rural past that had helped switch middle-class housing tastes to suburban homes on detached lots. It derived from the romantic English landscape architecture of the early nineteenth century. The style emphasized irregular, curvilinear shapes, which supposedly imitated nature. The middle class preferred scenery to nature and, indeed, tended to view nature as scenery. Sir Humphrey Repton, an eighteenth-century English landscape architect, enunciated the basic principle of the new school: "Nature abhors a straight line." The allegedly natural characteristics of the new art appealed to transcendentalist American devotees of a vaguely defined "nature."[18]

Andrew Jackson Downing, America's first landscape architect, introduced these new design concepts in his magazine, the *Horticulturist,* in the 1830s and 1840s. Downing drew on the romantic vision of the Hudson River school of landscape painters. He was also largely responsible for introducing the Victorian architectural taste, which dominated almost all nineteenth-century suburban housing. The new landscape design appeared first on the grounds of private estates and cemeteries in the 1830s. Beginning in the 1850s, it appeared in urban parks and new suburban subdivisions. Downing had led the agitation for Central Park in New York, the best known park in the new romantic style. He also landscaped the Mall in Washington with romantic curvilinear drives, a kind of miniature Central Park. In 1853, his protege, Alexander Davis, designed Llewellyn, New Jersey, the first American suburb planned on the new principles. Its wandering, tree-lined streets and detached lot homes, set well back from traffic, provided a model for later nineteenth century suburbs, which sought to avoid the "tyranny" of a gridiron layout.[19]

Privately owned cemeteries were the first urban open spaces planned in the romantic style. Health reformers, carriage owners, and intellectuals interested in romantic design built the first one, Mt. Auburn Cemetery in Boston in 1831. Other romantic style cemeteries followed soon afterwards, notably Greenwood in Brooklyn and Laurel Hill in Philadelphia. Later, after the Civil War, the idea spread westward to new cemeteries like Spring Grove, Cincinnati, and Forest Home, Milwaukee. Architects designed these "cities of the dead" as resting places from the noise and bustle of the living city. Corporations of lot-holders located them at isolated suburban sites in especially beautiful locations. Customarily their design emphasized vistas from rolling hills. Curving drives provided both access to grave sites and picturesque views. The cemeteries soon became important urban recreation places. As the only landscaped, carefully maintained lands available to the general public, they became popular places for Sunday afternoon picnics and for drives in fashionable carriages. One 1852 lithograph of Greenwood Cemetery in suburban Brooklyn shows more than half the visitors in carriages. Expensive suburban real estate subdivisions soon sprang up around the cemeteries. Their popularity with the new pleasure driving class was so great that some cemetery corporations banned non-lot-holders from them on Sundays.[20]

Actual and aspiring carriage owners began to pressure cities to create parks that would allow similar pleasure drives, without the ghoulish overtones and without the membership restrictions imposed by private cemetery owners. Although antedated by Philadelphia's Fairmount Park and Baltimore's Druid Hill Park, New York's Central Park became the prototype of the new parks. Wealthy carriage owners, who feared that the expansion of the city into midtown Manhattan would deprive them of rustic sites for leisurely carriage drives, led the lobbying for the new park. They first secured approval from the state legislature, fearing that city residents would resent paying taxes for an upper-class pleasure ground.[21] Frederick Law Olmsted and Calvert Vaux, a student of Downing's, won the competition to design the projected park in 1857. The plan followed Downing's romantic prescriptions by stressing an informal layout and picturesque vistas. Olmsted would go on to plan the most important urban parks in the country.

The main feature of the park was a series of drives reserved exclusively for private carriages. Olmsted banned omnibuses, hacks, and street railways from the park drives. To ensure uninterrupted riding Olmsted, himself a carriage lover, restricted this ordinary traffic to underpasses cut through the park. Non-elite riders lacked a view of the park, seeing only high stone walls as they passed through. Nor could passers-by on abutting streets see into the park in most places, because Olmsted isolated it with high walls along most of its periphery. The entire park appears to have been constructed with the end of providing a view from the carriage drives. The other obvious indicator of the upper class uses planned for the park was the prohibitions on all forms of ball-playing, street entertainment, and parades, all mostly lower-class forms of recreation.[22]

The 1863 John Buchanan lithograph (illustration 2.1) obviously exaggerated the drives, a measure of the importance that contemporaries assigned to them. The *Harper's Weekly* lithograph (illustration 2.2) suggests the high status of most carriage riders on the park drives. Walt Whitman caught the flavor of Central Park's carriage set when he described the scene at its Fifth Avenue entrance in 1879: "Private barouches, cabs, coupes and some fine horseflesh— lap dogs, footmen, fashions, foreigners, cockades on hats, crests on [carriage] panels, the full oceanic tide of New York's wealth and gentility."[23]

Real estate speculators learned valuable lessons from Central

Park. The streets adjoining the park, Fifth Avenue and Central Park West, became the fanciest residential locations in New York City. Indeed Tammany Hall, the city's Democratic political machine, wound up supporting the park, not just because it provided jobs for constituents during the 1857 depression, but also because Fernando Wood, the Tammany-controlled mayor, stood to make a windfall profit from real estate holdings near the park. Suburban developers elsewhere learned that parks were a sure fire device to distribute social values across otherwise undifferentiated land. The realtor who attracted a park for his subdivision frequently guaranteed its success. When cities sought to construct new parks, they found themselves in the midst of battles by real estate interests over park location. Subdividers wanted parks and parkways so badly that they often gave land to cities dedicated to that purpose.[24]

Olmsted, who believed in the classic American urban layout of low-density suburbs outside a high-density center, suggested some ways to plan parks to create class segregated residential areas at the outskirts of cities. In conjunction with his work on Prospect Park in Brooklyn, Olmsted developed a new urban, or more properly suburban, street form, the parkway. His report, *Observations on the Progress of Improvements in Street Plans, With Special Reference to the Park-way Proposed to Be Laid Out in Brooklyn* (Brooklyn, 1868), first coined the word "parkway." Olmsted suggested a suburban highway, with bans on wagons and common carriers restricting the roadway to private carriages. He also wanted to prohibit street railways because they contradicted its basic function as an upper class street. Cross streets would only be cut through the new highway at infrequent intervals to minimize interference with carriage traffic. The road included six rows of trees alongside the roadway, essentially making it a narrow, elongated park. Access streets to homes on the parkway would lie outside this strip of park land. The park strip was not just an amenity. It also served the legal purpose of preventing abutters from demanding access to the highway for other vehicles. Common law granted abutters access to all streets, but in this case, they would abut, not on the street itself, but on the narrow strip of city owned park.[25]

Olmsted, in his *Observations on the Progress of Improvements in Street Plans*, saw the new design as revolutionizing the structure of cities. The proposed 250 foot width, including strips of park would prevent the "stagnation of air and excessive deprivation of sunlight."[26] The parkway would foster "the separation of home and work, a trend of this century"(p. 18). Parkways were "for rest, recreation, refreshment and social intercourse. . . . designed with express reference to the pleasure with which they may be used for walking, riding, and the driving of carriages"(p. 18). Olmsted estimated that a parkway would quadruple the value of adjoining property and would be "the centre of a continuous neighborhood of residences of a more than usually open, elegant and healthy character."(p. 23). Such an atmosphere would be particularly suitable for "former country boys who have become wealthy in the city, but desire rural surroundings"(p. 27). Many well-to-do Brooklynites undoubtedly wished to believe in this self-image. Olmsted proposed that homes on the park strip should be "detached villas," with plenty of room behind them for stables (p. 27). Later, in other cities, Olmsted's followers would suggest restrictive covenants in deeds as the logical way of assuring that housing along parkways followed the appropriate pattern.[27]

Olmsted hoped to create and preserve middle- and upper-class suburbia by a massive public works investment in parkways. The prohibition of common carrier traffic assured class segregation, as well as preserving the appropriate "natural" feel. Those who could not afford their own carriages could not visit the newly developed suburbs, let alone buy homes there, unless they walked long distances. New York, ignoring Olmsted's plans for developing Washington Heights in northern Manhattan and the Bronx with parkways, adopted instead the gridiron street plan Olmsted detested, but most developers still preferred. Olmsted's planning style spread rapidly across the country, however, as other cities constructed limited-access parkways to connect large suburban parks or to allow an exclusive route for suburban carriage owners into downtown. The pattern of providing strip parks to limit access became commonplace. Even when park boards allowed access to common carriers or wagons, they paved the roads with thin macadam pavements which were only suitable for light vehicles. The purpose and function of these highways was similar to the Brooklyn original. Some also served the desire of the nineteenth-century middle class for speed, per se, a desire reflected in the beginnings of speed records for both athletes and vehicles.[28] Buffalo went so far as to license drivers to race on one of its Olmsted-designed parkways. Another early development was Grand Boulevard (originally "the Speedway") which Olmsted built between 1878 and 1883 to encircle Detroit.[29]

Almost invariably these parkways became the fanciest residential streets in their cities. When William Glazier wrote *Peculiarities of American Cities,* a travel account of American cities in 1884, he frequently noted the influence of these drives. He described the boulevard where Buffalo licensed racing this way: "Delaware Avenue is the leading street of Buffalo for private residences, and here much of the aristocracy do congregate"(p. 37). Glazier gloried in his rides along such boulevards in other cities as well: "I took one of those long and delightful drives which so exhilarates the blood and gives kind of a champagne sparkle to the mind"(p. 518). When Sylvester Baxter, Secretary of the Boston Metropolitan Park Board, wrote a lengthy report on boulevards and parkways in major cities across the country for *American Architect,* he praised the drives. Of Riverside Drive, New York, he commented that: "It commands prospects of scenery so grand as to deserve the appellation, imperial." In Chicago, he noted that parkways had attracted "palatial residences."[30]

Perhaps the strongest indication of the largely upper-class patronage of these parks and parkways comes from the 1880 Census. Buffalo reported that its two Olmsted designed parks had entertained only 125,000 visitors who had come by foot in 1879, while 700,000 came by carriage and 7,000 on horseback. Brooklyn reported that 1,253,972 people had visited its outlying parks by foot, 2,744,812 in carriages and 36,492 on horseback. Golden Gate Park in San Francisco, which had ten miles of light macadam drives, reported 260,000 carriages (hauling 748,000 people), 35,134 horseback riders, and 826,000 pedestrians. The statistics show that the parks primarily served carriage owners, an affluent group. Street railways could not enter any of these parks, so a visit involved a sometimes lengthy hike for all except members of each city's carriage-owning class.[31]

The park and parkway movement climaxed in the 1890s, coincident with the great wave of suburbanization associated with the spread of the electric trolley car. When Henry Whitney and Charles Francis Adams, Jr. first tried to make their Brookline real estate accessible, they had hired Olmsted to lay out a 200 foot wide boulevard, an elaborate extension of fashionable Beacon Street. A contemporary reported that "the broad, macadamized driveways bordering the tracks of the railway [are] being thronged every day with the equipages of the wealthy," and had attracted beautiful residences alongside them.[32] They overreached—Brookline remained beyond commuting distance from Boston for all but the very opulent. Adams and Whitney sold very few lots until they added a trolley car line. In the absence of fast transit, parkways by themselves could not develop much land, since very few people commuted by carriage.

A parkway, preferably located on a picturesque but otherwise useless strip of property such as a ravine, was the best way to attract wealthy people to a particular piece of accessible suburban land. As with the trolley, real estate developers across the country followed Adams and Whitney's leads on parkways. The municipality that probably built the most parkways for its size was Kansas City, Missouri, which embarked on a late, elaborate parkway system during the 1890s. Charles Francis Adams, Jr. owned much real estate in Kansas City and it may well have been his influence, as well as the chauvinism of a booming western city, which explained the large parkway system there.[33]

Table 2.3 shows the extent of the park and parkway movement. Almost all of the parks and parkways shown for 1916 were in place by 1890. Very few were built in the 1890s because trolleys were the preferred development tool. The climax of the movement, from the viewpoint of traffic segregation and movement, came in New York City and Boston in the late 1890s. Both built parkways several miles long, respectively the Harlem River Speedway and the Charles River Speedway, with even tougher travel restrictions than earlier parkways. Only trotting horses pulling sulkies could drive in the reserved center roadway (illustration 2.3). The Charles River Speedway (now Memorial Drive) developed the modern highway exit, designed to allow the trotters to slow down before joining the main stream of slower traffic (illustration 2.4). Northern Manhattan's Harlem River Speedway, which owed " its existence primarily to the efforts of the lovers of horseflesh,"[34] was carved out of bluffs along the Harlem River from 155th Street to Dyckman Street in 1896–97. New York City spent an estimated $2,250,000 to construct the two mile long road, removing 160 cubic yards of solid rock from the bluffs along the river, and placing a 15,000 cubic yard fill in the river. C. H. McDonald, an expert on building trotting tracks, laid out the drive and built deep concrete-lined trenches on each side to hold decorative trees. Builders rationalized the exclusive speedways by claiming they provided a general recreation, since spectators from the city could sit along the bluffs and watch the many informal races below.[35]

The justifications advanced by harness drivers for the policies excluding slower vehicles can only be called arrogant: "Certainly no personal or class interests are menaced by the present regulations or practices, since the [complaining] aldermen are just as much at

Table 2.3 **PARK ROADS IN MAJOR CITIES, 1890–1916**

City	Park Drives (Miles) 1890	Park Drives (Miles) 1916	Connecting Parkways (miles) 1916	Largest Park (acres) 1916	Miles from City Hall 1916
New York*	47	55	38	1,756	8
Chicago	87	51	63	543	8
Philadelphia	33	50	0	3,526	2
St. Louis	36	34	0	1,380	4
Boston	6	14	32	527	5
Baltimore	19	25	3	674	3
Cleveland	6	43	12	292	5
Buffalo	5	17	15	365	5
San Francisco	17	19	1	1,013	2
Cincinnati	12	20	0	1,000	6
Detroit	20	29	12	707	4
Washington	7	25	0	1,606	2
New Orleans	5	6	0	280	5
Minneapolis	17	26	26	586	3
Kansas City	0	18	21	1,334	9
Total	317	432	223	15,589	
Mean	21.1	28.8	14.8	1,039.3	4.7

*Includes Brooklyn.

SOURCE: Department of the Interior, Bureau of the Census, *Report on the Social Statistics of Cities in the U.S. at the Eleventh Census, 1890* (Washington, D.C.: Government Printing Office, 1895), 88–92; Department of Commerce, Bureau of the Census, *General Statistics of Cities: 1916* (Washington, D.C.: Government Printing Office, 1917), 53.

liberty to ride up the avenue as any other people, so long as they ride in a suitable vehicle. . . . Sense dictates a continuance of present conditions, because they ensure public convenience, comfort and concede a right to a large, if neglected class of rich."[36]

The new projects overstepped the bounds of public opinion. New York City trotting enthusiasts, including such wealthy notables as August Belmont, Frederick Vanderbilt, and Russell Sage, had earlier secured midnight passage of bills in the New York State Legislature authorizing the construction of roadways for trotters in both Riverside Park and Central Park. Neither project ever reached fruition. Working class groups objected to the loss of park land to elite groups. More important, from a political viewpoint, wealthy abutters, who did not mind more sedate driving in both parks, objected to the high-speed trotters and the sometimes raucous crowds they drew.[37] On the third try, the trotting groups selected a more isolated location, but the Harlem River Speedway still drew criticism. A letter to a New York City newspaper complained: "Thus the trotting fraternity, a small but wealthy and powerful class, secured the great public improvement, preempted the river bank and got the exclusive benefit of a vast public expenditure, while the crowded masses of the city cried in vain for sufficient parks, schools, baths and lavatories."[38]

A general demand for a more realistic municipal expenditure policy that gave low priority to Olmsted-style parks, led to a decline in park and parkway construction after the turn of the century. Most urbanites had enough experience with the new parks to realize, for example, that construction of Pelham Bay Park in a remote section of the Bronx was not going to create "a Newport for toilers"[39] as its promoters argued. Rather, the likely result was windfall real estate profits for some and a new resort accessible mostly to those who owned carriages. Many urban political machines had supported parks only to relieve unemployment, and as the depression of the 1890s faded out so did their support of the park movement. Developers no longer pushed as hard for parks, either. They did not loom as importantly as amenities in the age of the trolley, when most new suburban homes had yards.[40]

The end of the nineteenth century parkway movement was ironic. Olmsted style parkways and the speedways had developed all the fundamental elements of modern highway design: limitation of abutter access, restriction to one class of traffic, grade separation, and access/exit ramps. Yet cities stopped building them at precisely the moment that the first automobiles were beginning to appear on their streets.

The parkway movement reflected the most important aspects of the new wave of suburbanization. The new suburbanites idealized both a rural past and the speed and power of the new industrial age. The suburban boom of the 1890s contained many elements of this ambiguity. The high speeds of the trolley made quasi-rural homes on detached lots possible for the middle and upper classes. The parks and parkways represented a desire not only for nature, but also for the exhilarating feeling that high speeds on park drives offered. American cities devoted much more of their space to parks than did their European counterparts.[41] In part, higher incomes may have allowed higher taxes and greater park acquisition, but the design and use of the parks also suggests greater American class anxieties. Parkways served as status addresses to show new wealth. Suburbanites, who were becoming increasingly important politically during the late nineteenth century, learned several important lessons from their experience with parks and electric trolleys. Many came to believe that careful planning could enhance the urban environment, just as carefully planned park systems had enhanced middle-class, suburban life. Secondly, urbanites began to perceive technological advances as potential solutions to pressing social problems. In the future it would be much harder for cities to resist environmentally damaging new technology.

3

ANIMAL POWER, 1870–1900

O N NOVEMBER 9, 1872 Boston's central business district caught fire. The flames burned unchecked for thirty-five hours, destroying 776 buildings on 65 acres valued in excess of $73.5 million. The fire killed only fourteen people, but more than a thousand others saw their jobs go up in smoke. The flames were so intense that iron columns twisted and granite building stones turned to dust. While not as bad as the Chicago fire the previous year, the disaster devastated Boston's economy. Boston's building regulations, water supply, and fire department should have been adequate to prevent the fire. However, the Fire Department could not get its engines to the site of what should have been a localized blaze in time to prevent it from turning into a conflagration. In a rapidly mechanizing society, the fire fighters still hitched horses to their steam-powered pumps to get to fires; and that week almost all the horses in Boston were dead or sick from an equine epidemic, the Great Epizootic. The city had hired day laborers to pull the pumpers, but they were too slow. As a result, the Fire Department actually resorted to blowing up buildings to stop the onrushing flames. For want of a horse the city was lost. The tragedy shows the dependence of nineteenth century cities on animal power and one of the many limitations of that power source.[1]

Unfortunately, there has been no survey of horse transportation in American cities similar to F. M. L. Thompson's excellent essay, "Victorian England: The Horse-drawn Society."[2] Thompson found a great increase in urban herds in traffic in late-nineteenth-century English cities. The kind of pleasure riding described in the previous chapter grew, but more important was the increase in freight pulled by horses and passengers pulled in horsecars. Thompson noted that a vast increase in economic exchanges accompanied industrialization. He pointed out that these extra goods had to be delivered by horse power whenever they went to a recipient not adjacent to the tracks of a railroad. Not surprisingly, the steam railroads tended to own the largest stables of horses in English cities, since they provided local delivery. The number of horses increased as the British economy became larger and more complex.[3]

American steam railroads also increased their freight enormously from nearly 327 million tons in 1880 to more than 640 million tons in 1890. Horse-pulled local deliveries undoubtedly increased proportionately. One commentator wrote in 1872 that "Our dependence on the horse has grown almost *pari passu* with our dependence on steam."[4] Statistics from the latter part of the 1870–1900 period suggest increased traffic, but it seems impossible to get at the exact size of that increase. Contemporaries guessed that New York had 60,000 wagons in 1890 and 65,000 in 1895. Fifth Avenue, New York City, traffic counts showed that 5,460 vehicles traveled past Madison Square in 1885. The number increased to 6,300 in 1896 and 12,608 in 1904, a 120% increase over the nineteen years. Vehicles also became heavier. In 1885 only 9 percent of the vehicles weighed over three tons, but by 1904 21 percent weighed that much. Obviously, increased travel and tonnage demanded bigger horses and larger herds. American teamsters adopted larger, stronger Percheron horses in the 1880s, a sign of greater demand. Increased growth and wealth created much of the increased demand, but also, as more and more residents decamped for new suburbs, the downtown commute generated more and more traffic of all kinds.[5]

The Great Epizootic epidemic of 1872 underlined the significance of the horse in local economies. Editors of the *Nation* commented that "the present epidemic has brought us face to face with the startling fact that the sudden loss of horse labor would totally disorganize our industry and commerce."[6] The epidemic posed massive problems, in addition to Boston's conflagration. Not only did the movement of passengers and freight come to a standstill, but also cities could not even remove dead horses from the streets without other horses to haul them away. The fledgling American Society for the Prevention of Cruelty to Animals (ASPCA) sent Henry Bergh, its president, on tour of major American cities. Bergh urged municipal legislation both to regulate stables and to preserve the health of urban herds. Disease was not the only disaster that disabled horse transport. A horrible fire in the stable of the Second Avenue Street Railway in Manhattan killed most of its horses, disrupting service for weeks. While Bergh was more interested in the humane treatment of animals, he also made the economic arguments developed in the *Nation*, which urged:

> We now see that they [stables and horses] are not simply private property; they are wheels in our great social machine, the stoppage of which means widespread injury to all classes and conditions of persons, injury to commerce, to agriculture, to trade, to social life; and that sanitary inspection of horses and their dwellings during their life is just as necessary as sanitary arrangements for the removal of their bodies after death in every well-regulated municipality.[7]

A wave of stable regulations ensued as cities throughout the country began to exercise their police powers to prevent a recurrence of the epidemic. Business interests, probably led by insurance companies, usually led the drive for "humane" legislation. They could not afford the disruption of business if a stable fire or epidemic slowed freight deliveries or customer travel.[8]

Graph 3.1 indirectly suggests the increase in horse-pulled freight. On the average the number of teamsters increased by 328.4 percent in the ten largest cities during the thirty year period, while population went up only 104.5 percent. Thus, the amount of traffic within these booming cities was growing roughly three times as rapidly as population. By 1900, the first year in which the U.S. Census counted horses by locality, New York County (Manhattan) had over 130,000 horses, more than any other county in the U.S. More than 74,000 horses and mules pulled vehicles in Chicago, 51,000 in Philadelphia, and 32,000 in St. Louis. On average, the largest cities had one horse for every twenty-three people. Hauling freight typically required teams with more than one horse. In heavy hauling, horses worked only four hour shifts, shorter than a teamster's workday. In 1900 there were three horses for every teamster. Likely the number of horses was increasing more rapidly than the number of teamsters.[9]

The numbers are maddeningly sporadic and imprecise. It seems safe to generalize that in the pre-automotive era, large numbers of horses were necessary to move freight within cities; that the size of these herds increased rapidly; and that they posed great problems of cost, pollution, and traffic congestion.[10]

The private costs of the slow and accident-prone horse were most evident. There were public calls for "a cheap mechanical substitute for the horse" as early as 1868.[11] An 1875 study of freight facilities in

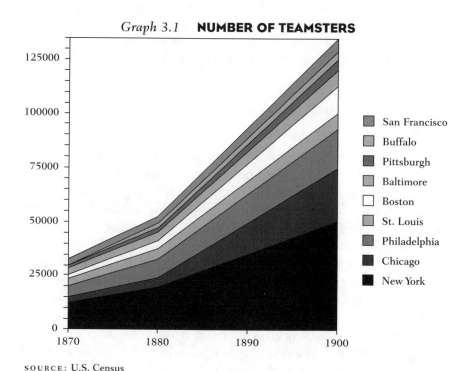

Graph 3.1 **NUMBER OF TEAMSTERS**

Legend:
- San Francisco
- Buffalo
- Pittsburgh
- Baltimore
- Boston
- St. Louis
- Philadelphia
- Chicago
- New York

SOURCE: U.S. Census

New York pointed out that it cost $7.50 a ton to ship freight all the way from New York to Chicago, but that local delivery costs added $5.00 a ton. It cost 22 cents a pound-mile to move freight by horse and wagon within cities in the 1890s, compared to 6 cents a ton-mile by steam railroad. The concept of depreciation accounts first appeared in American businesses with large stables of horses, like railroads. Their owners needed an accounting system that provided for the regular replacement of horses whose average life expectancy was four years. There was reason to worry about costs in the long run also. F. M. L. Thompson estimated that it took five acres of land to provide feed for each horse. Taking this estimate as a measuring device, farmers devoted more than one third of the land in the United States to raising crops to fuel the nation's horses. The dwindling supply of unused agricultural land in the United States may have placed an upward limit on the size of urban herds.[12]

Horses contributed little to private passenger transportation on the streets. Nobody rode horseback to the office. Who would want to arrive smelly in an age that feared the "great unwashed"? Driving to work was very uncommon. Owners could not park horses in the street, because they might run away, be stolen, or kick passers-by. Stabling horses at home and office required expensive urban real estate. Also, a horse required at least a stable hand to care for it, and usually a professional driver. A few wealthy commuters may have had their coachmen (and the U.S. Census showed that they were all men) deliver them to and pick them up for work. More than anything else, cost limited horse use. High prices put horses out of reach for any but the very wealthy for personal transportation. Mid-nineteenth century estimates included $1,200 for a tandem, the least expensive form of carriage, and at least $2,000 for a team of horses.[13] This was higher than the annual income of most engineers and doctors, to cite two upper middle class groups. Photos and lithographs of late nineteenth century streets show very few private carriages, except on the wealthiest streets or in parks.

Private carriage ownership did increase somewhat as urban elites grew. Their vehicles typically could travel as fast as fifteen miles an hour, much faster than delivery wagons. This introduced a new element of danger to urban streets. Increased carriage riding drew some hostile comment. In Charles Dickens's *A Tale of Two Cities*, the carriage powerfully symbolized the evils of the old aristocracy. *Harper's Magazine* serialized the novel, and book publication followed. The best seller appeared in 1859, a time when carriages were just becoming the vogue in both European and American cities. The key event in triggering Madame Defarge's rage, and, by implication, the terror that accompanied the French Revolution, was a carriage accident. A speeding aristocrat, the Marquis St. Evrémonde, brutally ran over a working-class toddler on a crowded urban street. In this episode the carriage symbolized, not just aristocratic affluence, but oppression. Dickens, excessively ironic, later had Sidney Carton travel to the guillotine in a tumbril, formerly an aristocratic equipage.[14]

The setting may have been eighteenth century, but the events are more like the heyday of the carriage in the nineteenth century, more likely to occur in Victorian London or New York than in pre-revolutionary Paris. Dickens acknowledged on the first page that he was writing a parable: "the period was like the present period." Dickens, who distrusted new wealth, and his American readers could easily confuse the evil Marquis St. Evrémonde with contemporary millionaires, whose vehicles were becoming increasingly common on big city streets. Strong class tensions accompanied the nineteenth-century increase in riding and driving. The carriage set had adopted deceptive politics to get their drives, a sign of unpopularity. Note the urchin in illustration 3.1 about to heave a snowball at the horses pulling the obviously wealthy young ladies. Popular hostility may have further limited carriage ownership.

Horse-drawn passenger common carriers had retained a role after the development of street railways, although on a much smaller scale than before. Hacks, forerunners of the modern taxicab, existed to serve a luxury trade, but were few and expensive. Fares ranged upwards from fifty cents a mile with extra charges for more than one person. Table 3.1 shows the relatively small number in operation in major cities.

Omnibuses also retained a role in the late nineteenth century. They shuttled between transportation terminals to serve passengers who could not carry baggage on a streetcar. Some hotels operated omnibus services to draw customers from these terminals. Passengers probably rode omnibuses most extensively on Fifth Avenue in

New York, where residents, for status purposes, had managed to have the city ban less expensive rail-operated common carriers. Omnibus fares remained expensive, typically twenty-five or fifty cents a passenger for relatively short rides. Washington, D.C. had more omnibuses and cabs for its size than any other city, largely because its relatively good paving diminished the speed differential between horsecars and street running vehicles.[15]

A comparison with means of passenger transportation in European cities is revealing. There, as here, cities banned steam dummies. Most Europeans did not emulate the American practice of placing quasi-rural homes on detached lots, lessening demands that could overcome the resistance to street railways. London, which allowed street railways, although not in downtown areas, continued to rely on omnibuses. These carried 115 million passengers in 1875 and 600 million passengers in 1890, long after they had disappeared from almost all American streets. Their survival rested on more than just housing tastes. The key to their success seems to have been the excellent street paving in London, which allowed an omnibus to operate at just about the same speed as a vehicle on rails. Lower European labor costs also made the smaller omnibuses somewhat

Table 3.1 **PUBLIC VEHICLES (HACKS) IN AMERICAN CITIES, 1890**

City	Population	Vehicles	No. of Persons per Vehicle
New York	1,515,301	1,500	1,010
Chicago	1,099,850	1,200	916
Brooklyn	806,343	86	9,976
Baltimore	434,439	350	1,241
San Francisco	298,997	442	676
Buffalo	255,664	94	2,719
New Orleans	242,039	132	1,833
Milwaukee	204,468	222	921
Washington	202,978	480	422
Minneapolis	164,738	100	1,647

NOTE: There was no data for, e.g., several large cities, such as Philadelphia, St. Louis, and Pittsburgh. License fees varied from $3.50 to $5.50, probably not enough to explain the variation in the numbers.

SOURCE: United States Department of the Interior, Census Office, *Report on the Social Statistics of Cities in the United States at the Eleventh Census: 1890* (Washington, D.C.: Government Printing Office, 1895), 43.

more practical. The higher omnibus levels in London and Washington, D.C. suggest again the intimate relationship of pavement and vehicle. Improvements in one went hand in hand with the other.[16]

Horses also created problems of congestion in the late nineteenth century, because a horse and wagon occupied more street space than modern delivery trucks. They also traveled at much lower speeds. Fewer of these long, slow vehicles than today's speedier, smaller cars could create a traffic jam. Downtown streets in most cities did not have the capacity for traffic at the levels shown in Table 3.2. These figures represented hourly averages over a week, and these streets were much more heavily traveled during rush hour peaks. Horses made street blockades worse than modern traffic jams. One early traffic analyst reported that a horse would fall, on the average, every 96 miles it traveled. When a horse actually dropped dead traffic was delayed even more. Sanitation departments took hours, sometimes days, to remove the carcasses. By the 1880s, New York City

Table 3.2 **WEEKLY TRAFFIC VOLUMES, 1885**

City	Location	Vehicles (both ways)	Hourly Average
New York	Broadway, near Pine	7,811	108.5
New York	Fifth Ave. near 25th St.	5,460	75.8
Philadelphia	Broad St. near RR. Depot	6,801	84.5
Philadelphia	Filbert St. near City Hall	5,075	70.5
Chicago	Wabash St. near Lake St.	3,367	50.5
Chicago	Clark St. near Madison St.	4,389	61.0
Boston	Devonshire St. near Post Office	5,362	74.5
Boston	Devonshire St. near Milk St.	4,926	68.4
St. Louis	Locust St. near Beaumont St.	3,247	45.1
New Orleans	Tchoupitoulas St. near Poydras St.	3,477	48.3
Washington	15th St. near Treasury	4,520	64.2
Buffalo	Main St. near Swan St.	2,923	36.3
Louisville	Main St. near Third St.	3,345	46.4
Omaha	Douglas St. near 15th St.	4,752	66.0

SOURCE: Francis V. Greene, "An Account of Some Observations of Street Traffic," *ASCE Trans.* XV (1886), 123–38. Employees of the Barber Asphalt Company made these observations from a second floor office at each site. They did not measure the same week in each city, but the time periods were close together. Weather conditions, pavement type, and street width varied from city to city.

SOURCE: New York City Board of Health, *Annual Reports*, 1875–190.

was removing 15,000 bodies annually. Horses could and did spook in traffic, rearing and tangling harnesses, further slowing traffic. Horses pulling a heavy load had to start slowly, which must have delayed even further the stop and go traffic of crowded streets. This problem became more complex with a team of horses, since all of them had to begin straining at the same time to start the load. The heavy burdens that teamsters often forced their animals to pull complicated matters. ASPCA founder Henry Bergh frequently recounted the story of the teamster who started a fire under a horse's stomach to get it moving with a heavy load.[17]

A motive power with a will of its own presented frightening safety problems. Graph 3.2 shows the soaring fatality rate attributable to the growing horse traffic of late-nineteenth-century Manhattan. Most of the victims were pedestrians, frequently children playing in the street. If illustration 3.2 is an accurate view, some street crossers climbed over wagons, rather than walking between the vehicles, presumably fearing that the horses pulling the wagon behind might kick or bite them. The rate of accidents seems to follow swings in the economic cycle, probably because people took more trips during boom times. When many riders switched from street cars to elevated

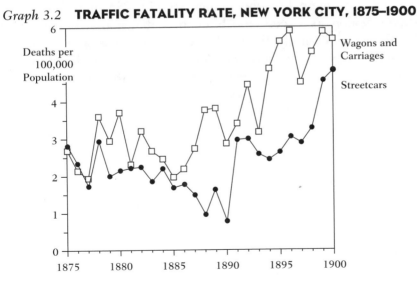

Graph 3.2 **TRAFFIC FATALITY RATE, NEW YORK CITY, 1875–1900**

SOURCE: Annual Reports of the New York City Board of Health

railroads in the 1880s, fatalities declined. When street railways increased speed after electrification in 1890, street railway fatalities increased also, still mostly pedestrians. It took a while for street railways to improve their brakes to cope with the extra speed of mechanical travel. Note that horse-pulled vehicles caused many more deaths, even after the street railways mechanized. This shows the danger of horses. Even at the relatively slow speed at which most traveled, horses caused accidents by biting, kicking, and bolting.

City leaders began to think about public works to ease traffic. As with most transportation problems, New York felt the pressure first. In 1867, the city built a short-lived pedestrian overpass across Broadway. Engineers later suggested widening streets by the construction of elevated iron sidewalks. *Scientific American* demanded such construction because "Streets in the lower part of the city are completely blocked three or four days out of the week."[18] One engineer, writing in 1896, argued that European cities had outdistanced American communities in modernizing their streets. He wanted American cities to make a larger investment in streets, since the lower freight cost in European cities was "enabling their merchants and manufacturers, by lessening the costs of hauling and handling goods within city limits, to control the markets of the world."[19] Lewis Haupt, the noted municipal engineer, suggested in 1889 that Philadelphia should widen its streets and build new diagonal streets to lower freight costs. Similarly, the Public Works Commissioner of Chicago recommended construction of an elevated loop for electric transit around the downtown business district in 1897 to simplify the movement of street-level freight traffic.[20]

Geographical obstacles like hills and rivers also delayed movement. Many cities undertook massive public works to overcome them. The new bridges of the late nineteenth century, like the Brooklyn Bridge and the Eads Bridge in St. Louis, had roadways for vehicular traffic. As with modern highway improvements, levels of traffic soon rose to meet their capacity. Jams ensued at their approaches. Ferry traffic continued to grow between New York and Brooklyn after the completion of the Brooklyn Bridge in 1883, and did not decline appreciably even after construction of the Williamsburg Bridge twenty years later.

Cities also began to regulate traffic. As early as 1866, New York's police had begun to control traffic at major intersections. Many cities had laws limiting wagon size and setting minimum wheel widths, but these seem to have as their object the task of preventing the destruction of street pavements, rather than facilitating traffic. Regulation seems to have become more organized in the 1890s, especially after bicycles began to contribute to the traffic problem. In 1897, at the peak of the bicycle craze, New York passed a comprehensive traffic code, the first in the nation. Trolley cars had the right of way. The ordinance banned the practice of backing carts up to the curb for delivery purposes, and even banned parking for too long periods of time. New York also established an eight mile per hour speed limit for bikes and other vehicles. The city required that they keep to the right, and that their drivers give hand signals before turning. The police expanded traffic control, claiming that they had stationed a six foot tall officer at every intersection on Broadway. New York's cable car company put a worker with red and green flags to direct the traffic in Broadway's Herald Square, a notoriously dangerous intersection, because cable cars had to go through a curve on momentum alone and their drivers were reluctant to brake in the curve. However, New Yorkers ignored the flag wavers, probably because they gave priority to their employer's vehicles. Other cities placed cops on horseback at intersections.[21]

Horse pollution attracted more attention than these safety and mobility issues. One urbanite described city streets as "literally carpeted with a warm, brown matting of comminuted [sic] horse dropping, smelling to heaven and destined in no inconsiderable part to be scattered in fine dust in all directions, laden with countless millions of disease breeding germs."[22] Another wrote: "In hot weather the city stank with the emanations of putrefying organic matter."[23] Each horse within a city daily dropped between ten and twenty pounds of manure, mostly on city streets. (See illustration 3.3.) Frequent urination added to the mess and stench. "Sanitary engineers [knew] that street washings are no improvement in character over ordinary sewage and occasionally the latter liquid may have the advantage."[24]

The horse counts in graph 3.2 show the magnitude of the problem. New York City horses, for example, probably passed between 800,000 and 1,300,000 pounds of manure a day. This totaled over

150,000 *tons* annually that required either public or private removal. Even when it did not land in the street, manure created a major nuisance near stables, which saved the wastes to resell as fertilizer. For example, the Central Park stable, hardly the largest in New York City, had a 30,000 cubic foot pile of manure next to it. Street railways sometimes had five- or six-story barns holding hundreds of horses. They allowed manure to pile up outside them for months. In 1883, a New York City Health Commissioner lost his job when he attempted to ban the piles.[25]

Not only was the manure esthetically unappealing, but it was also very unhealthy. Dust in the air from ground-up manure provided a likely vector for the bacilli that caused respiratory infections, the major killer in big cities. Tetanus posed another threat to public health since manure carried its virus. F. M. L. Thompson suggests that Victorian women may have worn long skirts to protect themselves from street filth, as well as to meet the demands of Victorian prudery. Decaying organic matter on city streets obviously frightened those who saw the "sewer gas" given off by decaying organic matter as a major health problem. These anti-contagionists blamed almost all illness on the mess.

The career of tuberculosis, the leading cause of death in the 1890s, suggests the extent of the problem. Doctors did not have an effective pharmaceutical treatment until the 1940s. Yet, the TB death rate declined significantly as the number of motor cars in cities increased, ending the dust hazard. Other changes, notably better nutrition, lower densities, and stronger public health regulations (quarantine, food regulation, and bans on spitting, for example) helped, but reducing dust was fundamental.

The career of George Waring, New York's famous street cleaning commissioner in the 1890s, illustrates the importance of sanitary reform to the public. Waring's first important project was building the drainage system in Central Park for Vaux and Olmsted. In the postbellum decades, he became the foremost advocate of the anti-contagionist school of public health. He argued that public health administration should properly rest in the hands of engineers who could build proper drainage, sewer, and water supply systems to eliminate "sewer gas." Waring attained national prominence in 1878 when President Hayes sent him to build a sewer system in Memphis, then enduring the most disastrous Yellow Fever epidemic ever suffered by a large U.S. city. Coincident with the sewer construction, the epidemic ended. Mosquitoes are the vector for Yellow Fever, and, although his work had little to do with their disappearance, Waring claimed credit. Confusing correlation with causation, he claimed getting rid of sewer gas had stopped the disease. As a result, his anticontagionist ideas received wide coverage in the contemporary press. He went on to make a substantial fortune as the patentee of several sewer designs and as a consultant to cities on sewer construction over the next twenty years.[26]

In 1894, New York's reform mayor, William Strong, appointed Waring as Street Cleaning Commissioner. He bolstered employee morale through the elimination of political assessments on salaries, the provision of white uniforms, and the creation of a department band. Mechanization and the more efficient management of labor allowed the Department to expand its operations to clean 144 miles of streets daily, compared to only 28 miles under the previous administration. Sweepers now cleaned most streets twice a day, and the more important ones three or even four times daily. Waring also discovered ways to reprocess street sweepings for resale as fertilizer, lowering costs still further. No shrinking violet, Waring ballyhooed a claim (based on fallacious statistical reasoning) that he had saved 60,000 lives because his street cleaning campaign reduced the city's death rate from 28.7 to 21.5 per thousand. He stated that proper street cleaning had reduced eye and ear infections and lowered the incidence of lung disease. Officials in other cities tried scare tactics like Waring's to attract popular support for street cleaning. For example, health officials in Rochester, New York claimed that if all the manure produced in one year by each of that city's horses were gathered in one place, the resulting pile would cover one acre of ground to a height of 175 feet. They claimed that the pile would breed sixteen billion flies, each a potential carrier of germs.[27]

The new public health concepts led to new assertions of municipal powers in the late nineteenth century. City governments had long since abandoned the notion that abutting householders would keep streets clean. City street cleaning departments could no longer announce, as the Kansas City Department did in 1880, that it would clean the streets only when the accumulation of filth became more than three inches thick. In the 1880s and 1890s, municipalities began to take this function away from ward administrators and centralize it, mostly following Waring's plan for a department headed by a civil service appointee, often an engineer. Sometimes they assigned street cleaning duties to the City Engineer's office.[28] Clean streets became the mark of a prosperous city: "Cities with disagreeable, repelling, improperly paved, noisy, and poorly cleaned streets cannot become nor remain successful cities. They cause men who are successful financially and socially to go to more attractive places."[29]

Another, more sanitary, form of animal-powered transportation attained success in the late nineteenth century, the bicycle. A primitive form of bicycle, the "dandy horse," which the rider propelled by pushing his feet along the ground, as with a child's toddle bike, had enjoyed a brief upper class vogue in New York, Boston, and Philadelphia during the winter of 1819. Fashionable gentlemen pushed these contrivances along the floors of dance halls indoors during the winter, but the idea did not last long into the spring. The dandy horse's clumsiness limited the vehicles to a passing fad. Riders could not balance on them on the badly paved streets of the day. One enterprising Philadelphian attempted to overcome this by riding his bike on the much smoother sidewalk, but the local police stopped him. Bans of bicycles soon spread to other cities, and bikes did not appear again until after the Civil War.[30]

French engineers developed a new form of bicycle, the velocipede, which appeared in New York in 1868, and soon spread as far west as Chicago. The velocipede represented a great improvement over the dandy horse. It was entirely metal and had solid rubber wheels, allowing for smoother operation. Pedals located on the hub of the front wheel powered the vehicle. American developers added springs, necessary for a smooth ride on rough American streets. Although primarily a fashionable toy, the early velocipede attracted some attention for practical travel. Boston had 5,000 riders by 1870. *Scientific American* suggested that thirty-foot-long tricycles pedaled by passengers might replace street railways. The velocipede fad also ended rapidly. Again most riders preferred ballrooms to urban streets. Their riders also encountered legal obstacles, most notably when the Central Park Commissioners banned bikes from the park drives.[31]

Biking continued on a small scale over the next twenty years, while entrepreneurs sought to perfect the vehicle. Albert Pope, the foremost American manufacturer of bicycles, first saw a velocipede at the Centennial Exposition in Philadelphia in 1876. He took out U.S. patents on most of the major improvements largely derived from European precedents. He introduced steel frames, which cost less and lasted longer, and brakes. In the 1880s Pope and others refined velocipedes into ordinaries, or high wheelers. The pedal remained directly on the wheel, but the high wheels, sometimes six feet in diameter, allowed faster speeds. This created detrimental side effects, because they made the vehicle less stable and limited the market to people whose legs were long enough to reach the pedal. The number of high wheelers grew gradually in the 1880s, reaching a peak of 100,000 in 1887. The absence of decent paving anywhere but cities confined these bikes to urban areas. Prices for these primitive, but fashionable vehicles were high; they cost about $125 in 1887. Many consumers still preferred to ride them indoors during the winter.[32]

Pope manufactured the first American version of the now familiar "safety" bicycle in 1889. It incorporated several advances over the high wheeler. Designers placed the pedals under the rider for maximum leverage. They introduced pneumatic tires, wire wheels, and ball bearings. The chain and sprocket arrangement which transferred power from pedal to wheels made gears possible. This gave the new bicycles greater hill climbing ability than their predecessors. By 1893 safety bicycles had completely replaced the old velocipedes. Over short distances, on smooth streets, a bicycle could travel twice as fast as a horse and carriage. Prices dropped rapidly as Pope and others began mass production. By 1895, manufacturers had reduced bicycle weight to twenty pounds. Bicycles only cost $100, a price halved three years later at the peak of the craze. In 1896, Americans owned more than four million bicycles.

Women adopted the new fad. Suffragists, like doughty prohibitionist Frances Willard, who learned to ride in her fifties, advocated the bicycle as a socially acceptable form of exercise for women. Traditionalists viewed biking women with some suspicion, since chaperones were usually too old to accompany bicycling parties, liberating them from traditional constraints. Bikers could hardly wear formal Victorian attire, either. Boston's Rescue League, a social purity group, complained that one third of the women that it had "rescued" were bike riders. The old fashioned moralists developed many of the fears that they later applied to women motorists.[33]

Evidently some urbanites commuted by bike in the late nineties, but it would be impossible to estimate the number. Apparently, only one urban traffic count included bicycles. In 1906, several years past the peak of the biking craze, Minneapolis' City Engineer found that bicycles accounted for more than a fifth of downtown traffic, four times as much as cars. Since the count included weekdays, some commuters probably rode them to work.[34] In addition to the problems of bad weather and storage at work, etiquette limited commuting. Accepted office attire, especially for women, precluded commuting by bike and riders worked up an unvictorian sweat. A few businesses like Western Union adopted bicycles for urban delivery. Cities began to mount traffic police on bicycles in the 1890s.

As with other forms of transportation technology, the bicycle existed in a close relationship with the surfaces on which it operated. In the early 1880s many fashionable bicyclists had taken their vehicles to Europe to find smooth surfaces. Great increases in smooth asphalt paving by American cities marked the 1880s and 1890s. Not surprisingly advances in bicycle technology followed on these paving changes. Because no rural area paved roads, bike riding was an almost exclusively urban phenomenon. Albert Pope helped found and contributed strong financial support to the League of American Wheelmen (LAW), the leading bicyclists' association. Both Pope and the LAW participated in the Good Roads movement of the 1890s and its urban counterpart. Pope even endowed the first professorship in highway engineering at MIT. This in turn fostered the increase in asphalt pavements. A few cities even put asphalt strips along one side of granite block streets to aid bicyclists. Although cities provided some smoothly paved streets, technical and social limits on bicycles restricted them. By comparison to Europe, few Americans rode bikes to work.[35]

There can be little doubt that the bicycle and, especially, horse power led to a great upsurge in urban street traffic in the late nineteenth century and especially in the 1890s. Historians have ignored this increase in animal powered vehicles, because it happened at the same time as the more spectacular arrival of the electric trolley and because it is difficult to document. New street traffic would lead to a series of changes in urban street design, in traffic regulation, and even in the definition of a street itself.

4

THE USES AND ABUSES OF STREETS

MAJOR CHANGES IN the technology and administration of streets accompanied the increase in traffic between 1870 and 1900. Cities began to lay asphalt and concrete pavements. They did so not only because of the increase in wagons, carriages, and bicycles, but also because they were easier to clean. The public and legal perception of the function of streets also evolved. The new suburbanites depended on streets for transportation only. Since their detached lot homes had porches and yards, they lost sight of the older functions of streets as places for recreation and social gatherings. The municipal engineers who took over public works administration also defined streets exclusively as arteries for traffic. The *Oxford English Dictionary* traces the first example of "artery" to mean street to an 1890s engineering periodical. This narrow, mechanical definition ignored the older functions of streets. Traffic movement was now the primary goal in street design. Street-using interest groups, like teamsters and bicyclists, fostered policies on streets which aided their vehicles. Traffic, an appropriate street use to suburbanites and these interest groups, seemed an abuse to residents of neighborhoods that valued streets for social discourse.

The evolution of pavements began immediately after the Civil War. Engineers introduced two new paving types, wood blocks and properly designed macadam pavements, as alternatives to inferior gravel and cobblestone pavements. Engineers designed these new pavements to serve the peculiar needs of horse-drawn travel. Cities also expanded the area surfaced with granite blocks, adding them to many more heavily trafficked streets. Macadam pavements dated to the English turnpikes of the early nineteenth century and appeared first in the U.S. during the turnpike boom of the 1820s. Yet, most streets that Americans called "macadam" probably bore little resemblance to the original.

Proper macadam pavements depended on alternating levels of stones of varying sizes meeting a detailed set of specifications. The older pavements often utilized gravel that was too large, too small, or not laid to sufficient thickness. High American wages made it prohibitively expensive to crush rock by hand. Engineers could only reduce high American labor costs after the adoption of blasting powder to break stone to the proper sizes. Steam rollers, a mid-nineteenth- century invention, provided an inexpensive way to compress them properly. This pavement provided a surface smooth enough for easy traction, yet rough enough to give a horse a foothold. Heavy wagons rapidly rutted macadam streets, so macadam had the additional feature of restricting traffic to light vehicles, mostly the pleasure carriages of the well-to-do.

Frederick Law Olmsted and Calvert Vaux laid out the first technically correct macadam pavements in the U.S. in Central Park in 1858. After the Civil War, E. P. North, Purveyor of Water for New York City (a job similar to that performed by municipal engineers elsewhere), laid a large amount of macadam pavement on the streets and boulevards favored by carriage riders in northern Manhattan. As other cities professionalized their public works departments, the new municipal engineers insisted on proper macadam specifications, like those in New York. They laid macadam primarily on suburban streets and parkways. While Graph 4.1 shows only a relatively small increase in macadam between 1880 and 1900, it seems likely that many cities inaccurately listed gravel streets as macadam in 1880.[1]

New construction of public works in the 1865–1873 period encouraged the development of another new form of paving, wooden blocks. Samuel Nicholson, the superintendent of a plank road turnpike in the Boston area, patented the most common type of wood pavement in 1858. Nicholson wood blocks offered the same foothold characteristics as a cobblestone or block pavement. The caulk on a horse's shoe could fit the wide crevices between each block. In addition, wood muffled the sound of iron horseshoes pounding on the street, a sound that some contemporaries thought damaged the nervous system. Since manufacturers could cut wood blocks to a uniform shape with a flat surface and the blocks wore more evenly than stone, wood blocks provided a smoother surface for rolling wheels than stone blocks or cobblestones. Nicholson's patent specified a plank foundation, which seemed to ensure a smoother, more stable surface.

Wood pavements lacked durability, but Nicholson claimed to have solved that problem by treating the blocks with creosote oil.

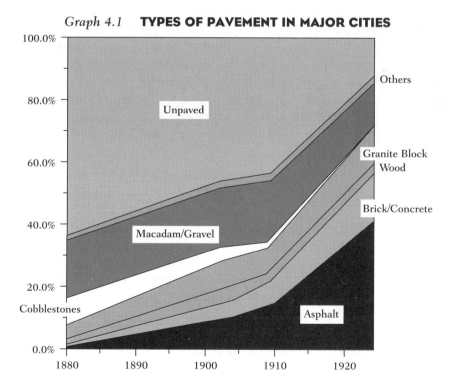

Graph 4.1 **TYPES OF PAVEMENT IN MAJOR CITIES**

He asserted that this process would prevent rot and deterioration for up to fifteen years. Wood blocks were also easy to repair. When one block had worn excessively, a worker could simply remove it and nail another one in its place. Nicholson pavements seemed highly successful when first installed, especially in western cities like Chicago and Detroit, which could obtain timber cheaply. Many cities invested heavily in wood blocks, usually at an exorbitant cost, since Nicholson's patents increased the price of the pavement greatly. Wood block suppliers often bribed city officials.

A series of disastrous failures in the early 1870s ended the wood block craze in almost all major cities. Contemporaries attributed the rapid spread of the Chicago fire of 1871 to the fact that the city had paved with wooden blocks soaked in highly flammable creosote oil. Streets acted to spread the fire, rather than serving as a fire break. Washington, D.C.'s "Boss" Alexander Shepard paved streets in the District with Nicholson blocks. The streets disintegrated within five years of their original construction. The District spent the next twenty years paying off bonds for pavements that no longer existed. The scandal was directly responsible for the loss of home rule by the District in 1878. In New York, William Marcy ("Boss") Tweed also had made a heavy investment in the disastrous pavements, although it was only a small part of his grander larcenies. Other cities across the country repeated this experience. Only Chicago and Detroit continued to pave with wood blocks to a large extent after these scandals. Some municipalities continued to lay wood block pavements in front of hospitals, where quiet was important, until the 1920s. Low initial cost seemed more important to their citizens than the high repair costs and possible hazards.

More important, engineers introduced asphalt pavements and concrete foundations in the postwar period. Concrete shattered under repeated blows from ironclad hoofs. It could, however, withstand weight better than any material of such low cost. So concrete became the foundation for many block pavements. Engineers usually covered the concrete with asphalt, a better wearing surface. Since cities laid concrete almost exclusively as a foundation, it does not show up in any of the statistical studies of pavements. Most street paving manuals written after 1885 recommended it in no uncertain terms. European cities had adopted concrete much earlier than that date, but Americans only began to produce durable Portland cements after that date. The development of the pneumatic drill, which made it possible to reach sub-street utilities buried under the concrete, helped.

Asphalt, which was second only to macadam as an urban paving type by 1900, was the most important new paving material. In 1871, E. J. DeSmedt, a Belgian chemist with asphalt paving experience in Europe, laid the first asphalt street in this country in Newark. Washington, D.C. became the first city to apply asphalt to any great extent after Congress turned management of the District over to the Army Corps of Engineers in 1878. DeSmedt became Inspector of Pavements for the District and supervised the highly publicized and successful replacement of the Nicholson blocks that Boss Shepard had laid on Pennsylvania Avenue. This installation convinced many cities that asphalt would work. While Washington and Buffalo probably switched to the new pavement most extensively, other cities, including San Francisco, New York and Philadelphia, began to lay asphalt to replace outdated cobblestone pavements.

Although asphalt remained the most costly type of pavement, advances in the asphalt industry between 1870 and 1900 considerably reduced its price. American investors began to import from the asphalt lake that Sir Walter Raleigh had discovered on the island of Trinidad in the sixteenth century. Research into the chemistry of asphalts made possible reliable, long lasting pavements. By 1900 advances in asphalt chemistry allowed the production of artificial asphalts, which were much cheaper and more predictable than the imported material. Asphalt firms also developed techniques to lay the new pavements by machine, avoiding the high labor costs associated with the various kinds of block pavements.

Accidental, or even inspired, technological innovation had little to do with the great increase in the quantity of paved streets in the late nineteenth century. European cities had introduced new paving techniques and materials long before American cities adopted them. Both Portland cement and good macadam pavements existed in Europe forty years earlier than they did in the U.S. Asphalt followed this pattern. Henry W. Halleck, later a well known Civil War general, had reported on the possibilities of asphalt pavements as early as 1841. Yet its adoption awaited DeSmedt's arrival in the United States thirty years later. Although the asphalt deposits on the island of Trinidad had been available for centuries, circumstances peculiar to the United States delayed its application.

American economic conditions differed from Europe: labor costs were higher, wood more readily available, the climate more prone to the freeze/thaw process that damaged pavements, and cities less well financed. Yet, the delays in deploying new street paving technologies seem to go beyond these factors. Changes in the administration of streets and in the official interpretation of the function of streets explain the adoption of smooth pavements better than technological innovation.

The administration of American street paving grew out of the traditional street uses of a pre-industrial city, where walking was the dominant means of transportation. Travel was only one form of communication for which urbanites used streets. As we have seen, they functioned also as meeting places for many activities. Open air markets met in the streets to perform a variety of economic needs. The first stock market in New York City met under a tree on Wall Street. Municipalities often looked the other way when entrepreneurs built market stalls in the roadway. Peddlers with hand- or horse- pulled carts became a familiar part of the nineteenth-century street scene. Urban residents did not go out to shop; rather the shops came to them. Homes lacked the refrigeration needed to store food. This necessitated daily shopping. Urban residents typically bought food and some dry goods from vendors who plied their neighborhoods in push carts. For residents of nineteenth-century row housing, streets served the sorts of purposes that yards fill for today's detached suburban homes. Each house obtained light and fresh air through streets.[2]

Observers have always commented on such uses of streets for social purposes in densely populated areas. Perhaps the best descriptions of the way in which inner city residents valued streets were in the massive social surveys of London that Charles Booth compiled in the 1890s. Booth noted that the "poor" gathered in the streets Sunday afternoons to drink, play cards, dance, and promenade.[3] The United States was no different. In fact, such street uses have continued in American cities in areas of high density. Jane Jacobs's influential book, *Death and Life of Great American Cities*, is a paean to the old style street. Jacobs claimed that in areas where such non-traffic street uses survive, they provide safer neighborhoods with a more viable local economy and healthier social life. According to her, children learn adult social roles more easily when social life for both adults and children occurs in the streets. David Nasaw, in *Children of the City at Work and Play* also found the streets a viable socializing environment for children in early-twentieth-century New York.[4] Presumably such benefits also derived from nineteenth-century street life, although urban reformers of that day believed that the street provided a bad environment for children. They were learning the wrong values (from the reformers' perspective) from the wrong people.

Nineteenth-century street administration reflected this view of streets. Paving was left entirely in the hands of abutters, who decided when, how, and by whom their streets should be paved. No city ever attempted to pay for streets by taxing vehicles that ran over them. Abutters rather than travelers were the primary beneficiaries of streets; therefore they paid for street improvements. The special assessment system developed earlier prevailed. The only function of the city was perhaps to provide engineering advice and, more importantly, coercive and borrowing power. When a majority of the abutters (or rather those holding a majority of the front footage) along a street decided to pave it, they would hold a block meeting to decide the type of paving. Then, they would petition the city or the ward's city councilor to solicit bids for a paving contract. The city would divide costs among the abutters in proportion to their front footage and enforce this special assessment against any minority owners who objected. The city also guaranteed payment to the builders. In some cities the contractor who laid the streets had to collect directly from the abutters, although with recourse to the municipal government for collection in case of default. More commonly, the city paid the contractor, then collected the special assessment either in a lump sum or in ten or twenty annual payments from the property-holding residents of the street. Such policies not only conformed with the perceived benefits from the street, but also fit in nicely with the decentralized, democratic ideals of Jacksonian American politics.[5]

The street systems that emerged from this form of private planning reinforced the social uses of streets. Residential areas in American cities usually had relatively wide streets, the better to function as playground and meeting place. A wide street symbolized wealth and health, since it provided additional light and air. Such wide streets might have helped traffic, but the system included precautions against this. Abutters kept the roadway relatively narrow and sidewalks wide. Some streets had "parking," a strip of land which was part of the street but rested between sidewalk and home. Residents might plant this strip but supposedly could not build on it. Cities only rarely enforced prohibitions against traffic impeding encroachments on sidewalks and streets, like market stalls. Americans built cities with gridiron plans that slowed traffic, but aided abutters. The gridiron made property values predictable, provided the maximum number of lots with street frontage and allowed square lots suited to the house building techniques of the time. Right angle street systems slowed radial traffic. Because the gridiron ignored topography, it often required steep grades, another impediment to traffic. Municipalities did not coordinate subdivision street plans, so traffic-calming gaps or jogs in gridiron thoroughfares were common.[6]

Abutters applied their control of street pavements to hamper traffic still further. They neglected pavements. As late as 1890 half the mileage of streets in major American cities remained unpaved. Abutters in residential areas almost invariably ordered the cheapest and least durable forms of paving they could find, typically gravel or cobblestones. Still another anti-traffic feature of the system was the requirement that the city or ward government pay for all maintenance or repairs out of general funds. Given the financial stringencies of most cities, this ensured rough streets safe from dangerous traffic in most residential areas. Most residents probably felt, as Lewis Mumford has noted, that pavements were for the rich and their horses, not for the average citizen.[7]

Some streets did evolve specialized traffic functions. Abutters in warehouse or industrial areas could and did provide heavy granite block pavements for wagons.[8] In carriage riding areas of a city, residents might order a macadam pavement, as for example, on one fashionable Baltimore street in 1856: "About 18 months since a number of enterprising residents of East Baltimore Street took active measures for the entire repaving of that frequented thoroughfare from Bond to Chapel Streets' which resulted in the structure of a fine, substantial and smooth bed, well graded for heavy rains, and proving a capital road, especially for light vehicles."[9]

In the post-Civil War period this began to change slowly. Not only did cities become larger, but increasingly, residential growth came in new suburban territories, with detached homes serviced by the new horse-operated street railways. Public attitudes toward municipal government changed also. In an age of large-scale industrialization, the democratic, decentralized principles of the Jacksonian period seemed outdated. References to cities as "machines" (interestingly enough this was also the name applied to the new, immigrant-based urban political organizations of the day) or as organisms appeared.[10] City governments started massive public improvements like bridges, railroads, and landfills to foster growth. The new sanitarian movement demanded increased municipal activity to improve public health. This, too, required increased public works expenditures to grade and drain streets, to provide sewers, and to offer a decent water supply.

A new attitude toward the purpose of streets also appeared. More and more urbanites came to view streets as arteries for transportation. Ease of travel rather than increased light and air for abutters became the justification for wide streets for suburbanites and some commercial interests. It is hard to imagine a pre-Civil War urbanite glorifying "progress" when he wrote about city streets as engineer Lewis Haupt did in 1877: "It may safely be assumed that facility of communication is one of the most potent elements of human progression and development, hence any obstacle to mobility, however small, becomes a bar to progress and ought to be removed."[11]

Other engineers also wrote of "easing tractive resistance" as the primary goal in paving design. Building smooth streets over which a wheel might roll more easily helped transportation. This bore little relation to the traditional goals in pavement design—drainage, cheapness, and a good foothold for horses. Nicholson claimed that his wood blocks would reduce wear and tear on horses and wagons by fifty percent. This suggests that he was aware of the new values encouraging mobility. As might be expected, New York City led the search for better pavements, experimenting with a variety of designs during and after the war. Gotham laid the first good macadam pavements, perfected the design of granite blocks, and experimented extensively with wood blocks.

New York City's size, density, and location on a narrow island created the worst street-related problems. In 1866, the city established the first modern Board of Health. While primarily concerned with the prevention of disease, at least two of its activities also eased street travel. The Board ordered encroachments removed from the streets and centralized control of street cleaning. The 1876 American Society of Civil Engineers' report to the city on transit recommended widening certain streets to improve traffic movement. Around this time, the city removed the trees bordering Broadway as traffic obstructions. In 1871, Philadelphians formed the Citizen's Association for the Improvement of the Streets and Roads of Philadelphia to lobby for better paved and cleaned streets. Concerns with traffic also mounted in Boston because of narrow streets and in Chicago, because of railroad grade crossings. As we have seen, both cities experienced massive fires in the early 1870s. Both cities widened some traffic-congested streets in the burned-over areas, but abutters successfully blocked most proposals.[12]

Americans also began to realize the need for proper street drainage. The gridiron plan, which ignored normal drainage patterns, had created many flooding problems in American cities. Buildings often blocked normal patterns and streets became the alternate way to drain urban land. Faulty drainage could cause flash floods, construction problems due to swampy soil, and epidemics (caused by insects breeding in stagnant pools of water). When Chicago became aware of the need for better drainage in the 1850s, it paved and raised the grade level of almost all its downtown streets. This costly process also required jacking every building in the central business district up to the new grade. After the war, cities increased their efforts to grade streets properly. Municipal engineers wanted to solve the public health problems that the new sanitarian movement had traced to faulty drainage.[13]

Streets also became the focus of several public services unrelated to travel. The new public health boards intensified pressures for water supply and sewers, the two oldest of street-associated utilities. These utilities depended on properly graded streets. Uneven surfaces made the construction of subterranean pipes difficult and imposed obstacles to the free flow of water or wastes through them. Perhaps most important, street railways refused to build on improperly graded streets. They feared having to rebuild their tracks if municipal engineers ordered a grade change. The wave of street improvements in the postwar years served to make these added utilities available, as much as to aid horse-pulled carriages and wagons.

In the ten years following the Civil War, cities also began some road improvements designed to foster deconcentration. New York spent $40 million developing streets and utilities for the largely unsettled area around Central Park. Chicago began major programs to drain and improve land on its outskirts. Radial streets also helped develop suburban land. Frederick Law Olmsted projected a series of "railroad avenues" to serve newly developed areas of the Bronx. Boston built Commonwealth Avenue as a feeder into the newly developed Back Bay. That new neighborhood had the widest streets in downtown Boston. In 1868, suburban communities in northern New Jersey jointly planned the Hudson County Boulevard. The bridges, parks, and parkways discussed earlier were a part of the same effort of encouraging suburbanization through public works.[14]

Policies toward new suburban areas began to change also. Previously, cities had refused to accept control of new streets unless improved. Now they began to ease control over subdivisions. For example, San Francisco in 1880 accepted the dedication of unpaved streets in new subdivisions. The city began to pay part of the street construction cost and to collect the balance through special assessments after settlement. Apparently the goal was to lower the cost of developing suburban land. The widespread annexations following the Civil War reflected the same goal. A central city could provide streets and street based utilities more rapidly than could an isolated suburb. Cities eased the restrictions on developers, usually accepting streets as easements, with little concern for their conforming with any street plan that the city already had or with grading or paving. This shifted much of the burden of suburban land improvements from developer to settler. Early suburbanites often discovered, to their dismay, that they had to pay repeated assessments for necessities like grading, curbs, sewers, and water supply. Later they paid again for other urban amenities like lights and pavements. Dividing and deferring expenses this way lowered development costs. Since developers profited significantly from these new policies, it seems likely that they greased the wheels of policy change.[15]

The policy of massive public works expenditures to encourage suburbanization encountered a temporary setback in the early 1870s because of scandals in public works spending, especially in New York City, and because of the panic of 1873, which ended the great postwar real estate boom in cities and triggered a national urban fiscal crisis. Most American cities had spent money lavishly for a variety of public improvements during the boom years. Almost uniformly, municipalities spent the public works money poorly. Contemporary engineering and administrative skills were inadequate. Many cities spent wildly for streets and street-associated utilities in projected suburbs, some of which would not receive settlers until long after the crash. Beside, machine governments often designed these works inadequately, requiring their complete reconstruction. Less corrupt governments also made major errors in design, since there was a lack of competent municipal engineers to supervise public works expenditures.[16]

The shenanigans of the Tweed ring in New York and of Boss Alexander Shepard in the District of Columbia illustrated the failures of the new public improvements policies. William Marcy Tweed occupied the post of Deputy Street Commissioner for New York City from 1863 to 1870. In practice, he dominated the department as the base for his political machine.[17] In his first four years in office, Tweed increased expenditures from $650,000 to more than $2 million. More important, he increased its payroll fourfold, frankly trading jobs for votes and, ultimately, for control of the city. The city's commercial and mercantile elite went along with Tweed, since they perceived the need for suburban expansion and better paved streets.[18]

Tweed overspent wildly, not just to line his pockets, but also to supply his followers with jobs. He also made many errors in judgment. His proposed rapid transit system involved extensive street widening and grading throughout Manhattan and called for placing the trains on forty foot high stone viaducts over the new streets. Tweed's biographer estimated its cost at $50 to $65 million, ten times the necessary amount. He spent more than $10 million a square mile to make street improvements in unsettled areas in the middle of Manhattan. When the city's growth slowed after the panic, much of this land remained unsettled. After the panic some abutters found themselves paying special assessments greater than the actual value of their property.[19]

In Washington, D.C., Alexander Shepard, a real estate developer whom President Grant appointed governor of the District in 1871, built a similar political machine. To counter the 1873 depression Shepard expanded public works appropriations. By shrewd manipulation of the jobs created, he managed to control the District's elective Council, especially its black members. Like some of Tweed's wealthy supporters, Shepard needed street and street utility improvements to make his suburban real estate accessible. Bad judgment about the means of improvement and about the city's future growth created a major scandal. Only three cities, all in the Midwest where timber was cheap, laid more miles of wood blocks than Washington, where, as we have noted, the wood rotted within five years. Shepard also made serious engineering mistakes in grading streets and laying sewers. In one case a lateral sewer, when completed, was ten feet lower than the main sewer into which it was supposed to drain. Shepard apparently assumed that ultimately the federal government would pick up the tab and, as a result, spent wildly. At one point he left the District government without money to pay its employees. After his regime, the District's indebtedness was higher than all but seven states. Bad engineering completely wasted one $5 million bond issue for street improvements.[20]

Other cities went through similar scandals, although on a smaller scale. Suburban Elizabeth, N.J. almost went bankrupt after 1873, and some developers there discovered that special assessments for unsold lots were higher than their market value. Cleveland and Newark also had major scandals over the Nicholson block pavements.[21]

The wave of overspending by American cities had severe repercussions on their administration and their politics over the next twenty years. While American urbanites still wanted to encourage suburbanization, the fear of mismanagement slowed expenditures on public improvements in most cities until the 1890s. In a few cities where machines controlled government during the 1873 depression they continued to spend money on public works to relieve unemployment in the mid-1870s.[22]

The structural reformers who emerged in the wake of machine misgovernment in the 1860s and 1870s seem to have acted more in reaction to machine rule than with any clearly specified goals of their own. They primarily cared about changes in the governmental form of cities and reducing municipal expenditures. James F. Bryce's best-selling *American Commonwealth* was perhaps the leading expression of these ideas. William F. Havemeyer, who took over New York's government following the fall of the Tweed Ring, provided an early example of this type of reform. Havemeyer's policy of vetoing street improvement bills (he vetoed 250 of them in three months in 1874) greatly hamstrung the growth of New York City. Grover Cleveland made his political reputation as mayor of Buffalo in 1882 by vetoing street cleaning contracts. During his term as mayor of Brooklyn, from 1882 to 1885, reformer Seth Low built a reputation on slashing expenditures and reducing taxes. There were many examples of similar mayors elsewhere.[23]

St. Louis's prominent municipal engineer, Robert Moore, summarized the ambiguities in the new movement nicely in the May 6, 1876, *Engineering News*. Some structural reformers wanted public improvements to encourage suburbanization. Moore noted that roads and streets were a measure of civilization and by that standard America, especially St. Louis, was less civilized than Europe. Still, to avoid costly municipal expenditures, Moore demanded controls on spending—controls that could only reduce the funds available for street pavements. His statement showed the negative side of the reform movement. Rather than suggesting some system of priorities to build improvements within financial constraints, he attacked all spending:

> We can plead in common with all American cities that the democratic form of our government, while it answers well enough for the state and nation, is not a good form of government for a city, at least without very decided modifications. . . . Our taxes are not levied, as they ought to be, by those who pay them, but are voted by those who pay nothing, and whose only interest in them is, after they are raised to divert as much as possible into their own

pockets. Our revenues are squandered in jobs. They are treated as a sort of poor fund for the relief of American beggars.[24]

In short, this reform movement emphasized reducing expenditures as the primary goal of municipal government. Many reformers agreed with Moore's longing for a return to a property suffrage. They wanted government dominated by taxpayers, although they admitted that there was no politically feasible way to attain that goal. They actively sought charter reforms designed to reduce expenditures. Some states had already imposed debt limits on their cities in reaction to bad investments in railroads before the Civil War. In the 1870s state legislatures extended such limits to restrict spending on internal urban improvements as well. The reformers also sought charter amendments limiting tax rates. For the first time, limits began to appear on special assessments. Municipalities could not assess property for more than half its value, an attempt to eliminate the overexpansion of services into undeveloped suburban areas.[25]

In local government structural reformers emphasized a variety of programs to foster efficient management. They reasoned that when Jacksonian politics diffused power among a variety of municipal agencies with popularly elected heads and gave ward governments important independent powers, it had made city governments too complex. The machine governments triumphed because they knew how to manipulate decentralized neighborhood needs to create policies for the entire city. The answer to this was to create a more centralized government headed by a mayor with veto powers, and staffed by a bureaucracy protected from popular control by civil service. Reformers like Carl Schurz cited municipal engineers as the leading example of a group who needed protection from political influences. They were among the earliest civil servants protected by the new laws.[26]

It is not correct, however, to describe the goal of this style of reform as just making municipal government more centralized and efficient. Many reforms begun in the name of making government less expensive actually served to disperse power still further. Reformers often belonged to political parties that were more powerful on the state than municipal level. In such cases they welcomed a greater assertion of state authority in local affairs. Usually this took place through frequent charter amendment, although occasionally states

took over municipal functions directly. Metropolitan boards to operate traditionally urban services were another form of assertion of
state power. Most of the metropolitan boards that states created held
responsibilities for parks or for utilities vital for suburban expansion.
New York briefly had one such board to control the city's police,
which allowed the state Republican party, a minority within the city,
plenty of patronage jobs.[27]

The boards under state or metropolitan control were mostly a
postwar phenomenon, although there was an older tradition of administrative boards within cities to deal with special issues like public health and education. In the reaction to machine governments,
reformers extended such boards to areas dealing with public expenditures. Since nineteenth-century cities often spent half their budgets on public improvements, reformers placed that function under
board control. Taxation and administration of the public debt were
two other areas that operated under board administration in most
cities.[28]

Reformers hoped that the boards would ensure the ability of a
conservative minority of taxpayers to veto expenditures. The terms
of board members overlapped those of the council or mayor that
selected them. Often new, restrictive charters required that both
political parties have representatives on the board. Sometimes at
least one board member had to have professional qualifications. For
example, statutes required that at least one banker sit on boards of
public debt. Additionally, civil service rules protected employees of
these boards. Some reformers suggested the District of Columbia
government as a model. After Washington lost home rule because
of the Shepard scandals, Congress turned its government over to a
Presidentially appointed board, which had to include one officer
from the Army Corps of Engineers. In practice, the Corps ran the
city. Local residents lacked any participation in the government.[29]

When the reformers strengthened the powers of mayors, created
administrative boards, and welcomed state intervention into local
affairs, they created a hydra-headed government that often had trouble functioning. Political machines did not disappear. Only they
could provide the informal kind of centralization needed to make
such a formally decentralized system work. The system did not necessarily reduce expenditures in the long run, although most cities

cut back spending for a few years after creating administrative boards. Civil servants did not object to spending *per se*. Engineers, for example, welcomed public works expenditures, which increased their power and responsibility. During the 1880s builders laid more miles of asphalt streets in Washington than any other city; the engineer-dominated District government encouraged and authorized the improvements. Other interest groups later came to dominate the boards. Suburban realtors, for example, sought appointment to boards of public improvements which built new streets or extended utilities.[30]

Reduced expenditures and changes in governmental structures were not the only results of the new conservatism that was affecting the nature and quality of urban streets. Since the new boards were reluctant to spend money, special assessments remained the principal way to finance streets. Although the boards had the authority to centralize control over streets, they did not exercise it at first. Abutter control seemed contrary to the structural reformers' concept of efficiency through centralization, but it also appealed to the part of their ideology that demanded taxpayer regulation of expenditures. While the public improvement boards could impose limits on the abutters' power, in practice they rarely challenged the old, decentralized way of doing business, except for occasionally tightening controls on street design. State legislatures and courts even extended the power of abutters over their streets during this time. In reaction to the new street uses and expenditures, legal theory extended the old form of abutter control to the new utilities.

These new governing bodies first increased controls over the pavement itself. Most state courts forbade cities to lay patented pavements. The reasoning was that when a city asked for bids to pave a street, as the law required, and specified a patented pavement, it actually bypassed the bidding process, since only one contractor might hold the patent right. High patent and promotional costs had doubled the cost of the old Nicholson wood block pavements. The courts hoped to prevent such expense. In doing so they protected abutters from excessive prices and assured them of options in choosing pavements. But the rulings also restricted the spread of new, smoother pavements, since patents covered many advances in brick and asphalt pavements. The restriction operated, in practice, to reinforce the traditional social values of streets by postponing the construction of smooth pavements necessary for extensive traffic.[31]

In the *Elevated Railroad Cases* of 1883, the New York State Court of Appeals introduced another form of protection for abutters. When the municipal government held the street in fee simple, the law had defined abutters' rights only as access to streets. An elevated railroad greatly damaged the value of an abutter's property without denying access. The physical structure of the elevated railroads cut off the streets from light and air, which contemporary public health beliefs described as "the great natural disinfectants," necessary for physical well-being. The trains themselves were noisy, smoky, and unsightly. Residents found it hard to resort to their streets for recreational or business purposes. By denying these street customs, the environmental monstrosities greatly depreciated adjoining property.[32]

The Court of Appeals forced the els to pay damages by extending the abutters' rights to include "light, air and access." If New York City had held only an easement in the streets, this ruling would not have been unusual, since abutters would still have held air and subsurface rights. In practice the court converted the municipal holding of streets from fee simple to easements as the law defined streets in most recently built suburban areas and in western cities. This concept reinforced neighborhood control of streets. Reformer John F. Dillon, author of the pioneering work *Treatise on the Law of Municipal Corporations,* described municipal holdings in streets, as "equitable easements in fee," in the new, 1890 edition of his treatise. This new legal definition gave abutters control over some forms of travel in the street. As with the new public improvement boards, when the conflicting reform ideas of centralization and taxpayer control clashed, local property rights triumphed. The legal doctrine in the *Elevated Railroad Cases* enabled residents to hamper new transportation modes that might turn their streets into highways. Significantly, New York City allowed no new steam-powered el lines in the crowded sections of Manhattan after 1883.[33]

Other states attained the same end by legislative enactments, rather than judicial decision. They began to require frontage consents for the construction of street railways. They passed such laws to extend abutter control where municipalities held the streets in fee simple. For example, the Illinois Legislature required in 1872 that street or elevated railways must obtain the consent of abutters holding of the front footage along their routes. Downtown Chicago residents complained in 1883 that transit companies were using consents from the suburban portions of projected routes to outvote them and destroy their enjoyment of the street. The Legislature responded by requiring that elevated and street railroads must have the consent, not only of most of the front footage owners for its entire route, but also most owners for each mile of street. This further protected inner city residents who were more likely to value streets for nontravel purposes. Other cities also followed these procedures.[34]

These new protective devices slowed the spread of smooth paving and rail transit. Still, American cities had longer, wider, and better paved streets than European cities of comparable size.[35] Most urban Americans continued to believe in policies to encourage suburbanization; street railway franchises had few restrictions and cities continued to build parks and parkways. The new rules on frontage consents delayed the spread of elevateds from New York City and Brooklyn. They did not delay the construction of street railways, a less threatening mode. Streetcar companies merely purchased frontage consents, in effect paying some damages to residents of the streets on which they operated. Abutters might collect damages from street railways, but only rarely could they enjoin their construction.[36]

Although els encountered vehement opposition, proposals for their construction occurred in many cities. Interestingly, John F. Dillon, an exponent of the power of abutters to block el construction, held stock in a company that projected an el line in St. Louis. Dillon's company blithely ignored his published legal views. Its prospectus argued: " The great cities of the world have been made illustrious by great public works. . . . The lofty destiny of a metropolis cannot be baffled by individuality, nor can measures of enterprise, initiated to promote its growth and advancement, be defeated by an opposition resting on a city lot or its uses."[37]

The contrast with public policy on streets and transportation in European cities illustrates the basic desire of Americans for suburbanization. In the U.S. legal restrictions on transportation were relatively short lived. In Europe, municipal governments retained exclusive control of street paving and there was no system of special assessments. This helped street running vehicles like cabs, private carriages, omnibuses, and wagons, but the municipalities did little to encourage suburbanization. Parisian administrators actively discouraged street railways by imposing high fares and prohibiting their construction outside the city fortifications. The administrators feared that suburbs would complicate defense of the capital in case of invasion. Similar motives probably explain the relatively small street railway system in Berlin. Such military concerns may also have explained the smooth paving in both cities. During the Second Empire, Baron Haussmann widened Paris's streets and laid the first asphalt, apparently for defense purposes. Armies could mobilize faster on better streets. Revolutionary urban mobs found it harder to build barricades from asphalt than granite blocks or cobblestones.[38]

The English experience resembled the continent's. London allowed abutters to delay the introduction of electric trolleys, but had excellent street paving. Social rather than military policy dictated this. British sanitarians demanded easily cleaned asphalt pavements and sometimes widened streets to eliminate slums. Urban geographer David Ward notes that many British reformers did advocate lower density suburban housing and a widespread street railway network, especially in the provincial cities, but complex economic reasons caused British suburbanization to lag behind American. The old taste for row housing lingered. Abutters could and did block transit improvements.[39]

J. W. Bazalgette, an important British civil engineer, frankly justified crowded tenement housing as good public policy in an argument unlikely for Americans:

> The condition of the few who can afford to live in well-built mansions, each as his separate castle leaves but little to be desired; but for the masses of the population who occupy smaller establishments, and more especially for the poorer classes, larger homes, laid out in separate tenements appear to offer many advantages. The streets of a city in which such houses prevail will be shorter, and the cost of maintenance and cleansing therefore less, than when the population is spread in smaller dwellings over a greater surface. The working classes are, moreover, thus brought into closer contact with their employers.[40]

The wave of suburbanization and the real estate boom that accompanied trolleys in the 1890s led to an increased interest in public works by American cities. This resembled the public works boom that had followed the introduction of horse-drawn street railways in the post-Civil War years. A new wave of urban social reformers, like Hazen Pingree in Detroit and Samuel "Golden Rule" Jones in Toledo came into power. They emphasized social justice issues more than financial conservatism. Unlike their predecessors, they desired strong municipal governments. Like their predecessors, they believed in centralized, bureaucratized municipal administration. Prominent among their demands was the suburbanization of American cities, a process that they believed would eliminate the social evils associated with the slums. Even in cities where they did not attain power, their ideas often prevailed. Cincinnati under Boss Cox, for example, encouraged the spread of trolleys and engaged in major street improvements.[41]

Reformers believed that centrally controlled streets were vital to deconcentrate cities. They sought gradually to take away abutters' control over streets and vest it in centralized city agencies to provide more efficient street systems and better paving. The reformers centralized control of streets by many devices. They strengthened boards of public improvements by giving more of their employees civil service protection and requiring that the boards staff themselves with professionally trained engineers.[42] Charles W. Norton, one advocate of municipal government by experts, argued that centralized administration would encourage suburban travel. Experts, who supposedly represented the city, would keep abutters, who wished to keep high-speed vehicles off local streets, from blocking suburban trolley lines: "Before the modern modes of transportation came into existence, the citizen might be supposed to have a peculiar interest in the street and roadway in front of his house, but now he is much more interested in the good condition and safe operation of the 200 miles of electric railway which maintains for him easy communication."[43]

When the earlier generation of conservative reformers had created these boards, it had given them the power to veto the type of pavements that abutters selected and to supervise street construction. Now boards began to apply those powers to restrict pavement choices to types like asphalt and brick, which served transportation better than recreation. They also found ways around the bans on patented pavements, to allow certain special asphalt preparations. Some cities started to install and maintain pavements themselves, rather than by contract, although abutters still had to pay special assessments. The controls extended to street layout also. In 1891 Boston's Board of Survey became the first board to receive the power to stipulate the layout of streets in new subdivisions.[44]

The new movement whittled down the principle of frontage consent considerably. In some cities, abutters could only veto pavement types while previously they had selected them. Many cities began to pay a portion of paving costs from general tax funds, an indication that they planned streets for general traffic, rather than abutters. Beginning in 1903, Illinois allowed its cities to pave without the abutters' consent. Courts began pull back on the extension of abutters' rights to include air and access, since it delayed the construction of street railways and els needed to create suburbs. This allowed construction of electrified el lines in both Boston and Chicago in the 1890s.[45]

Abutters retained considerable power, since the pace of change was slow. Even in the early twentieth century, they resisted change. After both the Baltimore fire of 1904 and the San Francisco earthquake of 1906, abutters blocked most proposals for street widening during reconstruction. As with the fires of the 1870s, only piecemeal change occurred.[46]

The municipal engineers, who exercised increasing control over pavement construction, evolved new standards of judgment. They began to produce a professional literature on pavements as they came to the realization that cities had invested a total of more than $850 million in street construction by 1900.[47] The only class of engineering works in the country with a higher investment was steam railroads. Table 4.1 shows a method of pavement evaluation from a widely read text written by George W. Tillson, an engineer in Brooklyn's Department of Highways. Tillson included two highly weighted variables in his scheme: "Little Resistance to Traffic" and "Favorableness to Travel." If the abutters who previously controlled pavement selection had ever prepared a similar formal rating system for pavements, both categories would have received a much lower weight. They preferred pavements that would slow down or limit traffic, since frequent travel interfered with the social uses of streets. They might, for example, have added categories for "favorableness to pedestrians" or "ease of play." The table showed that engineers valued streets for travel.

Tillson also included another highly weighted value, "Sanitariness," which greatly favored asphalt. This showed the engineers' well-known concern with public health, and the problem of horse droppings in the street. George Waring claimed in 1897 that he could reduce New York's street cleaning expenditures by half a million dollars annually and do a better job if the city adopted asphalt exclusively. Since asphalt was smooth, street cleaners could operate sweeping machines on it that would not have picked up filth in the grooves of the various block pavements. Even with control in the hands of abutters, the increased importance of health considerations might have resulted in an increase in asphalt streets.[48]

The engineers who staffed the agencies and boards responsible for street paving shared in the general idealization of suburban life. Often, they lived in detached-lot housing themselves. As noted earlier, they tended to view streets as arteries with a specialized mechanical function to perform. Many of them had a background working for railroads and this may have heightened their perception of streets as rights of way. Francis Greene, a prominent engineer, wrote

Table 4.1 **EVALUATION OF PAVING TYPES**

Quality	Weight	Granite Block	Asphalt	Brick	Macadam	Cobble-stone
Cheapness	14	2	4	3	7	14
Durability	21	21	15	13	7	15
Ease of Cleaning	15	11	15	12	5	2
Low Resistance to Traffic	15	7	15	12	6	4
Nonslippery	7	6	3	6	7	5
Easy Maintenance	10	10	6	6	3	2
Favorableness to Travel	5	3	5	4	5	0
Sanitariness	13	9	13	11	5	2
Total	100	69	76	67	45	44

SOURCE: George W. Tillson, *Street Pavements and Paving Materials* (New York: John Wiley and Sons, 1901), 167

in 1890 that "The streets of the city are built for the same purpose as railroads between cities—viz. to provide for the transportation of freight and passengers."[49] Other engineers had military training and designed streets after the model of Baron Haussmann in Paris, probably without realizing that his rationale grew largely out of security considerations. They also seem to have been more receptive to pressure from transportation and paving interests than from abutters. Some jumped back and forth between building streets for cities to doing the same for private contractors. Almost alone of the new engineering professional organizations, the American Society for Municipal Improvements admitted both professional engineers and entrepreneurs. This, too, inclined them to adopt the new pavements.[50]

In total, their training, living habits, and positions made them unable to understand the most important values of streets in older neighborhoods of cities. In 1896, Nelson P. Lewis, a prominent municipal engineer, expressed complete bewilderment at a petition from the residents of one street in Brooklyn. They requested an obsolescent cobblestone pavement for their street. He could only attribute the request to a desire to save money, by that showing the nearsighted view of his profession. The petition was an excellent summary of the non-travel function of streets, already forgotten by the suburbanizers:

> [Asphalt] . . . will reduce the value of property from twenty-five to thirty-five per cent on its present market value. We also protest because it will make _____ a thoroughfare from ____ to _____ for carts and vehicles of all kinds, including bicycles . . . , and the resulting noise will be so intolerable that it will make the street undesirable for private residences. The lives of our children would be in constant danger from reckless riders and drivers, if this private street is to be made a thoroughfare. We would prefer the privacy of the street as a residential street, and for the safety of our children who would not be menaced by the additional travel of bicycles and other vehicles.[51]

5

THE FAILURE OF THE
STEAM AUTOMOBILE

IN 1787 THE state of Maryland granted Oliver Evans, an unknown millwright, a patent for a steam automobile. Evans decided not to pursue the idea for the time being. Over the next seventeen years he devoted his energies to building the first American high pressure steam engines, mostly for milling and pumping machinery. A first rate mechanical inventor, he is best known for developing continual process flour mills. In 1804, Evans revived his automotive plans. By that date he had built several engines and believed that he had a reliable power plant. Also, by that date improved operating surfaces, vital to the success of any new transport mode, had appeared. On September 26, 1804, Evans wrote a letter to the Philadelphia and Lancaster Turnpike Co., owner of the nation's first turnpike, suggesting that steam wagons could increase its profits from eighteen to fifty dollars a day. The company rejected his idea. Although its roadway was an improvement over its predecessors, the company feared that Evans's heavy, but fragile engines would both ruin its light surface and be prone to topple over. Other investors refused to back Evans. Benjamin Latrobe, probably America's most prestigious engineer, condemned Evans's idea, complaining that high-pressure engines on wagons were dangerous, because they might explode. Latrobe delivered his intemperate attack in a speech to the prestigious Philosophical Society of Pennsylvania. Latrobe, who had invested in rival low-pressure engines, had the intellectual, economic, and political clout to frighten off most investors interested in Evans's ideas.[1]

Evans did not give up easily. When the Philadelphia Board of Health asked him to construct a steam dredge the following year, he took advantage of the opportunity to advance his automotive plans. The engine on the boat turned a crankshaft that the operator could connect by belts to either a paddle wheel or to the dredging machinery. To move the dredge from his workshop to the water, Evans placed it on a wheeled frame while another belt connected the crankshaft to the rear axle, thus producing America's first self-propelled road vehicle. On August 12, 1805, this peculiar forerunner of the Model T, unhappily named *Orukter Amphibolos* (amphibious digger), chugged around the streets of Philadelphia at four miles an hour. It thereby merited the dubious distinction of being America's first motor vehicle. Evans passed the hat among spectators to defray some of his research and development costs. Philadelphia's rough cobblestone streets proved too much for the *Orukter Amphibolos* and its wheels broke the first day.[2]

Several months later the Pennsylvania legislature banned steam wagons from turnpikes as Latrobe had requested, so Evans had to seek other operating surfaces. In 1809, he built a small, oxen-powered, wooden-railed tramway in Philadelphia, hoping eventually to power it with a steam engine, but this venture also failed. Evans spent the remaining fourteen years of his life trying to develop the idea of steam locomotion, but public opposition and a lack of capital frustrated his dreams. Later, he would bitterly entitle his autobiography, *Abortion of a Young Steam Engineer's Guide*.[3]

It will not surprise historians of technology that Evans did not operate in isolation. Nicholas Cugnot, a military engineer, had built a steam-powered artillery carriage in 1769, in France, where engineers had designed the best roads in Europe. English steam engine inventors had also thought about the transportation possibilities of steam. James Watt had patented a road vehicle and in 1801, Richard

Trevithick, who built the first high-pressure steam engines in England, had constructed a primitive vehicle. Erasmus Darwin, the British natural philosopher, had predicted the triumph of steam power in a bit of doggerel written in 1791:

> Soon shall thy force, gigantic steam afar
> Drag the slow barge or urge the rapid car.[4]

Even Evans's priority as the first American car builder is open to dispute. In 1791, Nathan Read, a Harvard professor, sought a U.S. patent for a steam vehicle. Some sources claim that Apollos Kinsey operated a steam carriage in Hartford in 1797. James Fitch, the steamboat pioneer, also had toyed with the idea. During the early years of the nineteenth century the concept of steam locomotion was obvious to anyone familiar with current technology. Nonetheless, steam power only achieved success on boats, which had a smooth operating medium.[5]

The *Orukter Amphibolos* was clearly a premature technology. The state of the art in both mechanics and metallurgy would not allow viable road vehicles. It would take another twenty years to build steam vehicles that would work, even on iron rails, the smoothest surface imaginable. Still Evans's failure pointed out problems that would plague advances in steam automobiles for the rest of the century. Any mechanically propelled wagon needed a flat operating surface; therefore, further advances awaited improvements in roads. Steam automobiles would always encounter the safety fears first raised by Benjamin Latrobe. Nineteenth-century Americans associated high-pressure steam engines with disastrous explosions and sought to regulate them, even on private property, and would not tolerate them on public streets. Automotive innovators, like Evans, also tended to blame their failures on the refusal of capitalists to support them, but prospective investors probably showed wisdom in avoiding such projects. They realized that there was little possibility of obtaining the social prerequisites for automobility—large public expenditures on streets and an end to adverse regulation. While steam locomotion made considerable advances in the ninety years after the *Orukter Amphibolos*, it would never overcome this trio of interrelated obstacles: the lack of smooth operating surfaces, public fears of possible boiler explosions, and the consequent inability to attract investors, even after inventors licked most of the mechanical problems.

The next wave of automotive innovation took place in the 1820s and 1830s, primarily in England, although there were some experiments in the United States modeled on the English trials. English roads were much smoother than American ones, so British inventors experimented with road vehicles for turnpikes as well as paved city streets. Goldsworthy Gurney, the most successful inventor, even ran a steam omnibus line on a suburban turnpike near Gloucester, England, and carried 3,000 passengers in four months. An innovative, safe tubular boiler powered this bus.[6]

William Hancock, another British engineer, operated several regular steam omnibus lines in the London area in the early 1830s. His longest lived trial conducted a daily service to Paddington that operated for 912 trips covering 4,000 miles in a 20-passenger bus capable of twenty miles an hour. In 1831, turnpike companies, anticipating that their horse-drawn business would suffer, lobbied prohibitively high fares for steamers through Parliament. Some early experiments ended after the steamers flipped over on turnpikes, where light macadam surfacing could not support their weight. In 1840, London officials banned steamers, not only because they feared explosions, but also because smoke and steam exhaust threatened the urban environment. Other British localities followed this example.[7]

The leading recent scholar of these experiments, David Beasley, argues that the turnpike companies, fearful of losing their horse-drawn patronage, raised fares unnecessarily and actually sabotaged the steamers. He claims that road steamers could have replaced Britain's embryonic railroads. These claims won't wash. Both Gurney and Hancock wanted to ignore or minimize turnpike tolls when they tried to attract investors. But, heavy, iron-wheeled steamers did require heavy, frequently repaired pavements. Also, at peak speed (about 15 m.p.h., comparable with contemporary railroads) the suction of turning wheels pulled gravel pavements apart, according to the analysis of later engineers. The higher tolls reflected, not just a fear of change, but also the greater damage that steamers did to the roadway. Both Gurney's and Hancock's trials showed a profit, but their accounting procedures were awry. They made little, if any, provision for maintenance or depreciation. We know from early-twentieth-century figures on technically much more sophisticated steamers that these vehicles had a life expectancy of about five years, with maintenance costing about 20 percent annually. Gurney's vehicles had several accidents, with one engine explosion killing five passengers. Although Beasley, his defender, claims sabotage, this kind of failure typified all early steam engines, whether stationary, on boats, or on trains. It does not require a conspiracy theory to explain why turnpike authorities charged them high rates and municipalities banned them.[8]

Poor pavements and turnpike bans were not the only, nor probably even the primary reason that steam land transportation evolved on rails rather than roads. Railroad operators had their own rights of way and thus could avoid public bans or resistance from fearful, horse-using customers. A private right of way also guaranteed a monopoly operation that was attractive to investors. Rails solved many technical problems that road operation presented because they could support much greater weight. Iron rails offered a smooth surface that minimized accidents and wear to fragile cast-iron parts. The early steam autos had difficulty turning because of the absence of efficient steering devices. Railroads solved this problem by avoiding it. Steering apparatus and differential gears on rear axles were not necessary since rails guided the locomotive. Engines changed direction only in broad, sweeping curves, or in switches, which operated by turning the tracks rather than the wheels. Flanges on wheels enabled cars to stay on the track in these turns. After English mechanic George Stephenson developed the modern rail system in 1825, automotive experimentation took a distant second place to rail locomotive design.[9]

The turnpike companies might have been smarter to encourage the new technology, pending improvements, but in these trials the technology was clearly premature. Relatively light road vehicles would not appear for another ten years. English inventors also developed both Ackerman (knuckled) steering gear and axles with differentials in the 1830s, but both came after railroads had established their supremacy. Better steel, which made for more durable parts, especially springs, and stronger boilers, did not became available until the 1860s. In the absence of a market for automobiles, engineers forgot these advances. Auto builders had to reinvent differentials and Ackerman gear independently sixty years afterward. Inventors could not attract sufficient investors to improve their prototypes sufficiently. Railroad construction drained capital from both auto experimenters and their best operating surface, turnpikes. The British toll road system, once the finest road network in Europe, deteriorated rapidly after the triumph of the railroad. The turnpikes remained in horrible shape until urban bicyclists began to complain in the 1880s that bad rural roads were limiting their vehicles to cities.[10]

Americans followed British developments closely. Prominent American engineers made research trips to England, imported English engineers, and, later, English locomotives. The English debate about the relative merits of road and rail traction received attention in periodicals like the *Franklin Journal*, America's foremost technical journal. In 1822, John Stevens, a leading builder of steamboat engines and a turnpike promoter, had suggested both railroads and a steam wagon–turnpike combination to New York State authorities, who were about to begin construction on the Erie Canal. The United States Congress reprinted the major Parliamentary report on steam vehicles in 1825. Americans also constructed some steamers. Thomas Blanchard built experimental road vehicles in Springfield, Massachusetts in 1825 and in Poughkeepsie, New York the following year. In 1828, two brothers named Johnson ran a steam wagon in Philadelphia. They lost control of their vehicle and destroyed it. William James, an associate of Hancock's, migrated to the U.S., where he continued his trials, running an experimental steamer in New York in 1829.[11]

Innovation in the United States peaked in the 1830s, beginning with Hanson Dyer in Boston in 1830 and Joseph Dixon in Lynn, Massachusetts in 1831. These inventors tested their prototypes on urban streets, since they provided slightly better operating surface than the shoddy macadam surfaces of American turnpikes. Turnpike promoters began to fear railroad competition, so the Fredericksburg-Potomac, Troy-Albany, and Boston-Worcester turnpikes all planned steam carriages in 1832. Also that year, the paradoxically named *American Railroad Journal* began publication, carrying on its masthead the slogan: "Steam Carriages for Common Roads."[12] These steamers so impressed one utopian novelist that she included them in her futuristic vision.[13]

Ultimately, this wave of innovation fizzled also. In an editorial, the *Franklin Journal* outlined the reason why steamers were even less successful in America than in England:

> That [steam] carriages can be made to run on hard level roads has never been doubted; but the unavoidable obstructions which must exist on the best roads, and even on the smoothest common pavements, would certainly, and rapidly, injure the machinery, whilst those elevations and depressions which must be encountered and overcome, if any good purpose is accomplished, would present difficulties which could not be obviated.[14]

Most of the inventors switched to building railroad locomotives. John Stevens, earlier in his life a turnpike promoter, became a railroad advocate. William James, whose New York steam carriages had appeared promising, began to design locomotives for the Baltimore and Ohio Railroad. J. K. Fisher, the most persistent of the early automobile builders, abandoned his 1840 design after other engineers pointed out that the British had failed on better roads. It is tempting to speculate as does Robert Fogel, the economic historian, that it would have saved money in the long run, if investors had channeled the funds placed in nineteenth-century railroads into road steamers, but the road vehicles of the 1830s were premature. The metallurgy needed to construct carriages light enough to operate on existing roads was years in the future. As in Britain, the American engineers preferred to blame external causes—for example, timid investors and the builders of inferior roads.[15]

Railroad development did more than channel innovative energy away from road carriages. It also created a set of public attitudes about high-speed vehicles on city streets and about steam engines generally. As we have seen, city governments limited steam railroads to private rights of way within cities, whenever possible, to avoid accidents with other traffic. Public fears of boiler explosions limited urban rail transportation developments.[16] The railroads seem to have suffered few urban boiler explosions, but these few had a spectacular impact on the public. The *New York Herald* noted, after an 1839 locomotive explosion: "Many a long year will scarce suffice to efface the scene from the minds of those inhabitants who witnessed the living mass of wounded and blackened wretches huddled together— the mangled remains of the dead lying in all directions. . . ."[17] This sensationalism followed an accident that claimed only two lives, and damaged no property other than the locomotive.

Like today's airplane crashes, nineteenth-century boiler explosions were spectacular and the fear of explosions was far greater than the likelihood of one actually occurring. Every city had its own memorable disaster. In Cincinnati in 1838, a steamboat, the *Moselle*, exploded, killing more than 100 people. Observers claimed that pieces had been blown over 800 feet in the air and that bodies rained down as far as a quarter of a mile away. A stationary boiler in Hartford exploded in 1854, killing 21 people, injuring 50 others, and starting a fire that caused major property damage. A compilation of boiler accidents for 1867 showed explosions in Milwaukee, New York, Chicago, Cleveland, Newark, Pittsburgh, Philadelphia, and Detroit, resulting in well over 50 deaths.[18]

Improving and regulating boilers became a major technical and political issue. Some reaction was likely to be nonproductive. Few were willing to dismiss the disasters as one Hartford minister described them: "a visitation from God." The crisis drew a lunatic fringe. A Dayton, Ohio inventor "demonstrated" that aeriform miasmatic columns carrying a latent caloric had a polar affinity for iron boilers. His solution was to provide copper covers for steam boilers, which he imagined would form a magnetic field opposed to the iron and avoid explosions. On a more serious note, the U.S. Treasury Department subsidized an 1836 scientific study of the causes of explosions. The national government, in an early example of the federal police power, began a system of inspection for steamboat boilers in 1838. Cities and states also devised elaborate inspection and licensing schemes for both boilers and their operators before the Civil War. Insurance underwriters began to sell casualty policies to owners of stationary factory engines, backed by regular checks by their own inspectors to minimize the dangers. These precautions notwithstanding, the infrequent explosions continued to be a source of public fear, and of opposition to steam carriages.[19]

Steam vehicle innovation revived in the 1850s, especially in New

York City, the locale of many street improvements. In 1851, J. K. Fisher, a prominent mechanical engineer, reentered the automotive field after an eleven year hiatus. Several New Yorkers interested in advancing American technology, including the editors of *Railroad Journal*, *Appleton's Mechanic's Magazine*, and *American Artisan*, formed the American Steam Carriage Company. Under its auspices, Fisher built a four-wheeled vehicle powered by a tubular boiler capable of speeds of up to fifteen miles an hour. When the driver wished to turn the carriage, he had to pivot the entire front axle, a very clumsy arrangement. The vehicle weighed only 1,400 pounds, which seemed to promise higher speeds. Unfortunately, such a light weight made the steamer too fragile to last, even on New York's relatively good roads. After early breakdowns, Fisher could not attract the capital needed to improve his prototype.[20]

Fisher reported on his ideas in the September 1852 issue of the *Journal of the Franklin Institute*. He claimed that the nub of the steam traction problem was bad roads and pointed out that railroads "were designed for loads too heavy for common roads." Fisher believed road operating steamers offered greater flexibility than rail operation, since each shipper would have a vehicle, could vary loads, and make point to point trips without delivering and picking up goods at a depot, thereby saving transshipment costs. He believed good roads were becoming available (1852 was the high point of the plank road boom) and that urban streets also showed a vast improvement. He predicted that, if steamers succeeded, cheap concrete pavements would become practicable, a shrewd observation since the primary obstacle to concrete was that it cracked when hammered by iron shod hoofs. Fisher believed in iron pavements and proposed a vehicle tax to finance them.[21]

Richard Dudgeon, a New York mechanic, operated a steam powered vehicle for several years beginning in 1853. He displayed an improved version at that city's Crystal Palace Exposition of 1857. The carriage seems to have been an awkward affair. Contemporaries described it as a "locomotive," appropriately enough, since it weighed a ton and a half and had 42-inch hard wheels. When Dudgeon attempted to operate on streets outside the Crystal Palace grounds, a hostile mob attacked him. Authorities prohibited further operation of the vehicle, ostensibly because it was too noisy. The customary safety and pollution fears undoubtedly contributed to the ban, since the engine burned two bushels of coal per trip. Ultimately, fire destroyed this vehicle when the Crystal Palace burned down. The police also banned an improved steamer that Dudgeon built in 1860, primarily because it exhausted live steam on the street. He finally secured special permission from the authorities in Bridgeport, Connecticut to test it there. Dudgeon's final (1866) model is still extant. Like Fisher, he never solved the steering problem and had severe difficulties with traveling range and pollution. Securing capital remained almost impossible.[22]

Other pioneers developed steam vehicles before the Civil War. J. K. Fisher reported on experiments by a man named Baltin, who built a steam carriage in 1856. It ran well enough, Fisher claimed, on the relatively few streets that Jersey City had paved decently, but could not operate with any speed or efficiency on rough, unpaved roads. Fisher, himself, built another steamer in 1859, a two and a half ton monster that once ran a mile in two minutes, forty seconds (22.5 m.p.h.). Steam fire engines led the wave of development. Moses Latta constructed the first one in 1851 when Cincinnati created the first professional fire department. Engineers in other cities, including Fisher in New York, imitated Latta's example.[23]

Fire engines applied their power principally to pump water, rather than for mobility, since it took too long to get up steam. Some fire department pumpers had the capacity to propel themselves at speeds up to eighteen miles an hour. Aldermen in some cities initially opposed steam fire engines on city streets because they feared an explosion, but later many cities allowed them. The fear of fires in nineteenth-century cities, largely built out of wood, overcame the fear of steam propulsion, especially after the great fire in Boston in 1872 showed the snags of relying on horse power in the most graphic manner imaginable. One other form of self-propelled vehicle, the steamroller, appeared before the Civil War. It suggests the potential of steam for moving very heavy freight around cities, a need that horses met very poorly.[24]

Fisher continued to publicize the idea of steamers, but was unable to attract capital after another prototype failed in 1860. With Alexander Holley, one of the more important mechanical engineers in the United States, Fisher wrote a lengthy essay on the "History and Progress of Steam on Common Roads in the United States" for an 1860 book by the English engineer C. F. T. Young. Fisher also advocated his ideas in a series of letters to the *New York Times* in 1863. Holley, who was a special contributor to the *Times* on technical matters, probably secured publication of his collaborator's letter. The prestigious *Scientific American* also endorsed the idea of steam carriages in 1866. Fisher's letters contained considerable foresight about a potential market. He suggested a system of suburban omnibuses, since street railways could not "go to every door." Also, individually owned steam carriages might provide wealthy suburbanites with a privacy and speed not possible on horsecars.[25]

Fisher analyzed the condition of contemporary paving accurately when he whined:

> It hardly needs to be added that the steam carriage must begin its career by underworking horses on roads made specially to suit the feet of horses; and that, in consequence of their toughness and softness have from four to twenty times the resistance [to the rolling of wheels] that will be found after steam is established, and the roads are made for wheels.[26]

Fisher continued to urge iron pavements as the ideal surface for steam vehicles, although he noted the possibilities of other pavements. For example, he knew that steam road rollers made cheap, smooth macadam surfaces possible. He never explained how iron streets could overcome the hurdles of cost, noise, and slipperiness. Fisher, like later engineers, did not perceive the reasons why urbanites preferred to have badly paved streets, without steam vehicles. When a carriage owner attacked his views in the *Times*, Fisher answered the most easily solved parts of the complaint, by stating that iron streets would save money in the long run because they would last longer. He asserted that condensers could solve the problems of noise and steam exhaust. He completely ignored the letter writer's major question: "How long would it take to make all our drivers skillful engineers?" a question that got at the most important worries of urbanites, who feared that speeding drivers would run over their children.[27]

Fisher also overemphasized the role that corruption played in municipal paving policies. He contended that corruption was the principal reason why municipal governments built pavements suited to inefficient horse-drawn transportation, rather than subsidizing suburbanization by providing smooth streets suitable for fast-moving through traffic. He charged that common councils adopted patented pavements, like the Nicholson wood blocks, only to enrich patentees who had bribed city officials. Encouraging street railways, rather than good pavements, also benefited street railway speculators by giving them a virtual monopoly on suburban traffic. Fisher made this jaundiced view of contemporary paving practice the basis of an attack on the existing forms of municipal government. He argued for more professional, centralized city administration. Fisher also anticipated the argument that municipal engineers would make thirty years later when they began to change urban paving policy by noting the adverse environmental impact of horses:

> But shall we all our lives endure one hundred and ninety-nine pounds of dirt [i.e., manure] from each hundredweight [of horse] when steam would reduce it to one pound because the improvement will not pay more patentees and speculators for introducing it? Are our streets sold to monopolists unconditionally so that we must endure all the filth which it may suit their supposed interests to inflict on us? Or must we endure it because our rulers are not engineers or men of science, but men without proper talent?[28]

Alexander Holley, Fisher's sometime collaborator, was indirectly responsible for the great improvements in steamers after the Civil War. Holley constructed the first Bessemer process steel mill in the United States at Troy, New York in 1865. Steel provided the strength needed to construct lightweight, yet durable vehicles. Thus the postwar years saw additional, more technically successful trials of steam autos.

The major innovator of this period was Sylvester Roper, a Boston engineer. Roper built a 650 pound steamer in 1863 that *Scientific American* reported could do twenty miles an hour. This four-wheeled vehicle allegedly burned only a penny's worth of fuel a mile. Roper developed an improved model in 1865, which weighed only 480 pounds and won a match race with a horse at Poughkeepsie, New York, covering a mile in two minutes, twenty seconds, almost 26 miles an hour. Roper's 1870 model, however, ran into political trouble. Boston aldermen, alarmed at the possibility of traffic accidents, sought to ban it. Roper built ten different models between 1865 and 1894 that received some public attention in demonstrations at racetracks or as novelties in circus parades.[29]

Many other designers tried prototypes in the 1860s and 70s. A New Englander, A. M. Spencer, had built two vehicles during the Civil War. Henry Alonzo House, a wealthy Bridgeport sewing machine manufacturer, developed a steam-powered, friction drive steamer in 1866 that he claimed could reach a speed of thirty miles an hour on flat surfaces. He drove this underpowered (only four horsepower) machine over a thousand miles before abandoning it. Again, there was popular resistance; House's contraption scared horses. Frank Curtis, a mechanic with experience building fire engines, operated a steamer in Newburyport, Massachusetts in 1866. When local selectmen ordered Curtis off the streets he moved to a neighboring town. His steamer weighed only 680 pounds. He claimed a speed of twenty-five miles per hour, a six to eight mile cruising radius, and only 2 2/3 pounds of coal consumption per mile. Two New Hampshire citizens also operated a steamer in the summer of 1868. A year later Sunapee, New Hampshire banned another experimental steamer. The craze spread westward also. A steamer scared residents and horses alike in Racine, Wisconsin in 1873.[30]

The technological history of the next twenty years is filled with stories of aborted steamers, many of which showed some technological progress. Most innovators simplified steering by adopting a single front wheel like a tricycle, rather than a pivoting front axle. Steel made stronger parts and driveshafts possible. Some innovators added gearshifts; others developed automatic feeding systems for cleaner burning coke. Experimenters in France had begun burning petroleum to heat boilers as early as 1873. Lucius Copeland, perhaps the most advanced designer, built several steam tricycles in Camden, New Jersey, Phoenix, and San Francisco during the 1880s. He adopted strong boilers weighing less than twenty pounds that he could start in five minutes and introduced solid rubber tires (illustration 5.1). The pattern of municipal prohibitions continued also. Northfield, Massachusetts, Chicago, Illinois, and Fleetwood, Pennsylvania all banned steamers.[31]

Several governmental bodies sought to encourage steam traction, primarily in rural areas. In 1878, the Wisconsin state legislature offered a $5,000 prize for a race by steam vehicles from Green Bay to Madison. Seven vehicles entered the race, but only two actually showed up. The winner averaged only five miles an hour on rough country roads, a sorry contrast to the speeds that some steamers achieved on good urban streets. The legislature paid only half the promised prize, because the winner "could not be considered a cheap or practical substitute for horses or mules upon the farms or highways of Wisconsin." In the 1870s, steam traction engines pulling threshers did appear in some rural areas, but these were basically stationary steam engines on wheels that could propel themselves at only two or three miles an hour. Even these low-speed vehicles, touring in the open countryside, encountered some resistance. New York State required that a rider on horseback precede them to warn oncoming traffic.[32]

Some city dwellers wanted to allow steam power either on automotive vehicles or on small dummy locomotives during the immediate postwar years. The *New York Times* called for a "mechanical substitute for the horse." Boston's Common Council had offered $5,000 for experiments on a "self-propelled steam power engine" in the late 1860s. These were unusual exceptions to the usual prohibitions. In the fourth (1890) edition of his *Treatise on the Law of Municipal Corporations,* John F. Dillon noted that Michigan allowed steam traction engines on rural roads, "but it seems to be doubtful whether a similar use of such an engine could lawfully be made without the consent, or at all events against a regulation of the municipal authorities." Steam enthusiasts were likely to be aware, not only of Dillon's position, and of the bans in many cities, but also of England's highly publicized Red Flag Law, which had completely ended the more advanced English developments. The law symbolized opposition to high-speed road travel. To stop the spread of steamers, Parliament required in 1865 that a man on foot, waving a red flag, must precede all road-operated steam vehicles. American venture capitalists would hardly be willing to invest in steamers after such a daunting precedent.[33]

Clearly, there were technical problems with all the steam vehicles developed in this country, but public resistance to the machines seems more important in explaining their failure. The standard complaint was that they were heavy and cumbersome, but this applies more to English than American steamers. Many British innovators built "road locomotives," designed to pull trains of vehicles on common roads. American inventors realized that cities would surely ban such trains and that adequate roads did not exist in the countryside. Instead, they emphasized light, speedy luxury vehicles, or, especially in the 1870s, omnibuses. Several succeeded in reducing steamer weight to the equivalent of the weight of a horse and carriage (illustration 5.1).[34]

The charges of cumbersome operation make more sense. Iron or wood wheels did make for a rough ride, but entrepreneurs could have imitated the rubber wheels that Copeland had adopted if a market demand had forced them to improve their product. Other schemers knew about them. Some pre-railroad English designers had experimented with rubber wheels and J. K. Fisher had suggested as early as 1863 that rubber tires presented a potential solution to the noise problem. Bicycle pioneers succeeded with solid rubber tires in the 1870s. Maneuvering steamers was always a problem, also. Tricycles presented a temporary solution to the steering problem, but here, again, it seems likely entrepreneurs would have rediscovered the Ackerman steering gear patented in the 1830s. Innovators were aware of the need for differential joints on the rear axle, and probably would have adopted them if their vehicles had evolved further, since the principle was well known.[35]

Operation of the vehicle presented other problems not so easily solvable. Steam engines were slow to start up, since it took a while to heat the water in the boiler. Starting in less than five minutes became possible only after Leon Serpollet developed flash boilers after 1900. A pilot light, like the one on a gas stove, always kept water heated in these boilers. A French engineer had patented boilers heated by petroleum as early as 1868 and several American innovators toyed with the idea. It seems likely that entrepreneurs would have developed such fast-starting flash boilers easily enough if the existence of a market had forced them to refine their vehicles. Hand feeding coal to the fire box also limited these steamers. Oil burning engines could have solved this fueling problem, but coal-using remedies were also possible. The *Engineering News* suggested in 1876 that it was possible to feed automatically small, pea-sized bits of anthracite coal, which could flow like water, to the boiler. High rates of water consumption limited early steamers to a six to eight mile operating radius, but later inventors extended this range considerably by adding condensers to recirculate the water. It also seems probable that market conditions would have created a chain of water supply stations, like the gas stations that emerged with the market for internal combustion engines.[36]

The weight of contemporary evidence suggests that steamers were technically feasible as a replacement for horses, clearly offering greater efficiencies for at least some urban travel tasks. The *Engineering News* did complain in 1876 that the heavy steam traction engines that rural American and British inventors had tinkered with, "[did not] promise much toward a Darwinian development into what will eventually be found to be employed in transporting passengers and light loads in the street." Yet, the article modified this position considerably by suggesting a series of essentially minor changes in design. A year later the same periodical suggested that steam trucks would soon appear in the streets. Robert Thurston, perhaps the most prominent mechanical engineer of his age, predicted success for steamers in his classic 1878 work, *A History of the Growth of the Steam Engine*. Three years later, when he became the first President of the American Society of Mechanical Engineers, he suggested in his inaugural address that the triumph of steam vehicles was imminent.[37]

The innovative entrepreneurs who later succeeded with internal combustion cars had believed that steamers would replace the horse in the 1880s. Hiram Percy Maxim, the technical brain behind several internal combustion auto producers of the 1890s, believed inventors could have built practical steam autos "in 1880, or indeed in 1870." Maxim believed steam autos had failed because no one foresaw their potential. Henry Ford later claimed that a bulky steam traction engine that he saw in rural Michigan in 1876 had triggered his interest in road locomotion. Charles Duryea, sometimes credited as the first American car builder, had known and written about steamers as early as 1882, but abandoned his plans because he did not feel the public saw their potential.[38]

Several other automotive pioneers built steamers before switching to gasoline. Elwood Haynes, another 1890s automotive pioneer, had previously abandoned steam as too dangerous. Ransom Olds, whose Oldsmobiles were the most popular gasoline make around the turn of the century, had built steamers in the 1880s. He tested them on the streets of Lansing, Michigan between three and four a.m. to avoid frightening his neighbors. When they still complained, he abandoned steam as too noisy and dangerous. Only Alexander Winton, among major gasoline auto innovators of the 1890s, left no record of a connection with the earlier pattern of steamers. Many French and German internal combustion pioneers, whom the Americans imitated, also had tried steamers.[39]

The pre-1890 steamers failed mostly because of regulation, not mechanical inefficiency. They delivered greater speed, lower operating costs, and less pollution than horses; but the public still feared them. The regulators reflected public opinion when they banned steamers because of their speed, smoke, steam exhaust, and potential for explosion. The constant repetition of bans in cities of every size, in every region of the U.S. shows the potency of the popular fears. It is striking that even the politically influential street railway companies could not get permission to switch to steam dummies, even on lightly populated suburban runs. If cities banned steam when confined to rails on a few major streets, they were hardly likely to allow it on vehicles whose owners could drive them anywhere. Any powered road-running vehicle destroyed the traditional, non-travel functions of urban streets.

It is hard to believe that steamers could not have replaced horses for at least some of the variety of tasks that those beasts performed. Perhaps as early as 1865 and certainly by 1880, they offered enough mechanical reliability. Light steamers won races with horses, led circus parades, and demonstrated their abilities at fairs. So private carriage or light delivery wagons could have been mechanized. Self-propelled fire pumps, threshers, and steam rollers demonstrated the ability of steam engines to move heavy burdens. Clearly, they would have been more economical than the twenty horse teams that urban teamsters sometimes had to assemble to move very heavy construction pieces or machines. The multiple horse teams of brewery trucks and omnibuses might well have been less cost efficient than steam, as well. The steamers were breakdown-prone, but so were the horses. Steamers required professional operators, but so did teams of horses and the early internal combustion cars. The inventions to improve steamers were on the shelf (or, more literally, in the dusty records of the patent office). The technology itself had matured by 1878 at the latest.

Public suppression was more important than mechanical inefficiency in explaining the failure of steamers. Strikingly, when cities allowed internal combustion cars in the late 1890s, they also allowed steamers. The 1890s gasoline-powered, internal combustion (i.c.) engine inventors chose that technology for more than just its greater technical potential. They feared a revival of both bans and consumer resistance to steam, even though steam worked better than i.c. in the 1890s. The switch of Locomobile (the leading American manufacturer) and Bollée (a leading French manufacturer) from steam to internal combustion just after the turn of the century marked the triumph of i.c. engines. As late as 1901 most American cars were steam-powered, as late as 1906 a steamer held the land speed record, and as late as 1917 steamers lingered on for some urban specialties, notably heavy trucking. If the nineteenth-century bans derived mostly from fear of steam, presumably those bans would have continued when cities allowed i.c. autos, but municipalities allowed both (with steamers facing somewhat stricter regulation). The rules typically required that steam car drivers hold a boiler operator's license, at a time when drivers of gasoline autos needed no license at all. Still, cities allowed the steamers and these licensing requirements were not extremely onerous, since professional chauffeurs drove most cars. Eventually the steam car makers failed in the early twentieth century, not because of regulation, or, as some critics have charged, because of mismanagement, but because they chose an inferior technology. The steamers might have been more efficient than horses, but they were inferior to internal combustion cars.[40]

There is no indication that American railroads earlier, or oil producers later, lobbied against steamers. The British historian David Beasley has argued that such lobbying explains the failure of steam engines and triumph of internal combustion engines in Europe. He claims that internal combustion cars triumphed "Because they consumed a product [petroleum] that capitalists had to market."[41] Beasley's claims deserve skepticism. First, petroleum derivatives could also heat boilers and likely would have replaced coal if steamers had stayed competitive much longer. It is hard to believe that the Roths-childs, who controlled most European oil supplies and who did in-vest in some of the pioneer French companies, could have controlled every European government. Moreover, coal producers also formed a politically powerful economic interest group. The American ex-perience does not bear Beasley out either, casting further doubt on his conspiracy thesis. Oil monopolists John D. and William Rocke-feller were among the earliest members of New York's carriage-riding elite to switch to cars, but they never invested in the early motor industry. In general, New York finance capitalists steered clear of automotive investments until the formation of General Mo-tors in 1909. The earlier steamer bans were local, not national. Pop-ular fears, at their most extreme in the shape of riots, not lobbying by interest groups like railroads, seem crucial in banning steam car builders when they sought to replace horses. The American inno-vators sought scapegoats for their failure, but never complained about railroads. If such opposition existed, they would have screamed about it. In the final analysis, internal combustion was and is a superior technology.

There is some evidence, admittedly shaky, that cities may even have banned experimental gasoline-fueled vehicles. British-trained Boston engineer George Brayton filed the first U.S. internal com-bustion engine patent. He became the leading American producer of these engines in the late 1870s. He apparently visualized auto-motive possibilities for them. Brayton's widow later claimed that Pittsburgh's City Council banned an omnibus powered by a Brayton engine in 1877. She also testified in a patent suit that the authorities in Pittsburgh and Providence banned prototypes built by his cus-tomers J. F. and W. J. Fawcett. A search of the minutes of the Pitts-burgh City Council for 1876, 1877, and 1878 produced no evidence for this. Possibly local health or safety officials did not secure a formal bylaw, but declared the new technology a nuisance and banned it under their police powers. Brayton's widow, testifying thir-ty years later, simply may have gotten the date wrong, or she may have misrepresented the past to inflate her husband's historical rep-utation.[42]

When Rochester patent attorney George Selden saw a German-made internal combustion engine at the 1876 Centennial Exposition, he immediately filed for an American patent on gasoline-powered cars. Selden later testified that he did no work on the car, because he was sure that cities would ban them. He did not finalize his patent until 1894, when the first European cars were being imported into the U.S. Some skepticism is warranted because Selden was a legal parasite, not an engineer. He never built an experimental vehicle, but sought to collect royalties on all American cars built before Henry Ford won a court case invalidating his patent in 1911. He likely deferred the patent to collect royalties on engineering developments that he was incapable of performing himself, rather than because he feared regulation. He could hardly have acknowledged such motives at a patent trial, so blaming regulation for delaying innovation better served his needs. If the testimony of Selden or Mrs. Brayton were accurate, it presents an indication that city dwellers did not want any powered vehicles on their streets, except those confined by rails to major arteries in the 1870s and 1880s. Even if both Brayton and Selden misrepresented the past, it is striking that both found urban regulation a plausible excuse for the lack of development. Clearly, such regulation, or even fear of it, could only retard innovation.[43]

By and large, historians have ignored the nineteenth-century experience with steam automobiles. Most of the literature has been written by automobile buffs, antiquarians seeking out historical oddities, or a few historians like Beasley who seek to argue the relative merits of steam and internal combustion technology. The latter often seem motivated by presentist concerns with the environmental damage created by the gasoline engine. They have missed the important point about the development, or rather, nondevelopment of steam autos. The resistance to steam autos came when the competition was with horses, not with internal combustion. This raises many questions about the way nineteenth-century urbanites viewed street travel. It shows a strangely conservative attitude toward some kinds of technological change in a society that allegedly worshipped it. For the student of urban transportation, the key questions about automobiles are not technological, but social. What changed in the decade between 1890 and 1900 to make powered vehicles, once anathema, acceptable? Why could the persistent automotive innovators suddenly get capital for their ventures, find an urban market, and expect a neutral, if not downright friendly, regulatory atmosphere in American cities, formerly a hostile environment? Why did the social, nontravel definition of streets lose its traditional power just before the turn of the century? Why did urban consumers become attracted to automobiles? These are crucial questions that the experience with steamers raises.

6

THE EMERGENCE OF THE INTERNAL COMBUSTION AUTOMOBILE: AN URBAN PHENOMENON

EUROPEANS INVENTED THE gasoline powered automobile. In 1860 the Parisian Jean-Joseph Lenoir built the first internal combustion (i.c.) engine for small, portable power sources. The internal combustion of gas promised to be much more efficient than the heating of water by an external heat source, as in steam engines. The German engineers Nicholas Otto and Gottlieb Daimler further refined Lenoir's machine over the next twenty years, eventually making lightweight, four cycle engines capable of 700 rpms with enormous mechanical reliability. The Silent Otto engine, introduced to America at the 1876 Centennial Exposition in Philadelphia, had sold more than fifty thousand units by 1894. American firms, notably those headed by George Brayton and Ransom Olds, also produced numerous motors, mostly for stationary engines or motorboats.[1]

The significant innovative paths for cars were in France and Germany. Both societies were, in large part, command economies, obsessed with improving roads and transport to ease military mobilization. They had excellent engineering schools. The French *Routes Nationales* were the best highways in the world and their German counterparts were not far behind. American urban planners often cited Paris and Berlin as models of street paving and design.[2] Adequate roads were a precondition for automotive experimentation. The U.S. and, for that matter, Britain, had poorer roads and engineering schools than France or Germany. Lenoir, Otto, Daimler, and others experimented with cars, but success only came in 1886. After four years of experimentation, Karl Benz built what scholars generally consider the first successful marriage of i.c. engine to vehicle, a tricycle, and he began to sell cars two years later. By 1895, when American inventors were showing their first prototypes, European firms had already sold more than 500 cars, some in the U.S. Major technical advances, all European, included carburetors, drive shafts, universal gears, and four-cylinder engines. In 1901 Benz eliminated the last vestiges of carriage design by placing the engine under a hood in front of its car.[3]

In 1900 the leading car producers were: France, 4,800; The United States, 4,000; Germany, 800; and Britain, 175. The American products were atavistic, however, including 900 heavy electric taxicabs, doomed to rapid failure, about 1,600 Locomobile steamers, also short-lived, and no more than 1,500 i.c. autos. American i.c. car design lagged behind the rest of the world, its devices were little more than small engines bolted on buggies. The most popular very early auto was the chain driven, Curved Dash Oldsmobile (illustrations 6.1 and 6.2).[4]

The world's automobile makers focussed on urban luxury vehicles. Only cities had large amounts of paved roadway and access to specialized materials, repair services, and mechanics. Breakdowns were so common that owners needed a full-time chauffeur, not so much to drive the car as to keep it in good repair. Only the great metropolitan centers of London, New York, and Paris had sufficient concentrations of rich individuals who could afford cars and chauffeurs. Almost all cars were open to the air: fair-weather vehicles that allowed their owners to show off their affluence in promenades down wealthy streets such as Fifth Ave. or the Champs d'Elysées; at each metropolis' opera; on fashionable park drives in Regent's Park, Central Park, or the Bois de Boulogne. A Sunday-afternoon spin through the nearby countryside, roads and weather allowing, was also a possibility. Some regulatory problems were overcome. Stuttgart police had arrested Karl Benz in 1882 for testing a car on their streets. Britain repealed the Red Flag Law to allow import of the novelties only in 1896.[5]

By 1900, Americans owned an estimated 8,000 automobiles (see table 6.1). This was more than France or Britain, but the ownership *rate* still lagged behind Western Europe. Within the U.S., urban residents were most likely to own cars. Historian Eric Monkkonen estimates that as late as 1910 urban residents were four times more likely to own cars than rural Americans.[6] The 1900 market for automobiles focused on New York City, the financial center of the American economy. By 1910 the city's per capita ownership was still higher than almost every state, but its leadership was much less pronounced as residents of smaller cities acquired cars. The less

Table 6.1 **REGISTRATION OF MOTOR VEHICLES (IN 1,000s) AND PERSONS PER MOTOR VEHICLE (PPMV)**

	1900		1910		1920	
	No.	PPMV	No.	PPMV	No.	PPMV
U.S.	8.0	9,526	458.0	196	8,131	13
U.K.	*	*	144.0	252	650	58
France	6.0	6,408	91.0	430	236	164
Germany	.9	62,633	50.0	1,299	119	573
N.Y.C.	2.4	2,457	31.2	153	213	26
D.C.	.1	3,484	6.3	52	34	13
Kansas	.2	6,681	10.5	161	294	7
Calif.	.8	18,955	44.1	53	583	6
Alabama	.04	45,725	1.7	1,212	74	32

*No data exist for 1900. In 1900, British persons per motor vehicle was probably lower than the U.S., but higher than France. P.P.M.V. based on the more accurate 1905 data was: U.S., 1,063; France, 1,749; U.K., 2,140 and Germany, 5,362.

SOURCES: National Automobile Chamber of Commerce, *Automobile Facts and Figures*; U.S. Bureau of the Census, *Historical Statistics of the United States to 1970*; U.S. Department of Transportation, *Highway Statistics Summary to 1965*; B. R. Mitchell, *European Historical Statistics* (New York: Columbia University Press, 1975). William Plowden, *The Motor Car and Politics, 1896–1970* (London: The Bodley Head, 1971), 453-4; R. J. Overy, "Cars, Roads and German Economic Recovery, 1932–8," *Economic History Review* 28 (August, 1975), 483; Jean-Pierre Bardou, et al., *The Automobile Revolution, The Impact of an Industry* (Chapel Hill: University of North Carolina Press, 1982), 15. Depending on availability, some European data are from a year or two after the date listed. Except for 1900, this should not create significant differences.

dense, but still urban District of Columbia had a higher rate of ownership than any state, or even New York City. As in Europe, only the very wealthy could afford automobiles.

State-level analysis confirms the urban focus of automobility in the early car era. Two states, New Hampshire and Maryland, have retained their first car registration records. In 1905 Baltimore residents (43% of Maryland's population) owned 68% of the cars in the state. That city's suburbanites owned most of the balance. Because of a legal peculiarity, most residents of Washington, D.C. also registered their cars in Maryland. If that state had actually included Washington, residents of that city would have provided only 20.3% of its population, but more than half its cars. Washington probably had more residents of great wealth than Baltimore. Washington also had exceptionally broad, well paved streets, the ideal locale for brittle early cars. Car ownership lagged far behind in rural areas, because cars could not yet handle poor rural roads, and the countryside had few very wealthy individuals. In 1909, the last date for which Maryland kept records, Baltimore and D.C. residents still bought a disproportionately large share of cars. Car purchases were up somewhat in rural Maryland, especially in the Chesapeake region, where plantation style agriculture tended to concentrate wealth.[7]

More rural New Hampshire followed an essentially similar pattern, although ownership was more common in its smaller commercial cities than in larger mill cities such as Manchester and Nashua. The mill towns had smaller elites in comparison to larger, more heterogeneous cities, like Washington or Baltimore. Urban dominance had lessened by 1911, however, with the greatest increases in car registration in the lowest density counties.[8] In general, early automobility seems strongly linked to wealth and urbanization.

U.S. cars designed for this urban market derived from the European experience. The transfer of technology occurred in five ways: technical press/trade periodicals, research trips to Europe, import of technical personnel, racing competition, and marketplace competition.

In the late 1880s American technical periodicals, most notably *Scientific American*, followed developments in Europe closely. An 1889 article describing a Benz automobile in *Scientific American* inspired Charles Duryea's first internal combustion experiments.

Americans knew about the European experience from other sources as well. William Durant decided to leave carriage production and produce autos after a close business associate returned from Europe and reported that the internal combustion auto was not a "noisy contraption," like the old steamers.[9]

In 1890 promoters of the 1893 World's Columbian Exposition, the Chicago World's Fair, announced in the popular and technical press a prize for the best mechanical road vehicle. The contest sparked the interest of early American innovators such as the Duryea brothers, Elwood Haynes, Charles King (who later built the first car in Detroit), and Alexander Winton. Only four cars actually appeared at the Fair (two electrics, a steamer built for circus parades, and, most significantly, an imported Daimler). Most fairgoers ignored these vehicles, but they apparently caught Henry Ford's eye and rekindled the interest of Ransom Olds in automobility. Haynes and the Duryeas completed the first successful U.S. built i.c. vehicles in 1893, but not in time to flaunt at the Fair.[10]

The Chicago publisher Herman Kohlsaat decided to introduce the new European fad to the U.S. by sponsoring a race in 1895, named after his newspaper, the *Times-Herald*. The race attracted national publicity, even in the *New York Times,* which praised French horseless carriages and called for Americans to develop their own, noting: "The work of extinguishing the horse and putting him in the company of the pterodactyl and the megatherium proceeds as well as could fairly be expected."[11] The *Times* urged New York State to repeal its equivalent of the Red Flag Law.

The *Times-Herald* race was anticlimactic after all the publicity build-up. Kohlsaat finally held the much postponed race in a snow-storm in December on park roads and suburban drives in the Chicago area, after Chicago's city government had authorized him to run mechanical vehicles on its roads. More than fifty inventors had planned to race, but ultimately only eleven entered and five showed up. Just two cars completed the race. Frank Duryea's car covered the fifty miles in nine hours, beating a Benz driven by Charles King. By European standards, this was a feeble show. [12]

Earlier in 1895 European firms had made their first investigation of the U.S. market. Emile Roger, Benz's agent in Paris, visited New York City. Roger found New York's pavements rougher than Paris's and wondered about his car's ability to survive on the irregular granite blocks. Macy's department store offered some Roger-Benz products for sale and even attempted to drive one to Chicago for the *Times-Herald* race, but the vehicle could get no further than upstate New York on the poor intercity roads of the time.[13] In the next four years more than thirty American firms began to produce cars. The major focus was on steam and electric cars, probably because proponents of these well-known technologies found it easier to attract capital. Most i.c. entrepreneurs could only finance small start-up operations in smaller industrial cities, especially in the midwest. The Duryeas, the Apperson brothers, Elwood Haynes, William C. Durant, Alexander Winton, Henry Ford, and Ransom Olds entered the industry in the late 1890s.

European vehicles continued to provide the measure of excellence for American automobiles even after these production efforts began. U.S. firms were not shy about recruiting foreign engineers and adopting foreign techniques. American markets attracted Louis Chevrolet, a French auto mechanic. Hiram Maxim, the engineer behind several New England auto makers, came from old England. Albert Champion, whose firm dominated the sparkplug business, migrated from France. Alexander Winton imported a French engineer when he decided to produce vehicles in 1898. After the engineer suggested a low-cost vehicle aimed at a mass market, Winton, who preferred the security of a luxury market, fired him.[14]

Americans also learned from foreign competitors operating in the United States. Daimler ran a factory for Mercedes cars in New York from 1904 to 1907. American firms only moved away from buggy style designs after facing this competition. The New York market was so attractive and American manufacturers seemed so weak that Fiat briefly contemplated moving to New York. The French manufacturers regularly displayed their wares at American motor shows and advertised them in the U.S. press. Renault introduced modern taxicab technology into New York City in 1907. Racing against European cars both in the U.S. and Europe also significantly refined American vehicles.

The gap closed swiftly. In 1904 the U.S. surpassed France as the largest car maker. By 1907 American firms produced more cars than all Europe. By 1908 the better American cars ran as well as the

French and German ones, although there were still hundreds of manufacturers turning out cheap, hastily made runabouts. In that year, Cadillac won a major British award for engineering, William Durant formed General Motors with the best-selling Buick at its core, and Henry Ford introduced the revolutionary Model T. American cars began to compete so successfully in European markets that, in 1912, French, German, and British car makers all petitioned their governments for tariff protection. Charles Kettering's development of the first marketable self-starter that year firmly established American technical supremacy. The U.S. was the supreme market for autos with triple the population of the major European industrial powers. Americans also needed cars more because they lived at lower densities, both inside and outside urban areas. American incomes, per capita, were the highest in the world. The U.S. also possessed vast domestic resources of cheap petroleum.

Initially, the American entrepreneurs relied on the urban luxury market, because American rural roads were, as one contemporary said, "the worst in Christendom." High wages and low population densities made American road construction expensive. U.S. governments did not worry about building good roads for military mobilization, a major concern in continental Europe. John B. Rae, the distinguished automotive historian, has suggested the interlocking nature of road development and vehicle transportation. Innovation in roads proceeded hand in hand with innovation in vehicles.[16] Contemporary municipal engineers were well aware of the road-vehicle relationship. As we have seen, the area covered by smooth asphalt and brick pavements increased substantially between 1890 and 1900 for reasons largely unrelated to improving travel. Not surprisingly, perceptive municipal engineers anticipated that automobility would increase the demand for asphalt and vice versa. One shrewd urban observer drew a parallel between new road surfaces and the role played by iron rails in the development of steam railroads. He wrote: "An asphalt pavement, for instance, converts the entire street surface into what for the motor vehicle is practically one broad road of infinite width—or what is equivalent of the rail in every property except that of guidance."[17]

American engineers repeatedly emphasized the importance of good pavements. Robert Thurston, by this date director of Cornell

University's pioneering school of mechanical engineering, wrote that "the transportation of merchandise must, in the early stages of the traffic, at least, be confined mainly to the cities or to business between cities connected by continuous stretches of good road."[18] In 1896, the *Engineering News,* the leading technical periodical, offered two reasons why the auto was more likely an urban technology. First, it cost more to store and feed horses on expensive urban land than on farms. Secondly, the editorial observed: "it is manifest to the engineer that power applied to the rims of the wheels of a vehicle depends for its efficiency very much more upon the nature of the roadbed than does power applied as a pull to the front end of a vehicle."[19] When only city streets were paved, primitive autos could only operate on city streets.

People associated with urban utilities early became aware of the potential of the auto for the well-paved urban market. This was especially true of those in the street railway industry or the electric light and power business that provided energy for the new trolley routes of the 1890s. Thomas Edison told the *New York World* shortly after the 1895 *Times-Herald* race that "it is only a question of time when the carriages and trucks in every large city will be run with motors."[20] Thomas F. Ryan, William C. Whitney, and other Wall Street operators associated with street railway holding companies, invested heavily in the new technology when they backed the Electric Vehicle Company in 1899, which they capitalized at over $200 million. Another magnate, Samuel Insull, was their agent in Chicago. They planned to concentrate their operations in very large cities, but failed disastrously because they chose an inferior electric technology and the 2,000 electric taxicabs that they produced proved unworkable.[21]

Several important manufacturers also had backgrounds in urban utilities. Henry Ford, the Chief Engineer of Detroit Edison, knew of the relationship between travel speeds and urban land values. He had invested in suburban real estate near River Rouge, reached by a new trolley car line. Ford favored suburbanization as an escape from what he perceived as the un-American residents of inner cities. Ford had argued about the relative merits of electric and internal combustion power with Thomas Edison at the annual Edison Company banquets in the 1890s. William Durant was best known as a carriage manufacturer, but he had also been active in Flint, Michigan's electric utility and in suburban real estate. These two people, with their awareness of the nature of the urban travel market, founded the two largest and most enduring auto firms. Amzi Barber, the leading asphalt manufacturer in the country, also invested in the auto business. His Locomobile Company was the leading auto manufacturer for several years around the turn of the century, but couldn't manage the switch from steam to gasoline power successfully. Bicycle manufacturers, whose vehicles depended on smooth operating surfaces, already knew of the importance of asphalt paved cities. For example, Alfred Pope, the leading bicycle maker and probably the leading financier of the good roads movement, began to make cars in 1897.[22]

The midwestern pioneers sought out plant locations near well paved cities. Ransom Olds built his first large factory near New York City, the largest auto market in the country. Elwood Haynes had trouble finding a level turnpike on which to operate his first vehicle near his Kokomo, Indiana home, so when he decided to open a factory, he moved to Cleveland. In *American Manufacturer and Iron World* Hiram Maxim predicted that the future automobile market would be primarily urban. At least one southern carriage manufacturer, on the verge of bankruptcy after a short fling at auto production, blamed the irregular topography and bad pavements of southern cities for his failure. When journalist Ray Stannard Baker argued for the universal adoption of the automobile in the July 1899 edition of *McClure's Magazine,* he claimed that manufacturers sold the highest number of autos in well-paved cities like Buffalo and Detroit.[23]

The general pattern of automotive innovation supports the paving-vehicle relationship. The auto developed first in the best paved European nations, Germany and France. It spread later to other technically advanced countries whose roads were inferior, like Great Britain and the United States. American innovation and early manufacturing were primarily urban processes. One expects innovation to take place in cities.[24] Only a very large city was likely to have the machine tool shops, carriage builders, rubber manufacturers, engine producers, and trained mechanical engineers that were vital to auto production. Within the large number of American cities possessing the technical infrastructure necessary for auto development, innovation seems to have concentrated in the better paved ones.

Cleveland, Buffalo, Detroit, and Washington had laid more smooth pavements on their streets than other large American cities. Except Washington, which had almost none of the industrial base needed to support auto manufacturing, all became major car producers. Other large cities with automotive pioneers and an appropriate industrial base, notably Springfield (Massachusetts), Hartford, Indianapolis, and Allentown, contained poor pavements and did not last long as car-making centers. All four, it should be noted, suffered from other locational disadvantages. The geographer Charles Boas has analyzed site patterns in the auto industry and noted the advantages of Great Lakes ports for the shipment of both raw materials and the finished product. This is likely a more powerful explanation of location, but worse paved Great Lakes cities, notably Milwaukee and Chicago, never became major auto producing centers.[25]

Urban street systems offered other advantages besides smooth pavements. By 1900 U.S. cities had built hundreds of miles of parkways (table 2.3). Urban areas developed in the late nineteenth century often featured Haussmann style boulevards like Commonwealth Avenue (Boston), Grand Boulevard (Detroit), or Prairie Avenue (Chicago). These roadways were perfect for the fragile novelties that very early auto manufacturers were selling. They lacked sharp corners or steep grades and they also had good pavements. None of the roads listed above allowed heavy teaming or public transportation, so competing traffic was light. The auto manufacturers usurped roads like these for proving grounds, and early purchasers avidly sought these venues. Many of the early elite New York motorists had initially shown their love of speed by racing trotters on the Harlem River Speedway.

While auto innovation also required advances in the technology of internal combustion engines, the existence of asphalt pavements in American cities eased the choice of motive power and the testing and marketing of prototype vehicles. But better pavements were not enough; favorable legislation was also a precondition for automobility, given the record of bans on the early steamers. Elwood Haynes and other early auto producers believed that guaranteed legal access to roads was vital to their success.[26]

While Western Europeans developed the automobile first, they came to own many fewer of them than Americans for an interlocking set of economic and regulatory reasons (table 6.1). The economic reasons for this are obvious. European national markets were too small in population and income to allow economies of scale in production on the Ford model. Regarding regulation, the British Prime Minister H. H. Asquith sought heavy horsepower-based taxes on automobiles in 1908, claiming that cars were "a luxury that is apt to degenerate into a nuisance." Britain also slapped heavy taxes on gasoline, an expensive imported product. France, Germany, and Italy followed the British lead in regulation. These rules changed European car design. If manufacturers wanted to sell vehicles other than heavy luxury cars, they had to focus on reducing horsepower and gas consumption. British Austin took over first place in British sales when it reduced the horsepower of its basic car from 20 to 7 hp. By the 1920s, such rules were probably more important than high tariffs in forcing U.S. cars out of European markets. European cities encouraged common carrier motor vehicles such as buses and taxicabs more than American cities. They also presented greater obstacles to private car ownership. Some municipal governments in France passed 6 m.p.h. speed limits. In 1912 the city government of Paris ordered gendarmes to shoot out the tires of speeding motorists. London and Paris required driving tests for motorists long before New York did.[27]

American cities regulated automobiles more favorably in the 1890s than they had earlier. Common councils rarely sought to ban gasoline autos as they had once banned steam autos, largely because urban residents had changed the way they defined street space. The auto did encounter some resistance based on the old ideas of street use, but in striking contrast to the old steam auto prohibitions, no American city government ever tried to ban the internal combustion auto. Cities that sought to restrain autos also found that evolving legal doctrines about the police powers of cities meant that their ordinances could not survive a court test. Thus, both courts and municipalities changed their regulatory attitudes. The most striking example of the change in the regulatory climate may be that cities even tolerated steamers like Locomobile in the new wave of innovation.

Another 1890s change eased automobility: city dwellers had become more accustomed to relatively fast vehicles on their streets. In 1900, *Popular Science Monthly* noted: "Prejudice against mechanically-propelled vehicles has gradually worn away, probably because of the introduction of cable and trolley cars, and at the present the majority desire to see the substitution of mechanical for animal power."[28] A survey of traffic on Fifth Avenue, New York City showed in 1902 that only two of the fourteen motor vehicles observed went faster than fifteen miles an hour. Twenty years earlier, urbanites might have violently opposed such speeds, but fifteen miles an hour was only slightly higher than the average speed of the trolley cars that now dominated many major urban streets. The speed no longer seemed quite so dangerous to many people.[29]

Also, the auto seemed less threatening to the urban environment in the 1890s, because the internal combustion engine did not have the bad public image that steam power conveyed to many Americans. Internal combustion engines could not produce monstrous accidents that scattered debris for blocks, as did steam boiler explosions. Improper gasoline storage did lead to some urban fires in the early days of the auto, but these made nowhere near the same impact on the popular mind that boiler explosions had made earlier in the century, perhaps because fire hazards were an accepted part of urban life. Cities did evolve ordinances on the storage of gas, but never regulated it as heavily as the steam boilers, which were subject to rigid inspection laws and licensing for operators. Just about the only law that hampered automobility to even a slight degree was a federal ban on carrying gasoline aboard ferryboats.[30]

Nor did the pollution of gas fumes offend urbanites as much as the sooty bituminous smoke that they associated with steam engines, although one early gasoline vehicle rider wrote: "I echoed inwardly the hope expressed by a fellow passenger that there was no bilious person present."[31] The early auto manufacturers overcame such qualms by putting mufflers with exhaust filters on their cars and, later, eliminating muffler cutouts. But, in comparison to the hue and cry that arose every time an isolated pre-1890 inventor tested his car on a city's streets, these complaints seem muted. The new steam autos of the period around 1900 succeeded only to the extent that they could overcome these traditional urban fears by burning cleaner fuels, usually gasoline, and building safer boilers. The Stanley Brothers widely ballyhooed their claim that not one of their boilers had ever blown up. Adding condensers helped, because steamers no longer exhausted live steam on the street.[32]

City residents were fed up with their rail transit systems and welcomed a potential competitor. The trolley car had not lived up to its expectations. Historians Paul Barrett, Mark Foster, and Scott Bottles have noted that transit riders in Chicago, Detroit, and Los Angeles hated the unresponsive, monopolistic street railway firms.[33] These hatreds extended throughout urban America. The novelist Theodore Dreiser wrote a popular muckraking novel about a greedy transit entrepreneur, modeled on Chicago's Charles Yerkes, claiming that he operated his lines on the principle that "The straphanger pays the dividends." Trolley companies overcapitalized themselves. They skimped on maintenance and scheduling to pay their financial obligations. Accidents and breakdowns were commonplace. Much rider resentment grew out of mismanagement, but more complaints grew out of the common carrier nature of rail transport. Southern blacks complained about segregated trolleys. Women complained that their fellow riders were rude, smelly "bustle-pinchers." For suburban commuters, the trolley ride contradicted all the values associated with the suburban dream. Trolleys were dirty, noisy, and overcrowded. It was impossible for middle-class riders to isolate themselves from fellow riders whom they perceived as social inferiors. Distancing themselves from blacks, immigrants, blue collar workers, and, in general those stereotyped as the "great unwashed," was often precisely why the middle classes had moved to the suburbs.

Also, changes in judicial attitudes toward late-nineteenth-century municipalities limited regulatory options. Under the leadership of prominent judges like Thomas Cooley and Stephen Field, state and federal courts began to exercise vast new powers of judicial review and to seek limitations on legislative activity. These judicial activists sought to whittle down the inherent police powers of city governments—that is, the municipal power to legislate for public health and safety.[34] The courts also sanctioned legislative review of municipal actions. Aggrieved urbanites could seek redress from actions by the local government in the state legislature or from several layers of judges. By 1900, activist judges had ruled against urban regulations that might impede automobility.

In transportation matters, shifting legal doctrines first manifested themselves in decisions dealing with street travel by bicycles, the technical and functional forerunners of the auto. Bicycles were private, not common carriers. They roamed freely over street surfaces, not bound to rails like street cars. Bicycles almost always traveled at higher speeds than their horse-drawn competitors. Since they moved quietly, with no hoofbeats, bicycles sometimes hit unsuspecting pedestrians who stepped off a curb in front of them. Just their novelty frightened some people. One person complained, albeit with tongue in cheek, of " . . . the swift and stealthy bicycle as deadly as the ancient war chariot, running people down or at least causing the nervous man to jump to one side like a tarantula."[35] The initial urban reaction to the bicycle had resembled the response to the steamers. "In 1878 the public hardly knew what to do with the bicycle, except suppress it."[36] Boston, New York, Newport, Brooklyn, Hartford, Chicago, Buffalo, and Washington all banned bikes for short periods of time.

Regulation of these bicycles, rather than the bans on steamers, formed the basis for the later legal reaction to the internal combustion auto. Bicycle manufacturers and the League of American Wheelmen, a fraternal organization of bicyclists, mounted an attack on the prohibitory legislation. Local L.A.W. chapters lobbied successfully to have common councils repeal the bans. Buffalo lifted its ban in 1885, the last major city to do so. These reversals came primarily in the political, not in the legal arena. They did not challenge the abstract right of cities to prohibit certain classes of traffic, such as steamers or too heavy wagons, from their streets.[37]

The leading early court case grew out of a bicycle manufacturer-backed challenge to a rule by New York's Park Commissioners that excluded bicycles from the fashionable carriage drives in Central Park. The suit complained that the Commissioners had wielded their power to regulate traffic in an unreasonable fashion when they had excluded bicycles. In 1883, the New York State Court of Appeals refused to overthrow the Park Commissioners' decision. The ruling justice wrote: "If I were acting in their place, I might not regard such an ordinance as necessary, but it is not in a legal sense so unreasonable as to warrant me in substituting my judgment for the judgment of the Commissioners."[38] He specifically compared this exclusion to the more reasonable urban prohibitions on steamers in the streets. Four years later, over the objections of New York's reform mayor, Abram Hewitt, the New York State Legislature finally overthrew the ban and allowed bicycles entry into the park.[39]

Judicial attitudes toward bicycles changed with the new, conservative legal doctrines, aiding bicycle-based mobility. After all, the bike was a somewhat harmless form of street travel; slow, light, and nonpolluting. Unlike horses, bicycles did not kick or bite passersby. Judicial changes took place primarily in cases growing out of accidents. Bicycle organizations often financed the litigation. At first, primary responsibility in tort cases rested with bike riders because of the novelty of their vehicles, but as urban street users (horses and people alike) became more accustomed to bikes, decisions diminished the responsibility of bikers. Judges declared that bicycling was reasonable, not especially subject to liability for accidents. The courts defined bicycles as ordinary carriages.[40]

Soon, courts began to apply this view of bikes to legislation also. When George B. Clementson wrote his 1895 treatise, *The Road Rights and Liabilities of Wheelmen,* he emphasized an 1892 Kansas case, Swift v. Topeka. This decision forced the City of Topeka to allow bikes on a downtown bridge. It defined bicycle riding as a common right. In his decision, the judge generalized about bicycles in a way that later courts could and did extend to automobiles: "They are not an obstruction to, or an unreasonable use of the streets of a city, but rather a new and improved method of using the same, and germane to their principal object as passageway."[41] John F. Dillon's magisterial *Commentaries on the Law of Municipal Corporations* illustrated the new attitude. In his 1890 edition, he stated that bans on self-propelled vehicles were legal, citing a precedent involving steamers. In the next edition, published in 1911, he commented that the courts would not uphold such bans.[42]

The increased willingness of the courts to pass judgment on the "reasonableness" of municipal legislation substituted the perception of a middle-class, professional group—the judiciary—for the perception of local aldermen, whose constituents might benefit from streets in other ways, not just as a "passageway." Judges upheld other police legislation that conformed to their social group's (i.e., middle class, likely suburban commuter) perception of the proper use of streets. While they favored commuters over abutters on ordinary streets, courts continued to sustain bans on wagons and common carriers in parks and on elite boulevards where they might interfere with upper-class carriages. To this day, New York City, Chicago, Washington, D.C., and Boston do not allow trucks and buses on some parkways.[43]

In the late 1890s, urban bicycle ridership expanded enormously. This created some trouble. For example, in New York's Lower East Side, the most densely populated spot on the globe, large numbers of children played in the street. They resented the middle- and upper-class bicyclists. One Lower East Side historian interviewed a woman whose oldest memory was being run down in the 1890s by "a well dressed man on a bicycle," apparently on his way to Wall Street. He lectured this four-year-old about playing in the street, rather than helping her. Eighty years later, she still burned with resentment. There were no parks or playgrounds in that neighborhood, so streets provided the only play environment. Local socialists opposed paving streets with asphalt, which they believed would attract bicyclists, but, like all American socialists, they were impotent politically. Children showed their resentment of having their turf invaded by sprinkling glass on the street, or even stoning bicycle "scorchers." Prohibition was no longer an alternative. The Lower East Siders hardly could have succeeded where upper-class park users had failed.[44]

Turn-of-the-century auto advocates applied the analogy of pro-bicycle decisions when they lobbied against urban attempts to ban the auto. In 1899 they convinced the Central Park Commissioners that it would be futile to continue a ban on autos, since automobilists could challenge it successfully in the courts. When Boston's aldermen passed an automobile prohibition, the lawyers of motorists convinced the mayor to veto it, because it would lead to a losing lawsuit.[45] Some state courts even threw out speed limits as infringements of individual rights, not surprisingly, given the anti-statist ideology of Gilded Age courts. The Illinois Court of Appeals went as far as to rule that Chicago could not license automobiles, since "such [a license] is imposing a burden upon one class of citizens in the use of streets which is not imposed on others."[46] Auto advocates, unable to see the other side of the coin, favored some restrictions on other traffic. After attacking the unsanitary nature of horses in

1901, *Automobile Magazine* advocated: "When the number of automobiles shall be increased sufficiently to warrant it, the horse may be wholly excluded from the boulevards, pleasure drives and parks."[47]

To some extent, changes in urban transportation policy grew out of outside factors, unrelated to travel needs. For example, a major reason for the increase in asphalt was because it lessened street cleaning costs. Judicial limitations on the police power developed for complex policy reasons, at best peripherally related to the urban transportation crisis. To a greater extent, the changes reflected new views of street use in low-density suburbs. More urbanites demanded improved transportation systems. The major change in the 1890–1900 decade was this increased taste for high-speed, street-using transportation. Most city dwellers for the first time saw mechanical vehicles in favorable terms. By 1899, serious thinkers about the future firmly believed that autos would primarily be private vehicles, that private ownership would increase greatly in the future, and that it would change people's lives for the better. This represented a dramatic shift in opinion toward autos from the prohibitions on mechanical vehicles that had prevailed through the 1880s.[48]

The bicycle and the trolley served the spread of the automobile in more ways than as precedents for favorable regulation. They showed the potential of technology for improving urban travel. They helped overcome the old fear of machines in urban streets. Until these forms of high speed or individual transportation actually existed, it was difficult for anyone to perceive a reason for automobiles, or to plan and encourage their deployment. The *Engineering News* urged the adoption of the mechanically powered vehicles to increase the speed and lower the cost of urban freight handling. It predicted that such vehicles would revolutionize urban freight transportation as the trolley car had revolutionized passenger transportation.[49] Hiram Maxim, a perceptive observer of the early auto scene, also believed that bicycles served as a precedent. He not only claimed that practical autos could have been built as early as 1870, but attributed the delay to an inability to perceive their potential:

> The reason why we did not build mechanical road vehicles before this, in my opinion, was because the bicycle had not yet come in

numbers and had not directed men's minds to the possibilities of independent, long-distance travel over the ordinary highway. We thought the railroad was good enough. The bicycle created a new demand which it was beyond the ability of the railroad to supply. Then it came about that the bicycle could not satisfy the demand which it created. A mechanically propelled vehicle was wanted instead of a foot propelled one and we now know that the automobile was the answer.[50]

Auto advocates argued that the car would increase the economic efficiency of cities in many ways and that the motor vehicle could improve street transportation as dramatically as the earlier innovations like the trolley and bicycle had succeeded in their narrow spheres. These advocates emphasized the auto's potential in freight and passenger transportation and pointed out that it would ease traffic jams, reduce accidents, and end pollution. The demand for the auto was not just economic; many urban reformers believed that the auto could solve the most pressing social problems of cities by relieving congestion and easing the development of low-density suburbs.

The arguments about economic efficiency appeared earliest. Because of the great increase in urban freight traffic in the 1890s, many engineers believed that the motor vehicle's primary field might well be freight haulage. Unlike passenger transportation, which the bicycle and trolley had revolutionized, freight traveled exclusively by horse power or by human powered pushcarts.

There seemed great room for improvement. In 1896 the *Engineering News* complained of the high cost of intra-urban traffic and made the incredible claim that railroads could carry some classes of intercity freight for as low as twenty-five cents a ton/mile while urban freight cost up to twenty-five cents a pound/mile. Such high transfer costs figured to raise the price of consumer goods considerably. The *News* cited the example of steam railroads that had reduced their intercity freight rates dramatically in recent years by lowering terminal costs. By analogy, local delivery costs might explain much of the difference between farm and urban prices for agricultural products. The *News* noted that transferring bulky commodities from shippers to commission agents to wholesalers to neighborhood markets involved repeated and expensive movements via slow, somewhat small, and clumsy horse pulled wagons. The article concluded that "The transportation of goods through city streets, therefore, is a problem which directly interests all classes and one which is well worthwhile to study and solve." It urged further development of both motor vehicles and asphalt streets.[51] Other articles in the technical press also suggested that light package delivery was where the motor vehicle would accomplish its first commercial success.

Despite the engineers' emphasis on freight, passenger transportation also offered promising applications for the automobile. Writers of the 1890s thought that the automobile would supplant the horse for private carriages, taxicabs, and omnibuses. Hiram Maxim believed not only that the auto would replace existing cab service, but also that it would develop an entirely new market for low-priced cabs. He predicted that many travelers who sought prices lower than the one dollar hack fare, but could afford more than the five cent trolley fare, would take taxis. Automobiles offered great advantages over the horse, even if operating costs were identical. The auto was easier to store at night. Owners could more easily predict maintenance and depreciation costs. Besides, repairing a broken auto would often be a simpler proposition than curing a sick horse. In 1896, the *Engineering News* saw little possibility that motor stages would ever replace trolleys, but *Scientific American* believed that their freedom from rails would eventually allow faster, more flexible, cheaper operation.[52]

Contemporaries debated the future role of the privately owned auto. Street railway companies initially did not fear the private car, since they thought it would function primarily as a luxury vehicle, like the horse and carriage. Others felt that the mystique and status of horse ownership would overcome the more utilitarian *"equus ex machina."* As late as 1907 the skeptical English periodical, the *Economist,* predicted "the triumph of the horse." Even the fragile early autos could serve the practical travel needs of many individuals, however. Motoring periodicals claimed that doctors could quadruple their house calls, and presumably their incomes, while sales agents could double the size of their territories. These periodicals reasoned that an owner could leave his vehicle at curbside while making a business call. A more cumbersome horse-pulled vehicle required much more street space than did the auto, could be stolen more easily and, because of the horse's propensity to bite and kick strangers, might even get involved in accidents while parked at curbside.[53]

The auto periodicals frequently debated the relative costs of horse and motor transportation for general travel beyond these special needs. Urban newspapers picked up on those debates, especially when auto industry public relations people circulated favorable stories. One forecast in an industrial periodical illustrated another argument for the auto. A few auto advocates believed that horses would become obsolescent only when auto manufacturers lowered the daily operating cost of their product below what it cost to operate a horse. They argued that the traffic jams which prevailed in the downtown sections of cities would reduce auto travel speeds to the level of existing horse-drawn transportation, so that, in cities, an auto could cover no more territory than a horse. This was a minority position, since most auto advocates argued that urban streets could handle many more cars than horses. Cars were shorter, faster, quicker starting, and more mobile laterally. On the same area of streets, the auto increased vehicular capacity. If the number of vehicles remained constant, the auto could relieve traffic jams and travel at higher speeds. Thus, the auto might cost more to operate per day but its greater speed would lower per mile operating costs, a more appropriate comparison.[54]

Automobile advocates also argued that, beside improving the economic efficiency of cities, motor vehicles would improve the urban environment. In this regard, they repeatedly emphasized that the auto would eliminate the pollution problem caused by horses. In the 1890s, a decade of heightened urban concern with public health, this was a potent argument. One motorist responded to complaints about the rising traffic fatalities by telling the popular *Appleton's Magazine* that cars would reduce tuberculosis fatalities by 20,000 lives annually in New York City alone by reducing dust. Other auto advocates blamed the constant clatter of iron horseshoes on stone pavement for the nervous disorders that seemed more common in cities than in the countryside. *Horseless Age* even argued that, "Given the greatly superior control of motor vehicles, the streets will be safer for pedestrians."[55] The periodical believed that the shorter braking and turning distances of cars compared to horses would enable drivers to avoid pedestrians.

Besides these narrowly economic functions, the automobile seemed to promise a way for turn-of-the-century Americans to get some of their most cherished social goals. In a sense, there was a "social demand" for the automobile, along with the economic one. The new middle class wanted other status objects in addition to suburban homes. The automobile, like the street railway before it, promised to ease suburban flight. Suburban historian Robert Fishman has pointed out the continuity: "The automobile has been essentially a tool in the attainment of a deeper goal which pre-dates the automobile era: the suburban ideal."[56]

Noted automotive historian James J. Flink has summarized this group's self serving beliefs about the automobile: "In a culture that invariably preferred technological to political solutions of its problems, automobility appeared to be a panacea for many of the social ills of the day . . . The ultimate answer to the tenement house slum was that everyone should buy a motorcar and commute to suburbia."[57] Auto owners tried to capitalize on these beliefs. Will Scarritt, President of the newly formed American Automobile Association, told *Munsey's Magazine* that the auto would help attain the desired social goal of suburbanization. *Horseless Age* claimed on the first page of its first issue in 1899 that cars would open more suburban land.[58] Frank Parsons, an urban reformer, predicted in 1901: "Automobiles, motor bicycles and possibly flying machines . . . will make it easy to travel fifty or sixty miles an hour in your own conveyance. No *respectable* family will be without its automobile or flying machine, and motor bicycles will be thick as mosquitoes on the Jersey coast. The country will be covered with a network of magnificent highways."[59]

Others even made the argument that autos would allow the poor to suburbanize. In 1902 Edward A. Bond, Highway Commissioner in New York State, claimed that good suburban roads would ease auto, bike, and trolley commuting, putting an end to the slum. He incongruously placed his argument in a political context; he believed that suburbanization would solve the problem of capital-labor relations. William Dix, writing in the reforming *Independent*, claimed in 1904 that cars would allow country homes for workers. In 1906, Frederick Coburn predicted that motor cars would turn the area between Portland, Maine and Washington, D.C. into a "Five Hundred Mile City," a prescient forecast. He praised the trolley and auto, which would allow "Decent-minded working folk . . . [to] live in a cottage colony, rather than a swarming tenement district filled with saloons and brothels."[60]

The rosy American forecasts of the new technology transcended any realistic prospect of automobility, suggesting that the new machines were more than just another transportation technology. In fact cars would create their own pollution, traffic mortality, and crowding problems. To understand the utopian visions that diminished resistance to the automobile requires an examination of the cultural attachment to horseless carriages that drove the rage for automobility.

1.1 Brick wheelways on a Washington, D.C. cobblestone street, still in place in 1971.

1.2 A wagon using trolley tracks for easier travel. Baltimore, 1904.

2.1 New York's Central Park as driving park, 1863. (THE NEW-YORK HISTORICAL SOCIETY)

2.2 New York elites in Central Park, 1874. (THE SMITHSONIAN INSTITUTION)

2.3 The Charles River Speedway, Boston, 1898. Note the spectators watching trotters in the reserved outer lanes. (THE SMITHSONIAN INSTITUTION)

2.4 The Charles River Speedway, Boston, 1898. Note the exit lane from the high-speed lanes on the left to allow trotters to slow down before joining slower traffic on the right. (THE SMITHSONIAN INSTITUTION)

3.1 Traffic chaos in New York City, 1884. Note the dead horse and the child flinging a snowball at traffic. (THE SMITHSONIAN INSTITUTION)

3.2 A blockade on Broadway, New York City, 1883. (LIBRARY OF CONGRESS)

3.3 The urban street at its filthiest, New York City, 1893.

5.1 An advertisement for Lucius Copeland's 1886 steamer. (THE SMITHSONIAN IN-STITUTION)

6.1 Curved Dash Oldsmobile, 1905. Oldsmobile, the American best seller, clearly has a backward design in comparison to the older Mercedes in illustration 6.2. The Oldsmobile still lacks headlights and a steering wheel. The engine looks like it is bolted onto a carriage. It provided less than one-tenth the horsepower, clearly more a horseless carriage than an automobile. (THE SMITHSONIAN INSTITUTION)

6.2 William K. Vanderbilt in his 1901 Mercedes, "The Red Devil." This Mercedes is truly an automobile, not a horseless carriage. Vanderbilt was hardly likely to go scorching in this bowler hat. (THE SMITHSONIAN INSTITUTION)

7.2 Conquest of nature: a car at the edge of the Grand Canyon, 1900. (SEAVER CENTER FOR WESTERN HISTORY RESEARCH, NATURAL HISTORY MUSEUM OF LOS ANGELES COUNTY)

7.1 John Jacob Astor and Mrs. A. Ladenberg in a high-society car floral parade in Newport, Rhode Island, 1899. (BROWN BROTHERS)

7.3 Touring pro-suffrage politicians in a 1916 Saxon. (AMERICAN MANUFACTUR-ERS ASSOCIATION)

7.4 Doctored photo showing cars on a Milwaukee street, c. 1912.

7.5 A suburban doctor and his family in a Curved Dash Oldsmobile, c. 1902. An early example of the "new baby, new car" motif in popular photography. (THE SMITH-SONIAN INSTITUTION)

7.6 Rauch and Lang ad using classical themes for the "car of social prestige."
Saturday Evening Post, 1912.

7.7 Pierce-Arrow as the car of sporting males. *Life,* 1910.

7.8 Pierce-Arrow as status symbol. *Life,* 1909.

Famous Hill-Climb of
HUDSON SUPER-SIX

In a hundred cities, Hudson dealers have won the local records with the Super-Six.

Not in America only. In several countries Super-Sixes have won the hill-climbing records.

But the Pike's Peak climb last September was the world's supreme test. There twenty great cars, all specially built, met for a race to "the top of the world." And the Hudson Super-Six made the best time of all.

What They Drove

The Super-Six, remember, is a small, light Six. It doesn't win by size. It won these tests just as it won all other worth-while records —by endurance.

This invention—patented by Hudson—has minimized motor friction. It thus added 80 per cent to the motor's efficiency. It nearly doubled the motor's endurance.

You don't care to climb Pike's Peak at the speed the Super-Six showed it could do. You don't care to go 102 miles per hour, as a Super-Six stock chassis has done.

Or 1819 miles in 24 hours, also with a stock chassis.

But you want the car which holds those records, if you buy a great car. Not because they prove capacity, but because they prove endurance—prove that no service you will ever demand will equal its capacity.

All-Round Ruler

But the Hudson is now more than monarch in performance. It is fully as distinctive in style and beauty this year, in finish, in equipment and in luxury. It has a new gasoline saver, in the form of radiator shutters, which, through controlling the heat of the motor in part, overcomes the disadvantages and waste of the present poor grade of gasoline. It has a patent pneumatic carburetor, exclusively Hudson, self-adjusting to every engine speed.

In whatever you prize most—performance, style, beauty or economy—you will find the Hudson leader. That's why it leads all other front-rank cars in sales.

Phaeton, 7-passenger . $1650
Cabriolet, 3-passenger . . 1950
Touring Sedan . . . 2175
Limousine 2925
Limousine Landaulet . . 3025
Town Car 2925
Town Car Landaulet . . 3025
(All prices f. o. b. Detroit)

HUDSON MOTOR CAR COMPANY, DETROIT, MICHIGAN

7.9 Phallic fantasies in advertising. *Scientific American,* 1916.

7.10 Cars attract mermaids. Another masculine fantasy ad, 1905. (NASCAR ARCHIVES)

7.11 Conquest of nature and suburban family themes in advertising. *Ladies Home Journal*, 1917.

THE SILENT Waverley Electric

UNMATCHED ELEGANCE— CONSTANT SERVICE YOURS IN THE LIMOUSINE-FOUR

With Full Four Passenger Capacity and Unobstructed View for the Driver.

Four grown people may ride in delightful comfort, without crowding or crushing of handsome gowns and wraps and without obstruction of the driver's view in this new four passenger electric.

Each occupies a separate Pullman chair, three of which face forward, with the fourth a "cosy corner" in front at the right—

—A novel, distinctive, luxurious and elegant arrangement to be found in no other electric, an arrangement which also insures the driver *full view ahead.*

Seat Plan— Patents Pending. Crosses show space for parcels, etc.

With more speed than your city ordinance allows and more mileage than any day requires. The Limousine-Four is always at your service in all weather. No blizzard that blows can keep it off the streets.

40 cells, 11 plate Exide Hycap or Philadelphia M.V. Style or 13 plate Gould or Waverley M. V. Style batteries. Edison or Ironclad Exide extra. Price complete, $2900.

Write for the Silent Waverley Electric Year Book, which describes and illustrates this superb car, together with the Waverley pleasure car line, the most complete made.

A de luxe production, valuable for its artistic beauty, it is free on request to those interested, as is also our Commercial Car catalog, showing models ranging from a light delivery wagon to a 5-ton truck. Address

THE WAVERLEY COMPANY
134 S. East Street, Indianapolis, Ind.
Chicago Branch, 2005 Michigan Avenue

7.12 Waverly Electric advertises rear seat tiller steering. The driver (rear left) is not watching the road. *Ladies Home Journal,* 1912.

7.13 Henry Ford entering the Detroit Electric that he bought for his wife. Note the backward facing front set and the steering tiller in front of the rear seat. (THE SMITHSONIAN INSTITUTION)

9.1 School lets out, Manhattan, 1916.

9.2 Posed photo from a school safety leaflet.

10.1 The Municipal Art Society 1904 plan for radials through Manhattan's gridiron. Only the extensions of Sixth and Ninth Avenues were ever built.

10.2 New York Mayor Gaynor's 1912 proposal for a new avenue between and parallel to Fifth and Sixth avenues.

10.3 Jules Guerin's vision of one of the boulevards proposed by Daniel Burnham in the 1909 plan of Chicago.

THE EPITOME OF POSSESSIONS: THE CAR IN POPULAR CULTURE

THE AUTOMOBILE, a metaphor as well as a machine, meant more to Americans than just another transportation mode, a tool to reach the suburbs. Very early in its history it became what French social critic Henri Lefebvre has called "the epitome of possessions."[1] The automobile symbolized wealth and psychic liberation for an enormous number of groups within American society. It also played a role in changing American patterns of gender identity. The advent of the automobile and government regulation of traffic took place in a culture that attached enormous emotional significance to the machine. One must examine the ways in which Americans discovered the car, and dreamed about its potential, at the turn of the century by looking at some of the cultural milieux which described it: newspaper stories, magazine articles, spectator events, advertisements, songs, photographs, films, and children's literature. Only through this framework can one understand the pattern of automobility that emerged.

To understand the cultural implications of motorcars, we must first understand the rapidly changing technology. Automotive design improved significantly in the first seventeen years of the century. Changes in the mechanical possibilities and cost of the machine conditioned much of the way Americans perceived it.

Owners would not be able to exploit cars for practical purposes, such as the journey to work, for many years. Before the advent of the Model T in 1908, most American car owners probably employed chauffeurs not just to drive their cars, but also to perform the all too frequent repairs needed by pre–mass production cars. In 1902 Harry B. Haines wrote a description of how to drive for beginners that reads more like a catalog of car repairs than instructions on how to apply the clutch, brake, accelerator, etc. Constant tire repairs probably represented the greatest hassle for early car owners. Tire changing required removal of the entire wheel, which took time and considerable strength. Demountable rims became standard around 1911, making changes much less physically onerous. However, the tires themselves only improved gradually. The industry added carbon black as a strengthener in 1912, invented high-pressure, cord tires in 1916, and developed well-based, low pressure tires in 1926. Smoother pavements in metropolitan areas also extended tire life, but before 1916, flat tires probably occurred every hundred miles or so. As late as 1910, one urban driver reported spending five times as much annually on tires as on gasoline.[2]

Other problems abounded. Hand-lit acetylene lamps, hand cranking, hand choking, and manual spark advancement all made car operation more complex than today. In 1912 Charles Kettering built the first electric system for production cars, including self-starter and electric lights, but it did not become standard equipment for several years after that. Manual gear shifting and primitive brakes required considerable physical strength. Hydraulic brakes and H-slot synchromesh transmissions did not become the norm until the late 1920s. Even steering required much strength and skill. Rubber firms did not add treads to tires until 1908 and tires remained 4–6 inches wide, so skidding was a recurring problem on the era's poor roads. The high center of gravity needed to clear obstacles in primitive, pre-1920s roads made rollovers all too frequent. High-speed turns often led to broken axles. Most manufacturers still installed some less than reliable hand tooled parts, even after Cadillac's famous demonstration of interchangeability in 1908. For most car buyers a modicum of mechanical reliability came only after Ford opened the first modern mass production plant in Highland Park, Michigan in 1910 and added a moving assembly line in 1913. Even then, frequent mechanical breakdowns imposed serious limits on the adoption of cars for commuting, probably the most common practical application of automobility.

Poor roads also hampered automobility. Cars could travel long distances on dirt roads only in the dry summer months. As late as 1913 road conditions in Michigan, a state with a reputation for good roads, remained so poor that Ford could only deliver cars by road to buyers within 100 miles of its Detroit factory.[3] Year round long distance travel only became possible in the 1920s. As late as 1928, drivers still published books on coast to coast travel that contained hints on how to avoid the worst dirt roads.[4]

Climate also limited commuting applications of automobility. Cars closed to the weather became the norm only after 1925.[5] Car manufacturers did not even offer hand-operated windshield wipers until 1916 and would not offer electric wipers as standard equipment until the 1930s. Large cities rarely cleared their streets of snow before 1915, despite a significant automotive presence. Advice columns in newspapers and periodicals before that date recommended that owners put their cars up on blocks for the winter. This suggests that consumers saw their vehicles primarily as recreational vehicles or status objects. Los Angeles had very high car registrations at a very early date, in part because its climate simplified driving for the journey to work or business purposes.[6]

As early as 1899, before most Americans had even seen a car, newspaper stories were reporting how the primitive vehicles were being used for ostentatious display. Elite New York auto owners formed the Automobile Club of America in a meeting at the Waldorf-Astoria Hotel. Its members included the socially prominent August Belmont, Alfred Vanderbilt, and Henry Clay Frick. They began a tradition of annual parades to flaunt their new machines. In one parade "society girls" in posh Newport, Rhode Island covered horseless carriages with flowers, perhaps the earliest example of car customizing (illustration 7.1). Ralph Epstein's survey of the records of two pre-1900 horseless carriage companies found that most purchasers described themselves as capitalists, manufacturers, merchants, or doctors—in other words, upper class.[7] The first popular song hinting at the affluent and romantic context of cars also appeared in 1899. That year U.S. drivers adopted the supposedly more romantic French word, *automobile,* rather than the more pedestrian British usage, *motor.*[8]

We can best understand the social impact and cultural context of the automobile with a local case study, emphasizing newspapers, the primary print medium for transmitting culture. A content analysis of the *New York Times* (table 7.1) suggests the complex way in which early-twentieth-century Americans received information about cars. Overall, the table seems to suggest a fairly balanced distribution of stories dealing with auto-associated problems (accidents, traffic, etc.) and more positive information (the doings of upper class drivers, industrial successes, races, etc.). But, these numbers are a little deceiving. Overwhelmingly, pre-1908 stories contained reports of elite travel in autos, covered on the society pages, a measure of the status associated with the new vehicles. Accidents and regulation led the coverage, but accident coverage often had a subliminal context implying that elites had received new

Table 7.1 **ARTICLES ON AUTOMOTIVE TOPICS IN THE NEW YORK TIMES**

	1900	1905	1910	1915
Number of Articles	32	288	1031	1728
Accidents/Regulation	28%	43%	27%	37%
Elite Use (Clubs, Tours, shows, *etc.*)	25	13	11	11
Industry/Technology	19	7	16	8
Racing	9	19	13	8
Roads	3	3	9	3
Traffic	0	2	1	11
Theft	0	2	2	3
Trucks, Buses, etc.	3	1	13	11
Foreign News	9	4	7	7
Miscellaneous	3	2	2	5

SOURCE: *New York Times Index,* 1900–1915. By 1915 stories were so commonplace that I only sampled, using the first quarter of the year multiplied by four. This may lead to some understatement of stories about roads, which were more likely to occur in the summer construction season. The *Times*'s coverage seems roughly similar to other papers, in New York and elsewhere. It is used here because its unique index facilitates content analysis.

powers over life and death on the street, or emphasizing the courage of motorists. Accidents might have drawn front page coverage before 1905, but appeared in the back pages after that. Death in the streets had become a routine part of metropolitan life.[9]

The *Times* printed some editorial complaints about speeding, pedestrian fatalities, and races on public roads, but noted that these were necessary evils required by the benefits of automobility. Cars promised high speed, private travel, less pollution than horses, new leisure possibilities, and suburbanization. Racing stories often dwelled favorably on the social class, courage, and skill of the racers. When racing became professionalized, around 1907–8, coverage diminished and editors also moved it to the sports pages.

Table 7.1 is also a little misleading in that the *Index* covered only news stories. The casual reader would have seen overwhelmingly positive coverage by looking at photographs or advertisements. These items may have had a greater impact than the news stories, since they were visuals in a sea of print.

The automobile and related activities received strong, primarily positive attention in the newspaper's new Sunday photographic section and in news photos. This coverage also diminished over time, as automobility became more commonplace. By 1906 photos of elite car owners were no longer news, but auto advertising was steadily expanding. During the peak spring buying season auto advertisements may have taken up more column inches than all the auto related print items. Also, after 1904 the *Times* printed an annual automobile section, mostly advertisements. Non-auto advertisers often put cars in their plugs as well. For example, department stores, temples of the emerging consumer culture, often advertised automobile delivery, a powerful symbol of status and novelty.[10]

Looking at the print coverage in more detail gives a sense of the perceptions that newspaper-reading Americans formed about the new technology. *Times'* readers first saw a front-page story about autos in 1896 when four cars (a bicyclist accompanied them) motored from Kingsbridge at Manhattan's northern tip to Ardsley, New York, thirteen miles away. The race's five judges included society eminences Chauncey Depew, John Jacob Astor, and Nelson Miles.[11] Readers could follow the adventure of other tours. Alexander Winton sold many cars to New Yorkers after his much publicized 48 hour run from Cleveland in 1899, which attracted more than a million spectators, many of whom were viewing a car for the first time. James Flink has noted Winton's clever employment of a press agent, Charles B. Shanks, to get newspaper coverage. Ransom Olds sold 750 Curved Dash Oldsmobiles in New York City after front-page coverage of a record breaking run from Detroit in 1902. The important Glidden reliability tours usually operated out of the City. In 1907, an estimated 50,000 residents gathered in Times Square to send off the entrants in the famous New York-Paris (via Siberia) race.[12]

Readers learned about the status connotations of the new machines from the doings of the elite Automobile Club of America, including coverage of its banquets, its Madison Square Garden Auto Show, races, its tours to summer resorts like Newport, and its parades. The newspaper played up A.C.A. press releases, including the members' chronic whining about the lack of good chauffeurs. The automotive escapades of elites were also titillating newspaper subscribers. The *Times* informed New Yorkers when Mrs. Bernard Baruch's chauffeur ran over a police officer in Central Park in 1901. Kaiser Wilhelm received coverage when he became a car buff (after his carriage lost a race to one) in 1903. The King of Belgium cracked the pages because he had learned to drive. When his daughter eloped in an automobile in 1904, it was front-page news. Society reporters told their readers when trotting enthusiast William Rockefeller traded his horses and carriages for cars in 1905. John Jacob Astor, another one time trotting horse owner, bragged to the public that "a stable of cars is coming to be recognized as the proper thing for a man of wealth."[13]

The press lavished attention on the most daring of the millionaires, William G. Vanderbilt. In 1902 he set a record by driving from Monte Carlo to Paris in 17 hours in his Mercedes, "The Red Devil" (see illustration 6.2). A week later he beat the Baron Henri de Rothschild in a match race on the streets of Paris. He won auto races in Vienna, Madrid, Newport, and Florida, briefly holding the world speed record for the mile. He sponsored the Vanderbilt Cup races, a major international competition. He relished speeding, and got into scrapes with the police in both Newport and New York. In 1907 he again hit the front page, when he caused an ugly international incident by running over a peasant child in Pistoia, Italy. Local authorities had to call out the Carbineri to rescue him from an enraged mob.[14]

Using the novel machines confirmed the courage, physical prowess, and elite status of car owners. Perhaps because so few women drove, women drivers rarely appeared in the *Times*, other than as oddities. In writing about drivers in general or, in referring to drivers whose gender they could not identify, reporters bestowed only masculine pronouns or adjectives. Cars symbolized masculine aggressiveness and wealth.

Newspaper and other photography reaffirmed the prestige messages about automobility. As early as 1896, *Cosmopolitan* ran a photo of wealthy New Yorkers inspecting a car at a suburban country club. The earliest published magazine photo of a family in a car appeared in the popular leisure magazine, *Outing*, which captioned the photo "Plaything of the Wealthy." A famous 1902 icon showed New York millionaire George Jay Gould's five formally clothed children in three approximately half scale, but fully operable cars, clustered around his large Panhard-Levassor. The Gould estate loomed in the background. The family chauffeur sat at the wheel of the imported car. The Gould photo foreshadowed what would become a twentieth-century commonplace: a photo of the whole family, often in their Sunday best, with a new car, a symbol of economic attainment.[15]

Photos showed auto pioneers, almost always men, almost always in suits, seated in their prototype vehicles. Some showed Mrs. Baruch or other high society women with their chauffeurs. Other images showed the Sultan of Morocco, the Czar, the Kaiser, and an array of other royalty in their cars. Many displayed a conquest of nature motif. Cars perched at the edge of the Grand Canyon, traveled through a tunnel bored in a Sequoia tree in Yosemite National Park, or climbed Pike's Peak (illustration 7.2). The *Times* showed many photos like these and editorially praised the motor car for its forays into deserts in the American west.[16] One car company generated widespread iconographic publicity for its model by driving it up the steps of the U.S. Capitol, a variant on the conquest theme.[17]

Presidential candidates, beginning with William Jennings Bryan in 1896, campaigned in cars, not just to increase mobility, but to prove their modernity, to attract crowds, and to generate newspaper photos. Progressive mayors like Tom Johnson in Cleveland and Sherburn Becker in Milwaukee also campaigned by auto. Becker even named his Pope-Toledo the "Red Devil," in the manner of Vanderbilt. By 1912 politicians were insisting on the indispensability of autos for campaigning. Suffragists barnstormed by car as a way to get positive publicity for their cause (illustration 7.3). Invariably such tours drew the local newspaper photographer, in part because editors perceived woman drivers as a rarity. Photos of Ford and other assembly plants also appeared. They still recur in history textbooks as evidence of the era's industrial growth. Then, as now, they were positive symbols of economic prosperity.[18]

Automobiles also became an important element of urban iconography. The Milwaukee Chamber of Commerce printed an album, circa 1912, apparently designed for distribution to visiting conventioneers (see illustration 7.4). The Chamber owned a collection of photos of city streets, all without traffic, which it had published to display unencumbered views of the city's largest buildings. In this album, it glued completely out of scale automobiles onto the photos, presumably to show the city's modernity and wealth. Similar postcards with fake automobiles had become a staple of small-town promotion by 1910.[19] At times, boosters even printed photos of jams, usually a taboo because they hinted at urban overcrowding, for bragging purposes. In 1917, the *Times* printed a spectacular overhead view of the backed up corner of Fifth Ave. and 42nd St., claiming that it was "The busiest intersection in the world."[20]

James E. Paster, who has surveyed many family snapshot collections in archives, estimates that individuals have taken billions of automobile photos for family albums since the 1890s. He found that the iconography of the popular family snapshot imitated the early-twentieth-century published images. Some family photos emphasized wealth, often by posing members next to new cars. Some illustrated mobility by showing people traveling, especially departing, by cars. These symbolized freedom and mobility. Americans marked changes in economic status by buying a new car, or by going someplace in one (illustration 7.5). Even the amateur family snapshots reproduced by Paster used low, frontal camera angles that exaggerated the size of the car, especially the hood and the engine underneath. Family members took the photos in daylight, with the sun behind the photographer. Camera technology forced this, but the resulting reflection made cars look especially shiny and new. According to Paster, few images showed old or dented cars. Clearly participants in the new age of mass photography romanticized cars in their snapshots.[21] Showing photos off to the unautomobilized reaffirmed wealth, status, and daring.

To viewers familiar with Thorstein Veblen, whose *Theory of the Leisure Class* enjoyed great popularity in the early years of the century, photos like the one of the Gould family might have suggested a negative theme: the popular dislike of conspicuous consumption by the wealthy. In other words, subscribers could read the photos of elite automobilists two ways: they might see success manifest in material possessions or they might see wasteful spending by the idle rich. Periodicals and newspapers sometimes published negative articles on this theme, with rashes of stories appearing in 1907 and 1911. For example, in a 1907 magazine short story the hero resisted buying a car (in his words, an "undemocratic, purse-proud, expensive contraption") because he feared that others might label him a wealthy dilettante.[22]

New automobilists attracted some censure as automobility percolated downward to other social classes. The *Times* blamed a 1911 wave of accidents, not on elite owners and their chauffeurs, but on new drivers like "the East Side butcher who buys a used car and joy rides."[23] Traditional moralists also complained; at least one small sect did not allow its members to drive because cars "exalted the heart."[24] The popular *Independent,* a religious journal, complained that spending on the auto detracted from more important things. Middle class men, it argued, were putting off marriage to buy cars. Once married, the pressure to provide cars likely became one of the pressures to consume that led to an increase in the divorce rate. Others complained that middle-class families deferred having children or had fewer children in order to purchase a car. One cleric griped that the money spent on cars would be better spent on cultural or religious activities. Some reformers felt that home ownership or savings accounts should have priority over status seeking. In 1910 the *Times* attacked autos as "an evil extravagance" for the middle class, especially when paid for by second mortgages on the home. *Harper's* printed a short story about some small-town shopkeepers who jacked up their prices to pay for new cars, ultimately bankrupting themselves. *Women's Home Companion* complained in 1911 that middle-class business executives were choosing to buy cars rather than send their children to college.[25]

Nothing infuriated whites concerned with limiting status symbols more than black drivers. The *New York Sun* headlined "White Race Saved" when Barney Oldfield, the race driver, beat Jack Johnson, the controversial black heavyweight champion, in a 1910 match race. The American Automobile Association, fearing that Johnson might further damage white masculinity by winning the race, had tried to prevent the event by threatening to ban Oldfield from racing. Johnson's biographer notes that white policemen in cities all over the United States harassed the boxer when he drove his car, especially when he carried white women. A theater manager in Indianapolis once threatened to kill Johnson when he took a white woman for a ride in his status object. Johnson's behavior threatened white middle class men on the interacting concerns of class, race, and sexuality. Later, the *New York Times* complained that blacks and Latins were bad drivers, with no supporting evidence.[26]

The middle class didn't buy these anti-consumption arguments—they bought cars instead. As one Muncie, Indiana woman later told two somewhat censorious sociologists who noted that her family had purchased a car before indoor plumbing: "You can't get to town in a tub."[27] The public wanted status symbols and wanted at least symbolic liberation from the constraints of everyday life. Thus, the moralists had little success. European governments did tax cars as luxury goods, but sumptuary regulation has never played well in the United States.

Advertising reinforced the print and photographic messages in the newspapers. Ads drew the reader's eye because ad agencies formatted their product differently from the rest of the paper. Ads exploited lush drawings, headlines, and empty space to highlight their message through contrast with the rigid, fine type format typical of newspapers. In fact the unstated economic purpose of the standard, unattractive newspaper layout was probably to make advertising, the key to the publisher's profit, look more attractive. Perhaps revenues from auto advertising explain the generally favorable treatment of automobility in the press. Publishers were probably reluctant to bite a hand that fed them.

By 1910 car companies were buying one-eighth and by 1917 one-fourth of the advertising in mass consumption magazines in the United States, a figure that was increasing annually.[28] To attract such important advertisers, other print media imitated the annual auto sections that appeared first in the *Times* and *Scientific American* in 1901. Corporate press releases, not "objective" journalism filled these sections. Press release journalism also dominated coverage of the auto industry in the business pages, and the descriptions of pioneer tours and races.

Truly aggressive marketing only came after Ford grabbed the bottom of the market with the Model T in 1908. The T was the prototypical modern car, whose owners were not just the stereotypical midwestern dirt farmers. In distant Paris, Gertrude Stein fell in love with her T, and even took a mechanic's course, so she could repair it herself. John Rae gives the following price series for brand new Ts: 1908, $850; 1910, $780; 1912, $600; 1914, $490; 1916, $360; 1921, $260. Sales grew at a nearly exponential rate: 1908, 5,896; 1910, 19,293; 1912, 78,611; 1914, 260,720; 1916, 377,036.[29] Henry Ford relied on price (50 percent below most competitors) and mechanical reliability to sell the car. Word of mouth, not print advertising, sold the T during its heyday. On those rare occasions when Ford did advertise, copywriters reserved the largest headline for price. Rivals and comedians joked about the supposedly backward style and unchanging features of the Model T, but it was a mechanical marvel in comparison to its competitors.

Ford marketed the Model T with a reverse psychology that avoided all suggestions of elegance. The style, which rarely changed, included such inconvenient oddities as no front door on the driver's side, gas tank under the front seat, and an awkward planetary transmission. Ford probably retained these design flaws because they served the vision of a cheap and reliable car for first time buyers. Even when he changed the T, for example, adding curved fenders in 1915 and electric lamps in 1925, Ford did not publicize the updates. Minimizing change helped drive the price down. Ford's values played especially well in traditionalist rural America. After a year's debate, one fundamentalist Dunkard sect banned Buicks, but not Model Ts, because they were not "haughty and sinful."[30]

The Model T was also a powerful car, something rarely noted because of its utilitarian image. Its high power-to-weight ratio and general mechanical efficiency often enabled the T to beat cars of double its weight and four times its horsepower in races. In 1909 it won a major New York–Seattle race. A race-prepared T beat the world record holding Blitzen Benz in a Detroit time trial in 1911. The makers of heavy touring cars feared the T enough to lobby racetrack operators to ban it. The track at Syracuse would not allow them. The operators of the Indianapolis 500 race required Ts to carry an extra 1,000 pounds of dead weight, ostensibly for safety purposes. The earliest adolescent street racers in Southern California preferred Model Ts. With modifications from reasonably priced racing kits, Ts dominated informal drag racing from its beginning around 1915 to the late 1920s. Many purchasers probably thought of the T as a muscle car, not just transportation.[31]

Other companies responded to the Model T first by resorting to exotic brand names, substituting image for performance. Chevrolet, Harroun, and Rickenbacker were early makes named after famous racers. Even Henry Ford had first come to the attention of New Yorkers as a world record racer.[32] Some firms chose animal names, suggesting that cars liberated drivers from the concerns of everyday life by making them as wild and uninhibited as animals. A few examples of this predated the T. In 1904 Peerless hyped a model with a massive 1120 cc. engine by naming it the Green Dragon. In 1905 Henry Ford's former partner, Alexander Malcolmsen, manufactured the Wolverine in 1905. By 1917 consumers could order Jackrabbits, Bearcats, Panthers, Eagles, Wasps, and Lions. These brand names also connoted either speed and aggressiveness, possibly both. Another ploy, obviously aimed at male drivers, involved naming cars after weapons or military leaders: Arrows, Flyers, Bullets, Rockets, Geronimos, Sheridans, and Grants.[33]

Many names had prestige connotations, since offering status was an obvious counter to Ford's functional style. Classical cars included the Phoenix, Vulcan, and Mercury. For the royally inclined, brands included: Imperial, Regal, Ruler, Sovereign, and Sultan. Non-regal, but still elite status came with Gentlemen's Speedy Roadster, Sterling, Premier, Continental, Saxon, Savoy, Success, Peerless, Playboy, Yale, and Harvard. A few manufacturers allowed men to drive women, at least metaphorically: Mercedes, Victoria, Dolly (manufactured, of course, by the Madison Company), Princess,

Queen, and Lulu. Rolls Royce, already established in the U.S. as a luxury car, labeled its hood ornament, a women in a flowing gown, "Spirit of Ecstasy."[34]

Advertisements also relied heavily on graphics. Before 1908, these typically consisted of simple illustrations of the products.[35] Sometimes, advertisers included photos of their factories. This symbolized a belief in quality manufacturing, a pragmatic appeal that made sense in a market where nervous consumers were often purchasing their first vehicle and leery of the investment. It also let buyers know that they were buying from a manufacturer, not one of the thousands of fly-by-night assemblers who plagued the early auto industry.

Competitive, post-Model T, marketing led to more elaborate ads. By 1912, the "plain and simple" style was appearing only in about a third of major magazine advertising. Ads first displayed cars against more decorative backgrounds. They depicted urban settings, typically the front of an upper-class mansion, a bank, or a classically designed government building. Traffic did not exist. In advertising copy rural or suburban roads violated reality by looking smooth, firm, and dust-free. Mansions, country clubs, or parks provided suburban locales.[36]

With the right product motorists could venture to farms, forests, beaches, national parks, mountains, or airports. Such ads showed a conquest of nature theme that must have played well in early-twentieth-century culture. Apparently advertising models never drove their cars to a factory, mine, or desert. Drivers looked prosperous: as a rule well dressed young men, but sometimes older, more substantial "banker" types. Senior citizens, farmers, and blacks never drove in this idealized world. Even the commonplace liveried chauffeurs fit the norms. All car drivers had perfectly shaped northern European noses. These drivers, almost without exception men, carried handsome women, impeccably dressed children, or other young men. Ads rarely depicted family motifs before the 1920s, although White Steamer tried to capitalize on this theme as early as 1911 and a few firms did so later. In general, the ads reeked of status.

In an age when cars were uncomfortable, slow, and unreliable; many manufacturers focussed their written claims on comfort, speed, and reliability. To some extent, this explains the focus on touring and racing in ads, since success in either implied reliability. Both themes also heightened the sense of adventure. Comfort derived, in part, from reliability but also drew from strength. Cars were heavy, built (or at least drawn or photographed) somewhat like locomotives. In the age of steam, consumers associated size with strength and power. Engineering considerations mandated large cars, but manufacturers also increased car size as a styling device to give cars a more substantial look. Ad agency illustrators made cars look larger in their copy by photographing or drawing them from a low angle with a strongly contrasting background.[37]

Manufacturers also tried to promise as much horsepower as possible, because that seemed to promise strength and reliability. First-time car buyers readily understood the analogy to horses. Advertisers frequently claimed silent operation, a sign of mechanical efficiency and elite dignity. Some affluent consumers wanted relatively quiet machines, akin to horses. Knight, once a major manufacturer, even named its model "The Silent Knight," not just to parody the Christmas carol, but because it ran with a peculiar sleeve valve system that made little noise. Marketing probably drove the design. Before the coming of the T, firms trying to substitute marketing for quality pretty clearly adopted the more exotic advertising techniques.[38]

Copywriters also emphasized fantasies of status and conquest. Cadillac tried for an upper-class market, running the pompous statement: "In every field of human endeavor he that is first must perpetually live in the white light of publicity whether the leadership be vested in a *man* or manufactured product."[39] The advertisement featured Roman style print with no capitals or punctuation, an allusion to imperial Rome and to the classical education of the upper classes. Rauch and Lang also deployed a classic motif, placing a Roman arch around the margin of its advertising copy (illustration 7.6). The ad drew on the historical allusion of Cosimo De Medici's coach, claiming that Rauch and Lamb sought the same quality in its "car of social prestige, built for people of unquestioned taste and judgement." Packard went after elites with a more understated message: "We build a good car and charge a good price for it. . . . Ask the *man* who owns one." Pierce-Arrow sought a more sporting, but still affluent crowd. Its plugs had little text, and normally featured young men with the accouterments of wealth, such as tennis rackets, golf clubs, or bejeweled women (illustrations 7.7 and 7.8).[40]

Historian Loren Baritz has summarized the visual effect of early auto ads: "They described a way of life: free, young, smiling, in tune with nature."[41] As a group, the ads reinforced notions of the prestige associated with car ownership. They taught that cars allowed adventure and liberation from the everyday world. Only one ad showed cars in traffic. None hinted at safety issues. Many romanticized racing. They also taught stereotypical gender values about both men and women. Typically men were in charge, women were spectators or trophies. The more graphic ads played to male fantasies of power, speed, and seduction (illustrations 7.9, and 7.10).

Only 4 of the 82 ads surveyed for 1907 and 1912 showed women drivers, and all but one of those ads appeared in *Ladies Home Journal*. These advertisers employed a very stereotypical approach, perhaps because male copywriters prepared the ads.[42] Oldsmobile bought the first car ads in the *Ladies Home Journal* in 1905, during a cyclical downswing. Winton, another company in difficulty, printed some ads with women drivers the same year. Babcock Electric ran ads in 1910: "She who drives a Babcock Electric has nothing to fear." Ads aimed at men never carried similar hints of the complexity of driving and repair. Men were expected to master them. Baker Electric ran a famous series of ads with drawings showing high society women at the wheel and even one of a woman dropping her husband off at the golf course. Cole claimed to be "the choice of American womanhood." Interstate, one of the first internal combustion cars with electric starter and lights, claimed in 1912 that its product "obeyed the will of a woman driver as readily, as easily and as simply as an electric coupe."[43]

Facing sluggish Model N sales in 1907, even the supposedly practical Henry Ford tried to appeal to women buyers in a way that he never tried with men. He noted the possibilities of the auto for romance. The ad claimed that the Model N was a "runabout built for two," added: "Two's company and a crowd frequently spoils a motoring trip," and closed: "Of course, you can scorch if you want to—40 miles an hour easily—but you won't want to. You'll get used to the soft purr of the motor and the gentle motion of the car." (Interestingly, cars never purred softly in the mainstream, male-directed ads.) The ad concluded with an endorsement from "a lady whose purse can afford anything she desires."[44]

Some subthemes occurred. A 1916 Willys ad showed a chauffeur saluting two women wearing riding pants and carrying riding crops. Buick printed two ads in the *Ladies Home Journal* in 1917 showing suburban women hauling their children (illustration 7.11).[45] The marketing-oriented car assembler Ned Jordan believed women made the key decisions in buying family cars. Yet, his attempt to market cars for women showed much condescension. In 1917 he announced that he would try to reach that market by adopting the ploy of the Parisian couturiers and selling "spring style models." Jordan also told his audience that they were buying "the enjoyment of something beyond mere transportation" and a "personal, individual, intimate car." Surprisingly, he labeled this supposedly women's car, "Playboy."[46]

Usually, advertising to women seems to have been the desperate ploy of companies in financial trouble, hoping that women were gullible enough to buy an inferior product. Interstate and Playboy sold second-rate cars, assembling parts made by other companies. Ford and Oldsmobile made these ads in slow sales years, hoping to get rid of obsolescent inventory before new models replaced them. Firms making electric cars turned to woman consumers after other manufacturers had established the supremacy of internal combustion. The electric firms rightfully feared bankruptcy. The slow, sedate, clean electrics required neither cranking nor shifting. Their ads implicitly assumed that women had inferior mechanical skills.[47]

Sometimes stereotyping women even led firms to regressive, unsafe engineering. In 1912 Waverly Electric and Detroit Electric, both failing companies, marketed cars that they claimed had been completely redesigned to meet the needs of women. Beside the backward electrical technology, each steered with an obsolescent, dangerous tiller. The driver operated the car from the rear seat. The front seat faced the back (illustration 7.12). The designers evidently believed that women drivers were more interested in seeing the faces of all their riders than the road. Henry Ford, whose marriage was not without considerable strife, actually bought his wife, Clara, a Detroit Electric, rather than a Model T (see illustration 7.13). At some subconscious level he may have preferred a dangerous design. A traditionalist like Ford also may have wanted to limit his wife's cruising range.[48]

All the advertising featuring woman drivers, also may represent attempts to shame males afraid to buy their first cars by suggesting

ɔotive technology had become so simple that even women
rate cars. Historically, technically innovative American
s have used women in this way. Two examples leap to
early electric illuminating industry subsidized a Broadway
eaturing women draped in light bulbs to show the safety
roduct to male consumers. Later, the nascent airline in-
stewardesses, rather than stewards, on airplanes hoping
men into flying.[49]

ss overtly commercial aspects of the popular culture also
automobility favorably without the incentive that paid
rtising gave newspapers. Popular songs presented the most
ntertainment statements about the romantic possibilities
of motor cars. Although hardly a best seller, Rudolph Anderson's
1899 song, "Love in an Automobile," illuminated many elements of
the car culture when probably fewer than two thousand Americans
owned cars. Anderson and later librettists of the automobile revolution wrote for a music hall audience in precisely those cities in
which elites were conspicuously consuming automobiles. Anderson
appealed to their fantasies:

When first I proposed to Daisy on a sunny summer's morn,
She replied, "you must be crazy," and laughed my love to scorn
Said I, "Now I've hit on a novel scheme, which surely to you
  may appeal.
Say wouldn't you go for a honeymoon in a cozy automobile?"
When she heard my bright suggestion, why, she fairly jumped
  for joy.

Her reply was just a question: "Oh joy, when do we start dear
  boy?"
Said I, "You will take 'bout half an hour to pack up your things
  and grip.
And then 'round the corner we'll married be, and start away on
  our trip.
We'll fulfill your dreams, barring mishap of course."

Anderson was writing about male sexual conquest: men can overcome the resistance of women by displaying their expensive new
machines. Daisy finds her rejected suitor much more satisfactory,
once she finds out that he has a car. To some extent, Anderson
portrays her as a golddigger—in 1899 the automobile was a *very* high

status item. The car (or, more precisely, its affluent owner) could liberate her from economic worries. The mention of marriage probably reflected a surface acknowledgment of Victorian moral sensibilities. The song gave a hidden message that cars could serve as places for sexual experimentation. The song also explicitly presented the auto as a place of male domination. The man owned it, drove it, and, if the breakdown predicted in the last line occurred, would fix it.

Gus Edwards and Vincent Bryan's 1905 smash hit, "In My Merry Oldsmobile" triggered a wave of automobile songs. Writers published more than 120 songs on automotive themes between 1905 and 1908, precursors of the more than 1,000 popular tunes written in this century on automotive themes.[50] This boom came during the pre-Model T period when ownership remained beyond most Americans' economic horizons. "In My Merry Oldsmobile"[51] contained a courtship theme somewhat more risqué than "Love in an Automobile": "You can go as far as you like with me, Lucille, in my merry Oldsmobile." "She says she knows why the motor goes; the sparker's awfully strong." "They spoon to the engine's tune, their honeymoon will happen soon." While Johnny Steele, the song's hero, did allow Lucille to steer the car, it was only so that he could "whisper soft and low" his proposition. The major auto themes recurred: the new status object provided a place for adventure, especially sexual adventure; it liberated riders from ordinary social controls, and it allowed men to conquer women. The song explicitly ridiculed Lucille's mechanical skills—Johnny owned and operated the car, even if he called Lucille "the queen of his gas machine." Bryan and Edwards subtly infantilized Lucille, by giving only Johnny a last name. Sheet music publishers sold tens of thousands of copies of "In My Merry Oldsmobile," even before Oldsmobile purchased 300,000 copies for distribution to its customers.

Composers often set these songs about the new, unconventional machines and the new unconventional morality to the new, unconventional ragtime beat. They continued the theme of the auto as romantic, male-dominated technology in such songs as "On an Automobile Honeymoon" (1905); "When He Wanted to Love Her (He Would Put Up the Cover)," (1915); or "Fifteen Kisses on a Gallon of Gas"(1906). Some songs had negative themes. A would-be middle class moralist like Irving Berlin could write: "Keep Away from the Fellow Who Owns an Automobile" (1912). His "Get Out and Get Under" (1913) ridiculed cars for unreliability, but that song also conveyed a more familiar message when car driving Al Jolson sang about having "visions of gold," when "Millionaire Wilson" advised him: "I have a daughter who is hungry for love—She loves to ride by the way." Above all else, auto ownership strongly symbolized financial success as another title suggested: "You Can't Afford to Marry Me if You Can't Afford a Ford."[52]

The embryonic film medium could not pass up glorifying the new machines either, even though that era's car owners rarely went to movies. Thomas Edison's 1900 short, *Automobile Parade,* came first. It displayed the new playthings of Newport's motoring elite. The film scholar Julian Smith has surveyed hundreds of pre-1920 films in the Library of Congress collection. To summarize his findings: Hollywood initially made short documentaries like *Automobile Parade* or the 1902 Biograph one reeler, *A Unique Race between Elephant, Bicycle, Camel, Horse and Automobile.* These movies showed off the mechanical novelty in very early tours and races. American theaters also played European comic films with anti-auto connotations, like *How It Feels To Be Run Over* (1900)[53]

Biograph's *Runaway Match* (1903) first exploited cars in a narrative film. This one reeler developed one of the classic auto themes: a rebellious couple elope in a car to avoid the heartless opposition of her rich father to their match. The film illustrated the values associated with automobility. The young can escape the tyranny of their elders. The technology allowed defiance of traditional courtship patterns. It democratized social relations by permitting a middle-class man to have the same freedom as the more affluent. Cars symbolized both wealth and liberation from control based on gender, class, or age. The negative stereotype of the car-owning plutocrat softened because the father became reconciled to his new son-in-law in the climactic scene.[54]

A 1905 film short, *The Gentlemen Highwaymen,* depicted the use of cars for highway robberies. The film hinted at the Robin Hood tradition—cars liberated the robbers from social control. Of course, in the standard moralistic Hollywood manner, the hero, driving his own car, finally captured the robbers. D. W. Griffith's 1909 short,

Drive for Life, began the genre of car racing movies. Smith describes these racing movies as giving film makers a way to depict male competition, "proving who was the better man."[55] A 1913 Biograph short, *Traffic in Souls,* featured white slavers showing off cars to entice young women into prostitution. The film could only have reinforced notions of masculine power associated with automobility, although, in the end, the hero foiled the kidnappers. In his well-known *Intolerance* (1916), the first feature-length film, Griffith inserted an extraneous car chase scene in which the hero, after a thrill-filled, high-speed race against time, delivers a pardon to the state prison, just beating the executioner. This represented explicit, not metaphorical liberation. Car chases, car races, and car courtships became important, enduring elements of popular movies.

Films could not ignore the dangerous side of automobility. The portrayal of risky accidents evidently enhanced the sense of adventure that many Americans found both in driving and at the movies. Directors usually depicted crashes as, to quote the title of a 1909 Edison film, *Happy Accidents.* They were plot contrivances to allow characters to meet one another, or to foil villains. Accidents, no matter how horrid, rarely killed anyone in either the action-adventure movies or the comedies. Julian Smith found that only four of the 110 film accidents that he viewed killed anyone, mostly a villain getting his just deserts. Slapstick accidents, a staple of early comedy like Mack Sennett's Keystone Kop series, trivialized crashes—they resulted from only the most manifest incompetence and never were lethal.[56]

Moviegoers learned the same things from films that they learned from advertising and popular music. Cars provided status, liberating drivers from the constraints of the everyday world by offering them romantic adventure.

Automobiles also fascinated the writers of children's literature. This genre, while hardly cerebral, performs the important task of passing values on from one generation to another. Kenneth Grahame wrote the most enduring and one of the few negative works, *Wind in the Willows* (New York: Grossett and Dunlop, 1908). The classic book, still in print, is also the theme of a ride at Disney World. Grahame's parable presents its leading character, Mr. Toad, as the model of the evil, car-loving plutocrat. The hero imagines himself when driving: "Toad at his best and highest, Toad the terror, Toad the traffic queller, the lord of the lone trail, before whom all must give way or be smitten into nothingness and everlasting night" (p. 68). Toad smashes up seven cars, is hospitalized three times, nearly squanders his fortune, and finally goes to jail for theft, all because of his infatuation with "The magnificent motor-car, immense, breath-snatching, passionate"(p. 36).

For Grahame the car symbolizes the evils associated with the idle rich, an appealing attitude in a society where attitudes toward the wealthy were, and are, ambivalent. Grahame presents the problem more as Toad's lack of self-control, than as automobiles *per se*. Americans might have overlooked the anti-auto implications of the book because Grahame, an Englishman, set Toad's adventures in English society and an English landscape. Americans may well have perceived Toad as a parody of decadent old-world nobility, more than as a parody of affluent American auto owners.

Victor Appleton, Jr. (a pen name for at least six hacks) wrote the best-known treatment of the automobile in American adolescent success literature, *Tom Swift and His Electric Runabout, or the Fastest Car on the Road* (New York: Grossett and Dunlop, 1910). This was the third in a long-running, still-in-print series. "Appleton" made himself the early-twentieth-century successor to Horatio Alger in creating fictional role models for male teenagers. He added inventiveness to the pluck and work ethic displayed by Alger's adolescents as preconditions for success. In the first two novels of the series Swift had enriched his family by cashing in on two inventions, an airship and a submarine.

In this volume, young Tom finds the solution to a still unsolved technical problem: increasing storage battery efficiency so that electric cars can compete with gasoline powered ones. He builds the car to race against his arch-rival, Andy Foger, owner of the fastest gasoline powered car in their county. Tom repeatedly shows the affluent Foger up. He forces Foger to strip his gears in an informal road race. Next, he foils working-class gangsters whom Foger has convinced to sabotage his runabout. Then he rushes cash to his father's bank in time to end a run inspired by Foger's father.

Finally, he carries off the prize in a 500 mile road race on Long Island, modeled after the real life Vanderbilt Cup races. The victory also marks Swift's triumph over Foger for the attention of Mary Nestor, their adolescent heartthrob. Tom seems more pleased by the $3000 cash prize than the success in romance. One suspects that this might not have been true had an adolescent written the novel. Nestor unhesitatingly goes to the victor and shakes Swift's hand, "even though it was greasy."

"Appleton" lays out a complex set of values for the adolescent male. Prowess, hard work, intelligence, and a clean life lead to success, technical (and economic), as well as romantic. Swift respects his father, although their communication seems limited to business and mechanical issues. "Appleton" portrays Swift as a warrior, good with his fists, clever in his machine, cruel at times (he evinces joy at the prospect of running over chickens and dogs), and proud of his abilities: in other words, he is the paradigm of male honor and daring. He promises a friend a ride "that will make your hair stand up" (p. 62).

Swift sympathizes with stereotypically inferior workers, immigrants, and blacks. Swift, a misogynist, bans women from his workshop, and always refers to his romantic interest as "Miss Nestor." Nestor, the only woman whom "Appleton" portrayed in the novel, lacks personality, even by the banal standards of children's literature. He only describes her in terms of general physical appearance: "beautiful" or "lovely," never in terms of character or of other attributes. She lacks interest in things mechanical. Women can only be spectators in the masculine world of invention and racing. Swift apparently views her more as a trophy, the symbol of his success, than as a person. By attracting her, he makes Andy Foger look bad.

Less successful juvenile writers also focussed on automobility. Howard Garis (under the pseudonym Clarence Young) published *The Motor Boys or Chums Through Thick and Thin* in 1906, the first of a 22 volume series that would run through 1924. The series included such epics as *The Motor Boys in Mexico, The Motor Boys on a Ranch,* and *The Motor Boys Go Over the Top.* Garis wrote about male bonding and adventure, often as mysteries. The novels celebrated mechanical prowess, especially driving and fixing cars, but not Tom Swift-style invention. The fourteen-year-old Motor Boys are resourceful, not inventive. They want cars to display social position and driving skill.[57]

Cars allow the Motor Boys to liberate themselves from the humdrum of everyday middle class life to travel and seek adventure. Racing to show their competitive instincts is as important to them as to Tom Swift. To judge from the title of the first volume, male bonding is even more important. They belittle danger, at one point claiming that motorcycles are "no more dangerous than horses." Racing also impresses the other sex. After one race, "Even the girls went wild with excitement."[58] However, this is almost the only context in which women appear. Here, too, they are the winner's spoils, at least metaphorically.

Tom Swift and the juvenile series literature shared the tunnel vision of the songs and movies. Accidents only happen to villains and are never fatal. Other than early versions of Swift's experimental prototypes, cars rarely break down, unless sabotaged. This contradicts all the expectations of real motorists during this era. Traffic jams and parked cars had become commonplace in big cities by 1914, but the novels written after that date depict neither. The youngsters do ask about road conditions before embarking on trips, but get lost or run into impassable rural highways only when the plot requires it. Since they drive open cars, rain sometimes forces them to seek shelter, opening up more plot contrivances. The novels equate automobility and social station. Strangers know the Motor Boys' social station because of their knowledge of driving. "Appleton" and Garis romanticize the real world of motoring. Grahame's parable may bear a closer resemblance to the real world, but, even there Mr. Toad's accidents, while commonplace, are never fatal.

Motorists bought more than just technology with their own machines. Clearly cars served a multiplicity of emotional needs beyond providing transportation. They granted an ersatz sense of both economic and gender status, in a culture where both were becoming harder to define. Consumers obtained a feeling of control and liberation in a society that was increasingly bureaucratized and regulated. Cars symbolized escape from the constraints of family and neighborhood. They asserted the owner's youth and modernity. Car buyers were up to date: they could travel to new leisure sites, move to the new suburbs, or pursue new courtship patterns. The important issue here is not whether or not cars really did these things, but that motorists believed they did. Drivers received psychic, not objective liberation, since the car, after all, carried with it a new set of obligations. Car payments firmly tied owners to the workplace in order to earn the cash needed for participation in the consumer culture. Traffic required obedience to norms. Breakdowns and accidents were commonplace. Nonetheless, the feeling of ownership was exhilarating. More than any other consumer good the motor car provided fantasies of status, freedom, and escape from the constraints of a highly disciplined urban, industrial order.

8

GENDER WARS

THE CONSTANT UTILIZATION of gender stereotypes in popular culture about autos suggests that the motor car served as a battlefield in the wars over gender roles that were so important in early-twentieth-century America. In the throes of massive economic and social change, men defined the cultural implications of the new automotive technology in a way that served the needs of their gender identity. In their efforts to exclude women from control of the new technology, automobiles were again more than just machines. Presumably, almost all Americans, except the most traditionally moralistic or those, like rural blacks, whose poverty excluded them from car ownership, sought both prestige and liberation through the new machines, but men sought it more.[1]

The sex of early drivers showed the masculinity of the new culture. Only two states have retained registration records. In 1905 only 1.8% of Maryland car owners were women, a proportion that would rise to only 9.1% four years later. Maryland's records also picked up most car owners in the District of Columbia. In 1905 21% of those registrants were women, and, in 1909, 15%.[2] New Hampshire's Secretary of State listed every licensed driver in the state in the 1907 *Annual Report* and listed all car owners in the

1907 to 1912 *Reports*.[3] In 1907 only 1.8% of the car owners were women. By 1911 the proportion of women owners had more than doubled to 4.8%, still a vast under-representation. These women seem primarily to have been wives who owned their family's second car, because they most frequently registered from the address of a man registrant with the same name. Women held 4.6% of the driver's licenses in the New Hampshire in 1906, about triple their rate of ownership. Thus, even in families that owned cars, few women drove.

Most of the women registrants of Maryland, likely also wives with an affluent family's second car, tended to live in Baltimore. In 1905, all three women car owners outside that city resided in its suburbs. In 1909 the largest number of women owners in Baltimore lived in the elite Roland Park neighborhood. Washington's much greater number of women owners mostly resided in the prestigious Northwest section. Presumably the District had a greater concentration of very affluent people and was more urbane. In Maryland, the more rural the area, the fewer women owners. About 10 percent of women had their cars registered by their chauffeurs, another sign of affluence. Strikingly, between 1905 and 1909, the proportion of women car owners in the District declined. This implies that automobility for women was less acceptable to upper-middle-class families, who could afford cars by that date, than to the elite families who had bought cars earlier.[4]

The New Hampshire data show a slightly different pattern. Women (like owners in general) tended to live in the state's smaller commercial cities, especially in the southeast, within easy rail travel of New England's metropolis, Boston. They were likely more urbane, possibly commuters or spouses of commuters. There were proportionately fewer women owners in the state's two large industrial cities, Manchester and Nashua, although both cities had far higher car ownership rates than the state's most rural counties. I suspect that this pattern describes the distribution of wealth in the state. Only very wealthy families could afford two cars and most women owners had husbands who also owned cars. The lower proportion of women owners in the mill cities may reflect both a lower median income and a stronger insistence on gender segregation. This insistence may have grown, not just from the manly image of industrial cities, but from the special anxieties of men in cities whose primary industry, textiles, employed large numbers of women. Greater employment opportunities for women may have created especially strong gender insecurities in men.

After Charles Kettering ended onerous hand-cranking by developing the self-starter in 1912 the proportion of women drivers increased somewhat, but never to a very high level. In 1914 women owned 15% of the cars in Los Angeles and 5% in Tucson. In 1917 only 8% of the drivers in Massachusetts were women and Southern California car dealers claimed that 23% of drivers were women, the highest rate in the nation.[5] A 1969 U.S. government survey showed that only 20.2% of the women interviewed (compared to 61.8% of the men) who came of driving age before 1916 held driver's licenses. Many of the women likely picked up licenses at a later date, perhaps when their families acquired a second car in the 1920s.[6] I would expect that fewer women drove in the generally poorer South, a more rural region with bad roads, few cities, and persistent nineteenth-century gender values.[7]

Presumably the economic benefits of early car ownership might have applied somewhat less to women, since many fewer women pursued occupations such as sales and medicine, whose practitioners were the first to adopt cars for work. Yet, on the surface, there is no reason why American women, fifty percent of the population after all, would not have sought the modernity, liberation, and prestige associated with automobility. To understand why not, we need to look at some changes in gender values that were occurring during the early twentieth century. It is important to remember that cultural definitions of gender are synergistic; i.e., when women seek to redefine their roles, implicitly they redefine men's roles and vice versa.

Since middle- and upper-class men seized control of the car culture, it is useful to examine their position first. The changes wrought by nineteenth-century industrialization profoundly threatened many traditional sources of male identity. Jefferson had predicated a republic of economically independent yeoman farmers as the key to the American dream. The traditional farmer was "his own man," theoretically controlling his productive enterprise and family with little interference from outsiders. Individuals allegedly succeeded or failed on their own merits. Farmers were supposedly rugged individuals: physically strong, knowledgeable about their business, and very honorable. Legally, a family's property almost always belonged to the man. Economically, his labor in the fields supposedly produced most of the family's income. He likely made the major financial decisions for the family. He provided for future generations by passing on the family farm and agricultural skills. Farmers expected their wives to be loyal and obedient, taking care of the household and raising many children. In times of war, the virtuous republican farmer, like Cincinnatus or Washington, could lay down his plow and take up his sword. Thus men were warriors also.[8]

Almost without exception these views were an oversimplified and fantastic vision of the past. Nonetheless, men believed this nostalgia and viewed early-twentieth-century society as a declension. Anxieties about manliness typified American culture at the turn of the century.[9]

The new corporate industrial order had changed the world. By 1870 half the male workers in heavily industrialized Massachusetts held the status of employee, no longer "their own man." The odds of men becoming farm owners, or even entrepreneurs, the urban equivalent of a farmer in terms of independence, were slim. In the industrial sector, machinery was deskilling jobs and doing work that had once required brute physical strength. Middle-class men now most likely held jobs in the growing white-collar office sector, which demanded obedience to corporate norms. These jobs did not allow the "traditional" male attributes of physical prowess, aggression, and independence. The new white-collar men were subservient bureaucrats, not independent proprietors or even agents.[10] Most attempts to redefine the new white-collar occupations as autonomous professions failed.

Industrialization also changed families in ways that apparently diminished traditional male roles. Unlike agricultural work, urban jobs normally separated work and residence. Typically, an employer's demands on a man's time took precedence over family demands. Middle-class careers demanded long hours at the office. Fathers no longer routinely passed job skills on to their children or to an apprentice. Rather, schools and mothers now socialized children for work. Apparently strong mother-son ties marked the middle-class

Victorian family, in part because fathers were often away at work, in part because Victorian mores made the home the woman's sphere. Society expected fathers to bring home a pay envelope, but little else. Historian E. Anthony Rotundo suggests that such female headed environments made young men insecure about their masculinity.[11]

In the nineteenth century women had begun to attend college in large numbers, had taken over some occupations (clerical work and elementary school teaching, for example), and had become a major force in literature and religion. Women also dominated the culture of consumption centered in the new urban department stores. The employment changes were likely especially threatening. Few of the new bureaucratic jobs required the brute physical strength and aggressiveness that were supposedly male traits. Many men feared competing with women in the new white-collar arena. Agitation for women's suffrage stiffened those fears.

Men responded by seeking to redefine masculinity to control the new jobs. They claimed that men were intellectually superior to women, especially in the disciplines of mathematics and science. These disciplines underpinned many new middle-class occupations, such as medicine, engineering, and accounting. Men argued that they were steadier and more efficient; women more nervous and excitable. They also claimed that women's reproductive responsibilities would interfere with professional careers. All this lacked persuasive evidence, but justified the sexual segregation (and male dominance) of almost all middle-class occupations.

Men added one new item to the roster of supposedly masculine traits: mechanical ability. Advocates of suburbanization claimed that one virtue of the single-family home was that men could fulfill their masculinity by tinkering around the house. They could find the pleasure of handiwork denied them in the new office jobs.[12] Harriet Beecher Stowe, in an 1870 novel advocating the new style suburban domesticity, wrote: "There is no earthly reason which requires a man, in order to be manly, to be unhandy."[13] This hints that mechanical skills may not have been considered a masculine trait that early, but were becoming so, since Beecher was a key arbiter of the new domesticity. Mechanical ability was becoming an attribute of gender, not social class. Margaret Marsh's recent *Suburban Lives* notes that the household division of labor was still being worked out during this period. Men were assuming responsibility for some elements of housework, especially those requiring heavy physical labor or mechanical skills, like minor house repairs and yard work.[14] The arts and crafts movement of the late nineteenth century also incorporated this gender value. Inventors, notably Thomas Edison and Alexander Graham Bell, became the new American heroes in the late nineteenth century.

Gender segregation became the norm in the new organization of work. In business, clerical jobs became defined as women's work and executive jobs as men's work. No longer could an executive secretary ride exceptional clerical skills to the top of a corporation as Andrew Carnegie had in the mid-nineteenth century. Men claimed that executive jobs required aggressiveness and decision making, both supposedly masculine attributes. In the health care professions, doctors redefined medicine as a "scientific" discipline and forced women out. They relegated women to the supposedly more nurturing, less scientific role of nursing. In education, universities increasingly served the function of technical training and so hired men as professors. Elementary school teaching, believed a more nurturing job, became women's work. In each case, men applied the newly defined "innate" gender traits to stake out the better jobs for themselves.

Nineteenth-century men also sought to create new institutions to salvage the traditional culture of masculinity. At mid-century the fraternal lodge, working class saloon, and elite social club emerged as all-male enclaves, which not only tolerated, but encouraged such traditional male pastimes as smoking, drinking, and swearing. Mark C. Carnes persuasively argues that the fraternal lodges placed great emphasis on rituals that symbolized initiation into all male adulthood and liberation from the female dominated world of childhood. At least one male fraternal organization, the Ku Klux Klan, placed "protection" of women high on its agenda. Klansmen feared economic competition with not just racial and ethnic minorities, but also women. The Klan and other vigilante groups of this period employed their new cars to terrorize blacks, immigrants, and political radicals. Cars allowed lynchers to take their victims beyond the jurisdiction of urban police departments.[15]

Sports became another new form of escapism that allowed men

to show traditional traits: aggressiveness, courage, and physical prowess. Once hunting and fishing ceased to be economic necessities for most Americans they became acceptable leisure activities for upper-class men. Fathers could no longer pass occupational skills on to their sons. However, teaching them atavistic hunting skills or taking them to watch tobacco chewing males hit balls in the ersatz rural environment of city stadia became important forms of father-son bonding. Athletes, not businessmen, became major role models for American boys in the early twentieth century—presumably businessmen were too effete. T. Jackson Lears describes these activities as an anti-modern, martial ideal.[16]

Purchasing cars was one area where men dominated the culture of consumption. The car became a masculine status object, driving a masculine skill, one of the few skills that fathers passed directly to their sons. Maintaining and operating cars required, in the early days, considerable physical strength, and always required some mechanical ability. The corporate bureaucrat could find the emotional equivalent of the skill, autonomy, and strength of the idealized farmer, traditional craftsman or small entrepreneur with his knowledge of cars and their upkeep. Increasingly males were defining their gender in terms of mechanical skill. Driving skill was like athletic ability. Supposedly, both were innately male traits requiring strength, steady nerves and good coordination. Driving also meant power. The driver controlled the car and the destiny of those in it.

Cars also provided liberation in several different ways. Men controlled their machines, a reversal of what happened in many new factory and office jobs, where machines set the pace for workers. In a society that still held frontier values, men could overcome their "Rooseveltian concerns with masculinity,"[17] by conquering space and seeking nature in their cars. Cars served as a private space. Only in private cars could proper middle-class men swear at complete strangers. Men smoked as they pleased in cars. They rapidly became places for sexual conquest. Driving, even in traffic, could be made competitive and aggressive, a false bravado.[18]

Later literary sources suggest the way in which many men have adopted cars to liberate themselves from the constraint of the new, twentieth-century family, bound by sometimes oppressively strong emotional ties. Sinclair Lewis was probably the first major novelist to sense the liberating possibilities of automobility for men. In his 1920 novel *Babbitt* (New York: Grosset and Dunlap, 1920), the title character takes long car rides to relax, away from his bickering wife and teenage children.[19] For George F. Babbitt, "The motor car was poetry and tragedy, love and heroism" (p. 11). He believed that parking "was a virile adventure, manfully executed" (p. 29). Babbitt's car made him feel "superior and powerful, like a shuttle of polished steel, darting in a vast machine" (p. 45). The car was "an aspiration for knightly rank" (p. 63).

The theme has persisted in later twentieth century novels. A Robert Penn Warren character noted the impact of cars on men in southern families: "a man could just git up and git, if'n a notion come on him."[20] For John Updike's Rabbit Angstrom, trapped in an unsatisfying marriage, "his Ford's stale air is his only heaven."[21] Dean Moriarity, Jack Kerouac's youthful male rebel, symbolically claimed that he was born in the back seat of a Model T.[22] William Faulkner once described the red sports car of a Mississippi man: "alien and as debonair, as invincibly and as irrevocably polygamous as its owner."[23]

Men defined driving in terms of values that they proclaimed as masculine. When men claimed mechanical ability as a gender trait, implicitly they excluded women from automobility. Men claimed that the key emotional traits needed to drive—steady nerves, aggression, and rationality—were masculine. Women may well have read these traits differently, equating steady nerves with a lack of emotion; aggression as a form of bad manners, at best, or bullying, at the worst; and rationality with selfishness. The distinction between mechanical ability and brute strength was probably less than obvious—changing tires required strong arms more than mechanical ingenuity.

This process of coopting relevant physical and emotional traits was crucial to dominating the car culture. Women car advocates sensed this from the start. The first woman to drive in New York City told a *New York Times* reporter: "I don't understand why women are so nervous."[24] She perceived the limitations implicit in existing gender values. Men not only embraced the auto enthusiastically as a symbol of traditionally masculine values, but also actively sought to exclude women from the car culture. They likely feared, as one man complained in the *Literary Digest* that "the automobile has given women too much confidence."[25]

Men controlled almost all the media for the transmission of culture outside the family. As we have seen, newspapers, magazines, popular songs, and films customarily portrayed drivers as men and described drivers generically with masculine pronouns. The largely masculine world of racing became a major focus in these media. They highlighted the courage of the pioneer motorists, while downplaying the risks of automobility. The behavior of the advertisers was especially startling. They knew that women played a significant role in most family car purchase decisions, but still preferred to demean rather than flatter them. They preferred stereotypical to rational marketing and profits, a measure of the power of gender values.

The culture ignored famous women motorists, including writers like Emily Post and Edith Wharton, record setters like Joan Newton Cuneo and Alice Huyler Ramsey, and heroic ambulance drivers like Gertrude Stein and F. J. Linz. Car companies sometimes subsidized these pioneers for publicity purposes. Maxwell, for example, underwrote Alice Huyler Ramsey's pioneer cross-country trip.[26] Florence Woods generated much publicity for her father's car firm in 1900, when she became the first woman licensed to drive in Central Park.[27] These publicity gimmicks emphasized the practicality and ease of motoring (with an "even a woman can do it" motif that might shame men), as much as the possibilities of motoring for women. The early car companies never emphasized famous women drivers in advertisements, although they sought endorsements from well known men.

A few men suggested a legal ban on women drivers. Cincinnati experienced a major controversy in 1908 when a woman driver ran over the City Treasurer. Mayor Markbreit proposed a ban, saying, "The only proper machine for a woman to run is a sewing machine." A newspaper condescendingly commented: "A woman with strong nerves and good muscular development might run a car as well as a male chauffeur." When Magistrate C. F. House of the Bronx fined Lillian Siddens for reckless driving in 1915, he told her: "In my mind no woman should be allowed to operate an automobile. In the first place she hasn't the strength, and in the second, she is very apt to lose her mind."[28]

Yet early accident studies showed that women drivers had an accident rate half of men's.[29] Edwin Cornell, President of New York City's Highways Protective Society, was a hero of the early auto culture. He refused to sweep the danger of accidents under a rug and his organization did the first statistical analyses of traffic safety. Cornell, despite knowing the safety record, wanted to eliminate women drivers, arguing that: "Any nerve specialist will tell you auto riding has a sad effect on motherhood."[30] Even for this hard-headed observer of the car culture, gender values took precedence.

Anti-feminist Montgomery Rollins made the most comprehensive attack on women motorists in the popular magazine *Outlook* in 1909. Rollins knew that men had accidents at a much higher rate than women. He argued that men who were breaking the law should be excluded from the statistics, because the courts would punish them. Without empirical data, he argued that women had a higher rate of accidents, *while driving legally*. He acknowledged that some women were strong enough to control cars, but only one in a thousand. Since license examiners could not distinguish between the one strong woman and the 999 others, "the only proper protection is to withhold them [licenses] from all." Rollins felt that women were flighty, "not trained to think of two things at once," because they had not learned to play baseball as children. He made the further unsubstantiated generalization that women drivers believed that the etiquette of the streets was like the etiquette of the drawing room and expected men to yield to them. The "natural hysteria" of women turned crises into accidents. He also cited the folkloric accident in which a woman driver hit another car, because she swerved to avoid a dog. Preconceptions about gender roles seem all that mattered.[31]

The proposals to prohibit women drivers failed. The car companies might demean women customers, but they still opposed any legislation that might limit any potential market. States preempted driver licensing, so cities like Cincinnati probably could not have enforced bans, even if city councils had passed them. Car company lobbyists, a potent force at the state level, blocked all unfavorable legislation. Presumably the very early woman motorists, an affluent lot, could have litigated such restrictions successfully.

Gender conscious males found other ways beside legal bans to restrain women drivers. The pioneering, prestigious Automobile

Club of America in New York City banned women members. This elite club probably had the best garage and repair facilities in New York for several years after the turn of the century. Women automobilists, mostly, according to the *Times,* commuting shoppers from affluent suburbs like Tuxedo Park, New York, talked about forming their own club. The A.C.A.'s Milwaukee counterpart, for which we have a detailed roster of members, was equally masculine. More strikingly, the American Automobile Association, which then sanctioned car races, banned women race car drivers in 1909, after Joan Newton Cuneo beat the famous racer Ralph DaPalma in a meet at New Orleans. Likely, the AAA sought to protect masculine prerogative rather than feminine safety.[32]

Cuneo, suffering from the delusion that racing was merely a recreation, rather than the expression of a warrior cult, took her ban like a good sport. She told *Outing Magazine:* "Would that I could cultivate some suffragette tendencies and fight for my rights. But I can't—having instead tried to keep the women's end in automobiling sweet, clean and refined. I drive and race just for the love of it all." Cuneo tried to stand the male argument about nervousness on its head by noting; "Whenever I feel nervous or out of sorts, I get into my car and drive off my troubles." She also subtly attacked the overly aggressive, masculine values of racers, by telling her interviewer that the most enjoyable thing that she did with her racing Lancia was to take children from a New York City orphanage on their annual outing to Coney Island.[33]

Many men tried ridicule to limit women drivers. In 1916 the *Times's* automotive section reprinted as a humorous anecdote the story of some English male truck drivers who tried to convince a wartime woman replacement to oil her spark plugs. One early woman driver reported that young boys applauded when they watched her changing her tires. Another sought out deserted locations to do routine repairs to avoid snide comments from male kibitzers. Although she played its importance down, Joan Newton Cuneo noted that intimidation from male drivers, especially cabbies and truckers, was commonplace in big cities. In 1916 the *New York Times* interviewed cab driver Edward Flinckner, who claimed that he always yielded the right of way to women, because they were so unpredictable.[34]

Wealthy urban women, like men, often wanted their cars for

recreational touring vehicles. Press interviews and memoirs by eight pioneer transcontinental travelers suggest the social difficulties they encountered. To judge from residence and education all came from upper-class backgrounds. Seven of the eight came from the New York area. Still, men made the open road inhospitable for them. Women motorists asking for directions were fair game for practical jokers. One woman driver complained about "the cynical observations" of male drivers. She claimed that traffic police fled in mock terror to safety islands when they saw her. Street corner "loafers" made them feel uncomfortable by staring. When touring women drivers emerged from their cars, well dressed downtown passers-by often ignored them, assuming from their road attire that they were working-class women in the wrong place. Many hotels would not admit women travelers. Those that did often made them feel uncomfortable, sometimes unconsciously, as the western hotel whose lobby had a large (and ignored) sign banning chewing and spitting tobacco.[35]

Not surprisingly men exercised such social control primarily within families. The pioneer women tour drivers all sought permission from their parents or husbands before embarking on their adventures. If they were lucky, their husbands consented, sometimes for odd reasons. Alice Huyler Ramsey, a Vassar graduate, who lived in Montclair, New Jersey, an elite suburb, was the first woman to drive coast to coast. She, like the other transcontinental pioneers, claimed that she was "born mechanical." She was the only girl in the manual arts class in her high school before going off to Vassar.[36] Her husband, a car-hating horse lover, bought her a Maxwell because he did not like the way she handled the family's horses. He did not object to her trip, as long as she brought his sister along as a chaperone. Men apparently had more objections to their daughters' driving, especially if unchaperoned. President Roosevelt refused to buy his pugnacious daughter Alice a car and publicly quarreled with her when she borrowed a friend's car to go out for a spin by herself.[37]

Perhaps a 1911 *Harper's* article best pointed out the marital tensions inherent in automobility: "The women automobile drivers of Detroit have hit on a novel method of keeping track of their husbands, by driving them to their places of business in the morning and calling for them when the day is done."[38] If the automobile symbolized liberation and men were driving to escape traditional social constraints, they must have feared that their wives or daughters, whom prevailing values confined much more sharply, would also adopt the technology as an escape. Sexual jealousy clearly laid behind these fears. The usage of the word "fast" to describe a morally loose woman first appeared in American slang in the early years of the car culture.[39]

The objections to women driving increased after the arrival of the Model T in 1908 made automobiles available for more of the middle class. Virginia Scharff, the leading scholar on these matters, has noted increased masculine defensiveness in the automotive press after that date. Probably middle-class men, who perceived their economic position as precarious, felt more threatened by women drivers than the wealthy car owners of previous times.[40] There are several accounts of early drivers prohibiting their wives from driving, including one where the woman lost all her mobility, because the family had sold its horse and buggy, which she could drive.[41] One proponent of woman drivers quoted an apocryphal suburban daughter in a 1913 essay: "Oh, I'd love to drive a car, but father doesn't think I could drive it. He wants me to drive an electric, and they don't go either fast or far enough."[42] One pioneer woman motorist attacked a husband who did not approve of his wife driving: "His real reason is, without doubt a wholly selfish one—he fears her proficiency and doesn't want her to use the car as often as she would wish were she capable of its operation."[43]

How did women perceive cars differently from men? We can infer some things about women car owners from the New Hampshire and Maryland records of the types of cars that they chose to buy.[44] Vivian Ball of M St., NW in the District of Columbia owned the largest car registered by either men or women in 1905, a fifty horsepower Thomas. In 1909 the largest Maryland cars belonged to nonresidents Joan Newton Cuneo (a 50 hp Rainier) and famous actress Anna Held (a 45 hp Mercedes). They were typical. Women owners preferred more powerful, heavier cars (see tables 8.1 and 8.2). This choice likely reflected a greater interest in touring, in mechanical reliability, and in status. Women drivers, probably wealthier than men, also chose better makes (often Cadillacs or Packards) than men, who were more likely to buy cheap, assembled cars, especially in rural areas. The women showed better technical judgment.

In 1905 a quarter of women car owners in Washington, D.C. owned underpowered (less than 2 horsepower) electric cars, the great exception to the rule that women preferred power. Such cars could operate better on the District's wide, smooth, asphalt streets than on poorer pavements elsewhere. Few women in Maryland owned electrics and no woman in Maryland or the District bought

Table 8.1 **WOMEN CAR OWNERS**

City	Date	(Number)	(Percent)
Baltimore City	1904	3	1.6
Maryland (outside Balt.)	1904	3	8.8
D.C.	1904	24	21.0
New Hampshire	1907	27	1.8
Baltimore City	1909	27	11.3
Maryland (outside Balt.)	1909	13	6.5
D.C.	1909	24	15.0
New Hampshire	1911	214	4.8

SOURCES: *Annual Reports of the New Hampshire Secretary of State,* 1907 and 1912; Automobile Registration Applications, State of Maryland, 1905 and 1909.

Table 8.2 **SIZE OF CARS BY OWNER'S GENDER**

		Median Horsepower of Cars	
City	Date	Women Owners	Men Owners
Baltimore City	1904	12	10
Maryland (outside Balt.)	1904	16	12
D.C.	1904	16	10
New Hampshire	1907	—	—
Baltimore City	1909	40	26
Maryland (outside Balt.)	1909	30	22
D.C.	1909	35	22
New Hampshire	1911	35	25

SOURCES: *Annual Reports of the New Hampshire Secretary of State,* 1907 and 1912; Automobile Registration Applications, State of Maryland, 1905 and 1909. The Washington, D.C. figures are for nonresident registrations issued by Maryland.

one in 1909.[45] The heavy marketing of elect   ag-
azines found few pigeons among the w   New
Hampshire's rugged roads. Only three o   car
owners registered electric vehicles. No

Strikingly, woman drivers avoided   s becoming the dominant American mak   amp-
shire four times the proportion of r   . The
T had a reputation as a man's ca   ysical
strength to steer and shift. Since   he left
side, drivers had to clamber acros   r shift,
a major obstacle for a skirt wearer. The   der the
driver's seat, a smelly arrangement. What is more, Henry Ford adopted the self-starter much later than other manufacturers. Finally, T
ownership tended to be concentrated in rural areas, where fewer
women drove.

Some women moved into the driving occupations during the
World War I years. An impressionistic 1915 magazine survey found
a few women adding to their family income by taking passengers on
the family car as a jitney (quasi taxicab) during rush hours. The
survey found a few women mechanics, truck drivers, and cabbies,
mostly widows who had inherited their husband's business. A 1916
article claimed that many New York women were taking courses in
auto mechanics. Many other women moved into these jobs when
the U.S. went to war in 1917. A few elite women drivers, of whom
the writer Gertrude Stein was probably the best known, volunteered
as ambulance drivers in France. Others formed a Woman's Motor
Corps in New York City to aid the war effort. Men speedily resegre-
gated the motoring occupations after the war.[46]

For women, as well as men, automobility initially denoted
wealth. When *Munsey's* published one of the first articles in a popular periodical on autos in February 1900, it emphasized elite Parisian car fanciers. The article included three photos of woman drivers,
one in a car that the story described as "the machine in which fashionable Paris takes the air in the Bois de Boulogne."[47] Upper-class
leisure magazines like *Outing* printed photos of elite women, almost
always chauffeured, in autos.[48] Elite woman often notified the *Times's* society editor of their doings. The car represented social pre-
tension to the less affluent as well. In 1904 the New York City Police
Department asked an officer's wife to ride in a borrowed car

as part of a decoy operation to identify children who were stoning cars. Mrs. McGillicuddy insisted that they buy her a duster and an appropriate hat, so she could look "like a real millionaire's wife."[49] Etiquette manuals suggested that women should ride in the back seat, even if their husbands were driving. This must have created the impression of having a chauffeur.

Writers in popular magazines, mostly men, made much of the possibility that the new motor car could ease life for suburban housewives. The suburbs probably had a larger concentration of women drivers than rural areas, but the number was still tiny. Women drivers tended to reside in big cities.

On the surface, the automobile offered utility to women in the newer, more isolated suburbs, especially the ones served by expensive, irregular commuter rail, rather than by trolley car. As a household technology, the automobile held some promise for ending the isolation of suburban housewives. A 1907 *Suburban Life* article fantasized about the possible virtues of suburban automobility.[50] The puff piece concluded with an allusion to the anti-modern aspects of automobility, even for women: "out in the suburbs are the true Happy Hunting Grounds of the motorist." It seemed primarily concerned with the recreational possibilities of cars, posing a woman at the wheel for photos labelled: "Getting close to nature with the motor car," "The up-to-date way of making calls," "A swift run over country roads," and "A delightful way of entertaining one's friends." It sensed the liberating possibilities of driving as well, captioning others: "Independent of coachman and chauffeur," "When 'mere man' is only a passenger," and "A woman's hands can manage even the biggest machine." Hilda Ward, the piece's author, also noted the possibilities of cars for shopping and commuting. She further claimed that "The most unruly of suburban children can be diplomatically governed" by depriving them of automobile outings. She also believed that automobiling soothed her nerves, allowed her to sleep soundly, and gave her a hearty appetite.[51] What more could suburban wives, whom the *Times* called "wide awake women of today,"[52] desire? Yet, Ward was the only woman writer who claimed that cars improved life for suburban housewives.

In 1913 C. H. Claudy wrote a much-cited six part essay, the "Motor Emigrants" in *Home and Garden*.[53] Claudy followed the adventures of a fictional urban small businessman and his family, as they moved from a big city to a suburban home, a twenty-minute drive from the commuter rail station. He engaged in much financial sleight-of-hand to show that the move actually saved money. He claimed that suburban real estate was a better investment than the bonds in which the family had put its savings and justified the added cost of a car. Included on the plus side of the fantasy ledger were several hundred dollars made by the family's children through gardening and chicken-raising, healthy activities that they could not pursue in the city. The fictional family also saved large medical expenses in the supposedly healthier suburbs.

Mr. Spence, the essay's businessman hero, finally bought his wife, unhappy over her isolation, a car, ostensibly to enable her to make social visits in the suburbs and allow shopping trips, even to the big city. Thus Claudy shows her car as liberating Mrs. Spence. The details of the story suggest, however, that it was merely another form of suburban entrapment. Mrs. Spence now must drive her children's produce to market, do shopping that a servant had once handled, and maintain a large piece of machinery. When the family takes a motor camping vacation trip, she cooks over an open fire and washes their dishes in a stream, hardly romantic motoring. Close examination of the financial records cooked up by Claudy, show that the largest economy in the auto-based suburban life is a reduction of Mrs. Spence's clothes budget by $800 a year, because the Spences do not go out as much in the country. One wonders how a real world Mrs. Spence might have felt about this.

In this respect the automobile resembles the other new household innovations of the twentieth century. The washing machine, the gas range, and the vacuum cleaner all made housework less physically onerous. They also increased the time spent in housework because the expectations of household members rose more rapidly, according to scholars like Joann Vanek and Susan Strasser.[54] To Mrs. Spence's contemporaries, a car meant driving the children places, a vacation with its own form of housework, and more time spent in shopping. Cars hardly liberated the suburban woman from her work.

In any case, most husbands resisted letting their wives buy cars to end their isolation. These advocates of suburban automobility for women, while mentioning access to the city *for shopping* as one possibility for cars, generally downplayed that motive. Instead, they focussed on the car as a way to allow greater social activities for women within the suburbs, as a way to increase the recreational access to nature, and as a way to improve household efficiency. Presumably, this set of activities seemed less threatening. Nonetheless, almost all suburban husbands would not buy Claudy's argument, because mobility threatened to liberate their wives and daughters too much, in a world that many perceived as already having too many gender threats. Men wanted to control the family car.

Many suburban women shared the evangelical notions of domesticity and separate spheres. They feared the central city and did not care about access, except perhaps for shopping or formal entertainment. To be sure, cars offered them greater privacy and freedom from the formal urban etiquette (speak softly, only look straight ahead, never talk to a man) governing street behavior. Still, cars with woman drivers also attracted attention, something that the well-mannered sought to avoid. Many suburban housewives craved respectability, but good manners limited the fun of leisurely automobiling. Etiquette books advised women drivers to bundle up in hats, dusters, and veils; and to cover their faces with cold cream. Alice Huyler Ramsey complained that the approved attire made her and her companions look like "a quartet of nuns." Respectable women did not have disheveled hair. Sunburns suggested farm wives, a hopelessly déclasse lot. Theodore Roosevelt once violated the norms of hospitality by refusing to admit one of his daughter's friends to his Oyster Bay, New York house. She had shown up with her hair in disarray after a long, unchaperoned car ride.[55]

Etiquette books advised woman drivers not to scare pedestrians and animals, to drive slowly enough to avoid throwing dust, and not to flaunt their car's power by passing others at an excessive speed. Injunctions on the necessity of chaperones constantly recurred, an indication that chaperonage was in trouble. Dorothy Dix, the popular newspaper writer on manners, warned parents that the auto was a "devil wagon." *Harper's Weekly* warned parents of the dangers of car riding for their daughters in an article entitled: "Where is Your Daughter This Afternoon?"[56] In all, the social conventions of early-twentieth-century suburbia limited the joys of automobility for women.

According to Virginia Scharff, many feminists viewed technology as cold, rational and oppressive.[57] To this group, woman drivers threatened to open the separate sphere that they had worked hard to carve out as theirs. Driving blurred gender behaviors, offending traditional middle-class women. Not surprisingly, then, early women drivers often encountered hostility from other women. Some ridiculed women drivers as "mannish."[58] Two of the pioneer women cross country drivers reported such hostility. In strange cities, they resorted to the expedient of asking women, "who looked like they had daughters at home," for the name of a respectable hotel. Some lectured the young women on their appearance and location, or, alternatively, fled in silence, as if the young hotel seekers were street walkers.[59]

Male fears of the liberating possibilities of cars were not unfounded. Some younger women drivers sought autonomy from family and community control, wishing new freedom in courtship and dating. Historians Beth L. Bailey and Ellen Rothman have noted the emergence of a new style of courtship between 1890 and 1925.[60] The "going out" style of dating replaced traditional, parentally supervised courtship that involved the man calling on the woman in her parents' house. Cars enormously eased the transition to the new style by allowing the young to get away from the bounds of family and neighborhood. Cars also provided privacy for "petting," one attribute of the new style.[61]

Considerable conflict attended the spread of dating, which did not become the norm for middle-class America until the 1920s. The automobile served as the locus for this change; courtship, to borrow the title of Bailey's book, moved from the front porch to the back seat. Abundant masculine fantasies in songs and films hinted this possibility for automobiles before 1920, as do other sources, some written by women. Alice Roosevelt's constant, much publicized, conflicts with her father over joy riding clearly reflected her desire for and his fears of sexual liberation. In 1904 the New York Times printed an account of a bizarre accident involving a car that ran off the road with all its occupants drunk. The driver, a chauffeur, had "borrowed" his employer's car and picked up a male friend and two shop girls, whom the reporter hinted were prostitutes.[62] Clearly, these working class couples sensed the possibilities of the car for joy riding long before they could afford it.

The revolution in sexual mores traditionally attributed to the 1920s had earlier roots. Progressive Era purity reformers betrayed considerable anxieties over changes in sexual mores. Presumably real behavioral changes underlaid the anxieties. James McGovern has found clear examples of the emergence of the stereotypical 1920s fast woman or "flapper" in the pre-World War I years. When Alfred Kinsey surveyed American women on their sexual behavior in 1953, 18% of those born before 1900 (i.e., they would have been over 17 in 1917) reported that they had engaged in premarital sex in cars. How much, when, and why remain open issues.[63]

There were juvenile series books, written by women, for girls, that suggested the liberating possibilities of cars. Of course, they did not directly discuss sexuality, an obvious taboo for this genre. Between 1910 and 1917 Margaret Penrose (a pseudonym for Lillian Garis, the wife of Harold Garis, author of the Motor Boys series) wrote the ten-volume Motor Girls series, the best known of this obscure genre.[64] These works presented a different view of automobility than the Motor Boys serials. Penrose encouraged adolescent girls to learn to drive by insisting that it was simple. The Motor Girls turned cranks, replaced tires, and did other repairs with aplomb. The Girls easily coped with road emergencies. Part of the books' appeal to adolescent girls undoubtedly was that they handled these automotive crises as well as the Boys.

Still, the attitude toward mechanical repairs is a little ambivalent. In one book, the Girls solve a mechanical problem that the Boys cannot, but elsewhere a Motor Girl calls on a butler to turn on the lights in a living room.[65] The protagonists are not above charming men into doing needed repairs. The writers also show ambivalence on other issues. Barbara Thurston, the leader of a motoring group, has the intelligence and leadership abilities to fight forest fires successfully and deal with small town cops at speed traps. Still, she confesses that she is "too stupid" to understand politics. She hopes that "some day" girls may have the chance to be "as patriotic as boys." Ironically, this is just before she breaks up a spy ring in Washington D.C.[66] The contrast between competence and insecurity bewilders.

The Girls prefer a different style of motoring from the Boys. They must retain some behaviors that set them off from the Boys. Otherwise, they'd lose their identity as girls. They like touring, not racing. The key difference can be found in a 1910 novel where a motor girl describes driving: "The car went noiselessly—the perfection of its motion was akin to the very music of silence."[67] The Boys prefer their cars noisy, like racing cars, and even disconnect mufflers. They like motorcycles, a taboo for the Girls. The Girls do not watch races, the Boys' fantasies to the contrary notwithstanding. They can hold their own in informal road races, but profess not to like speeders.[68] The girls choose not to compete in the warrior cult of racing. They employ different driving manners than the boys. For example, they slow down when passing to avoid "dusting" the other driver.[69]

There were significant gender-based differences in plot. The automobile allows the Girls travel and adventure, but of a different sort. While the Motor Boys travel coast to coast, visit ranches in Arizona, tour Mexico, and go over the top of World War I trenches; the Motor Girls travel to Hudson River mansions, visit Newport, and sightsee in Washington D.C. They seek prestige as well as adventure, with their cars an entree to politicians, millionaires, and foreign dignitaries. Most often boys and romance await them at their destinations, along with mysteries. Cars are more utilitarian for them than the Boys, a way to get to adventure and status, rather than the center of their lives. They enjoy showing off their skills to gawking men, but they do not aggressively seek competition.

Girls played little, if any role, in the lives of the Motor Boys, but boys always accompanied the Motor Girls, not because their mechanical skills were superior, but for romantic interest. While it would be incorrect to describe the Girls as man hungry, dances with socially correct young men often await them after their trips. Penrose and the other authors included chaperones on the Girls' trips. This set limits on their adventures. It is hard to imagine the Motor Girls going over the top in the Argonne in their dusters and veils, accompanied by chaperones. The Girls do not like chaperones, finding them "a necessary evil,"[70] but bad things happen when they do not have one. In one novel an "impudent" boy tries to share their picnic lunch.[71] In another, a man who is socially unacceptable strikes terror into an Automobile Girl's heart by proposing marriage when he gets her alone in his car.[72] So, they normally consult with the chaperone before embarking on a trip.[73] Since these were fictional works, the chaperones always say yes. The proposal episode hints at the sexually emancipating possibilities, while formally rejecting them.

Given the generally romantic theme of their adventures, the bow in the direction of chaperonage was a way of reassuring parents that the books were acceptable. Parents rarely creep into the books. When they do, they seem more oppressive than the chaperones. Adolescent readers undoubtedly also perceived the absence of parental authority as a measure of the liberating possibilities of cars. For the Girls, as for the Boys, autos were symbols of generational change and modernity. The publisher advertised the series as "tales that all wide-awake girls will appreciate."[74]

A more explicit, but unusual, hint that young women sought sexual liberation can be found in popular music. Song writer Kerry Mills, presumably writing for other young women, clearly suggested different sexual mores in "Take Me Out for a Joy Ride":

> Take me out for a joy ride, a girl ride, a boy ride.
> I'm as reckless as I can be, I don't care what becomes of me
> Let's go out on the parkway, the dark way, the lark way
> All afternoon we'll sit and spoon on that long joy ride.[75]

Mills displayed no cant of male sexual conquest in this unusual song. Women, at least the women who sang Mills' song in urban music halls, apparently also welcomed the chance to speed into the countryside, to flout the social conventions of the era.

Overcoming the social pressures against driving and the financial requirements for car ownership made automobility impossible for most young women. They could participate in automobility through the new dating system, without owning the cars themselves. In a society that could and did place severe limitations on the freedom of women, they could shift courtship into cars controlled by men more easily than they could get cars themselves. Many young urban women evidently preferred this to the old style parentally controlled courtship. The larger society still claimed hegemony over young women, but they could choose an alternative courtship style, which they preferred, even though they still could not exercise full control. To paraphrase Virginia Scharff, they may have sought more to control the back seat than the car itself.[76]

In conclusion, for men of the motoring classes, automobility was close to irresistible. Cars offered an emotional substitute for the perceived loss in status that they attributed to economic change. Unfortunately, most men carried the love affair with cars too far, seeking the exclusion of women and adopting risky driving behaviors. For middle-class women, attractive as driving might be, there were other, more important battles—suffrage, legal rights, and limiting parental control. The motor car probably looked like another form of suburban entrapment by household technology to some women. Cars eased the change in courtship patterns, but this change did not require ownership or driving. The battle to control the car culture was one sided, because only one side really waged it. Worshippers of the car, driven by the powerful emotions associated with gender and status identity, would dominate the regulation of and planning for the new machines in cities.

9

RED LIGHT, GREEN LIGHT

ON SEPTEMBER 13, 1899, wealthy New York City realtor H. H. Bliss stepped off a trolley car at the corner of Central Park West and 74th Street. Cabbie Arthur Smith, driving a new electric vehicle, tried to pass the trolley on its right side, since he did not want to follow a slow wagon on the left. Smith killed Bliss, the first of the more than 2.7 million Americans sacrificed on the altar of automobility.[1] The accident illustrated all the problems of introducing autos into crowded city streets. Drivers like Smith resented having to drive at less than top speed and thought of the streets as arteries for travel. For example, earlier that year, Smith's fellow cabbie Arthur Driscoll had weaved through Fifth Avenue traffic, supposedly at the unheard of speed of 35 m.p.h. He was trying to earn a fifty dollar tip by making a train connection. Driscoll nearly caused several accidents as pedestrians and horses scattered in terror. He became the first New Yorker arrested for speeding.[2] Autos surprised urban pedestrians, accustomed to trolleys, which followed rails, or to horses, which traveled slowly, and whose clanging horseshoes announced their coming. Too many drivers behaved like Smith, or Driscoll, or Mr. Toad.

The debarking trolley passenger, Bliss, thought of the street as a walkway. Not surprisingly, it never occurred to him to look. He likely never saw what hit him. More than 200 New Yorkers died in street accidents involving horses that year, mostly because a frightened horse ran away, or spooked and kicked someone. In a case like Bliss's, it is possible that a horse would have stopped or turned to avoid him. Smith allowed himself neither the time nor space to avoid Bliss. Neither the courts, nor the press attached any responsibility to Smith, or to later drivers who had similar accidents, as long as they attempted to stop.

The urban traffic revolution first took place on New York City's already crowded streets, making it the ideal location for a case study of the emergence of traffic. In 1900, Paris was the only city in the world with more cars. As late as 1905, the *New York Times* estimated that better than 45 percent of the nation's cars were in New York State or New Jersey, most of those in the metropolis. As late as 1910, the city had more motor vehicles per capita than the nation as a whole (see table 6.1). *American City,* the most important professional journal for municipal officials, noted in 1915 that most American traffic regulation had originated there.[3]

New York's traffic mortality rate (see graph 9.1) followed an uneven pattern in the early twentieth century. Traffic fatalities doubled between 1902 and 1907, largely because more powerful motors increased trolley car speeds. New York's rate was roughly in line with other major cities, slightly better than Chicago, slightly worse than London or Paris.[4] A Minneapolis traffic count also suggested that the real problem was not cars, per se. In 1906 downtown streets in that city averaged only one vehicle every ten seconds during the work day (approximately one quarter of Fifth Avenue, New York, traffic volumes). These probably created only enough traffic to jam major downtown intersections briefly at peak travel times. Nearly three-fourths of Minneapolis' street running vehicles were horse-drawn and 21 percent bicycles. The city's fewer than 700 autos only generated 5 percent of traffic.[5] New York autos might have accounted for double that proportion, still a small part of total volume.

The problem may well have laid more with the mixture, rather than amount of traffic. Five different travel modes (pedestrians, bicycles, street railways, horses, and autos) with five different sets of operating characteristics could only increase accidents. In almost all cities, but in Manhattan only on Tenth Avenue, railroad grade crossings added a sixth element.[6] Horses, trolleys, and, to a lesser extent, cars, were noisy. Cars traveled faster than trolleys or horses, but could brake and swerve more rapidly. Bicyclists, pedestrians, and all sorts of drivers could have lapses in attention spans and might even be drunk. Throughout this period, a huge proportion of drivers were new to their tasks. In collisions trolleys were likely the safest for occupants, bicycles the most dangerous. Henry Ford once told New Yorkers that cars did not scare well-bred horses. If so, New York's horses must have been an ill-bred lot, because horse-related fatalities increased nearly 50 percent between Bliss's death and 1907. Late-

Graph 9.1 **TRAFFIC FATALITIES, BY CAUSE, NEW YORK CITY, 1902–1915**

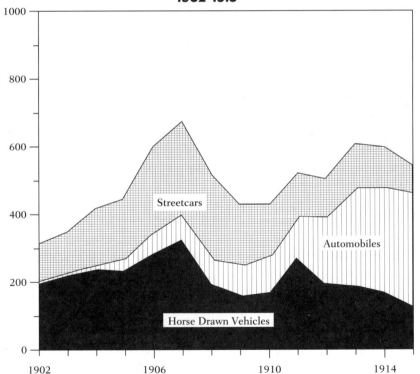

SOURCE: Annual Reports of the New York City Board of Health

twentieth-century data suggest that the highest urban traffic mortality rates occur in third world cities, where precisely this mix of traffic still occurs.[7]

Cars hitting pedestrians, especially children, became a major new form of accidents, and over the next dozen years a war raged between automobiles and youngsters for the control of New York's streets. Not surprisingly, the cars would win the hostilities. The first skirmish came in 1901 when a chauffeur driving H. R. Root and S. H. Sterns to their Wall Street offices, hit a two-year-old who had been playing on a Lower East Side street. The victim was Louis Camille, the son of Italian immigrants. Neighborhood residents assaulted the chauffeur, whom police rescued. The police exonerated the chauffeur, who claimed Camille had run in front of his car. To Camille's neighbors, the issue was an invasion of their turf. Young Louis was playing in the kind of recreational space where urban children had amused themselves since the invention of cities. At least, in his case there was no pathetic neighborhood-wide search for the relatives of an unknown victim, an all too common scene in an age when few people carried identification. Probably three quarters of the auto's victims were pedestrians, mostly children playing in the street, inattentive to the new vehicles. Motorists killed more than a thousand New York children before World War I. In 1910, 195 of the City's 376 traffic accident victims were children. In 1913, 149 of 534. Cars killed children in other cities as well, but at a much lower rate. In Los Angeles, for example, only 9 percent of traffic fatalities in the same period were children. Los Angeles had much lower densities, so many children had yards as play locations. Today, fewer than 20 percent of motor vehicle fatalities involve pedestrians.[8]

Gotham's poorer neighborhoods, which lacked parks and playgrounds, provided most of the victims of the new status symbols. Residents of those neighborhoods retaliated against the new, upper-class invasion by attacking motorists. Within five years of the Camille incident, the *Times* reported thirty-four anti-auto incidents, including stonings, firecracker throwings, shootings, and full fledged riots. It reported the death of only one driver, slain by the irate father of a victim. The most violent outbreak happened in Hoboken, where police became involved in a shootout with neighborhood residents after rescuing a teamster who had run over a child. Fortunately, neither the victim's neighbors nor the police hit anyone.[9]

Almost invariably anti-auto incidents had overtones of class warfare. The most publicized case came in 1903. Her chauffeur was driving Mrs. H. Gottschall in her open electric car through East Harlem, then an immigrant Italian neighborhood, en route to an afternoon tour of the bucolic parkways in the Bronx. Neighborhood children stoned the car, hitting the wealthy Mrs. Gottschall in the head, and knocking her unconscious for three days. There was a hue and cry in New York's middle-class press, replete with ugly ethnic slurs and attacks on the police for failing to control Italian youth gangs. The police responded by conducting a huge man (or, rather, boy) hunt in East Harlem, questioning all adolescents into whom they had a hook.

To end the police pressure, neighborhood children fingered a perpetrator, Joey Russo, then three and a half years old. The police, seeing an out from the newspaper attacks, solemnly arrested Russo and booked him downtown. Since it is wildly improbable that a child that young could have concussed Mrs. Gottschall, the entire episode was likely a ploy by the neighborhood and police to placate angry motorists and newspapers. They fingered someone whom the court system would never send to jail. The usually staid *Times* had a field day with the story, printing a satirical attack on nativist fears of ethnic gangs. The editorial claimed that young Russo had belonged to the much feared "rubber nipple" gang.[10]

Suburban and rural residents also resented wealthy urban motorists. In the countryside drivers injured not only people, but also chickens and dogs. Urban based drivers also deepened the ruts in rural roads and threw vast amounts of dust into the air.[11] Suburanites also resented the annual late spring invasion of autos, the playthings of the urban rich. New Jersey briefly tried to ban cars with New York registrations (technically, the legislature directed the prohibition at all nonresidents, but politically, there was no doubt that the target was wealthy New York scorchers). Suburban sheriffs routinely set up Sunday afternoon speed traps and even shot at speeders. Tarrytown, N.Y. police severely injured one woman speeder when a rope, which they had stretched across the road, yanked her out of the driver's seat. Some constables clearly overreacted, but, when affluent motorists whined that all suburban regulation was a form of extortion, as an Oyster Bay Roosevelt did in a letter to the *Times,* they overstated the case.[12]

New York's suburbs were not alone. Glencoe, Illinois laid a three-inch-high brick speed bump across its main road in 1905 to slow speeders from nearby Chicago. James Collins, the marshall of suburban Glen Echo, Maryland, nearly started an international crisis by shooting out the tires of cars and arresting motorists from the District of Columbia, even those with diplomatic immunity. Secretary of State Elihu Root actually requested that Secretary of War William Howard Taft send in troops to protect motorists from the pistol packing sheriff. One suburban town that clearly applied a speed trap to draw revenues was Seabrook New Hampshire, which was on the road from Boston to the popular Hampton Beach resort. Seabrook's constable handed out 295 of the 311 traffic tickets issued in New Hampshire in 1911, all but three of them to out-of-state drivers.[13]

The worst squabbles ended when suburban motorists and realtors, who realized that automobility increased property values, pressured local authorities to treat drivers better, around 1907–8. Suburban road houses, which benefited from touring city residents, likely lobbied suburban constables as well. The arrival of the Model T in 1908 allowed many suburbanites and wealthy farmers to own and poorer farmers to dream about car ownership. After that date rural/suburban newspapers stopped calling cars "devil wagons" and rural anti-automobility, especially its suburban manifestations, declined.[14]

The attack on the auto was not entirely based on location and social class. One group of evidently well-to-do urbanites, who did not own cars, also demanded a halt to the menace. In 1902 Horace Parker, a Fifth Avenue resident and leader of an anti-speed organization, surveyed 20,000 New Yorkers, primarily in upper- and middle-class neighborhoods where automobility and suburbanization might seem desirable social goals. Ninety-five percent of those surveyed favored restricting autos to eight miles an hour, a rate roughly comparable to horse speeds and not completely incompatible with the social functions of streets. Parker overstated the threat, claiming that the vast majority of drivers exceeded existing speed limits and that pedestrians already had long waits before crossing streets.[15]

Until 1905, even the *Times* attacked autos, editorially calling them "devil wagons," demanding the 8 m.p.h. speed limit. The resolutely middle-class *Times* not only attacked the "idle and vicious poor" for stoning cars, but also the "idle and vicious rich . . . speeders of automobiles."[16] It sympathized with the rioters: "There is one thing that travels faster than the swiftest automobile yet invented and that is a bullet. It would not be well for the drivers of automobiles to induce the belief that firearms offer the only really efficient protection against them."[17]

The *Times* was not alone. The well known anti-vice crusader Dr. Charles Parkhurst attacked the "haughtiness and self-complacent nonsense" of auto owners in a sermon: "It does not stand to reason that in a democratic country, 95% of the population should be tyrannized and run over by the other half."[18] Woodrow Wilson, then President of Princeton University, blistered car owners in a 1906 speech: "Of all the menaces of today, the worst is the reckless driving of automobiles." Wilson warned affluent drivers that their callousness was breeding socialism in the U.S. He said that, "as a Southerner," he could understand those who took the law into their own hands and shot hit-and-run drivers.[19]

The anti-automobilists were right about the arrogance of motorists on issues of street use and speed. The car owners fought almost any regulation. Auto enthusiast Xenophon P. Huddy wrote the first U.S. legal treatise on regulation of the auto in 1906. Huddy's views reflected those of motoring organizations like the Automobile Club of America. Huddy opposed all regulation, arguing that the normal workings of tort litigation would force motorists to be more careful. He believed that the only guarantee of safety needed was the ordinary caution mandated by the common law. In other words, motorists would stop speeding when the specter of other speeders losing lawsuits to those they injured made them more cautious. He noted approvingly that courts put the burden of proof in allegations of speeding, or other forms of reckless driving, on the police or on plaintiffs. As a rule lawyers could destroy their testimony about speed on cross examination. This doctrine also would have prevented a requirement for speed governors on the engine, a proposal bandied about by some anti-automobilists.[20]

Huddy did not believe that states could require driving tests, although he was aware of European precedents. To Huddy, pedestrians, children, and horses lacked any special claim on the streets.

He opposed any taxation on autos that did not apply equally to horse-drawn vehicles, although he noted that most state courts had upheld registration laws. He approvingly cited an Ohio Supreme Court decision, which ruled that the state legislature could not set a speed limit, because that was a prerogative of localities. Interestingly, lawyers would get speed limits in New York City thrown out on the opposite ground—the state legislature had set a higher one. Clearly the automobilists could afford wily, effective lawyers.[21] Huddy was not alone: Car maker Alfred Pope complained that speed limits were "invidious class legislation."[22]

Huddy wrote in 1906, before the great traffic jams, but his values lingered. When James Rood Doolittle wrote the first history of the auto industry in 1916, he expressed similar sentiments. Doolittle cited drunken drivers whom the courts had excused from liability for an accident because they were driving below the speed limit. To him, "the solution to the problem is to repeal the [speed] laws and call reckless drivers before the scale and sword of the Blindfold Goddess, Justice, standing on the Common Law."[23]

Car owners also campaigned effectively in state capitols. In Wisconsin urban motorists defeated a 1907 proposal for an 8 m.p.h. speed limit that farmers had sought.[24] The elite Milwaukee Auto Club led the successful lobby against the measure. Of the city's estimated 900 motorists (about two-thirds of Wisconsin's drivers), 209 belonged to the Club. The 1910 Milwaukee City Directory listed occupations for 180 of them. Eighty-nine described themselves as manufacturers, managers, executives or merchants, obviously high-status jobs. Fifty-three came from "footloose" occupations likely to want autos: doctors, attorneys, building contractors, or insurance sellers. Some attorney members had strong political connections. Many others, including much of the Club's leadership, came from the auto industry, including sixteen dealers, three repair shop owners, and eight parts suppliers. The latter included A. O. Smith, one of Milwaukee's wealthiest manufacturers, who made body frames for many carmakers.[25]

The pattern of dealer domination suggests that in many ways the Milwaukee Auto Club, and others like it, reflected what the auto industry wanted. Clearly, it made sense to lobby through dealers with local connections. The state's three auto manufacturers (Jeffrey, the maker of Rambler, was the largest) also lobbied. Many state legislators received their first car trips when Club members gave them free rides outside the Capitol. The Milwaukee Club took the lead in forming a permanent lobbying group, the Wisconsin Automobile Association, composed of dealer created local clubs around the state.[26] There were other examples of auto club/industry collaboration. For example, Henry Ford financed the lawsuit against Detroit's first registration law.[27]

The various auto clubs manipulated the federal system to their advantage, playing local, state, and national regulation off against each other. Some states (notably Maryland and New Jersey, rural states bordering major metropolises) initially required nonresidents to register cars. The auto clubs, dealers, and manufacturers jointly stopped this by lobbying for federal registration, which would have ended state control and registration income. The main lobbyist for the abortive proposal for a federal takeover of motoring registration was the National Automobile Chamber of Commerce, a dealer and manufacturer group. The N.A.C.C. also played an active role in starting motorists' clubs and safety organizations. Likely, the car dealer members kept the clubs focussed on legislative issues, rather than questions of consumer rights. The safety groups typically focussed on driver or pedestrian education, not issues of regulation or car design. It would not be until the 1950s that the American Automobile Association, a mass membership group unlike the old elite clubs, began to function like a consumer group. Before that date the automobile groups, whether elite clubs or supposedly more democratic associations, concentrated on regulatory, educational, and road-building issues.[28]

New York City residents also ran into state legislative and judicial obstacles when they sought to regulate street traffic. Early in the debates judges decided that neither pedestrians, trolleys, nor horses could claim any preference in street travel to autos. The City enacted a 12 m.p.h. speed limit, compatible with other street uses and safer for drivers, too, at a time when accident reports frequently cited rollovers and blown tires as causes of accidents. As we have seen, courts threw out the City's speed limit in 1908, saying that the state-enacted 25 m.p.h. limit superseded it. At least they did not void all speed limitations, as happened in Connecticut. New York's auto clubs and, according to the city's Police Commissioner, the auto industry behind them consistently opposed other proposed speed limits. They successfully resisted the imposition of state license tests and even minimum driving age laws until 1919, eleven years after Massachusetts passed the first permanent laws in the U.S.[29] The New York City-based Automobile Club of America actually wrote the state's first motor vehicle law.[30] Also, the state courts initially refused to enjoin road races.

In evidentiary law, state courts followed Huddy's prescription, shifting the burden of proof to witnesses and the police, who typically lacked the background to evaluate driving technique or speeds closely. Professional chauffeurs and their passengers could be much more convincing, especially when they claimed to have read a particular rate off the speedometer. When the city's auto fatality rate soared in 1911, The *Times* claimed that it was because the New York State Superior Court had voided legislation aimed at hit-and-run drivers. The Court had ruled that requiring drivers to stay at the scene of an accident violated their constitutional protection against self-incrimination. The *Times* likely exaggerated, since increased traffic alone probably explained the changes. The courts did uphold one law. The New York Appellate Division decided that motorists who hit passengers alighting from trolleys, could not claim contributory negligence if the passenger did not look before stepping onto the street.[31]

The *Times* took an especially strong stance against racing. After the winner of the Paris-Berlin Race in 1901 averaged 47 m.p.h., the paper suggested that "the ultimate velocity has been attained." To the editors that speed represented the maximum, because accidents invariably killed drivers if their machines broke down at that speed, as had happened to several in that ill-fated race. Neither farm animals nor pedestrians could get out of the way. The editorial discussed one child killed during the race who, because of the dust thrown up by the speeding cars, probably never saw the car that hit him. The driver told reporters that he could not see the child either. The *Times* even asked the Auto Club to disband after Club members killed two spectators while exceeding the speed limit during a Club sponsored race on Southern Boulevard in the Bronx.[32]

In October 1904 William K. Vanderbilt held the first Vanderbilt

Cup, the equivalent of a modern Grand Prix, on public highways on Long Island. Residents, supported by the *Times,* objected to the race both as a symbol of the dangerous speed mania that gripped automobilists and as a hazard to Long Island residents who sought to travel on their own roads. The *Times* castigated the Nassau County Board of Supervisors and local courts for allowing the race to proceed. When the race was over, the *Times* commented that the race was "utterly futile" from the view of improving the new technology. The paper editorialized that it "clearly infringe[d] the public right for a few rich men and their servants." The paper went on: "It's a terror and a juggernaut, like that which led the nobility and privileged classes into the excesses which precipitated the French Revolution."[33]

But, that was the last time the *Times* applied the rhetoric of class warfare to attack the automobile. One sign of the impending change was that, editorial opposition notwithstanding, the first Vanderbilt Cup received front page attention and favorable reporting, especially because nobody died. The race attracted an estimated 200,000 viewers, probably the largest crowd ever to see a sporting event in the New York area until very recently. The lack of fatalities may have disappointed them. On another occasion, Barney Oldfield, the famous race driver, told a reporter that spectators only went to such races in the hope of seeing someone killed.[34]

The favorable popular response to the race may have affected editorial judgment. The *Times* shortly after that praised "The All-Conquering Auto," urged urban mothers to keep their children off the streets, and even opposed speed limits.[35] Accident coverage took a different tone also. It rarely reached the front page and lacked the emotionalism or respect for the victims present in earlier stories. A June 18, 1905 story described an accident between a car and a rag peddler on the Lower East Side: "The air was filled with wheels, rags, and Italians." After a chauffeured car ran over seven-year-old Antonio Pasquetrette on July 7, 1907, triggering a stone throwing mob, the *Times* speculated that he might have been hitching a ride on the fender, thus transferring blame to the victim.[36]

Why the shift to callousness? Perhaps by 1905 car prices had come down and reliability had gone up to the point that the *Times*'s writers and editors either had bought or were about to buy autos. In other words, mere affluence may have replaced opulence as a pre-condition for ownership. Auto registration nationally increased more than ten times over between 1900 and 1905, a sign of declining prices. When newspaper editors can afford cars, the joys of speed can hypnotize them, too. The powerful car culture was taking hold. After 1905, coverage in the newspaper expanded and reflected a different outlook on cars. The paper reported positively when automobiles gave the first powerful, highly publicized demonstration of their utility by providing emergency services and supplies to San Francisco after the 1906 earthquake. The *Times*'s business section began to follow the booming, highly profitable auto industry closely. After the turnout at the Vanderbilt Cup races, the sports section gave much more space to car racing. The society pages continued to follow the deeds of wealthy motorists.

The *Times* also began to attract larger amounts of automobile advertising. It had been running an advertising laden annual auto section since 1900 to coincide with New York's prestigious auto show, but, around this time, it began to pick up advertising daily. Suburban road houses started to advertise to touring motorists in the newspaper also.[37]

In 1905, the *Times* gave a positive endorsement to the second Vanderbilt Cup, especially praising the increase in the winner's speed from 52 to 70 m.p.h. In 1906 the paper printed remarks by an A.C.A. member who criticized Woodrow Wilson's attack on automobile plutocrats, and claimed that autos "broke down class distinctions." When Charles Parkhurst attacked motorists, editorials accused him of trying to stir up class warfare. The *Times* did continue to report on especially arrogant motorists. For example, in 1914 it printed a story on a chauffeur who had skidded onto a sidewalk and knocked a pedestrian down. The chauffeur, Otto Harf, kicked and slugged the wounded man before driving off.[38]

Cities reacted to the increase in accidents by increasing police patrols. Philadelphia created a ten-member traffic squad, the first specialized squad in the nation for the Christmas, 1904 rush.[39] Ultimately, 6,000 officers would staff New York's Traffic Bureau, formalized in 1907. Other cities followed in New York's wake as they professionalized their forces. Cities also mechanized police in response to the new conditions. The Boston Police bought a Stanley

Steamer in 1902. In 1903 the New York Police Department purchased three bicycles. After the Gottschall incident, detectives borrowed an elite touring car from a police commissioner and deployed it successfully on a trip through several working-class neighborhoods as bait to entrap adolescent stone throwers. Large-scale motorization of police came much later.

Police control was not enough. Urban streets needed new rules and behavior to augment familiar traffic customs. One major expectation persisted from the nineteenth century, keeping to the right side of a street. Clearly that was no longer enough, as traffic grew and the mix became more complex. Wealthy Manhattan socialite William Phelps Eno convinced Police Commissioner Francis V. Greene to issue the first comprehensive set of rules of the road in the U.S. in 1903. Eno, a car owning millionaire, was the first American to develop a significant interest in traffic regulation, in his case as a hobby. He claimed to have participated in the drafting of Paris's pioneer traffic code, on which he modeled his New York proposals. He later served as a traffic adviser in London. Although an amateur, Eno operated in many ways like a professional traffic engineer. He consulted in several cities, wrote five books on traffic control, and helped create the first professional organization. In 1933 he endowed a university traffic engineering program at Yale, his alma mater.[40]

Eno's rules called for slower traffic to stay to the right and for faster vehicles to stay to the left, especially when overtaking street cars. Wagons could no longer back up to the curb (side loading was the alternative) and parked vehicles had to be next to the curb and face in the same direction as traffic. These dictums largely re-enacted regulations passed in 1897, at the height of the bicycle craze, but already forgotten. The new rules also banned parking within ten feet of corners. Drivers had to set their brakes when parked. The directives expected drivers to give hand signals before stopping or turning. Trolleys had the right of way on their tracks (transit operators were already complaining that vehicles making left-hand turns were stalling trolleys). The Eno rules expected traffic officers to give priority to north-south over east-west traffic, which probably only reinforced their existing behavior. During this period police also attempted to crack down on the storage of wagons in the street and to prohibit some left turns from Fifth Avenue. New York's Board of

Aldermen augmented the rules to ban drivers under the age of 16, to require lights on cars at night, and to set a twelve miles per hour speed limit downtown.[41]

Other cities passed much simpler bylaws, also in 1903, typically requiring a visible license number, imposing a speed limit of eight miles per hour or less, and requiring lamps and horns. Philadelphia mandated an inspection by the Bureau of Boiler Inspection, even for internal combustion cars. Chicago required drivers to turn off the engines in parked cars. Cleveland ordered motorists to stop for frightened horses. Evidently, the rules had little impact initially. Cleveland's Chamber of Commerce suggested a set of rules almost identical with those already on the books in 1906, a sign that the police were not enforcing the first set. When Boston police checked registrations at a roadblock in 1904, they found that barely half the cars that they stopped had the license plates mandated by state law. Paul Barrett estimates that one third of Chicago's motorists never bothered to register cars and routinely defied all traffic laws.[42]

In 1905 the New York City police imposed a new system of Eno-designed rotary traffic control on the chaos of Times Square. Traffic officers and barriers prohibited crosstown traffic between 42nd and 46th Streets. The system required vehicles entering the Square from the north or west to proceed south on the west side of the square until they reached 42nd Street, where they might turn left. The rules banned wagons from this turn and forced them to proceed further south. Traffic from the east or south had to proceed north on the east side of the square until it reached 46th St., where westbound traffic could make a left. In other words, traffic moved around Times Square in a giant one-way, rotary pattern. The police also painted lines to guide pedestrians across the street and built safety islands for streetcar passengers. Pedestrians faced rules requiring them to cross at corners.[43] Ernest P. Goodrich, New York's first traffic engineer, claimed that motorists stopped for the lines only because police told them that their superiors had authorized them to shoot at the tires on cars that crossed the line without a sign.[44] The city did not fund the program adequately, so Eno paid for the first 100 traffic signs and to print copies of the rules.

The new rules did not embody all Eno's ideas. He had wanted to establish a rotary system of control at all intersections like the one at Times Square. For example, he proposed handling traffic at the corner of Fifth Ave. and 42nd Street by placing a pole or small tower in the center of the intersection. The proposal required that all traffic swing around the tower in a circular pattern, as though in a rotary or traffic circle. Eno thought that this would allow traffic to flow continuously through the intersection, a motorist's dream. Wisely, the police did not buy his reasoning. The effect would have been to take eight lanes of moving traffic and compress them into two lanes while swinging around the center of a narrow gridiron intersection. At even moderate volumes, there would not have been enough space for traffic to interweave, inevitably causing gridlock. Beside, the rotary scheme, like most motorist-designed traffic plans, made no provision for pedestrians.

Cabbies, teamsters, and motorists led a firestorm of protest against the 1905 rules, which they believed violated their freedom and, presumably, their masculinity. They defied regulations, especially in Times Square, and successfully lobbied the City Council to get rid of the police-imposed system. New Yorkers continued to speed, continued to obstruct trolley tracks, and continued to park wherever they wanted. Other cities sought to impose similar rules before 1910, normally at the behest of trolley companies. Pressure from car owners, teamsters, and cabbies killed these rules, in large part because drivers perceived them as impositions on their freedom by the hated street railway monopolies.[45]

Municipalities salvaged some changes in traffic behavior from the wreckage of regulatory failure. Drivers did honor a rotary system in Columbus Circle, New York. Boston and Philadelphia, with probably the narrowest streets in the country, successfully adopted one-way traffic rules for some streets. In 1908, when Times Square traffic went from unbearable to impossible, even New York's rule-hating cabbies recognized the wisdom of adopting Eno's system. Ultimately, the plan of one-way rotary traffic would be adopted all over the world, most notably in the monumental circles of Washington and Paris. It still was not a good way to handle pedestrians. Later, poet e.e. cummings would complain that traffic had stranded him in the middle of a Parisian rotary for two and one half hours. By 1910, most motorists had conceded urban crosswalks to pedestrians and most adult pedestrians had conceded the middle of the block to cars.

Some Boston wag even introduced a new word to English, "jaywalker" (from "jay," meaning hick or rube).[46]

While opposing regulation, the motorists now showed some sensitivity to the need for better behavior. Their periodicals called out for safer driving. Wealthy automobilists encouraged YMCAs to start driving and mechanical schools, albeit primarily for chauffeurs. The press encouraged first-time drivers to attend such schools, advising them that the ten-minute lesson given by new-car sellers was not enough. A few traffic experts thought otherwise. F. E. Rankin of Detroit believed that the high proportion of first-time drivers explained much of the accident rate. Nonetheless, he thought the best way to learn was to put a new driver right into traffic and "let him take his chances."[47]

Not all motorists attacked the laws prohibiting hit-and-run and drunk driving. Motoring periodicals attacked both behaviors. New York drivers had rejected the police inspired attempts to impose hand signals, but those devised by the Auto Club of Southern California in 1910 eventually found national acceptance, when motorists accepted their utility. Most car buyers probably wanted head lights, tail lights, and good brakes before states required them. H. H. Bliss, the first auto fatality, did not die in vain. Both regulation, *and custom* now prevented passing trolleys on the right.

All this notwithstanding, automobiling groups generally continued to resist governmental regulation. They even attacked Eno's mild, far-sighted, pro-mobility regulations. At times, they could be downright regressive, as when some anglophiles suggested switching to left-hand driving on the British model. The Chicago Motor Club claimed that rules forcing slower speeds in front of schools were merely another attempt to harass motorists. The automobile clubs promised to enforce reasonable speed limits among their members when they lobbied against speed laws. Once, the Automobile Club of America even offered to lend its members' cars to the New York City police for speed law enforcement. However, *Horseless Age* could not find a single case where an auto club had actually expelled a member for speeding.[48]

In general, motorists wrote the early rules, even when they were a tiny fraction of the traffic. Perhaps this was not surprising. Traffic required some commonly observed behaviors and, given the elitist, warrior mentality of early drivers, they were unlikely to follow any rules unless they consented to them. Teamsters, cabbies, downtown merchants, transit companies, and even a few safety crusaders had some input into the process, but the elite drivers wrote the rules, and wrote them to help mobility, much more than safety. The others, especially pedestrians, had to take the place designated for them.

Motoring groups financed educational campaigns to change the street behavior of children. New York safety crusaders even resorted to the foreign language press to publicize the dangers to school-age children. They urged immigrant mothers to watch their children when they went out, or keep them in the home, an impossibility for many. They even sought to trigger feelings of shame among ethnics, claiming at one point that German-American mothers did the best job because especially few of their children died in traffic. The New York public schools responded to the crisis by running traffic safety campaigns for their pupils. They discouraged students from playing in the streets and employed older children as school crossing guards. The police initially arrested children who violated the new anti-play rules, forcing their parents to go to the precinct station and bail them out. Police Commissioner Woods mercifully modified this policy, telling his officers to bring them home instead.[49]

The first wave of regulatory and educational programs in the 1903–7 period had some impact. From 1907 to 1909 traffic fatalities in New York declined, mostly because of rules requiring trolleys to adopt air brakes. Horse-related accidents also declined and the rate per vehicle went down (although not the absolute number of deaths). Bicycles virtually disappeared in all American cities, eliminating one of the least safe elements of the confusing traffic mix. Since pedestrians, especially children, were the most likely victims of all types of street accidents, the decline also suggests that they were changing their behavior in response to the motor car (see graph 9.1).

The rate of auto fatalities among children declined after 1910. Most behavioral changes occurred at the individual or family level. It was not hard to figure out that children, probably the biggest losers in the rise of traffic, needed new habits. Traffic forced parents to confine children to the home or subject them to strict traffic discipline at an early age. I am writing this while seated on the stoop of

Table 9.1 **STREET TRAFFIC, 1913**

City	Street	Daily Vehicles	
		1885	1913
New York	Fifth Ave.	910	8,605
New York	Broadway	1,666	3,277
Washington	Fifteenth St.	753	4,687
Chicago	Clark St.	731	4,691
Chicago	Wabash Ave.	561	3,794
Philadelphia	Broad St.	1,133	6,176
Philadelphia	Filbert St.	845	5,184
St. Louis	Locust St.	541	3,496
Buffalo	Main St.	487	2,941
Boston	Devonshire St.	821	5,410

SOURCES: Table 3.3; T.W. Howard, Isaac Van Trump, and C.G. Anderson, "Report on Traffic on Streets and Roads," *Proceedings of the American Society for Municipal Improvements* 12 (1913), 146–47. Engineers compiled the two data sets different ways and sometimes at different intersections, so they are only roughly comparable. Clifford Richardson, "Street Traffic in New York City, 1885–1904," *American Society of Civil Engineers Proceedings* 32 (May 1906), 382–91 found traffic counts 50% higher than this in 1913 on Fifth Ave., an indication of how imprecise the counts were.

my house in one of Boston's inner suburbs. I am watching a parent two houses up the street teach his eighteen-month-old toddler, who is not yet toilet trained, how to walk. Every time she steps off the curb, he swats her. Nursery school teachers still exploit the popular game, Red Light, Green Light, to teach children about obeying rules. In motor age America, children require street discipline at an early age. They have since the coming of traffic.

Traffic posed increased danger when it soared after the 1908 advent of the Model T, and not only in New York. New York's mortality rate began to creep upward again in 1910, likely because of rapid expansion in the city's car fleet. In St. Louis and other cities, the growth in car registrations was nearly exponential (see graph 9.2) after 1908. In St. Paul, auto registrations went from 1,100 in 1911 to 4,500 in 1915.[50]

Also, the car was becoming more than just a leisure toy. Suburbanites were beginning to commute by car. When the National Auto Chamber of Commerce surveyed urban car buyers in 1909, almost all respondents claimed that they had purchased cars mostly for recreational purposes. Seventy percent said that they sometimes commuted, especially when the weather was nice.[51] In 1914 Saxon ran the first ad in the *Times* appealing to commuters: "Straphangers, the Saxon sets you free!"[52] In 1917 75% of New York City's car buyers preferred closed to open cars, far higher than the national norm. Commuters preferred the closed cars, which they could drive year round. Commuting implied not just more cars, but also more trips, longer trips, and the loss of street space to parked cars. Manufacturers added ignition and door locks to American cars about 1912, suggesting that many people wanted to leave their cars unattended all day in the street, as commuters do. Photos of downtown streets in popular periodicals and *American City* rarely showed parked cars before 1910. After that date they were commonplace and it was unusual to see a photo of a downtown street on a weekday after 1916 in which parked cars did not line both sidewalks.

Separate traffic counts on suburban roads (now described as arteries) outside Boston (1909–1912), Baltimore (1910–1913) and St. Louis (1913–1914), showed car travel increases respectively of 131%, 1,741% and 67%.[53] Massachusetts suburban traffic increased by another 121% in 1913 and 1914.[54] As early as 1912 the *New York Times* claimed a family with an annual income of $2000 could afford a car.

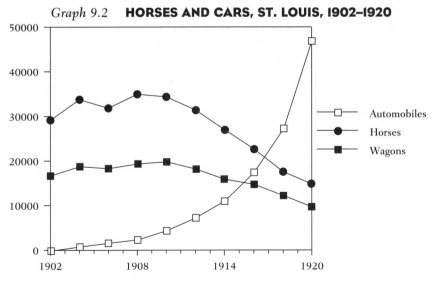

Graph 9.2 **HORSES AND CARS, ST. LOUIS, 1902–1920**

SOURCE: John Henry Mueller, "The Automoblie: A Sociological Study." (University of Chicago Ph.D. Diss., 1928), 140

The consequent move to the suburbs was booming property values.[55] Wealthy Chicagoans with summer homes on the North Shore, and, likely, summer residents of suburban resorts in other cities, gradually began to extend their stay there, commuting in their new cars.[56] Still, most commuters stayed within reach of transit. The National Automobile Chamber of Commerce claimed that there were only 135,000 urban families who relied exclusively on cars to commute as late as 1920, a tiny fraction of the all downtown travelers.[57]

A few other new mechanical vehicles were appearing. Urban cab companies were prospering and steadily switching to i.c. autos after 1907, but this did not lead to much of an increase in traffic, since high fares, fixed by law, limited the market for taxi rides. The number of cabs actually declined between 1910 and 1920, because speedier, more durable mechanized cabs could cover more territory.[58]

Motor trucks also put in an appearance. A careful cost accounting presented at the 1910 convention of the American Society of Mechanical Engineers suggested that, for light loads (under 2½ tons), trucks cost less to owners per vehicle mile than wagons. Five hundred New York truckers staged a parade in 1912.[59] Some factories, either those engaged in nuisance trades that were banned downtown or those requiring large amounts of land that was unavailable downtown except at a very stiff price, had already chosen suburban locations near railroads or waterways. The new steel mill cities of Gary, outside Chicago, and Homestead, outside Pittsburgh, were probably the leading examples of this. Even the light trucks available before 1917 could only reinforce that movement. *Harper's Weekly* reported that two factories in New York in 1913 had cut off all ties to the railroad, moved to the suburbs, and relied exclusively on trucks, but these harbingers of change were isolated exceptions before the 1920s. When Graham Taylor toured industrial satellite cities in 1915, he reported that in Norwood, near Cincinnati, executives commuted in autos from the central city and avoid living in the mill town.[60] None of the pre-1920 traffic counts showed that more than 10 percent of traffic consisted of trucks, and these were likely replacements for wagons. Major truck-dependent industrial suburbanization awaited the development of the Liberty truck during World War I and the massive state road building programs after the conflict.

Fifth Avenue Coach in New York purchased the first urban buses from the French firm DeDion Bouton in 1907. Only 500 buses, mostly domestic makes, were running on American streets as late as 1920. Companies operated bus services only on elite streets like Fifth Avenue and Riverside Drive, from which trolleys were banned. The bus firms sought an elite ridership, forbidding standees and charging ten cents a ride, twice the normal transit fare. No city, except New York, had more than thirty buses in operation in 1920. Because of its ability to dodge traffic, some transit operators sensed that the bus had the potential to replace rail-bound trolleys,[61] but this did not happen until larger buses became available in the 1920s. Almost exclusively then, the surge in urban automobility came from commuters in new, private automobiles, mostly Model Ts.

The *Saturday Evening Post* coined a new word in 1910, "traffic jam," a sign of surging traffic.[62] When Edward Hungerford, the popular travel writer, toured American cities in 1913, he found impassable conditions in many cities. He reported that Pittsburgh and San Francisco, cities with central business districts on peninsulas, limiting entries to a few main streets or bridges, faced diurnal traffic jams. Narrow colonial streets posed the obstacle in Boston and Philadelphia. In Cleveland, Hungerford reported, traffic was destroying the value of property on once upper-class Euclid Ave. Philadelphia, facing a similar crisis on posh Wissashickon Drive, had sought to ban, not just trucks and trolleys, in the traditional manner of elite urban streets, but also "automobiles of the more indiscriminate sort."[63] The growth of traffic far outpaced the growth in car registration and population, according to *American City Magazine*.[64] Evidently urbanites were not only buying more and more cars, but also taking more and larger trips (see table 9.1).

Hungerford reported that Fifth Avenue in New York and Chicago's Loop District had become hopelessly snarled in rush hour traffic. New York's elite motorists liked to drive on Fifth because the city had banned street railways from that street and it was too far from the waterfront to draw much freight traffic. As a result, its traffic had grown by a factor of eight and a half, while that on Broadway had merely doubled. Hungerford claimed that a Wall Street millionaire with a midtown home had given up commuting by car to take the subway.[65] In both 1915 and 1917 time tests showed that

Fifth Avenue rush hour pedestrians were moving faster than cars. In the latter year, The Fifth Avenue Association, a merchant's group, commissioned a traffic study. It claimed that gridlock especially at Fifth and Forty-Second, was costing stores $750,000 a day.[66] New York's influential Chamber of Commerce had already complained that traffic delays in Manhattan were forcing shippers to switch other American ports.[67]

Permanent twice-daily traffic jams spread to every large American city in the summers of 1914 and 1915. Newark, to cite one example, reported a 48 percent increase in traffic between 1913 and 1915 at its major downtown street intersection, now reduced in travel lanes because of shopper and commuter parking.[68] The jams did not only affect car drivers. Chicago trolley lines, for example, claimed that speeds within the Loop had declined 45% by 1915.[69] We have no registration or traffic figures for Atlanta, but Howard Preston found that the number of garages went from 3 to 27 between 1909 and 1915. Gasoline sales more than doubled during that period, sure signs of booming traffic. In 1908 Atlanta drivers purchased twice as much gasoline in May as January. In 1915, they purchased only 10 percent more in May.[70] Gasoline consumption increased by a factor of six between the two years, probably faster than car registrations. This suggests that drivers were putting more miles on their cars and driving them year round, a pattern consistent with the rise of commuting.

In Washington D.C., where parked cars occupied 30 percent of the downtown street space, rush hour car speeds declined below 6 miles per hour, presumably making trolleys even slower.[71] Trolley cars, often carrying more than a hundred passengers, frequently found themselves stalled behind one car with one driver, waiting for a gap in oncoming traffic to make a left-hand turn. Cabbies lost passengers, who found walking short distances quicker or took rapid transit, in cities where it was available. The 142,000 pedestrians who now competed with 25,000 cars to cross the corner of Fifth Ave. and 42nd Street in New York, or the estimated 340,000 who danced through cars in Times Square daily in 1915 also found their pace slowed by traffic. Everyone complained.

On July 1, 1914 L. P. Draper of Los Angeles picked up a passenger at a trolley stop in his Ford Model T and dropped him off several blocks later, after charging him a nickel. Draper had invented a new urban transportation mode, the jitney (the name came from a slang expression for a nickel), which would spread across the country to incorporate 62,000 vehicles by the summer of 1915.[72] San Francisco had a thousand, Milwaukee had 350, and Dallas had 500. Seattle's 500 jitneys carried 49,000 passengers daily at their peak. More than 1500 jitneys in Los Angeles carried 150,000 passengers daily. The Los Angeles Electric Railway Co. blamed them for a decline in ridership from 139.8 million riders in 1913 to 117.3 million riders in 1916. In Atlanta transit ridership declined from 71 million in 1913 to 65 million in 1915. In both cities ridership rose after bans on jitneys. Clearly, jitneys represented a major addition to urban traffic, pushing many cities over the threshold into the age of the traffic jam.[73]

The jitneys found an economic niche between cars, whether taxis or privately owned vehicles, and trolleys. A driver, usually a Model T owner, plied main streets leading to the central business district, picking up three or four passengers to take downtown for five or ten cents. Some jitneys operated with regular customers, offering door-to-door service, like a van pool today. Service was erratic: many drivers were unemployed workers using the family car to earn a few bucks while they job hunted. Some jitney drivers were commuters themselves, picking up a few riders on the way to work in the morning and a few others on the way home at night. Jitneys excelled at providing late night "owl" service, when cabs and transit did not run. "Gypsy" and regular cabs illegally offer similar service late at night in outlying neighborhoods of New York City today.[74] Jitneys also delivered the kind of crosstown service to shopping or recreational sites that trolley companies usually avoided.

Riders liked jitneys for many reasons. Because they allowed multiple ridership, they were cheaper than urban cabs, which typically charged 70¢ for the first mile and 40¢ for each mile after that. Because jitneys made fewer stops and could maneuver in traffic, they were faster than trolleys. In Atlanta, jitney trips were between 150% and 200% faster than trolley trips for commuters. Jitneys also guaranteed their riders a seat. All-black lines soon sprang up in Southern cities, whose riders could avoid the stigma of Jim Crow laws on southern transit systems. Likely, other jitneys took only white riders. Evidently, jitneys were also popular with women who sought to avoid the jostling and general discomfort of trolleys. Car owners using jitneys could avoid the hassles of parking downtown.[75]

The jitneys sought to keep their hauls as short as possible, so they concentrated on inner city neighborhoods. Here, they could charge the same fare as trolleys, despite their much lower carrying capacity. As we have seen, the real estate developers who had developed most transit companies had insisted on a flat fare, despite distance traveled, to promote the sale of suburban lots. In other words, short-haul, inner-city customers effectively subsidized longer haul suburban customers. Inner-city riders, usually the last to board trolleys, wound up straphanging. They preferred jitneys. They had seats, door to door service, faster speeds, did not subsidize suburbanites, and participated in the glamour of auto travel. In Los Angeles, the trade union newspaper, the *Record*, supported jitneys and argued that trolleys were obsolescent.[76] Encouraging jitney use might have improved the efficiency of urban travel and reduced jams, by limiting the number of one-car, one-passenger trips.

This never happened. Politically potent transit firms and taxi owners lobbied against the intruders. They sought regulation in the form of inflated insurance requirements, fixed routes, rigid schedules, and exorbitant license fees. They sought what they wanted from every possible governmental body, including state legislatures, state utility commissions, judges, and city councils. Typically they achieved success at the state, rather than local level. The transit owners usually argued that jitneys had unfair privileges, because other common carriers had to meet these stiff requirements. However, fixing routes and schedules reduced jitneys to the speed of trolleys. Requiring part time jitneys to carry the same insurance and have the same licenses as full time cabs destroyed their cost effectiveness, especially if cities restricted the issuance of cab licenses. Within three years, it was all over. The other interest groups had lobbied or sued jitneys out of business in every big city in the U.S.[77]

There would be no middle ground in urban transit between big, fixed-route common carriers and private cars until the paratransit revolution of the 1970s (inspired in part, by the rediscovery of the jitney experience by transportation economists). Jitney riders complained, none more bitterly than southern blacks, who blamed discrimination for rules shutting down black-serving, black-operated jitney lines in cities like Norfolk. Blacks wanted the freedom of automobility, even in jointly occupied jitneys, rather than Jim Crow streetcar service. A few cities allowed taxicab companies serving blacks only, because regular cabs refused to pick them up, but cabs were expensive. Likely only whites had the economic and political clout to get licenses.[78]

The jitneys probably accelerated the permanent jamming of traffic, but jams did not go away when cities banned them. Some, maybe most, jitney riders switched to private cars, not back to transit. Private auto registrations and travel continued to soar. Commuters reduced street space significantly by filling the sides of downtown streets with parked cars. Auto periodicals first began whining about a parking shortage in 1916, suggesting that, by that date, motorists had already taken over one third or more of the space in downtown streets to store their vehicles. Increased traffic brought both increased fatalities and slower travel times. Powerful interest groups complained. Trolley companies found their speed cut in half in the central business district. Downtown merchant groups began to worry about the ability of shoppers to reach their traffic-stranded doors. Commercial interests complained that the jams were increasing freight costs.[79]

Baltimore, Chicago, Cleveland, Detroit, and St. Louis all started traffic squads around 1911, following the lead of New York and Philadelphia.[80] Police Departments did not like assigning one-quarter or one-third of their officers to traffic duty. Putting a police officer at every crowded downtown intersection was both expensive and inefficient. Officers did not like traffic duty, which required them to be "a cross between a city directory and a football referee."[81]

Police, business groups, and transit companies tried a variety of solutions during the Model T era. At the insistence of the Fifth Avenue Association, New York briefly banned left-hand turns. Drivers ignored the rule. At the behest of downtown stores Chicago tried a short-lived 60 minute parking limit in 1911. Los Angeles tried one later. The stores figured that the limit would reserve parking space for shoppers making short stops, at the expense of commuters, who tied up space all day. Both cities revoked the limits after car owners protested vigorously. Parking bans at fire hydrants and near corners had more success. Detroit deployed the first "boulevard" stop signs in 1915 to give traffic on main streets the right of way. Initially motorists ignored them. Neighborhood groups did not like them either, since they increased vehicle speeds and made no provision for pedestrians.[82]

Few cities were willing to imitate the one-way streets in Philadelphia and Boston. New York's traffic advisers wanted to make some crosstown streets one way, but this did not happen until much later, because shopkeepers on individual streets feared losing customers. Pioneer traffic engineer E. P. Goodrich estimated that painting center lines (first done in Trenton, Michigan, near Detroit) and lane dividers improved speeds by 50 percent by channeling traffic better. Drivers often ignored the painted safety areas for passengers waiting for trolleys, so most cities followed San Francisco's lead and built raised safety islands. Some motorists even opposed them on the theory that they encouraged jaywalking.[83]

Enforcement of traffic laws continued to be weak. The regular courts had little time for the flood of traffic offenders and often voided regulations limiting parking, requiring obedience to stop signs, or banning left turns. Chicago created the first traffic court in 1916 and New York followed suit, but these were not of immediate help. They allowed police to issue summons, instead of immediately arresting miscreants, did not require bail, and scheduled hearings in advance. While these were "progressive" measures, they may have made things worse, not better, because they intimidated drivers less. Joseph Sabath, the Judge of Chicago's pioneer traffic court, probably typified judicial attitudes on traffic cases. He believed that his job should be educational, not punitive, and let almost all offenders off with a lecture. Sabath preferred to concentrate on community educational campaigns. The lack of appropriate legislation also tied Sabath's hands. Some offenders were boys as young as thirteen, but Illinois, like almost every state, did not license drivers until the 1920s. Obviously, judges could not threaten license revocation. Sabath recognized that drunk driving was a major menace, something that police only recognized around 1915, but it was not yet illegal in any state.[84]

As traffic jammed and fatality rates resumed their upward march, urban demands for state legislation, especially driver's licenses, resumed. William G. MacAdoo, New York's Police Commissioner, worried about the large number of inexperienced drivers, but rightly believed that auto companies had aborted requests for effective licensing.[85] The real pressure against regulation still came mostly from motorists and their clubs, who still would not support any regulation that they thought might interfere with their driving rights in the slightest. There were countervailing groups. The transit companies were anxious to speed up traffic and often subsidized traffic police, bought traffic signs, and paid for traffic engineering studies. Later they would buy and provide electricity for the first traffic lights in some cities. They influenced, in part through consultant contracts, many early traffic planners. Some early traffic reports did note that cars took between 10 and 20 times more street space per passenger than trolleys and that it was unreasonable for one motorist to delay 100 trolley riders. Street railway companies primarily sought to ban left-hand turns and driving on trolley tracks, but they had little success. The urban public hated the politically connected monopolies. The one area where they had some success, banning jitneys, was an exception.[86]

Downtown business groups also wanted greater mobility, but they were unsure of their agenda. They tended to be tax conscious and traffic solutions were expensive. They wavered between favoring and opposing left-hand turns. They generally favored parking limits, but did nothing to create them in the face of consumer resistance. In New York City, some mercantile groups wanted to reroute trolleys to stop them from making left-hand turns, but this ran afoul of the trolley companies. Usually, business groups favored one-way streets, but would never stand against the merchants on any block, who opposed one-way proposals for their street. Downtown stores had an interest in encouraging the culture of consumption and restricting a consumer good like the auto ran against the grain for them.[87] Working-class groups shared the culture of consumption and offered less resistance to automobility than their European counterparts. For example, after the failure of Seattle's general strike in 1919, union members turned to consumer cooperatives as an alternative form of organization. One goal of these new consumer organizations was to finance car purchases.[88]

The best regulatory results seem to have come, not from police or interested amateurs (usually motorists like William Eno), but municipal engineers, who worked out a moderately successful system by trial and error. Traffic was a hot topic in their press after 1914 with frequent reports on practices in different cities. During this period innovation gradually switched from New York to midwestern cities like St. Louis, Cleveland, and Detroit. The engineering network guaranteed that, eventually, cities would develop uniform rules. Uniformity made for greater safety. In 1916 *American City* printed the rules developed by a national conference of safety experts, rules that ultimately prevailed nationally.[89] Many cities appointed their first traffic engineers and began to call on engineering schools to train people in the new specialty.

Engineers began to do regular traffic counts to formulate appropriate answers. New York engineer F. Van Z. Lane applied the first modern solution based on traffic counts on the Brooklyn Bridge, one of New York's biggest bottlenecks. He increased traffic speeds on the bridge 30 percent (according to his account) by eliminating overweight wagons, which his studies showed produced most of the slowdowns. He also added an electric signal light system for street cars. He placed a one-way, rotary system at the plazas approaching the bridge, which forced some vehicles to take a longer approach, but improved the flow. Lane's policies regulated wagons, pedestrians, and streetcars to improve safety and motoring mobility. This engineering approach succeeded where traffic police alone had failed. Systems analysis provided the solution.[90] Ultimately, engineers, not police, would develop the traffic rules.

Traffic signals were an obvious solution to the technicians. As early as 1902, *Municipal Journal and Engineer* had noted their potential. Residents of several cities suggested borrowing the familiar railroad system of red and green lights when the traffic crisis of 1914 broke out. Lights on poles would be more visible than police officers. They cost less than stationing a cop on every corner and they could be synchronized to speed up the flow. In 1908 Toledo and shortly after that Detroit equipped mid-intersection traffic police with manually controlled semaphores, which had a green sign saying "go" and a red one saying "stop." The midwestern cities avoided lights because they were more costly and hard to see in the daytime.[91]

New York enhanced this system by adding lights to the semaphores. The police placed tall semaphores at major intersections on Fifth Avenue and advised cops at intervening corners to follow the semaphore, the first attempt at traffic synchronization. The Traffic

Squad found the system unworkable and the hard to see lights of little help. They were abandoned within a year. The Cleveland Police unveiled the first modern red/green light at the corner of Euclid Ave. and 104th Street. in 1914. The local street railway, which wanted to improve traffic flow through a major junction, paid for it. Cleveland also tried a crude progressive control system in 1916, borrowing the idea from New York. Detroit officer William Potts finally developed the modern green, yellow, red light system in 1920.[92]

Police Departments initially (1917–1920) preferred to build crow's nest towers in the center of intersections, where individual cops could control their intersections. This proved a costly flop. Detroit, New York, and other cities abandoned them after Crouse-Hinds, the railway signal firm, developed a lens allowing greater daytime visibility in the early 1920s. Electrical systems allowed much more accurate synchronization. Initially, drivers obeyed the lights because a police officer was present. Once they came to believe that the system increased mobility, the officers could be phased out. Optimists believed that the lights would permanently accelerate traffic. New York even placed tiny statues of Mercury, the Roman god of speed, on Fifth Avenue's first traffic lights.[93]

American drivers did learn that traffic flowed better if everyone followed the rules. The volume of traffic impressed an Italian immigrant arriving in Boston in 1917. The willingness of thousands of motorists to stop whenever a police officer raised his hand astonished him.[94] The reaction of motoring groups to legislation seems amazingly callous and short sighted. Still, it is important to remember that those same groups urged good behavior, "Safety first," in the words of the time, on their members. They did point out that traffic flowed better for all, if drivers obeyed officers, and, later, lights. They urged their members to avoid high speeds in traffic and to avoid driving drunk. The insistence of motoring groups, Judge Sabath, and several police commissioners on education campaigns helped. In the long term, developing traffic rules on a consensual basis, substituting apparently impartial machines (the lights) for police officers whose judgment was human, therefore suspect, and educational campaigns did improve driving safety in the U.S.

The early regulation, engineering, and education programs succeeded to the point that American urban traffic became the safest in the world. The auto fatality *rate* dropped steadily in the thirty years following 1915. Still, the *number* of fatalities continued to increase with soaring automobility. The key difference between European and American traffic mortality rates today lies in the much lower proportion of pedestrians killed in the U.S. Suburban homes with yards, a housing style more common in the U.S. provided an alternative play space. The cost of automobility was the greater social control of traditional street users, which destroyed the livability of inner-city neighborhoods designed in the pre-automobile years.

American drivers still do kill themselves and other drivers at higher rates by almost any measure than western Europeans. Health experts implicate speed and drinking in nearly three fourths of accidents today. The reasons for today's bloodbath are evident in the early auto culture. Men and the few women who drove could still engage in atavistic anti-modern impulses. Drunken driving did not disappear and is still poorly regulated. Adolescent joyriding became a popular pastime. In 1917 more than a thousand cars were stolen in New York City alone, very few by professional thieves. For many drivers, trapped in an increasingly bureaucratized, impersonal society, cars became outlets for their aggressions. Weekend country touring, often at high speeds, became a popular pastime. Speed governors, rigid licensing programs, and traffic or parking bans downtown offered solutions obvious to contemporaries, but Mr. Toad's mentality ruled. The motorists secured minimal regulation at the expense of those who walked or played in the street.

Each traffic control improvement did improve traffic flow, but only temporarily. The nearly insatiable American demand for cars has always increased traffic beyond the capacity of any control system. It is probably unfair to blame early-twentieth-century engineers for this. How could they have envisioned the enormous growth in automobility throughout the century? Even the contemporary auto industry kept arguing that it had reached the saturation point for cars and that ownership rates would not increase further. The great irony of traffic control was that the engineers, measured their success much more by improvements in mobility than safety. Yet these improvements did not end congestion and, ultimately, their primary achievement was to improve safety.[95]

10

THE MOTOR BOYS
REBUILD CITIES

DEVELOPING TRAFFIC CONTROL was not enough. Many urbanites also wanted to reconstruct their cities to encourage suburban automobility. Cities planned reconstruction in two ways. First, designers prepared
fantasy plans, which in effect declared traditional cities obsolete by calling for rebuilding downtown
around the car. These fantasies involved leveling entire neighborhoods for grand boulevards, huge public
plazas, and elevated highways. The fantasies came
from the pens of utopian novelists in the Edward Bellamy mode, auto clubs, construction oriented politicians, and architects. Almost all proponents were
car-loving males, trying to create a high-speed urban
environment for their machines. Second, municipalities continued traditional organic, ad hoc city planning presided over by city engineers, who sought to
plan new suburban territory around cars, and to re-
trofit downtown to the new technology through repaving, street widening, and bridge construction programs. Both responses assumed the possibility of
reconciling traditional cities with automobility.

Fantasy is always more interesting than reality,
and an examination of early-twentieth-century urban

plans shows why they had the power to, in Daniel Burnham's words, "stir men's minds.[1]"

In his brilliant history of nineteenth-century urban planning, Stanley Schultz has shown that most planning visions originated from urban utopian writers. These typically middle- or upper-class male novelists visualized a perfect future made possible by technological changes and by better control of urban development. Bostonian Edward Bellamy wrote the most popular, *Looking Backward,* in 1887.[2] Bellamy and his dozens of imitators loved nineteenth-century cities and technology for the wealth that they had created, but hated the social conflict, crowding, and pollution that accompanied economic growth. They wanted to rebuild for better health and social control.

The utopians had predicted the coming of the motor car as early as 1836 and carriage maker Chauncy Thomas's *The Crystal Button; or, Adventures of Paul Prognosis in the Forty-ninth Century* proposed rebuilding cities around this yet unimplemented technology in 1878. Thomas built his fictional city of Tone around eight double-decked streets, radiating out from a huge central plaza. Only pleasure vehicles and pedestrians could travel on the upper deck.[3] The utopians welcomed cars, which they believed would encourage suburbanization. Most visualized huge (up to forty million population) cities with gigantic downtown skyscrapers. The working class lived in high-rise tenements, usually set in parks. The utopians never envisioned traffic-choked streets destroying the big downtowns that they thought vital to urban success. Mechanized transportation, especially cars and another novelty, subways, would speed traffic over the wide, densely populated landscape. By 1895 most other utopians had usurped Thomas's ideas about wide suburban radials, double decker streets (with the top deck always reserved for private cars), and separate pedestrian walkways. The new walkways appeared either as arcades or elevated, moving sidewalks.[4]

Bellamy himself did not envision cars. In his version of the year 2000 Bostonians still got around by horses and walking. He was unusual in believing in a decentralized city, although one built around "miles of broad streets, shaded by trees."[5] All sidewalks had portable awnings for rainy weather. Each neighborhood had its own civic square, surrounded by "colossal" government buildings. Urban adornment was the highest form of art. New technology such as telephones and pneumatic tubes for package delivery helped eliminate the need for a traditional downtown. Centralized planning eliminated the need for social parasites like the banks, insurance companies, and mercantile groups (jobbers and wholesalers), who historically had created downtown. Bellamy clearly envisioned that better technology and better planning could improve cities. Bellamy's closest follower, Boston journalist Sylvester Baxter, had no trouble integrating the primitive motor cars of the 1890s into Bellamy's futuristic vision.[6]

These fantasists manifestly affected city planning in the early twentieth century. Urban utopians had strong followings in New York, Boston, and Chicago, homes to the leading American architecture/city planning firms. New York had nearly elected the visionary Henry George mayor in 1886 (he finished ahead of Theodore Roosevelt, the Republican candidate, but behind Abram Hewitt, the Democratic victor). All three cities had Nationalist Clubs, which sought to turn Bellamy's urban rebuilding plans into reality. Baxter, president of the Nationalist Club in Boston, was an important figure in that city's planning movement. He served as a publicist for park and City Beautiful designs for planners such as Frederick Law Olmsted and Charles Eliot.[7] Utopians also had some influence in Chicago. Frank Parsons, who had predicted universal family car ownership in 1901, spoke for Chicago's many urban populists, including the dreamer Henry Demarest Lloyd. Architect-planners in all three metropolises did not miss the future implications of automobility.[8]

Motorists also floated many grandiose plans for rebuilding cities around cars, even in the pre-Model T era. They wanted to create costly auto expressways, free from pedestrians and cross traffic. They proposed very costly elevated car-only highways. The most grandiose of these, an engineering impossibility, would have run down the center of Manhattan through the second story of existing buildings. Despite pedestrian refusal to use an experimental pedestrian overpass, New York's Auto Dealer's Association wanted such overpasses on every corner in Manhattan. Another writer suggested that pedestrians would walk on overpasses if provided with escalators. Increased mobility for cars justified the inconvenience to pedestrians and the cost.[9]

Auto commuters also wanted to take over public spaces for parking. They succeeded in turning Cadillac Square in Detroit and market squares in Dallas, Boston, and Newark into parking lots. Philadelphia briefly allowed drivers to park horizontally in the middle of Broad Street. William Eno wanted to level the Plaza at the corner of Fifth Avenue and 59th Street for a parking lot. Similar proposals aimed at Cincinnati's lovely Fountain Square narrowly failed. Washington's bureaucrats wanted to carve parking lots into the mall. The motorists expected cities to pay for these fantasies from general funds, and opposed gasoline, registration, or horsepower taxes. The public rejected almost all their proposals, often with considerable scorn.[10]

Manhattan Island seemed to present an especially juicy terrain for advocates of rebuilding for automobility. In 1904 the Municipal Art Society suggested evicting "hundreds of thousands" of people for five downtown radials.[11] (See illustration 10.1). In 1907 the Civic Improvement Commission, a group of Manhattan business leaders from the motoring classes, suggested new, broad diagonal avenues to approach the Brooklyn Bridge. Their glitzy illustration showed only nineteen vehicles on the traffic-free, divided-approach plaza.[12] Nine were cars, although cars constituted less than a tenth of New York's vehicles at that date. The sketch revealed no wagons, trolleys, buses, or pedestrians. Clearly these visionaries were thinking about rebuilding to encourage privately owned cars.

William Gaynor, a mayor elected by public-works loving Tammany Hall, proposed a new north-south avenue for Manhattan in 1910 to relieve the jams on Fifth Avenue. Gaynor wanted to build a 100-foot-wide road, which would have been New York's broadest avenue, from Eighth to Fifty-Ninth Streets, carved out of the middle of each block between Fifth and Sixth Avenues. The artist's fantasy of the new avenue showed a gutted Bryant Park (located between 40th and 42nd Street between Fifth and Sixth Avenues) and only 46 vehicles on thirteen blocks, at a time when Fifth was probably carrying more than 10,000 vehicles a day (illustration 10.2). Although cars did not yet account for half of Manhattan traffic, 37 of the 46 vehicles were cars, all closed touring cars of the sort favored by Manhattan's elite motorists. There were no trucks, wagons, trolleys or buses, although the illustration shows them jamming a cross street. Only seven cars had parked in the thirteen blocks. Clearly this was a dream for motor boys and girls, with unlimited parking, plenty of open road, and few slow vehicles. Gaynor announced that he expected to raise the estimated cost of $40 million by asking property holders to contribute their buildings and land. He said that whatever property that they had left would increase in value because it fronted the new avenue. There were no Santa Clauses out there waiting to give the mayor their Manhattan real estate.[13]

In their *Central Park: a History and a Guide,* Henry Hope Reed and Sophia Duckworth list eleven visionary proposals to "improve" it before 1925. Their book includes a remarkable artist's depiction of what the Park would look like if all the city had followed all the suggestions. Radio transmission towers dominate the parkscape. Trolley tracks, moved into the park to speed traffic on Central Park West, cut off pedestrian access from the West Side. Visionaries had added a fifty thousand seat stadium, a music hall, an outdoor music stand, and a large Memorial Hall, designated for military trophies. Veterans could reenact World War I battles in trenches cut into the North Meadow. Hangars and an air strip cover the west side of the park in the Eighties. Not surprisingly, the most serious proposals for gutting the park came from motorists, who would have filled the pond and built no less than four new drives, a 30,000 car parking lot, and a garage. There might have been a few trees left.[14] Reed and Duckworth missed one spectacular proposal: futuristic architect Ernest Flagg wanted to sell the park off for building lots and apply the money to construct a ten-mile-long clone of the Champs Elysees up the center of Manhattan.[15]

Most architects who did grand city plans shared the motorists' values. Architect Daniel Burnham, the most influential planner in the early twentieth century, loved cars. He had leased his first one in 1903. In the tradition of evasion of responsibility that character-ized early motorists, he carefully included a proviso in the lease that made the lessor responsible for speeding tickets. He owned three cars by 1905, one customized with leather seats and red satin head linings. He frequently toured Europe in motor cars. He knew the most optimistic forecasts on the future of the car, having sat next to Henry Ford at a formal banquet in 1907 while Ford expounded on the coming people's car. When starting his 1905 San Francisco plan, he drove around to familiarize himself with the city. In other words, he thought first from a driver's perspective.[16]

Burnham praised cars and took an optimistic view of their future at the London Town Planning Conference in 1910.[17] Other twentieth century architects emulated Burnham. Frank Lloyd Wright, at this time a near disciple of Burnham's, designed one of the first suburban homes with a garage in 1904. Wright's influential Broadacre City utopia (1935), centered on elevated highways, had a great influence on mid-twentieth century planning. He once told a group of French architects that Chicago was the most beautiful city in the world, because of its uninterrupted parkways, saying "You can drive nearly all day on them."[18] This suggests that for Wright, as for Burnham, the purpose of urban street systems was to provide high speeds and beautiful vistas for drivers.

The French architect Le Corbusier, arguably the most influential urban designer for mid-twentieth-century America, summarized the fantasies of early twentieth century architects about cars in this schizophrenic 1924 quote:

> Then came the autumn season. In the early evening twilight on the Champs Elysees it was as though the world had suddenly gone mad. After the emptiness of summer, the traffic was more furious than ever. Day by day the fury of the traffic grew. To leave your house meant that once you had crossed the threshold you were a possible sacrifice to death in the shape of innumerable motors. I think back twenty years, when I was a student; the road belonged to us then; we sang in it and argued in it, while the horse-'bus swept calmly along.
>
> On that first day of October, on the Champs Elysees, I was assisting at the titanic reawakening of a comparatively new phenomenon, which three months of summer had calmed down a little—traffic. Motors in all directions, going at all speeds, I was overwhelmed, an enthusiastic rapture filled me. Not the rapture of the shining coachwork under the gleaming lights, but the rapture of power. The simple and ingenuous pleasure of being in the centre of so much power, so much speed. We are a part of it, we are part of that race whose dawn is just awakening. We have confidence in this new society, which will in the end arrive at a magnificent expression of its power. We believe in it.[19]

Le Corbusier had an insight into the traditional uses of streets that many middle-class Americans lost with the coming of the auto. Even with this insight Le Corbusier, like car-owning Americans, worshipped technological change, the key to middle-class lifestyles, too highly to allow non-arterial functions for city streets. The residents of old inner-city neighborhoods, urban villages, faced a choice; move to the suburbs or live at the "centre of power and speed." Clearly he and other architects viewed the city mostly as a race track and geometric fantasy for car owners, not a pedestrian-friendly environment.

In most American cities, business leaders, likely motorists, turned to City Beautiful plans, featuring the geometric fantasies and massive rebuilding plans of Daniel Burnham and other architects. These plans encouraged automobility by building formal grand boulevards on the model of what Baron Georges Haussmann had done in Napoleon III's Paris. These ideas permeated the architects who dominated the early planning profession. When City Beautiful planners held a national conference in 1915, the overwhelming consensus was that the car could solve most urban problems. Only the German architect Walter Hegemann dissented, predicting total congestion.[20]

Aesthetically the roots of the City Beautiful movement were in Burnham's neoclassic architecture and baroque plan for the 1893 Chicago World's Fair. He first applied those concepts to a city in the 1901 MacMillan Plan for Washington, D.C., which restored L'Enfant's original mall with right angle roads and grand vistas. Burnham cleared the romantic curvilinear roads and heavy planting of the Mall that Andrew Jackson Downing, Frederick Law Olmsted's mentor, had laid down in the 1850s. Downing had designed a mall that looked and functioned like Central Park. Burnham wanted a more rigidly geometric plan, surrounded by classical buildings and monuments, as befitted the capital of a new empire. Planning Historian M. Christine Boyer notes that the classical style connoted "communal unity" and were "an ideal paradigm for disciplinary order."[21] Architectural historian Carl Condit once described the Burnham-planned mall as "the work of a demented neo-platonist looking for a pure form to express the inhumanity of government."[22]

Municipal groups, like chambers of commerce, commissioned Burnham-style City Beautiful plans all over the U.S. in the next fifteen years. These plans usually had four elements. City Beautifiers wanted a civic center, most commonly a public square framed by neoclassic buildings. Many cities built civic centers on this model, with the best-known examples in Cleveland (a 1903 Burnham design) and Denver. Second, the City Beautiful advocates suggested radial grand boulevards in the Haussmann style to cut through the old gridiron street plans. These planners justified boulevards more on aesthetic, than traffic moving grounds. Third, the fantasists suggested linking suburban roads into circumferential highways (a suggestion that was normally beyond the political power of the city, given the governmental fragmentation of metropolitan America). The suburban highway plans often did affect state or regional planners indirectly. For example Edward Bennett's 1911 plan for Brooklyn suggested boulevards across Long Island, in pretty much the form that the Island's highway network would take in the 1920s.[23] Fourth, the plans, especially after critics like Herbert Croly complained that they were too grandiose, dealt with a broad variety of other urban issues, including playgrounds, suburban park reservations, finances, health, union railroad terminals, etc., but with much less emphasis than on the civic centers and boulevards.[24]

These business community–funded plans appealed to affluent urbanites for several reasons. American cities were, in fact, an ugly hodgepodge. The new plans promised organization in cities to those who worried about the social order. The appeal to classical Roman motifs struck a responsive chord in those who thought of America as a republic, and an even more responsive one in those who thought of America as an empire. The auto-loving business leaders who sponsored City Beautiful plans wanted to drive to work through imperial vistas, rather than crowded streets, or Olmsted-style romantic landscapes. In cities competing for commercial supremacy, imperial symbols also showed dominance over a hinterland. Some hoped that beautification might even attract tourists. Burnham was particularly good at appealing to these sentiments. He proposed to redesign the Chicago waterfront to look like the Seine or the Thames, with lagoons like the canals of Venice and a yacht club on the lake. These improvements, he claimed, would attract wealthy people from other cities, who would otherwise become expatriates in beautiful European cities. Chicago, he believed, should look like an imperial capital, because "The [commercial] domain over which Chicago holds sway is larger than Austria-Hungary, or Germany or France."[25] San Francisco merchants hired Burnham to beautify their city in part because they worried that Los Angeles might attract more immigrants from the east coast, because it was more visually attractive.[26] The plans had a generally anti-urban tone. Boston's, for example, quoted Cowper's verse: "God the first garden made, and the first city, Cain."[27]

The wide radial roads cut through gridirons were the most important element of the plans, especially the most widely publicized, the 1909 Burnham Plan for Chicago. Planners advocated them for aesthetic reasons, noting that the roads provided incredibly long vistas, as a rule focussed on the civic center or a major downtown monument. Burnham wrote: "There is true glory in mere length, in vistas longer than the eye can reach, in roads of arrow-like purpose that are unswerving in their flight."[28]

City Beautiful dreamers also liked traffic circles, such as the rotaries suggested by William Eno, most often built around an imposing monument at the end of a Haussmann-style boulevard. They expected to inspire awe and a sense of order among residents and drivers. Sometimes the Beautifiers planned radials to clear or wall off poor neighborhoods. Duane Street, an 1890s radial built through New York's Lower East Side, had eliminated the notorious Five Points slum. Atlanta's 1917 planner claimed that one radial would wall off an expanding ghetto. Virgil Bogue's 1911 Seattle Plan proposed a radial that would eliminate an emerging "oriental" neighborhood. When New York's Municipal Art Society projected long radial approaches to the new Manhattan Bridge, it hoped to demolish Chinatown.[29]

While preparing the *Plan of Chicago,* Burnham had talked to Jane Addams, whose Hull House settlement house served the poorest neighborhoods in the city. He promised her that his finished plan would increase access to the lake shore for working-class Chicagoans. Instead the plan cut the shore off with a boulevard. It made no provision to cover over the railroad tracks that also reduced access to the beach. Burnham's final report said not a word about immigrants, Hull House, or Addams. Although Chicago had the highest traffic fatality rate in the nation and many, if not most, of the victims were inner city children, the *Plan of Chicago* never mentioned playgrounds.[30] This was a plan made for the motoring classes, who had paid for it.

Burnham's projected City Beautiful radials were clearly car movers, often eight lanes or more wide with a ban on trolleys and, sometimes, trucks. Yet the early plans did not specifically advocate these boulevards as auto roads and later ones played down that element. The remarkably lush twilight paintings by Jules Guerin that accompanied Burnham's plan of Chicago showed almost no traffic on the boulevards, like the New York City fantasies of the same period (illustration 10.3). In five paintings of future Chicago it is possible to identify 117 horse-drawn vehicles and only 11 automobiles.[31] Guerin showed only open cars, not the closed touring cars of affluent suburban commuters. None were parked. The cars were also disproportionately small, so that pedestrians tower over them. Visually Guerin's roads were geometric objects, not trafficways. In sum, the paintings downplayed the future of the car. Every scholar who has looked at the plan has noted that Burnham planned for car travel,[32] even though he only mentioned automobiles twice, in passing, in the text of the plan.[33] Also striking was the total absence of discussion or illustration of any rail-based public transport at a time when Chicago already had not just trolley lines but also an elevated system. There was no loop of elevated railroads, Chicago's most obvious landmark, in Guerin's paintings and Burnham suggested no future transit alternatives. This could only be the vision of people who planned mostly for autos.

Why weren't cars mentioned in the *Plan of Chicago,* if providing roads for automobility was so clearly one of its functions? Burnham knew that traffic and its attendant problems were increasing, as did the wealthy business leaders who funded the *Plan.* The reasons were undoubtedly political. Wealthy car owners were not popular. Cities had rejected their ad hoc plans for rebuilding with elevated highways, pedestrian overpasses, and traffic rotaries and especially the 1904 and 1907 efforts to cut new diagonal roads through densely populated Manhattan neighborhoods. If Burnham had clearly labeled his *Plan* as an attempt to automobilize Chicago, it might have drawn a very hostile reaction. Neighborhood residents might have lacked the political clout to restrict cars, but they clearly could have blocked expensive reconstruction plans.

Other City Beautiful planners who espoused automobility also avoided making that view apparent because they did not want their plans associated with these unpopular motorists.[34] Even so, few of the Haussmann/Burnham style city plans ever materialized. A few cities built sterile civic centers, destined to become hangouts for derelicts. Where the radials took park land or were built on landfill, cities sometimes completed them. Some highway builders constructed boulevards in suburban areas, where land condemnation costs were cheaper and developers and abutters believed that they would boom property values. Finance provided a major obstacle. States limited the indebtedness of cities and clearing existing housing out of the gridiron was not only unpopular with those evicted, but also expensive. Seattle's voters rejected Bogue's plan, in part because of cost, in part because of its grandiose nature, in part because that city's existing Olmsted style parkways better satisfied residents.[35] Ten years after Burnham published the plan of Chicago, the city had only built two elements of the plan: Lake Shore Drive, built on landfill, and the double decker street along the Chicago River, which shipping and hauling groups wanted.

The professional journals for city engineers seemed little impressed by the Burnham plan, perhaps because similar proposals had been around for years. It was the climax of an aesthetic impulse, not the start of something new. Many examples had already appeared. Boston had built Commonwealth Avenue, the first U.S. clone of a Haussmann boulevard, thirty years earlier. The German city planner J. Stubben had spelled out city planning precepts remarkably like Burnham's to the American Society of Civil Engineers in 1893. St. Louis architects and engineers had proposed radial roads feeding into a new public square in front of the new Union Station in 1894. New York had opened up transit- and freight-free Riverside Drive in the late 1890s. Senator Francis Newlands of Nevada exploited his political clout to get the District of Columbia to open Connecticut Avenue as a 150-foot wide boulevard through Northwest Washington to his new upper class subdivision in Chevy Chase. Strikingly, the District chose to do this, rather than build an Olmsted-style parkway through roughly parallel Rock Creek Park, a sign of declining interest in Olmsted-style planning. Pittsburgh had sliced the shoulder of a cliff for Grant Boulevard, a wide carriage road from its suburbs to the Triangle in 1901. In 1905 the *Engineering Record* reported that

London planned to cut two radials through its downtown district at a cost of £23 million. That journal called for Haussmann-style boulevards the same year. In 1907 both *Municipal Journal and Engineering* and the prestigious *Engineering News* ran major stories on city planning, reviewing the latest European and American plans.[36]

The two most significant radials actually built were the Grand Concourse in the Bronx and the Benjamin Franklin Parkway in Philadelphia. Histories of road building in the 1920s and 1930s note that the Haussmann-style Grand Concourse (finished in 1907) had the greatest impact on post-World War I road designers.[37] New York City built this artery, not downtown, but in the rapidly developing Bronx. The Concourse carried eight lanes of traffic with only the two outside lanes open to freight. Raised islands separated the unreserved lanes from the main roadway. There was no trolley line on this boulevard and underpasses were used to accommodate major crosstown streets (i.e., those with trolley lines). While some trees were planted on the islands, there was no abutting park strip, like parkways.[38]

Perhaps the most expensive example of a new radial was Philadelphia's fifteen million dollar Benjamin Franklin Parkway. The city's engineers took the new planning precepts seriously, leveling twenty blocks through the gridiron in the heart of the central business district to build a diagonal. This road, despite its title, was not a parkway, but a grand boulevard with vistas of City Hall and the Philadelphia Art Museum at opposite ends. The city banned commercial traffic, but allowed too many cross streets for it ever to become an express road. Philadelphia took from 1903 to 1914 to finish this radial.[39]

Traffic jammed the new radials soon after completion, because abutters had unlimited access, side streets crossed them at grade level, and parking ate up their outside lanes. The radial boulevard was not an efficient traffic mover. William Wilson, the most recent defender of City Beautiful ideas, argues that it is unfair to blame Burnham and other planners for not anticipating the surge of traffic, but that defense is spurious.[40] By definition, planners should be prescient. Burnham's Chicago plan did not even depict the present accurately, let alone see the future, if it is taken at face value. The Olmsted style parkways provided an alternative model that moved cars better than grand boulevards, because they limited access and isolated cross traffic. City beautiful planners ignored them. To be sure, the City Beautiful plans were more comprehensive than the ad hoc improvements cities traditionally had built, but how important was a comprehensive plan if it were too costly and impolitic for implementation? Civic centers, monumental rotaries, and radial highways without any park amenities provided short-run traffic help, at best.

The popularity of the City Beautiful movement bemused municipal engineers, bound by the real world of budgets, cost accounting, and debt limits. They had recommended similar diagonals in the nineteenth century, when cities could have mapped them before development raised land costs too high. Business groups, who had demanded the gridiron without radials, because it maximized the number of sellable lots and made real estate values more predictable, had convinced city councils to turn the engineers down. Now, the same business groups were plugging City Beautiful schemes, which included radials that they had rejected earlier. Adding those radials after the fact would have involved expensive demolition of existing buildings. High costs were a key reason so few City Beautiful plans came to fruition.[41]

The engineers responded to the demands of motorists with the kind of ad hoc, organic planning that was normal in the United States. The municipal engineers were hardly likely to question any new technology and they never saw a building project that they did not like. After all, they named their professional organization the American Society *for* Municipal Improvements. They rarely fantasized about the distant future, but thought incrementally.[42] They emphasized repaving, street widening, and bridge construction (including railroad overpasses). Cities also added a new item to their physical plant, playgrounds, largely in response to the car. They also authorized at least one of the old, Olmsted-style parkways.

Changing street pavements came first. Granite block and cobblestone pavements were already in decline, but the propensity of cars to skid on those surfaces hastened their disappearance. As early as 1908 every municipal engineer speaking about paving at the annual convention of the American Society for Municipal Improvements noted the need to repave for automobility. In 1909, when Charles Duryea visited Atlanta, a city that had paved less than a third of its streets, he told unhappy local motorists that this would limit them to the "extravagant sporting period" of driving. Shortly after that, Atlanta began an asphalt paving campaign.[43] By 1915 auto loving Los Angeles claimed that it had paved all its streets.

Dirt and macadam gravel pavements posed difficult problems in the motoring age, even if smooth. The suction of rapidly turning car wheels threw up vast amounts of dust on such roads, destroying them. Cities and suburbs treated these roads with asphaltic tars, initially to lay the dust, later to hold them together. Often the gravel, granite, and cobblestone streets became foundations for new asphalt surfaces.[44]

The car also required expensive snow removal programs, since car owners could not replace their vehicles with sleds, as had horse owners. By 1915, New York City was hiring up to 24,000 temporary workers after each snowstorm.[45] This was another sign of the growing business and commuting use of cars, since leisure drivers would not bother to go out in such weather.

Engineers did not build the first heavy-duty chassis suitable for trucks and buses until World War I. Still, some earlier urban trucks were very heavy and posed special problems. In 1916 a New York City municipal engineer reported on a thirteen-ton truck that pulled a steel-wheeled trailer. This monster actually cracked granite blocks.[46] The few trucks were not heavy by today's standards, but they had a greater impact on pavements because of their very rigid suspensions and solid rubber tires. Cities did try to regulate them because of the way in which they destroyed pavements. By 1914 at least Boston, Buffalo, Cleveland, Cincinnati, Los Angeles, Minneapolis, and Washington D.C. charged trucks a license fee that escalated sharply with size, limited vehicle width, and required wide tires.[47]

Engineers dealt with the added weight of more traffic and heavier vehicles by laying concrete foundations eight or nine inches deep. Since horses still made up a major portion of traffic, they covered the concrete with asphalt, brick or, rarely, wood blocks. Horse owners preferred the bricks because the cracks between bricks gave a grip for hoofs. Also, bricks proved less slippery than granite blocks in rainy weather. Wayne County paved one mile of the suburban extension of Woodward Avenue, one of Detroit's main streets, with an experimental concrete pavement in 1910. Concrete was more frequently laid in the 1920s, by which time horses had almost completely disappeared.[48]

The municipal engineering manuals recommended increasing the standard street width, so repaving projects frequently included some widening, usually by cutting back on sidewalks, a relatively inexpensive expedient. New York widened 23rd Street, an important crosstown street, in 1910. Two years later, the city cut back Fifth Avenue's sidewalks to add two new ten-foot lanes for traffic. Later the city widened Madison Avenue, a project favored by merchants on that street, but opposed by residents. Baltimore widened its streets a little after the great fire of 1904 and San Francisco did the same after the earthquake, but only on a piecemeal basis. Public works departments in other cities also cut back sidewalks. High condemnation costs limited most building demolition to the occasional elimination of bottlenecks. Municipal engineers also increased the radius of downtown curbs to allow cars to turn more easily. This made it slightly more difficult for pedestrians to cross the street. Widening streets often meant cutting down street trees. Abutters objected, but the demands of suburban commuters and shoppers for parking spots almost always took priority. Thus, urban residents not only lost the use of the street itself for social, recreational, and commercial purposes, but much of their sidewalk and many trees as well. Even the limited success of these street widening programs suggests the political power of automobility, since abutters had only allowed widening under the rarest of circumstances in the nineteenth century.[49]

As early as 1907, a far-sighted writer in *Municipal Journal and Engineer* had noted that street improvements had not eased traffic mobility, but "the result has appeared to be exactly the opposite."[50] Fifth Avenue traffic did not speed up at all after the 1912 widening, because parked cars and added traffic drawn by the wider roadway occupied the new space. Still, the *Times* recommended another major street widening program in 1913.[51] Municipal engineers, by occupational predilection builders, paid little attention to the increased traffic generated by wider, smoother streets.

Cities also built many bridges. New York built three costly bridges over the East River and ten over the Harlem River between 1898 and 1910.[52] The city planned bridges both to relieve the traffic-congested Brooklyn Bridge and to open newly annexed suburban territory in Queens and the Bronx. Cities cut up by railroad tracks, like Atlanta and Chicago, built viaducts over them. Washington bridged the narrow Rock Creek Valley and Milwaukee the Menominee.

State governments emerged as major actors on the metropolitan street scene. Drivers and car companies had reinforced the rural good roads movement, which dated back to the 1880s. Under pressure from good roads enthusiasts, most states had created their first highway departments between 1890 and 1910, before the auto was a factor. The national government also took some steps toward good roads during this period, woefully underfinanced to be sure, but a harbinger of the future. Suburban counties and townships picked up their share of growing state highway funds. Thus, state support hastened road construction by counties and townships on the periphery of big cities. Real estate developers hoped that good suburban roads would attract car commuters.[53]

The states did not fund the new road agencies well initially, preferring to limit their function to providing expert advice to towns or counties. In 1906 local governments spent only $75 million on the 2,150,000 miles of rural road in the U.S., compared to the estimated $300 million cities spent on 200,000 miles of streets. As of 1913, highway agencies of all the states had run up only $136 million in total debt, $100 million of it in New York State. Rural groups, which dominated most state legislatures, did not want to pay property taxes for roads (whether city-to-city or suburban or asphalt paved) that primarily benefited urban drivers. States would only resolve highway financing with gasoline taxes segregated for highway construction, beginning in Oregon in 1919.[54]

Urban landowners did not like paying property taxes, the primary source of state revenues, to finance rural or suburban roads. The *Times* complained that New York State had not spent a penny of its massive $100 million 1912 bond issue in cities, although urbanites paid more than half the state's revenues. New York was not alone. The Cleveland Chamber of Commerce complained that repaving for the motor car was causing the city to run a deficit. The tax conscious Chamber was especially upset because the Ohio state legislature refused to appropriate anything to help, even when city streets were part of state routes. Ohio also insisted on keeping all car registration fees for itself, not even letting Cleveland charge its own fee.[55]

States adopted dust-free, auto-friendly asphalt pavements slowly. By 1913 only four heavily urbanized states had more than 1,000 miles of roads (urban streets excluded) paved with asphalt. New York had laid 3,169 miles; Massachusetts, 1,337; Ohio, 1,066; and Maryland, 1,042. This was more than three-fourths of the asphalt highway in the entire country. Suburban Los Angeles County pioneered; it had used state funds to spray asphaltic oils on suburban gravel roads to reduce dust as early as 1898. Evidently most states preferred to spend their limited budgets on dirt or gravel farm-to-market roads, a measure of rural dominance of state legislatures. These roads were of little value to urban drivers.[56]

A few state officials saw into the future. New Jersey hired the famous engineer General George Goethals, fresh from his success in completing the Panama Canal, as chief engineer in 1917. Goethals expected to build a limited access motor highway from New York City to Philadelphia, complete with a bridge over the Delaware and a tunnel under the Hudson. An article reviewing his plans noted: "You can't get automobile or truck efficiency out of horse capacity highways."[57] Still, New Jersey would not build such a road for 35 years.

New York and Massachusetts funded the two largest highway programs. While neither state allowed the expenditure of funds in cities, there can be little doubt that their systems served urban motorists. Both planned a three-tier road system. Suburban arteries around major cities formed one tier. In addition, each built recreational roads that also served some big-city suburbs. The Massachusetts one ran from Boston to Cape Cod. In New York the recreational system included stretches from Buffalo to the shore of Lake Ontario, in the Adirondacks, and from New York's city line into Westchester and Long Island. Finally, these states built city-to-city roads. Peter Hugill, the leading historian of these highways, has noted that they primarily benefited "elitist owners of Mercedes-style automobiles."[58] Governor William Sulzer of New York defined the new asphalt highways as "arteries of the industrial life."[59] There can be little doubt that easier suburbanization was a primary reason for these newly paved arteries.

Suburban counties spent their own funds and state road money to help motor commuters. Cook County (Chicago) planned a suburban boulevard system in 1903. Burnham included the proposal in the *Plan of Chicago,* where it became a very highly praised element of the plan. Los Angeles County voters approved a $3.5 million road bond issue in a 1908 referendum. Baltimore County also approved extensive radial road building.[60]

States also created private and public authorities to build suburban roads. Boston and Chicago had special metropolitan park authorities charged with suburban parkway construction. Both had their roots in metropolitan sewer and water districts created in the nineteenth century. These authorities served the goal of allowing suburban towns to obtain urban services without annexing themselves to the central city. Both special authorities had the power to tax throughout the metropolitan area that they served, including the central city. Governors appointed the administrative boards of both, isolating them from the control of central cities, which had the bulk of voters in metropolitan areas. Both had built radial parkways through the suburbs to their parks in the 1890s (see table 2.3). These roads eased car-based suburbanization, at least for a while. But their roads rarely restricted access in the manner of traditional Olmsted-style parkways. While the park districts banned trucks, trolleys, and buses, they allowed too many cross streets and did not restrict abutters from access. In the 1920s, developers had lined most older parkways with homes, significantly slowing traffic.

The park authorities did pioneer in a governmental form, special authorities, which would provide many highway improvements in metropolitan areas in the 1920s. However, only three cities authorized new radial parkways immediately before World War I. Kansas City approved the Blue Valley Parkway, and Washington, D.C. mapped the Rock Creek Parkway, but neither city funded completion for a long time.[61] Parkways were largely an abandoned style.

The first new suburban road was privately owned, an oddity. In 1908 William Vanderbilt started a turnpike company to build the twenty mile Long Island Motor Parkway. He wanted a venue for the Vanderbilt Cup race and a drive for wealthy car enthusiasts in the *Great Gatsby* country on the North Shore of Long Island. Vanderbilt built a luxury hotel modeled after a French palace, the Petit Trianon, at the road's terminal at Lake Ronkonkoma. In 1914 *House Beautiful* claimed that the road made Long Island "a motorist's paradise."[62] Tolls paid for the limited access suburban run. Vanderbilt constructed 65 overpasses to allow uninterrupted car movement. Since horses were excluded, his engineers laid an early reinforced concrete pavement. They also built the first banked curves on any highway in the world. The professional journals for engineers ignored the Vanderbilt road, probably because it seemed like a rich man's hobby. Municipal engineers probably saw little that they could copy in its limitation of abutter access, tolls, and ban on freight and horses.[63]

The New York State legislature set up a special authority to build the more influential Bronx River Parkway in 1907. This revival of an old Olmsted plan would keep the parkway ideal alive until the 1920s. It ran from the south Bronx into suburban Westchester County. The wealthy New Yorkers who sought its construction (including Madison Grant, President of the Bronx Zoo) saw it as a multiple purpose road. The parkway and park lands on either side of it would stop pollution of the Bronx River, pollution that was poisoning zoo animals that drank the water. Grant hoped to restore the natural beauty of the sadly decayed Bronx River, once the subject of James Rodman Drake's popular mid-nineteenth-century song, "My Old Romantic Bronx."[64]

The Bronx River Parkway also provided a venue for fast driving, since the park strips limited access and very few streets crossed it at grade level. It opened south central Westchester County for commuter settlement. The road finished at Kensico Lake, allowing New Yorkers access to their Croton Reservoir watershed for recreation. The right of way averaged more than 600 feet wide. This allowed four lanes (forty feet) of traffic and at least 200 feet of park land on either side of the road, not a bad neighborhood amenity. The legislature allowed the road's commissioners to bill New York City for three quarters of the expected $4 million cost, but those funds were not forthcoming for years. After the excesses of speedway construction in the 1890s, Olmsted-style parkways had lost their appeal to a city government that was hardly anxious to build a road that would mostly increase real estate values outside the city.[65]

In 1912, as traffic jams were becoming the norm, the City finally appropriated $35,000 to survey the road. The Bronx River Parkway

Commission had already obtained half the land for the 300 to 1,000 foot wide right of way by taking recreational land in Bronx Park, by utilizing land atop the Croton Aqueduct, and by accepting donations from realtors in the north Bronx and Westchester. The realtors correctly anticipated that the road would attract car-owning suburbanites to their subdivisions. When completed, the road did triple the value of real estate at its northern end, where it cut driving time to the city by more than half.[66]

The Commission could not get appropriations to finish the Parkway until state courts forced New York City to pay its assessments. New York Mayor Hylan sued the Commission because acquisition and construction costs exceeded $10 million, more than doubling estimates, but the courts refused to rein in construction. Westchester realtors, powers in the Republican Party that controlled the state legislature, also blocked New York City's attempts to have the special authority's charter revoked. The Bronx River Parkway kept Olmsted's vision alive, while most cities planned Haussmann-style grand boulevards to create easy suburban travel.[67]

The Bronx River Parkway set a pattern for later highway design and administration, largely because the municipal trade press covered the new highway from its inception.[68] *American City* devoted nine major articles to parkways in the 1920s and seventeen in the 1930s, but only one between 1904 and 1920. The only pre-1920 article dealt with the Bronx River Parkway. The parkway passed Olmsted's design concepts on. Engineer Jay Downer, who served as secretary of the Commission, became the designer of the pioneer Westchester County parkway network in the early 1920s. He and Gilmore Clark, the Bronx River's landscape architect, would publicize the parkway idea in professional circles.[69]

Both ultimately worked for Robert Moses, the nation's leading highway builder in the mid-twentieth century. Moses borrowed the Olmsted design from the Westchester County system when his first special authority began to build highways on Long Island in the mid-1920s. New York City legislators prevented the state from giving Moses' special authority a blank check like the Bronx River Commission had obtained, but Moses borrowed the toll idea from the Vanderbilt Motor Parkway to finance his parkways. By the late 1930s Moses was building pure traffic movers, without providing any significant parks for abutters. His Henry Hudson Parkway (1939) had only an 18-inch strip on either side in many places. Moses' parkways inspired the German autobahns, the Italian autostrada, state turnpikes, and ultimately the U.S. interstate highway system.[70]

The City Beautiful boulevard schemes proved a design dead end. Olmsted-style parkways were superior on several counts. Limiting access was the key to speeding movement, but grand boulevards usually had many cross streets and driveways entering them. Thus, Chicago's new park boulevards and Boston's pseudo-parkways rapidly jammed in the 1920s, when suburban traffic burgeoned. The parkway provided the enduring model for twentieth-century highways. Parkways also proved more feasible politically, because providing string parks alongside the roadway diminished neighborhood resistance. Tolls on motorists, not property taxes on non-users, paid for them. The Olmsted style has probably produced greater neighborhood stability as well. If the Bronx is any example, property values have held up better on Mosholu Parkway, an Olmsted-style parkway, than the Grand Concourse. The latter, once the most fashionable street in the borough, is now largely a burned out shell in its southern portions. In Boston property values have held up better on Olmsted-designed 1880s Fenway parkways, than on the outer parts of Beacon Street, built as a suburban boulevard in the 1890s.[71] The tragedy of Olmsted-style limited access highway building would come after World War II, when, following Moses' lead, urban road planners forged the political alliances and legal tools to level neighborhoods for limited access highways without giving them open recreational space.

The early-twentieth-century planners did accept one set of ideas aimed at relieving the impact of automobility on inner-city neighborhoods.[72] Most of the City Beautiful plans asked for programs of playground construction based on programs advocated by a national reform organization, the Playground Association of America. This organization cared about safe play opportunities for inner-city, working-class children, but they wanted more than safer streets. The best-known scholar of the organization argues convincingly that their rhetoric about social justice concealed another motive. The Association sought social control by directing the play opportunities of inner-city, especially immigrant, children, to "Americanize" them away from their parent's alien political, social, and economic beliefs. One pre-auto playground advocate wrote that the street was where "the devil uses his most destructive ammunition to blast and demolish human character."[73]

Reformers had started building playgrounds in a few cities before the coming of auto traffic, which also suggests that controlling play was more important than safety. However, most playground construction came after the new hazards posed by the upsurge in street traffic. Hundreds of children were dying on the streets. These reformers convinced cities to build schools with playgrounds and to add them to older schools, if necessary on the roofs. Municipalities switched park funds away from Olmsted-style scenic parks like Central Park to smaller, neighborhood sites for active recreation during the progressive era.[74]

In 1909 New York's Park and Playground Association even asked that the city set some blocks aside as traffic-free play streets. They especially sought the block of Ludlow Street between Rivington and Houston Streets on the Lower East Side. By their count 10,750 children lived on that block, including better than 500 preschoolers. Strikingly, the reformers couched their appeal in terms that might attract the support of motorists. Police Commissioner Arthur Woods and the playground reformers argued that setting aside play streets would improve traffic flow on major avenues.[75] They expected that children would abandon traffic ways for the safer play streets. By 1916 the New York police were reserving thirty-two streets each summer for recreation. Few other cities adopted New York's program, but New York's population density was unique. Playground reformers even had the Committee on Congestion of Population in New York, a pioneer planning group whose efforts would eventually lead to land-use zoning, recommend a ban on all traffic below Chambers Street in Lower Manhattan.[76] There was no way motorists or downtown businessmen would accept this restriction.

The journey to work generated the worst jams, so decentralizing workplaces would have diminished traffic. Reducing downtown population densities offered the most effective way to reduce traffic jams, but property interests would tolerate only the most trivial limitations on the development of downtown land. The Committee on Congestion of Population recommended a zoning law with height limits, but the city enacted no law until later. No downtown zoning law has lasted very long in the U.S. without being riddled by exceptions. Guerin's paintings for the *Plan of Chicago* showed almost all buildings in downtown Chicago eight stories tall, including sites where Burnham, himself, had built taller buildings. The text of the plan never mentioned height limits. Again, the likely explanation was political. Burnham undoubtedly knew that the wealthy downtown business community, which financed the plan, would not countenance any limitations on their property. The downtown business leaders wanted to have it both ways. They wanted higher buildings, but also wanted to speed home to the suburbs in private automobiles. Higher buildings automatically drew more traffic. Nobody was willing to confront the dilemma.

Policymakers avoided the issues, even the vaunted progressive era municipal experts. A look at some progressive era municipal administration textbooks is revealing. Most knowledgeable urban reformers knew about the adverse impact of the auto on traditional street uses, but still commented favorably on the influence of high-speed, mechanical transport. Charles Beard's classic, *American City Government,* said that workers could not possibly afford suburban homes. Long hours, low wages, and irregular employment confined them to high-density, inner-city neighborhoods. Also, Beard revealed some insight into the inner-city functions of streets. He described them as "meeting-places" and "playgrounds," as well as traffic arteries, and noted the increased importance of playgrounds as part of a municipal park policy because of the changed conditions of street use. Despite this, Beard still argued for auto-favoring policies like pro-mobility traffic regulation and the increased adoption of asphalt.[77]

Other municipal reformers took similar positions. Delos Wilcox in *The American City: A Problem in Democracy* and Charles Zeublin in *American Municipal Progress* argued similarly to Beard.[78] When Edith Abbott, Chicago's distinguished housing reformer, wrote a history of Chicago housing in the 1930s, she was well aware of the disastrous impact of the auto on street life, especially play opportunities in older Chicago neighborhoods. Yet, she praised the automobile because it had solved the horse caused problem of street filth.[79] The reformers' attitudes toward the auto reveal the motoring instincts of middle-class urbanites. The reformers saw the problems of automobility, but could not bring themselves to criticize the new status objects.

A few reformers suggested that the auto might have a "trickle-down" housing effect. Tom Johnson's protege, Frederick C. Howe, believed that increased travel speeds would relieve slums, a key plank in his mentor's platform. Howe developed a sophisticated theory of housing improvement. He argued that, when middle-class Americans abandoned their inner-city homes to motor in from the suburbs, they left behind a stock of relatively new, decent housing for the immigrants to take over. Though immigrants might overcrowd this housing, it still offered greater privacy, more space and lower densities.[80] Edward Bennett, Burnham's collaborator on the *Plan of Chicago,* shared this view. In his 1917 *Plan of Minneapolis,* he claimed that he was encouraging suburbanization for the "well-to-do," so that housing prices closer to downtown would decline and allow more "workingmen" to own homes.[81]

Adna Ferrin Weber, an early and influential urban demographer, knew that the suburban movement that accelerated in the 1890s was primarily a middle-class phenomenon. He argued that reformers must seek reduction of working hours and the creation of low-cost building associations to open suburbs for lower class urbanites. Weber praised the suburban flight of the 1890s, pointing out the status and concerns of those who sought new homes at the city's edge:

> The "rise of the suburbs" is by far the most cheering movement of modern times. It means an essential modification of the process of concentration of population that has been taking place during the last hundred years and brought with it many of the most difficult political and social problems of the day. To the Anglo-Saxon race life in the great cities cannot be made to seem a healthy and natural mode of existence. The fresh air and clear sunlight, the green foliage and God's clear blue sky are dear to the heart of this people, who cannot be reconciled to the idea of bringing up their children in hot, dusty, germ-producing city tenements and streets.[82]

The new middle class, or "Anglo-Saxon race," in Weber's terms, believed that, since transportation technology had eased their flight to the suburbs, it could aid those who, in reality, could not afford to obtain decent housing also. They manipulated the rhetoric of reform politics to justify transportation policies that aided their class. This succeeded for several reasons. Reformers could not admit that thirty years of housing reform had failed or that changing the environment of poor people was not the answer to changing their behavior. To be sure, nineteenth-century housing laws had lowered death rates, even in the worst slums, but Weber's "Anglo-Saxons" still feared the high crime rates, ethnic politics, and alien religions of the slum districts. Support for policies favoring technological changes, like the automobility, allowed middle-class residents to flee the center city, and, simultaneously, believe that there was no self-interest in their policies.

The rhetoric of aiding the working classes also served an important political function. Richard Wade and others have noted the new political geography of industrial cities, in which the middle-class periphery opposed the lower-class inner city.[83] Suburban reformers might attract some votes from the central core of a city by arguing that their policies also favored citizens from those districts. Progressive reformers often sought the cooperation of working-class organizations, especially trade unions, in forming reform organizations. Since both feared the continual growth of big business, they were not a totally incompatible pair of bedfellows. Arguing that transportation policies would lower inner-city densities also might lure immigrant voters into their bed. But, as John D. Buenker's interpretation of urban politics argues: "All too often, their analyses of the urban malaise involved firmly rooted, nativist, racist assumptions that held the urban immigrant working class to be the major cause." While arguing the cross-class utility of faster transportation, Weber's "Anglo-Saxons," applied the new methods of travel to create class-segregated suburban havens. To understand their politics, one must watch their feet, not their mouths.

The motor car provided not just access to the rapidly expanding middle-class suburbs, but was a status item in its own right tied to notions of gender, status, and individual freedom. Sinclair Lewis perhaps summarized it best when he wrote in *Babbitt*: "A family's motor indicated its social rank as precisely as the grades of the peerage determined the rank of an English family."[84] The motor car carried a powerful cultural image. No wonder it bewitched everyone in metropolitan America. One expects film makers, advertisers, and utopian novelists to have fantasies, but the car also entranced newspaper editors, municipal engineers, planners, and public officials. Automobility blinded them, just as it blinded advertisers, who needlessly antagonized potential women consumers; industrialists, who sometimes rejected profitable cars at the lower end of the market to make prestige items; and drivers, who ignored the dangers of automobility. Both men and women saw liberation in the car. Blacks saw freedom from Jim Crow laws. Whites saw freedom from sharing transit with blacks. Who could argue with such a panacea?

The long-term result of these decisions has hardly fulfilled the utopian vision. When Americans made the car an idol, they relied on a machine to solve problems not reconciliable by a machine. The liberating effects have been powerful and important, especially for groups traditionally bound by relatively strict social control, but they also chained consumers to the jobs needed to pay for their cars and put their lives at risk. Suburban homes are nice, but the overall urban environmental effects have been horrible. In many ways downtown neighborhoods are less livable now than they were in the nineteenth century. For one thing the buildings are seventy years older and deteriorating rapidly. For another, nineteenth-century architects designed them without space for recreation or for social gatherings outdoors, functions filled by streets unencumbered with traffic. Today, those streets serve primarily as storage spaces and racetracks for motor cars that are absolutely incompatible with traditional street functions. The modern American metropolis is a socially and politically fragmented, gas-guzzling environmental nightmare. Central business districts have deteriorated and inner-city neighborhoods have sadly decayed. Ironically, the automobile is the third leading cause of death in America. Traffic jams have gotten worse. In the rush hour a pedestrian can still beat a car up Fifth Avenue, unless mugged. Replanning cities to serve Daniel Burnham's geometric fantasies made not a large dream, but a large nightmare.

NOTES

PREFACE

1. Clay McShane, *Technology and Reform: Street Railways and the Growth of Milwaukee, 1887–1900* (Madison: State Historical Society of Wisconsin, 1975).

2. Cambridge: Harvard University Press, 1962.

3. Noel Perrin, *Giving Up the Gun: Japan's Reversion to the Sword, 1543–1879* (Boulder: Shmambala, 1980).

4. John B. Rae, *The American Automobile* (Chicago: University of Chicago Press, 1965); James J. Flink, *America Adopts the Automobile, 1870–1910* (Cambridge: MIT Press, 1970). Rae and Flink did pioneering work of enormous value. I relied heavily on them for information derived from industrial sources and motoring periodicals.

5. Cambridge: MIT Press, 1971.

6. Barrett, *The Automobile and Urban Transit: The Formation of Public Policy in Chicago* (Philadelphia: Temple University Press, 1988); Scott Bottles, *Los Angeles and the Automobile* (Berkeley: University of California Press, 1988); Howard Preston, *Automobile Age Atlanta: The Making of A Southern Metropolis, 1900–1935* (Athens, University of Georgia Press, 1979).

7. Henry J. Case, "Rise of the Motor Car," *Harper's Weekly* 50 (January 13, 1906): 57.

8. See note 6 above.

9. August 8, 1905.

I. URBAN TRAVEL BEFORE THE TROLLEY

1. Michael Feldberg, "The Crowd in Philadelphia History: A Comparative Perspective," *Labor History* 15 (Summer 1974), 329–30; *Philadelphia Public Ledger*, March 13, 14, 1840.

2. Ibid.; John W. Reps," *The Making of Urban America* (Princeton: Princeton University Press, 1965), 160–74. For a comparable, but less violent reaction in Chicago, see Christine Meisner Rosen, *The Limits of Power: Great Fires and the Process of City Growth in America* (New York: Cambridge University Press, 1986), 36–37, 166.

3. Robert West Howard, *The Horse in America* (New York: Follett Publishing Co., 1963), 78; George Rogers Taylor, "Beginnings of Mass Transportation in Urban America, Part 1," *Smithsonian Journal of History* 1 (Summer 1966), 35–37; Lewis

Mumford, *The Culture of Cities* (New York: Harcourt, Brace, 1938), 57; Gideon Sjoberg, *The Preindustrial City* (Glencoe, Ill.: Free Press, 1960), 323; Comments of George W. Tillson in "An Informal Discussion: Will the Street Paving Materials of The Present Be Used in the Pavements of the Future?," *Transactions of the American Society of Civil Engineers* 33 (August 1907), 711–12. The latter source will hereafter be abbreviated *ASCE Trans*. For a map illustrating this urban structure, see Stuart Blumin, "Mobility and Change in Ante-Bellum Philadelphia," in Stephen Thernstrom and Richard Sennett, eds., *Nineteenth Century Cities* (New Haven: Yale University Press, 1969), 187.

4. Olmsted, Vaux Co., *Observations on Improvements in Street Plans, With Especial Reference to the Parkway Proposed to be Laid Out in Brooklyn* (Brooklyn, 1868), 8–15; R. J. Forbes, *Land Transport and Roadbuilding 1000–1900* (Leiden: E. J. Brill, 1957), 113–18; Henry C. Moore, *Omnibuses and Cabs, Their Origins and History* (London: Chapman & Hall, Ltd., 1902), 187; Mumford, *The Culture of Cities*, 91–98, 124–25.

5. Carl Bridenbaugh, *Cities in the Wilderness* (New York: Ronald Press, 1950), 12–22, 153–70; George W. Tillson, *Street Pavements and Paving Materials* (New York: Wiley, 1901), 9; Christopher Tunnard and Henry Hope Reed, *American Skyline* (New York: Mentor Books, 1956), Part I.

6. Bridenbaugh, *Cities in the Wilderness*, 21–22, 160–70; John Duffy, *A History of Public Health in New York City 1625–1866* (New York: Russell Sage Foundation, 1968), 176–95; Carl Bridenbaugh, *Cities in Revolt* (New York: Knopf, 1955), 34–35; L. M. Haupt, "The Growth of Cities, as Exemplified in Philadelphia," *Proceedings of the Engineer's Club of Philadelphia* 4 (August, 1884), 150; J.H. Hollander, *The Financial History of Baltimore* (Baltimore: The Johns Hopkins Press, 1899), 79.

7. Howard, *The Horse in America*, 79–81,129–36; Haupt, "The Growth of Cities," 150; C. St.B. Davidson, *History of Steam Road Vehicles* (London: Her Majesty's Stationery Office, 1953), 9; Wharton J. Lane, "The Early Highway in America, to the Coming of the Railroad," in Jean Labatut and Wharton J. Lane, eds., *Highways in Our National Life* (Princeton: Princeton University Press, 1950), 71.

8. Bridenbaugh, *Cities in Revolt*, 235–45; City of Detroit, Rapid Transit Commission, *Vehicular Traffic in 1930* (Detroit, 1930), 18–20; George Rogers Taylor, *The Transportation Revolution 1815–1860* (New York: Rinehart & Co., 1957), 26–30; Howard, *The Horse in America*, 127; Haupt, "The Growth of Cities," 150–53; Lane, "The Early Highway in America," 171.

9. Ibid.

10. Mumford, *The Culture of Cities*, 211; Delos Wilcox, *The American City: A Problem in Democracy* (New York: MacMillan, 1904), 31; Forbes, *Land Transport and Roadbuilding*, 203–204; Stanley Kutler, *Privilege and Creative Destruction: The Charles River Bridge Case* (New York: Lippincott, 1971), 155–81. The twentieth century form was the public authority, not the private corporation.

11. Bridenbaugh, *Cities in the Wilderness*, 17–21; Bridenbaugh, *Cities in Revolt*, 235–45.

12. J. L. van Ornum, "Theory and Practice of Special Assessments," *ASCE Trans.* 38 (1898), 338–49; Hollander, *Financial History of Baltimore*, 38, 79–80, 155; Bridenbaugh, *Cities in the Wilderness*, 17, 153–70, 313–25; Bridenbaugh, *Cities in Revolt*, 28–32, 235–48.

13. Bridenbaugh, *Cities in Revolt*, 235–45; J. L. van Ornum, "Special Assessments," 338–49; Hollander, *Financial History of Baltimore*, 38; N. P. Lewis, "The Theory and Practice of Levying Assessment for Benefit," *The Municipality* 1 (December 1900), 32–33; Mumford, *The Culture of Cities*, 187.

14. Moore, *Omnibuses and Cabs*, 182, 187, 205–16; Howard, *The Horse in America*, 138; John W. Boettjer, "Street Railways in the District of Columbia," (M.A. Thesis, George Washington University, 1965), 9–10; Haupt, "The Growth of Cities," 150; Taylor, "Beginnings of Mass Transportation in America, Part I," 41; Albert C. Rose, "The Highway from the Railroad to the Automobile" in Jean Labatut and Wharton J. Lane, eds., *Highways in Our National Life*, 81.

15. Haupt, "Growth of Cities," 135, 150–55; Taylor, "Beginnings of Mass Transportation, Part I," 41–47; Mumford, *The Culture of Cities*, 211; Glen E. Holt, "The Changing Perception of Urban Pathology: An Essay on the Development of Mass Transit in the United States" in Stanley K. Schultz and Kenneth T. Jackson, eds., *Cities in American History* (New York: Knopf, 1972), 324–25; Frederick W. Speirs, *The Street Railway System of Philadelphia, Its History and Present Condition* (Baltimore: Johns Hopkins University Press, 1897), 10–11; Boettjer, "Street Railways in the District of Columbia," 9–10; John Noble and Co., *Facts Respecting Street Railways: The Substance of a Series of Official Reports from the Cities of New York, Brooklyn, Boston, Philadelphia, Baltimore, Providence, Newark, Chicago, Quebec, Montreal, and Toronto* (London: P. S. King, 1866), 15–18; St. Louis Board of Public Service, *Report on Rapid Transit for St. Louis* (St. Louis, 1926), 34; *New York Times*, June 10, 1866; Kenneth T. Jackson, *The Crabgrass Frontier: The Suburbanization of the United States* (New York: Oxford University Press, 1984), 33.

16. Taylor, "Beginnings of Mass Transportation, Part I," 35–37; Haupt, "Growth of Cities," 150; Chamber of Commerce of the State of New York, *Rapid Transit in New York and Other Great Cities* (New York, 1905), 6; Jacqueline Marion Overton, *Long Island's Story* (Port Washington, 1929), 199–200; *New York Times*, June 10, 1866; Mumford, *The Culture of Cities*, 210–211; Jackson, *Crabgrass Frontier*, 27–33.

17. Clay McShane, "Transforming the Use of Urban Space: A Look at the Revolution in Street Pavements, 1880–1924," *Journal of Urban History*, 5 (May, 1979), 280–87.

18. Fisher, "Railways and Other Roads," *Journal of the Franklin Institute* 24 (September, 1852), 154–55; John Geise, "What is a Railway?," *Technology and Culture* 1 (Winter, 1959), 69, 74; Greville and Dorothy Bathe, *Oliver Evans, A Chronicle of Early American Engineering* (Philadelphia: Historical Society of Pennsylvania, 1935), 169, 200; Charles Frederick T. Young, *The Economy of Steam Power on Common Roads* (London: Aitchley & Co., 1860), 52–54; Lewis B. Haney, *A Congressional History of Railways* (New York: Augustus M. Kelley, 1968 reprint of the original 1908 edition), 15–26; *Roads and Railroads, Vehicles and Modes of Travelling* (London: John W. Parker, 1839), 266–67.

19. Haney, *Congressional History of Railways*, 26–62; Edward Hungerford, *Men and Iron: The History of the New York Central Railroad* (New York: Thomas Y. Crowell Co., 1938), 120–22; Edward Hungerford, *The Story of the Baltimore and Ohio Railroad* (2 vols., New York: G. P. Putnam's Sons, 1928), 1, 34–35; George Rogers Taylor, "Beginnings of Mass Transportation in Urban America, Part II," *Smithsonian Journal of History* 1 (Fall 1966), 47; Fisher, "Railways and Other Roads,"

154–55; Beckles Wilson, *The Story of Rapid Transit* (New York: D. Appleton and Co., 1914), 35–36, 184. Contrafactual historian, Robert Fogel suggests [*Railroads and American Economic Growth: Essays in Econometric History* (Baltimore: Johns Hopkins Press, 1964), 2–14] that some of the funds investors channeled into railways might have been more profitably spent seeking a steam vehicle for turnpike use. The suggestion is not susceptible to verification.

20. Haupt, "The Growth of Cities," 150; Q. A. Gilmore, *A Practical Treatise on Roads, Streets and Pavements* (New York: D. van Nostrand, 1876), 232–33; "Restriction of Traffic on Highways," *Engineering Record* 41 (February 10, 1900), 122; Jackson; *Crabgrass Frontier*, 29. The technical problems associated with flush rails were not worked out for another twenty years.

21. Hungerford, *Baltimore and Ohio Railroad*, 1, 34–35, 143; Gilmore, *Treatise on Streets*, 24; Haupt, "The Growth of Cities," 158–61; S. A. Howland, *Steamboat Disasters and Railroad Accidents in the United States* (Worcester: Warren Lazell, 1846), 298–302; Taylor, "Beginnings of Mass Transportation, Part II," 50; John Ashcroft, *The Laws in Relation to the Inspection of Steam Boilers Passed by the States of New York and New Jersey* (New York: John Ashcroft, 1868), 52–55; John G. Burke, "Bursting Boilers and the Federal Power," in Melvin Krainzberg and William H. Davenport, eds., *Technology and Culture: An Anthology* (New York: Schocken Books, 1971), 106: *Report of the Special Committee Appointed by the Common Council of the City of New York Relative to the Catastrophe in Hague Street on Monday, February 4, 1850* (New York: McSpedon & Baker, 1850), 3; Hungerford, *New York Central*, 120–25. The Park Avenue trench was covered when electrification eliminated the risk of smoke asphyxiation.

22. "The Buffalo and Niagara Falls Railroad Co. v. the City of Buffalo," 50 *Hill* 211–12 (1843).

23. T.C. Barker and Michael Robbins, *A History of London Transport: Volume One, the Nineteenth Century* (London: George Allen and Unwin Ltd., 1963), 100–101; Frank Crowell, "The Railroad Facilities of Suburban New York," *Engineering Magazine* 10 (March, 1896), 1029; Edward E. Hale, "The Congestion of Cities," *Forum* 4 (January 1888), 531–35; Mumford, *Culture of Cities*, 216; Taylor, "Beginnings of Mass Transportation, Part II," 31–54; Charles J. Kennedy, "Commuter Services in the Boston Area, 1835–60," *Business History Review* 36 (Summer 1962), 153–70; Jackson, *Crabgrass Frontier*, 35.

For a list of all the commuters on one suburban railroad, which clearly shows their social status, see Richard Nelson, *Suburban Homes for Businessmen on the Line of the Marietta and Cincinnati Railroad* (Cincinnati: Nelson & Bolles, Land Agents, 1874), 18 *et seq.*

24. Henry Binford, *The First Suburbs: Residential Communities on the Boston Periphery: 1815–1860* (Chicago: University of Chicago Press, 1985), 129–30. The walking figures deceive a little because communities near downtown Boston refused annexation, even this early.

25. Taylor, "Beginnings of Mass Transportation, Part II," 39–51.

26. As quoted in Jackson, *Crabgrass Frontier*, 29.

27. Ibid.; Haupt, "The Growth of Cities," 150–61; George Hilton, *The Cable Car in America* (Berkeley: Howell-North Books, 1971), 14–15; St. Louis Board of Public

Service, *Report on Rapid Transit*, 34; Speirs, *Street Railway System of Philadelphia*, 10–14; John W. Boettjer, "Street Railways in the District of Columbia" (M.A. Thesis, George Washington University, 1963), 13–23; Barker and Robbins, *London Transport*, 1, 90–91; Binford, *The First Suburbs*, 130, 141–42.

28. Sam Bass Warner, *Streetcar Suburbs: The Process of Growth in Boston, 1870–1900* (New York: Athenaeum, 1973), especially pages 17 and 35, seems to me to overemphasize the importance of street railways for suburbanization. David Ward, *Cities and Immigrants* (New York: Oxford University Press, 1971), 130; Richard J. Hopkins, "Status, Mobility, and the Dimensions of Change in a Southern City; Atlanta, 1870–1910," in Jackson and Schultz, eds., *Cities in American History*; and John Burchard and Albert Bush-Brown, *The Architecture of American; A Social and Cultural History* (Boston: Little, Brown and Co., 1961), 121–33 suggest some of the other elements necessary for suburbanization.

See J.W. Bazalgette, "Presidential Address," *Minutes of the Proceedings of the Institution of Civil Engineers* (London) 76 (1884), 18–20, for a justification of this housing pattern in terms of cheaper housing and easier access to employment for the "working classes."

29. As quoted in John W. Noble & Co., *Facts Respecting Street Railways*, 27.

30. James Willard Hurst, *Law and the Conditions of Freedom in the Nineteenth Century United States* (Madison: University of Wisconsin Press, 1967), 8–10; Lawrence Friedman, *Contract Law in America* (Madison: University of Wisconsin Press, 1967), 74–75 document both the legal weakness of cities and the general pattern of municipal encouragement of private entrepreneurs seeking to use new technology. For a compendium of street railway franchises, see Delos Wilcox, *Municipal Franchises* (Two vols., New York: *Engineering News* Book Department, 1911), vol. 2. It should be noted that in many American cities, the municipality does not control the streets in fee simple, but only holds an easement. Ownership is actually held by abutting property. In such cases, street railway companies had to secure permission from a majority of abutters, as well as the municipal government. On New York ridership and the more stringent regulation prevailing in Europe, see John P. McKay, "Comparative Perspective on Transit in Europe and the United States," in Joel Tarr and Gabriel Dupuy, eds. *Technology and the Rise of the Networked City in Europe and America* (Philadelphia: Temple University Press, 1988), 3–5.

31. Edward P. North, "The Influence of Rails on Street Pavements," *ASCE Trans.* 37 (June, 1897), 70. See John F. Dillon, *Treatise on the Law of Municipal Corporations* (1st. ed., Chicago: James Cockroft & Co., 1872), 541–43 on the legal necessity of preserving the street surface for other users.

32. On the design of rails, see two editorials in *Engineering News* 19 (February 4, 1888), 80 and 17 (May 28, 1887), 341.

33. Dillon, *Law of Municipal Corporations* (1st. ed.), 541–43; Warner, *Streetcar Suburbs*, 56, 60, 73; Ward, *Cities and Immigrants*, 94–107, 134–39; Holt, "Development of Mass Transit," 329–30; Taylor, "Beginnings of Mass Transportation, Part II," 51; Jackson, *Crabgrass Frontier*, 103.

34. J. K. Fisher, "Letter to the Editor," *New York Times*, August 21, 1863; Hilton, *The Cable Car in America*, 14–15; Gary Levine, "History of the American Steam

Car" (Ph. D. Diss., St. John's University, 1971), 56–57; Alex I. Holley and J. K. Fisher, "History and Progress of Steam on Common Roads in the United States" in C. F. T. Young, *Steam on Common Roads* (London: n.p., 1860), 364–65; Howard, *The Horse in America,* 175.

2. THE SEARCH FOR OPEN SPACE: TROLLEYS, PARKS, AND PARKWAYS

1. Robert Fishman, *Bourgeois Utopias: The Rise and Fall of Suburbia* (New York: Basic Books, 1987), ch. 1; Kenneth T. Jackson, *The Crabgrass Frontier: Suburbanization in the U.S.* (New York: Oxford University Press, 1985), ch. 3. Land, it should be noted, cost less in the U.S., and incomes were higher.

2. Charles V. Chapin, "History of State and Municipal Control of Disease" in Mayzick P. Ravenal, *A Half Century of Public Health* (New York: American Public Health Association, 1921), 134–36.

3. Ibid., 139–40; J. M. Gregory, "The Hygiene of Great Cities," *Engineering News* 7 (January 10, 1880), 10.

4. James H. Cassedy, "The Flamboyant Colonel Waring," *Bulletin of the History of Medicine* 36 (March and April, 1962), 163–76.

5. George Waring, Jr., "Essay Upon Sanitary Science," *American Architect* 11 (November 10, 1877), 359–60.

6. Stephen Smith, "Vegetation a Remedy for the Summer Heat of Cities," *Popular Science Monthly* 54 (February, 1899), 444.

7. Octave Chanute, et al., "Rapid Transit and Terminal Freight Facilities," *ASCE Trans.* 4 (1875), 15, 33; "The Future of Great Cities," *The Nation* (February 22, 1866), 232; *New York Times,* May 24, 1867, June 10, 1866; "Rapid Transit in the Metropolis," *Harper's Monthly* 57 (September, 1878), 624–26; St. Louis Elevated and Rapid Transit Railway Co., *Exhibit Presenting and Illustrating the Work Contemplated, Its Plans and Public Uses and Benefits to Ensue From It* (St. Louis: Times Printing House, 1883); Hugh Mercer Blain, *A Near Century of Public Service in New Orleans* (New Orleans: New Orleans Public Service Co., 1927), 52; Haupt, "Rapid Transit," 144; T. C. Martin, "Electric Street Cars, Part I," *Street Railway Journal* 3 (February, 1887), 198–99; Charles Loring Brace, *The Dangerous Classes of New York and Twenty Years Work Among Them* (Montclair, N.J.: Paterson Smith, 1967 reprint of the original 1880 edition), 56; David Ward, *Cities and Immigrants* (New York: Oxford University Press, 1971), 134.

Several very hilly cities, e.g. Cincinnati and Pittsburgh, used inclined planes, another application of steam power, to overcome unusual geographical obstacles, but these were a minor part of the overall transportation situation. See John H. White, Jr., "The Mt. Adams & Eden Park Inclined Railway, 'The Kerper Road,' " *Bulletin of the Historical and Philosophical Society of Ohio* 17 (October, 1959), 242–76 and "The Cincinnati Inclined Plane Railway Company; The Mt. Auburn Incline and Lookout House," *Cincinnati Historical Society Bulletin* 27 (Spring, 1969), 7–22.

8. John W. Boettjer, "Street Railways in the District of Columbia," (M.A. Thesis, George Washington University, 1963), 43; Barry Temkin, "Oats and Iron: Horse Drawn Transportation in Milwaukee 1850–1890," (B.A. Thesis, University of

Wisconsin, 1970), 66; *New York Times,* January 10, 1876; "Steam on Street Railways," *Engineering News* 4 (March 10, 1877), 59; J. B. Knight, "Steam on Street Railways," *Franklin Institute Journal* 102 (June, 1877), 379–80; T.C. Martin, "Electric Street Cars, Part I," 198–99; *Motive Power for Street Cars* (New York: John Stephenson Co., 1889), 40–42; John H. White, Jr., "By Steam Car to Mt. Lookout: The Columbia and Cincinnati Street Railroad," *Bulletin of the Cincinnati Historical Society* 25 (April, 1967). I am indebted to Mr. White, Curator of Land Transportation Emeritus at the Smithsonian Institution's National Museum of History and Technology, for leading me to many of the sources on steam dummy engines.

9. Ibid.

10. Frank G. Carpenter, *Carp's Washington* (reprints of his newspaper column for the year 1882, edited by Frances G. Carpenter, New York: McGraw-Hill, 1960), 8; *Street Railway Journal* 4 (March, 1888), 97; George W. Hilton, *The Cable Car in America* (Berkeley: Howell-North Books, 1971), *passim.*

11. Hilton, *The Cable Car in America,* 14–15. For a description of the difficulties with horsecars in another city with unusual geographic problems, see Leslie H. Blanchard, *The Street Railway Era in Seattle* (Forty Fort, Pa.: Harold Cox, 1968), 3.

12. *Additional Burdens on Street Railway Companies, Arguments of Henry Whitney and Prentiss Cummings Before the Committee on Cities and the Committee on Taxation of the Massachusetts Legislature* (Boston: Press of Samuel Usher, 1891); Louis P. Hager, ed., *History of the West End Street Railway* (Boston: privately printed, 1892), 11–18; Frank J. Sprague, "The Future of the Electric Railway," *Forum* 12 (September, 1891), 120–30; Blanchard, *The Street Railway Era in Seattle,* 4–8; Robert M. Fogelson, *The Fragmented Metropolis: Los Angeles 1850–1930* (Cambridge: Harvard University Press, 1967), 35–39; Harold C. Passer, *The Electrical Manufacturers 1875–1900* (Cambridge: Harvard University Press, 1953), 218–47.

13. Blain, *Public Service in New Orleans,* 58. Anthony Sutcliffe, "Street Transport in the Second Half of the Nineteenth Century, Mechanization Delayed" in Joel Tarr and Gabriel Dupuy, eds, *Technology and the Rise of Networked Cities in Europe and America* (Philadelphia: Temple University Press, 1988), 32–35 argues that investor fears of urban bans delayed the introduction of trolleys for ten years or more. This argument makes little sense for the United States, where streetcar entrepreneurs had been financing experiments in electrical traction from the early 1880s and were very aware of its possibilities. It works better in western Europe, where, by Sutcliffe's account, inner city property owners feared that rapid transit would transfer value from their land to the city's outskirts.

Washington, D.C. and, to a limited extent, New York forced entrepreneurs to use third rails in conduits, a costlier system than overhead wires.

14. Sylvester Baxter, "The Trolley in Rural Parts," *Harper's Monthly* 97 (June, 1895), 61.

15. As quoted by Frederick C. Howe in his introduction to *Tom Johnson, My Story* (New York: B.W. Huebsch, 1911), xxxi.

See also St. Louis Board of Public Service, *Report on Rapid Transit for St. Louis* (1926), 38; Edward S. Mason, *The Street Railway in Massachusetts* (Cambridge: Harvard University Press, 1952), 4, 5; West End Street Railway, *Annual Report for the Year Ending December 31, 1900* (1901), 1; Edward E. Higgins, *Street Railway*

Investments (New York: Street Railway Publishing Co., 1895), 6; Ernest Pendleton, "Cincinnati's Traction Problems," *National Municipal Review* 11 (October, 1913) 617–20; Zane L. Miller, *Boss Cox's Cincinnati* (New York: Oxford University Press, 1968), 6; Delos Wilcox, *Municipal Franchises* (2 vols., New York: *Engineering News* Book Department, 1911), 2, *passim*; Tom L. Johnson, "Free Street Car Transportation," *Municipal Journal and Engineer* 12 (September, 1902), 109–12. The outstanding work on street railways and urbanization is Sam Bass Warner, Jr., *Streetcar Suburbs: The Process of Growth in Boston, 1870–1900* (New York: Atheneum, 1970). *Municipal Journal and Engineer* will hereafter be abbreviated *MJ&E.*

16. Roy Rosenzweig and Betsy Blackmar, *The Park and the People, A History of Central Park* (Ithaca: Cornell University Press, 1992), 219–22; Foster Rhea Dulles, *America Learns to Play: A History of Popular Recreation 1607–1940* (New York: D. Appleton-Century Co., 1940), 240.

17. Lewis Mumford, *The Culture of Cities* (New York: Harcourt, Brace, 1938), 98, 124–25; Allen Nevins, *The Emergence of Modern America* (New York: MacMillan, 1927), 219; Robert West Howard, *The Horse in America* (New York: Follett, 1965), 207–10; Constance McLaughlin Green, *Washington, Capital City 1879–1950* (Princeton: Princeton University Press, 1963), 13–14, 47; *New York Times*, June 10, 1866; Ezra M. Stratton, *The World on Wheels; or Carriages, With Their Historical Associations from the Earliest Times to the Present* (New York: privately published, 1878), passim; F. M. L. Thompson, "Victorian England: The Horse Drawn Society," (London: n.p., 1970), 17; Dulles, *American Learns to Play*, 240.

18. Wolfgang Sachs, *For the Love of the Automobile: Looking Back Into the History of Our Desires* (Berkeley: University of California Press, 1992 translation by Don Reneau of the original 1984 German edition.), 152. Norman T. Newton, *Design on the Land* (Cambridge: Harvard University Press, 1971), 207–20.

19. Marsha Peters, "The Natural City: Landscape Architecture and City Planning in Nineteenth Century America" (M.A. Thesis, University of Wisconsin, 1971), 21–48; Elizabeth Barlow and William Alex, *Frederick Law Olmsted's New York* (New York and Washington: Praeger Publishers, 1972), 31; Reps, *The Making of Urban America*, 325–26; 339–48; John Burchard and Albert Bush-Brown, *The Architecture of America: A Social and Cultural History* (Boston: Little, Brown, 1961), 100–107, 121; Anselm Strauss, *Images of the American City* (New York: Free Press, 1961), 217; Christopher Tunnard and Henry Hope Reed, *American Skyline* (New York: New American Library, Inc., 1956), 83–89. Downing wanted the mall to be a "landscape garden and drive."

20. Reps, *The Making of Urban America*, 325–26; Richard Nelson, *Suburban Homes for Businessmen on the Line of the Marietta and Cincinnati Railroad* (Cincinnati: Nelson and Bolles, Land Agents, 1874), 18; William Glazier, *Peculiarities of American Cities* (Philadelphia: Hubbard Brothers, 1884), *passim*. For the lithograph of Greenwood Cemetery, see David Schuyler, *The New Urban Landscape: The Redefinition of City Form in Nineteenth Century America* (Baltimore: Johns Hopkins University Press, 1986), 48–49.

21. Rosenzweig and Blackmar, *The Park and the People*, 16, 46, and 217.

22. Tunnard and Reed, *American Skyline*, 108–10; Reps, *The Making of Urban America*, 330–37; Barlow and Alex, *Olmsted's New York*, passim, esp. 37–38; *New*

York Times, June 10, 1866; Melvin Kalfus, *Frederick Law Olmsted: The Passion of a Public Artist* (New York: New York University Press, 1990), 2; Schuyler, *The New Urban Landscape,* 4–5. The drives and bridle paths had speed limits to exclude the less fashionable, more dangerous trotters. Informal trotting races also drew an undesirable working class audience. The immigrant *Irish Echo,* whose readers were hardly likely to own race horses, endorsed park access for trotters to provide its readers with a spectator sport. See Rosenzweig and Blackmar, *The People and the Park,* 244.

23. Walt Whitman, *Autobiographia, or the Story of a Life* (New York: Charles L. Whitman, 1892), 155.

24. John Mullaly, *The New Parks Beyond the Harlem* (New York: The Record and Guide, 1887), 26–37; Nelson, *Suburban Homes on the Marietta and Cincinnati Railroad,* 131–32; Tunnard and Reed, American Skyline, 110; Sylvester Baxter, "Parkways and Boulevards in American Cities, Part III," *American Architect* 62 (October 29, 1898), 35; F. L. and J. C. Olmsted, *The Projected Park and Parkways on the South Side of Buffalo* (Buffalo: Buffalo Park Commission, 1888), 28; Rosenzweig and Blackmar, *The Park and the People,* 56.

25. Barlow and Alex, *Olmsted's New York,* 7, 35; Schuyler, *The New Urban Landscape,* 40–41, Tunnard and Reed, *American Skyline,* 110; Olmsted, Vaux Co., *Observations on the Progress of Improvements in Street Plans, With Special Reference to the Park-Way Proposed to be Laid Out in Brooklyn* (Brooklyn, 1868), 27–29. Alexander Davis, the romantic architect and associate of Andrew Downing, labeled the main drive in his planned suburban community at Llewellyn, N.J. (1853), "Parkway," but Olmsted seems to have been the first to use the word in a generic sense.

26. Olmsted, Vaux Co., *Observations on the Progress of Improvements in Street Plans, With Special Reference to the Park-Way Proposed to be Laid Out in Brooklyn,* 18. Subsequent references to page numbers in this work are in parentheses in the text.

27. Olmsted specifically suggested the use of such covenants when he planned his first suburban community, Riverside, outside Chicago in 1869. See also a letter from John C. Olmsted to J. M. Frink, President, Board of Park Commissioners, Seattle (January 4, 1909), reprinted in Seattle Board of Park Commissioners, *Parks, Playgrounds and Boulevards of Seattle, Washington* (Seattle, 1909), 147.

28. Sachs, *For the Love of the Automobile,* 119. The *Oxford English Dictionary* traces the use of the word "record" in the sense of record-setting or record-breaking to the 1880s.

29. United States Bureau of the Census, *Social Statistics of Cities, Tenth Census* (1880) (Washington, D.C.: Government Printing Office, 1886), vol. 19, 496; William H. Wilson, *The City Beautiful: Movement in Kansas City* (Columbia: University of Missouri Press, 1964), 5; Tunnard and Reed, *American Skyline,* 108–10; "The Riverside Drive Viaduct over Ninety-Sixth Street, New York," *Engineering Record* 45 (April 12, 1902), 343–45 Glazier, *Peculiarities of American Cities,* 64; Jacob A. Cantor, "Streets of Old New York," *MJ&E* 12 (May, 1902), 64; A. C. Schrader, "Parks and Boulevards" *Journal of the Western Society of Engineers* 5 (June, 1900), 157–64; Detroit Rapid Transit Commission, *Vehicular Traffic in 1930* (Detroit, 1930), 20; Cynthia Zaitzevsky, *Frederick Law Olmsted and the Boston Park System* (Cambridge:

Harvard University Press, 1982), *passim*. Architectural historian Jane Holtz Kay has suggested that the curvilinear design of these roads may have been a traffic calming device to slow carriages. While the curves slow autos today, I do not believe that they would have slowed most nineteenth-century carriages, which had a top speed of about 15 miles per hour. They would have slowed fast trotters, vehicles that Olmsted wanted to keep out of the park badly enough to impose a speed limit. Curvilinear roads conformed to romantic design concepts, regardless of traffic, since paths in romantic gardens and, supposedly in nature, always curved.

30. Sylvester Baxter, "Parkways and Boulevards in American Cities, Part I," *American Architect* 62 (October 8, 1898), 11; part I, p. 35.

31. United States Bureau of the Census, *Social Statistics of Cities, Tenth Census* (1880) (Washington, D.C.: Government Printing Office, 1886), vol. 18, 475, 503; vol. 19, 806. Central Park was an exception. A majority of visitors came by foot, but, by that date it was accessible by el and high-density housing surrounded it.

32. Hager, *History of the West End Street Railway Co.*, 12.

33. Charles Francis Adams, Jr., *An Autobiography* (Boston and New York: Houghton-Mifflin, 1916), 184–88; Baxter, "Parks and Parkways, Part II," 27; James B. Crooks, *Politics & Progress, The Rise of Urban Progressivism in Baltimore 1895–1911* (Baton Rouge: Louisiana State University Press, 1968), 138; Green, *Washington, Capital City*, 17, 49; James Jensen, "Parks and Politics," *Park and Cemetery* 12 (October 1902), 383–84; Mullaly, *The New Parks Across the Harlem*, 26–37; "Boston's West End Improvement," *Engineering News* 14 (October 22, 1887), 292; "Essential Features of a Park System," *Municipal and Paving Engineering* 10 (March 1896), 171; "Hudson County Boulevard," *Engineering Record* 29 (March 24, 1894), 271; Albert A. Pope, *Relation of Good Streets to the Prosperity of a City* (n.p., n.d. [1890?]), 17; Wilson, *The City Beautiful Movement in Kansas City, passim*.

34. "The Harlem River Speedway, New York City," *Scientific American* 86 (February 6, 1897), 89.

35. Ibid., 89–90; "The Harlem River Speedway," *Engineering Record* 29 (July, 1897), 350–51; "New York's New Speedway," *Municipal Engineering* 13 (December, 1897), 376; William T. Pierce, "The Charles River Speedway of the Boston Metropolitan Park System," *Engineering Record* 51 (April 29, 1905), 496–98.

36. "Editorial," *Rider and Driver* 17 (March 11, 1899), 8.

37. Rosenzweig and Blackmar, *The Park and the People*, 366–67; Rebecca Reed Shanor, *The City That Never Was: Two Hundred Years of Fascinating and Fantastic Plans That Might Have Changed the Face of New York City* (New York: Penguin Books, 1988), 180–82.

38. As quoted in "Editorial," *Rider and Driver* 17 (March 18, 1899), 8.

39. Mullaly, *The New Parks Across the Harlem*, 211.

40. Jensen, "Parks and Politics," 383–84.

41. Jon C. Teaford, *The Unheralded Triumph: City Government in America, 1870–1900* (Baltimore: Johns Hopkins University Press, 1984), 52–59.

3. ANIMAL POWER, 1870–1900

1. Christine Meisner Rosen, *The Limits of Power: Great Fires and the Process of City Growth in America* (New York: Cambridge University Press, 1986), 176–79.

2. Thompson's essay, the Inaugural Lecture for the Chair of Modern History,

Bedford College, October 22, 1970, is available in pamphlet form at the Library of Congress.

3. Ibid., 18–19.

4. "The Position of the Horse in Modern Society," *The Nation* 15 (October, 31, 1872), 277.

5. Col. George E. Waring, "Street Cleaning," *City Government* 3 (October, 1897), 117; Francis V. Greene, "Construction and Care of Streets," *Engineering and Building Record* 21 (March 1, 1890), 196; Clifford Richardson, "Street Traffic in New York City, 1885–1904," *ASCE Proc.* 32 (May 1906), 384; Robert West Howard, *The Horse in America* (New York: Follett, 1963), 175. The 1904 New York street count showed that autombiles were still less than 5 percent of traffic

6. "The Position of the Horse in Modern Society," 277.

7. Ibid., 278.

8. Ibid., 277–78; Zulma Steele, *Angel in Top Hat* (New York: Harper, 1942), 68–69, 56–79, and 171–74. It is a striking commentary on the priorities of the elite members of this humane society that they waited another ten years before finding another group to prevent cruelty to children.

9. Census Office, Interior Department, *Statistics of Population in the United States: Ninth Census* (June 1, 1870) (Washington, D.C.: Government Printing Office, 1872), 775–804; Census Office, Interior Department, *Statistics of Population of the United States at the Tenth Census* (June 1,1880) (Washington D.C.: Government Printing Office, 1890), 860–909; Census Office, Department of the Interior, *Report on the Population of the United States at the Eleventh Census: 1890* (Washington, D.C.: Government Printing Office, 1897), 544, 630–743; Bureau of the Census, Department of Commerce and Labor, *Occupations at the Twelfth Census* (Washington, D.C.: Government Printing Office, 1901), 428–79; Bureau of the Census, Department of Commerce, *Thirteenth Census of the United States, Taken in the Year 1910*, Agriculture (Washington, D.C.: Government Printing Office, 1913), 441–46.

10. Ibid.

11. *New York Times,* August 6, 1868.

12. Albert A. Pope, *The Relation of Good Streets to the Prosperity of a City* (n.p., 1890?), 20; Thompson, "Victorian England, The Horse-drawn Society," 19; Octave Chanute et al., "Rapid Transit and Terminal Freight Facilities" *ASCE Trans.* 4 (1875), 39.

13. Roy Rosenzweig and Betsy Blackmar, *The Park and the People, A History of Central Park* (Ithaca: Cornell University Press, 1992), 213–16. These are 1863 prices that likely came down as horse prices dropped in the late nineteenth century and manufacturers, notably Studebaker, began to mass produce buggies. This topic requires much further investigation, grounded in local sources.

14. Charles Dickens, *A Tale of Two Cities* (New York: Signet, 1980 reprint of the original, 1859 edition), 114–15, 362.

15. Carl Baedeker, *The United States, with an Excursion Into Mexico* (New York: Scribner's, 1893), xxii; Greene, "Construction and Care of Streets," 197; "Growth of City Traffic," *Engineering News* 18 (October 15, 1887), 273; Richardson, "Street Traffic in New York," 385.

16. T. C. Barker and Michael Robbins, *A History of London Transport, Volume I, The Nineteenth Century* (London: George Allen & Unwin Ltd., 1963), *passim,*

esp. 271; David Ward, "A Comparative Historical Geography of Streetcar Suburbs in Boston, Massachusetts and Leeds, England: 1850–1920," *Annals of the Association of American Geographers* 54 (December, 1964), 477.

17. Thompson, "Victorian England: The Horse Drawn Society," 8–12; Greene, "Some Observations of Street Traffic," 130; Richard Harding Davis, "Broadway," in *Great Streets of the World* (New York: Charles Scribner's Sons, 1892), 6; Kenneth T. Jackson, *Crabgrass Frontier, The Suburbanization of the United States* (New York: Oxford University Press, 1985), 106; "Through Broadway," *Atlantic Monthly* 18 (December 1866), 717, 726; Steele, *Angel in Top Hat*, 72; J. Robert Clair, "The Safe Operation of Teams and Wagons," *National Safety Council Transactions* 16 (1927), 881–86. Professor Allan G. Bogue of the University of Wisconsin has illuminated several of the problems of the horse as a power source to me by recounting anecdotes from his youth when he drove teams.

18. "Bridge Over Our Downtown Side Streets," *Scientific American* 62 (February 8, 1890), 82.

19. Stevenson Towle, "Pavement Construction and City Growth," *Engineering Magazine* 12 (October 1896), 59.

20. John A. Miller, "Certain Effects of Bridges on Traffic Conditions," *ASCE Trans.* 88 (1925), 127–39; *New York Times,* June 10, 1866; "Bridge Over Our Downtown Side Streets," 82–83; *Nation* (February 22, 1866), 252; Towle, "Paving Construction and City Growth," 59; "Need of Repaving Chicago," *Municipal Engineering* 13 (October 1897), 239; Lewis M. Haupt, Municipal Engineering—A Study of Street Pavements," *Journal of the Franklin Institute* 28 (December 1889), 444; "Plan to Prevent Street Crossings," *Municipal Journal and Engineer* 16 (January, 1904), 33.

21. "Restriction of Traffic on Highways," *Engineering Record* 41 (February 10, 1900), 122; George Waring, "Street Cleaning," *City Government* 3 (October, 1897), 117; "Plan to Prevent Congestion at Street Crossings," *Municipal Journal and Engineer* 16 (January 1904), 33; "New York City Bicycle Ordinance," *Municipal Engineering* 13 (September 1897), 146–47; "Editorial," *City Government* 2 (June 1897), 176–77; "Street Traffic Regulations," *Municipal Journal and Engineer* 23 (December 20, 1897), 577–78; Ernest P. Goodrich, "Traffic Engineer's Reminiscences," *Institute of Traffic Engineers Proceedings* 21 (1946), 105.

22. "Editorial Comment," *Automobile Magazine* 1 (October, 1899), 87.

23. George E. Waring, Jr., *Street-Cleaning and the Disposal of a City's Wastes* (New York: Doubleday and McClure Co., 1898), 13.

24. "Sanitary Pavements," *Engineering Magazine* 10 (October 1895), 163.

25. Rosenzweig and Blackmar, *The Park and the People*, 296; Joel A. Tarr, "Urban Pollution—Many Long Years Ago," *American Heritage* 22 (October 1971), 65–69, 106; Lawrence H. Larsen. "Nineteenth Century Street Sanitation: A Study of Filth and Frustration," *Wisconsin Magazine of History* 52 (Spring 1969), 239–47; George W. Hilton, *The Cable Car in America* (Berkeley: Howell-North Books, 1971), 15; Interview with Jonathan Gradess, August 8, 1973; Raymond H. Merritt, *Engineering in American Society 1850–1875* (Lexington: University of Kentucky Press, 1966), 167. I am indebted to Professor Tarr for providing me with a copy of the footnotes for his *American Heritage* article which led me to many of the sources on this problem.

26. James H. Cassedy, "The Flamboyant Colonel Waring" *Bulletin of the History of Medicine* 36 (March and April 1962), 163–68; Harold Bolce, "The Horse vs. Health," *Appleton's Magazine* 11 (May 1908) Hilton, *The Cable Car in America*, 15. Ironically, Waring died when he contracted Yellow Fever after the U.S. Army sent him to Havana in 1898 to plan a sewer system to rid that city of the disease. Cassedy (163–68) attributes the triumph of the contagionist theory of disease in the public mind with the failure of this sewer system, followed by Walter Reed's successful proof that flies carried the germ that caused the disease.

27. Waring, *Street-Cleaning*, 1–4, 14, 20–21, 42, 98–99; Larsen, "Nineteenth Century Street Sanitation," 247; "Reduction of the Death Rate in New York City," *Municipal Engineering* 13 (November, 1897), 292–93; Tarr, "Urban Pollution," 66–67. Waring's figures were distorted by two miscalculations, that New York continued to grow at its 1880–90 rate from 1890 to 1897 and that the entire reduction in the death rate was due to improved street cleaning.

28. Merritt, *Engineering in American Society*, 167; Tarr, "Urban Pollution," 69–70; Larsen, "Nineteenth Century Street Sanitation," 245–47; United States Bureau of the Census, *Social Statistics of Cities, the Tenth Census*, 1880 (Washington, D.C.: Government Printing Office, 1886), 556; Emmons Clark, "Street Cleaning in Large Cities," *Popular Science* 38 (April, 1891), 748–55.

29. J. W. Howard, "What Pavements Do for a City," *Municipal Engineering* 18 (June 1900), 357.

30. Norman L. Dunham, "The Bicycle Era in American History" (Ph.D. Dissertation, Harvard University, 1956), 4–41.

31. Ibid., 47–121. Dunham cites the *Scientific American* of October 10, 1868 on the proposed thirty foot long tricycle.

32. Ibid., 175–94.

33. Ibid., 397–437, 469–77; Albert C. Rose, "The Highway from the Railroad to the Automobile," in Jean Labutut and Wharton J. Lane, eds. *Highways in Our National Life* (Princeton: Princeton University Press, 1950), 85; Hiram Percy Maxim, *Horseless Carriage Days* (New York: Dover Publications, 1962 reprint of the original 1936 edition), 1.

34. *Annual Report of the City Engineer of Minneapolis* (Minneapolis, 1906), 16–17 as cited in Eric H. Monkkonen, *America Becomes Urban: The Development of U.S. Cities & Towns, 1780–1880* (Berkeley: University of California Press, 1988), 291.

35. Dunham, "The Bicycle in American History," 301–302; Philip P. Mason, "The League of American Wheelmen and Good Roads" (Ph.D Dissertation University of Michigan, 1957), *passim*; Pope, Relation of Good Streets to the Prosperity of a City, 16–20; "Editorial," *City Government* 2 (June 1897), 177; L. W. Rundlett, "Bicycle Paths," *Proceedings of the American Society for Municipal Improvements* (1897), 318–27; Joy J. Jackson, *New Orleans in the Gilded Age: Politics and Progress 1880–1896* (Baton Rouge: Louisiana State University Press, 1969), 264–66; James Rood Doolittle, *The Romance of the Auto Industry* (New York: The Klebold Press, 1916), 16–17; Walter J. Somers, "The Asphalt Trust Turned Down," *Municipal Journal and Engineering* 16 (January 1904), 18; Donna-Bell Garvin and James L. Garvin, *On the Road North of Boston: New Hampshire Taverns and Turnpikes, 1700–1900* (Concord, New Hampshire: New Hampshire Historical Society, 1988), 192.

4. THE USES AND ABUSES OF STREETS

1. The material in this and succeeding paragraphs derives from my essay, "Transforming the Use of Urban Space: A Look at the Revolution in Street Pavements, 1880–1924," *Journal of Urban History*, 5 (May 1979).

2. Charles A. Beard, *American City Government* (London: T. Fisher Unwin, 1913), 242, 343–48; Lewis Mumford, *The Culture of Cities* (New York: Harcourt, Brace, 1938), 187; Delos Wilcox, *The American City: A Problem in Democracy* (New York: MacMillan, 1904), 15; Buffalo City Planning Commission, *Recreation Survey of Buffalo* (Buffalo, 1925), 60, John F. Dillon, *Treatise on the Law of Municipal Corporations* (Chicago: James Cockroft & Co., 1872), 504–505.

3. Harold W. Pfautz, ed., *Charles Booth on the City: Physical Patterns and Social Structure* (Chicago: University of Chicago Press, 1967), 193, 197, 305–306.

4. Jane Jacobs, *The Death and Life of Great American Cities* (New York: Vintage, 1961), 29–88; David Nasaw, *Children of the City: At Work and At Play* (New York: Oxford University Press, 1986), *passim*.

5. Dillon, *Treatise on the Law of Municipal Corporations* (1872 ed.), 481; Ross D. Netherton, *Control of Highway Access* (Madison: University of Wisconsin Press, 1963), 18–23; Carl Bridenbaugh, *Cities in the Wilderness* (New York: Ronald Press, 1938), 317–18; Nelson P. Lewis, "The Need for a Systematic Paving Program," *American City Magazine* 9 (July 1913), 1; Victor Rosewater, *Special Assessments: A Study in Municipal Finance* (New York: Columbia University, 1883), 9–25, J. L. Van Ornum, "The Theory and Practice of Special Assessments," *ASCE Trans.* 38 (1898), 338–42; N. P. Lewis, "Some Observations on General Taxation and Special Assessments," *American Society For Municipal Improvements Proceedings* 4 (1901), 132–33; Christine Meisner Rosen, *The Limits of Power: Great City Fires and the Process of Urban Growth in America* (New York: Cambridge University Press, 1986), 56–57; John M. Goodell, "City Engineering Problems," *Engineering Record* 47 (January 3, 1903), 22; Samuel Nicholson, *The Nicholson Pavement* (Boston: Henry W. Dutton & Son, 1859), 28–29; Lawrence M. Friedman, *Contract Law in America* (Madison: University of Wisconsin Press, 1965), 74–75; Robert C. Wood, *Suburbia, Its People and Their Politics* (Boston: Houghton-Mifflin, 1958), 33–35, N. F. Lewis, "The Theory and Practice of Laying Assessments for Benefit," *The Municipality* I (December 1900), 32–33. These practices varied somewhat from city to city.

6. Mumford, *The Culture of Cities*, 84–87; Albert A. Pope, *The Relation of Good Roads to the Prosperity of a City* (n.p.; 1890?), 16–17; N. P. Lewis, "The Need for Systematic Repaving Programs," 9; Nelson P. Lewis, "Planning Streets and Street Systems," in Arthur H. Blanchard, ed., *American Highway Engineers Handbook* (New York: John Wiley, 1919), 365–402; Lewis M. Haupt, "On the Best Arrangement of City Streets," *Franklin Institute Journal* 103 (April 1877), 257; Walter Wilson Crosby, "Preliminary Investigations," in Blanchard, ed., *American Highway Engineer's Handbook*, 148; Werner Hegeman, *City Planning in Milwaukee, What it Means and Why it Must be Secured, a Report Submitted to the Wisconsin Chapter of the American Institute of Architects, the City Club, the Milwaukee Real Estate Association, the Westminster League, the South Side Civic Association* (Milwaukee, 1916), 8–9.

7. Mumford, *The Culture of Cities*, 93–98.

8. Q. A. Gilmore, *A Practical Treatise on Roads, Streets and Pavements* (New York: D. Van Nostrand, 1876), 168; Lewis, "Some Observations on General Taxation and Special Assessments, 133.

9. *Baltimore Sun*, September 12, 1856.

10. The earliest reference that I have seen to the idea of cities as an organism is a newspaper quote from the early 1870s in William H. Wilson, *The City Beautiful Movement in Kansas City* (Columbia: University of Missouri Press, 1964), 3. "The Position of the Horse in Modern Society," *The Nation* 15 (October 31, 1872), 278 referred to cities as "great social machines." The *Oxford English Dictionary* attributes the first use of the word "machine" in a political context to an article in the 1876 *North American Review*.

11. Lewis M. Haupt, "On the Best Arrangement of City Streets," *Franklin Institute Journal* 103 (April 1877), 252.

12. Emmons Clark, "Street Cleaning in Large Cities," *Popular Science* 38 (April 1891). 749; Lewis Mumford, *The Highway and the City* (New York: Harcourt, Brace, 1963), 178; Martin, "The Financial Resources of New York," *North American Review* 127 (November–December 1875), 440; Merritt, *Engineering in American Society, 1850–1875*, 163; Octave Chanute, et al., "Rapid Transit and Terminal Freight Facilities," *ASCE Trans.* 4 (1875), 34–40; Gilroy. *Street Pavement Report*, 22, 29; Robert Moore, "Municipal Engineering in St. Louis," *Journal of the Association of Engineering Societies* (March 1892), 125–27; Frank G. Johnson, *The Nicholson Pavement and Pavements Generally* (New York: W. L. Rogers & Co., 1867), 11, 82, 89, 94; Robert Moore, "Street Pavements," *Engineering News* 3 (May 6, 1876), 146; Gilmore, *Treatise on Roads, Streets and Pavements*, 76, 137, 203; John H. Sargeant, "Street Pavement—Past, Present, and Future," *Journal of the Association of Engineering Societies* 6 (September 1887), 331; Citizens Association for the Improvements of the Streets and Roads of Philadelphia, *First Annual Report* (Philadelphia: L. Moore & Sons, 1871); Christine Meisner Rosen, *The Limits of Power: Great Fires and the Process of City Growth in America* (New York: Cambridge University Press, 1986), *passim*.

13. Committee on Science and the Arts, the Franklin Institute, "Report on the Best Modes of Paving Highways," *Journal of the Franklin Institute* 36 (September 1843), 145–47; Stanley Buder, *Pullman: An Experiment in Industrial Order and Community Planning, 1880–1930* (New York: Oxford University Press, 1967), 5; "A Review of Chicago Paving Practice," *ASCE Trans.* 66 (1910), 1; Raymond H. Merritt, *Engineering in American Society, 1850–75* (Lexington: University of Kentucky Press, 1969), 89–90; Ross D. Netherton, *Control of Highway Access* (Madison: University of Wisconsin Press, 1963), 41–43; Martin, "The Financial Resources of New York," 432; Thomas F. Gilroy, *Report of the Department of Public Works of the City of New York on Street Pavements* (New York: Martin B. Brown, 1892), 29; "The Future of Great Cities," *The Nation* (February 22, 1866), 232; Christine Meisner Rosen, "Infrastructural Improvement in Nineteenth Century Cities: A Conceptual Framework and Cases," *Journal of Urban History* 12 (May 1988), 212.

14. Williard Glazier, *Peculiarities of American Cities* (Philadelphia: Hubbard Brothers, 1884), 39, 313, 492–93; William R. Martin, "The Financial Resources of

New York," 427–43; Elizabeth Barlow and William Alex, *Frederick Law Olmsted's New York* (New York and Washington, D.C.: Praeger, 1972), 45; Sylvester Baxter, *Boston Park Guide* (Boston: The Author, 1895), 3; "Hudson County Boulevard," *Engineering Record* 289 (March 24, 1894), 271.

15. United States Bureau of the Census, *Social Statistics of Cities*, 10th Census (1880) (Washington, D.C.: Government Printing Office, 1886), Vol. 19, 805; William Jackson, "Government of Boston," *Journal of the Association of Engineering Societies* 11 (March 1892), 135; Sam Bass Warner, Jr., *Streetcar Suburbs: The Process of Growth in Boston* 1870–1900 (New York: Athenaeum, 1970), 156–60; N. P. Lewis, "Planning Streets and Street Systems," 385; Dillon, *Municipal Corporations* (1872 ed.), 476–78; "Municipal Co-operation, Possible Substitute for Municipal Consolidation," *Engineering News* 41 (February 16, 1899), 104–106; Martin, "Financial Resources of New York," 427–43; Moore, "Street Pavements," 146; Samuel Whinery, "The Effect of Street Paving on the Abutting Property," *Engineering Record* 25 (May 21, 1892), 418; Kenneth T. Jackson, "The Crabgrass Frontier: 159 Years of Suburban Growth in America," in Raymond A. Mohl and James F. Richardson eds., *The Urban Experience* (Belmont, California: Wadsworth,, 1973), 207.

16. "The Future of Great Cities," *The Nation* (February 22, 1866), 232.

17. Harold Zink, *City Bosses in the United States* (Durham: University of North Carolina Press, 1930), 96.

18. Alexander B. Callow, Jr., *The Tweed Ring* (New York: Oxford University Press, 1965).

19. Ibid., 187; Martin, "The Financial Resources of New York," 437; Thomas F. Gilroy, *Report of the Department of Public Works of the City of New York on Street Pavements* (New York: Martin B. Brown, 1892), 439.

20. Constance McLaughlin Green, *Washington Village and Capital* 1800–1898 (Princeton: Princeton University Press, 1962); Monte A. Calvert, "Manifest Functions of the Machine" in Bruce M. Stave, ed., *Urban Bosses, Machines and Progressive Reformers* (Lexington, Mass.: D.C. Heath, 1972), 49–50.

21. Ernest Adam, "Topic of Street Pavements in the City of Newark and of Pavements Generally," *Proceedings of the American Society for Municipal Improvements* (1903), 180; Sargeant, "Street Pavements-Past, Present and Future," 331; N. P. Lewis, "The Theory and Practice of Laying Assessments for Benefit, Part II," *The Municipality* 1 (February 1901), 30–31.

22. On the general pattern of expenditures, see Terence McDonald, *The Parameters of Urban Fiscal Policy: Socio-economic Change and Popular Culture in San Francisco, 1860–1896* (Berkeley: University of California Press, 1986).

23. Melvin G. Holli, *Reform in Detroit, Hazen Pingree and Urban Politics* (New York: Oxford University Press, 1969), 162–66; Seth Low, "The Government of Cities in the United States," *Century Magazine* 42 (September 1891), 731; Jon C. Teaford, *The Unheralded Triumph: City Governments in America, 1870–1900* (Baltimore: Johns Hopkins University Press, 1984), 42–82.

24. Moore, "Street Pavements," 146.

25. "The Wooden Pavements of Chicago," *Engineering News* 4 (October 20, 1877), 287; Dillon, *Treatise on the Law of Municipal Corporations*, 21–30; Holli, *Reform in Detroit*, 161–69; Martin, "The Financial Resources of New York," 432;

Moore, "Street Pavements," 146; "Road-building: An Informal Discussion," *ASCE Trans.* 41 (June 1899), 126; and Eric H. Monkkonen, "The Politics of Municipal Indebtedness and Default, 1890–1936," in Terrence J. McDonald and Sally Ward, eds., *The Politics of Urban Fiscal Policy* (Beverly Hills: Russell Sage Press, 1984).

26. Dillon, *Treatise on the Law of Municipal Corporations*, 21–25; William Jackson, "Government of Boston," *Journal of the Association of Engineering Societies* 11 (March 1892), 133–37; Low, "Government of Cities in the United States," 730–38; "Street Pavements in the City of Newark," 180; Holli, *Reform in Detroit*, 161–69; E. B. Guthrie, "Government of Buffalo," *Journal of the Association of Engineering Societies* 11 (March 1892), 145. For a review of Carl Schurz's ideas, see "Engineers as Commissioners of Public Works," *Engineering News* 31 (February 1, 1894), 82; Teaford, *The Unheralded Triumph,* chs. 3 and 6.

27. Moore, "Municipal Engineering in St. Louis," 124–31; Sylvester Baxter, *Boston Park Guide* (Boston: The Author, 1895), 2; Warner, *Streetcar Suburbs,* 29–31; Wilson, *The City Beautiful Movement in Kansas City,* 34; "Municipal Co-operation, a Possible Substitute for Consolidation," *Engineering News* 41 (February 16, 1899), 104–106; Callow, *The Tweed Ring,* 225–28.

28. Teaford, *The Unheralded Triumph,* 66–80.

29. Jackson, "Government of Boston," 133–35; Francis M. Scott, "Government of the City of New York," *Journal of the Association of Engineering Societies* 11 (March 1892), 138–43; Warner, *Streetcar Suburbs,* 29–31; Guthrie, "Government of Buffalo," 145; Moore, "Municipal Engineering in St. Louis," 129–31; "Engineers as Commissioners of Public Works," 82; Lewis M. Haupt, "Municipal Engineering - A Study of Street Pavements," *Journal of the Franklin Institute* 128 (December 1889), 458.

30. Callow, *The Tweed Ring,* 225–28; Warner, *Streetcar Suburbs,* 329–31; Haupt, "Municipal Engineering," 458.

31. Dillon, *Treatise on the Law of Municipal Corporations* (1872 ed.), 384.

32. John F. Dillon, *Commentaries on the Law of Municipal Corporations* (4th edition, Boston: Little, Brown & Co., 1890), 834–56. Future citations to Dillon will list the date of the edition used. The quote on fresh air as a disinfectant is from J. W. Howard, "Why Good Paving is Essential to the Success of a City, Part II," *Paving and Municipal Engineering* 10 (April 1896), 305. The most prominent of the Elevated Railroad Cases was Story v. New York Elevated Railroad Co., 90 N.Y. 122 (1883). The expression "fee simple," denotes almost absolute ownership rights.

33. Dillon, *Commentaries on the Law of Municipal Corporations* (1890) , 834–59; Ross D. Netherton, *Control of Highway Access* (Madison: University of Wisconsin Press), 41–43.

34. Netherton, *Control of Highway Access,* 41–46; Frederick W. Speirs, *The Street Railway System of Philadelphia: Its History and Present Condition* (Baltimore: Johns Hopkins University Press, 1897), 14; Warner, *Streetcar Suburbs,* 78; Robert David Weber, "Rationalizers and Reformers: Chicago Land Transportation in the Nineteenth Century" (Ph.D. Dissertation, The University of Wisconsin, 1971), 178–87.

35. Teaford, *The Unheralded Triumph,* 227–28.

36. Weber, "Rationalizers and Reformers, Chicago Local Transportation in the Nineteenth Century," 35, 178–79. See graph 4.1 for the paving statistics.

37. St. Louis Elevated and Rapid Transit Co., *Exhibit Presenting and Illustrating the Work Contemplated, Its Plans and Public Uses and the Benefits to Ensue From It* (St. Louis: *Times* Printing House, 1883), 10.

38. Sylvester Baxter, "Berlin: A Study of Municipal Government in Germany," *Bulletin of the Essex Institute* 21 (April, May, and June 1889), 55–61; Green, *Washington, Village and Capital,* 354; George Keegan and F. T. Wood, *Transportation Facilities of London and Paris* (New York: New York Railways Co. and Interborough Rapid Transit Co., 1913), 87–88.

39. T. C. Barker and Michael Robbins, *A History of London Transport, Volume I: The Nineteenth Century* (London: George Allen and Unwin Ltd., 1963), 192–297; Pfautz, ed., *Charles Booth on the City,* 188, 283; Asa Briggs, *Victorian Cities* (New York: Harper Colophon Books, 1970) 227–28, 323; David Ward, *Cities and Immigrants* (New York: Oxford University Press, 1971), 139; David Ward, "A Comparative Historical Geography of Streetcar Suburbs in Boston, Massachusetts and Leeds, England: 1850–1920," *Annals of the Association of American Geographers* 54 (December 1964), 488–89; J. W. Bazalgette, "Presidential Address," *Minutes of the Proceedings of the Institution of Civil Engineers* (London) 76 (1884), 20.

40. Ibid., 18.

41. Holli, *Reform in Detroit,* 157–61, 169–81; James B. Crooks, *Politics and Progress, The Rise of Urban Progressivism in Baltimore 1895–1911* (Baton Rouge: Louisiana State University Press, 1968), 109–157; Zane L. Miller, *Boss Cox's Cincinnati* (New York: Oxford University Press, 1968), 103–104. Not all reformers of the progressive period fall into this category. A substantial number were structural reformers in the old sense. There is little need to differentiate them too closely in this work, since their policies on suburbanization, transportation, and streets did not differ too greatly.

42. Holli, *Reform in Detroit,* 304; Tom L. Johnson, "Free Street Car Transportation," *Municipal Journal and Engineering* 11 (June 1901), 282; "Engineers as Commissioners of Public Works," 82.

43. Charles W. Norton, "City Government by Fewer Men," *World's Work* (October 1907), reprinted in William Allen Nelson, ed., *Charles W. Norton, the Man and His Beliefs* (New York: Harper & Brothers, 1926), 756.

44. Haupt, "Municipal Engineering," 458–62, 491; Moore, "Municipal Engineering in St. Louis," 124–31; David Molitor, "Municipal Public Improvements and the Laws Governing Them," *Municipal Engineering* 13 (December 1897), 331–35; Charles Carroll Brown, "Municipal Ownership and Municipal Control," *Municipal Engineering* 14 (January 1898), 1; David Molitor, "An Outline of Municipal Laws Governing Public Works," *Municipal Engineering* 14 (January 1898), 10–20; Guthrie, "Government of Buffalo," 147; William Jackson, "Government of Boston," 136, "Engineers as Commissioners of Public Works," 82; Committee on City Planning of the Boston Chamber of Commerce, *Report on City Planning in Relation to the Street System of the Boston Metropolitan District* (Boston, 1914), 3–4.

45. Dillon, *Commentaries on the Law of Municipal Corporations* (1911 edition), N. P. Lewis, "Some Observations on General Taxation and Special Assessments," 132–33; *Municipal Journal & Engineering* 14 (June 1903), 296; Bell, "Street Paving in New Orleans," 51; Difference of Opinion Regarding the Pavement Promoter,"

Municipal Engineering 17 (July 1899), 392–93. Of course electric el trains also seemed less dangerous than their steam engined predecessors.

46. Rosen, *Limits of Power, passim.*

47. John W. Alvord, "The Paving Problem in General," *Municipal Journal & Engineering* (July 1904), 4.

48. John S. Billings, "Municipal Sanitation; Defects in American Cities," *Forum* 15 (May 1893), 3–4, 310; Emmons Clark, "Street Cleaning in Large Cities," *Popular Science* 38 (April 1891), 754–55; George E. Waring, Jr., "The Relation of Street Cleaning to Good Paving," *Engineering Magazine* 12 (February 1897), 781–85.

49. F. V. Greene, "Construction and Care of Streets," *Engineering and Building Record* 21 (March 1, 1890), 196.

50. Fred P. Spalding, *A Textbook on Roads and Pavements* (New York: John Wiley and Sons, 1894), 1; Williston Fish, "The Evolution of City Street," *Street Railway Review* 10 (August 15, 1900), 445–46; J. W. Howard, "Why Good Paving is Essential to the Success of a City," *Paving & Municipal Engineering* 10 (April 1896), 227–31; James Owens, "The Controverted Questions in Road Construction," *ASCE Trans.* 27 (1892), 604.

51. Nelson P. Lewis, "From Cobblestone to Asphalt and Brick," *Municipal and Paving Engineering* 10 (March 1896), 234–35.

5. THE FAILURE OF THE STEAM AUTOMOBILE

1. Grenville Bathe and Dorothy Bathe, *Oliver Evans, A Chronicle of Early American Engineering* (Philadelphia: Historical Society of Pennsylvania, 1935), 5, 19, 98–99; Thurman Van Metre, *Early Opposition to the Steam Railroad* (Pamphlet in the Library of the National Museum of History and Technology, n.p., 1924?), 13–15; Gary Levine, History of the American Steam Car" (Ph. D. Dissertation, St. John's University, 1971), 43; L. Scott Bailey, "The Other Revolution," in Editors of *Automobile Quarterly, The American Car Since 1775* (New York: L. Scott Bailey, 1971), 18–22; Carroll W. Pursell, *Early Stationary Steam Engines in America* (Washington, D.C.: Smithsonian Institution Press, 1969), 114.

2. Bathe and Bathe, *Oliver Evans,* 108–109; Bailey, "The Other Revolution," 18–22.

3. Bathe and Bathe, *Oliver Evans,* 169; John B. Rae, "The Internal Combustion Engine on Wheels," in Melvin Krainzberg and Carroll W. Pursell, Jr., *Technology in Western Civilization* (2 vols., New York: Oxford University Press, 1967), 2, 122.

4. As quoted in C. St. B. Davison, *History of Steam Road Vehicles* (London: Her Majesty's Stationery Office, 1953), 8.

5. John B. Rae, *The American Automobile* (Chicago: University of Chicago Press, 1965), 2: Bailey, "The Other Revolution," 12–16; Levine, "History of the American Steam Car," 40; Rudolph E. Anderson, *The Story of the American Automobile* (Washington, D.C.: Public Affairs Press, 1950), 11.

6. Anthony Bird, *Roads and Vehicles* (London: Longmans, Green, 1969), 4; Henry C. Moore, *Omnibuses and Cabs, Their Origins and History* (London: Chapman & Hall, 1902), 41–45; C. F. T. Young, *Steam on Common Roads* (London: n.p., 1860), 198–99, 211, 400; Davison, *History of Steam Road Vehicles,* 9; Lewis H. Haney, *A Congressional History of Railways* (New York: Augustus M. Kelley, 1968 reprint of

the original 1908 edition), 64; Charles Frederick T. Young, *The Economy of Steam Power on Common Roads* (London: Aitchley & Co., 1860), 219.

7. Ibid.

8. David Beasley, *The Suppression of the Automobile: Skulduggery at the Crossroads* (New York: Greenwood Press, 1988), 1–22.

9. Young, *The Economy of Steam on Common Roads* (London: n.p., 1860), 220–49; Bird, *Roads and Vehicles*, 59; Davison, *History of Steam Road Vehicles*, 11–12; Haney, *A Congressional History of Railways*, 38; *Roads and Vehicles and Modes of Travelling* (London: John W. Parker, 1839), 266.

10. Davison, *History of Road Steam Vehicles*, 11–12; Bird, *Roads and Vehicles*, 30, 59; Stephen Black, *Man and Motor Cars, an Ergonomic Study* (New York: Norton, 1966), 16.

11. "Col. John Stevens," *Dictionary of American Biography*, vol. 17; "Some Account of the Various Projects for Propelling Carriages by Means of Steam," *The Franklin Journal* 5 (March 1828), 185–89; James Rood Doolittle, *The Romance of the Auto Industry* (New York: The Klebold Press, 1916), 12: Bailey, "The Other Revolution," 220–25; Haney, *A Congressional History of Railways*, 22–26, 63; Levine, "A History of the American Steam Car," 45; Robert Mills, *Substitute for Railroads and Canals Embracing a New Plan of Roadway; Combining the Operation of Steam Carriages, Great Economy in Carrying into Effect a System of Internal Improvement* (Washington, D.C.: James C. Dunn, 1834); Beasley, *The Suppression of the Automobile*, 58.

12. Levine, "History of the American Steam Car," 45; Bailey, "The Other Revolution," 25; Alex I. Holley and J. K. Fisher, "History and Progress of Steam on Common Roads in the United States," in C. F. T. Young, *Steam on Common Roads* (London: n.p., 1860), 352.

13. Mary Griffith, *Three Hundred Years Hence* (1836) as cited in Stanley K. Schultz, *Constructing Urban Culture: American Cities and City Planning, 1800–1920* (Philadelphia: Temple University Press, 1989), 22–23.

14. "Some Accounts of the Various Projects for Propelling Carriages by Means of Steam, 186.

15. Bailey, "The Other Revolution," 24; "Col. John Stevens." *Dictionary of American Biography* 17; Robert Fogel, *Railroads and American Economic Growth* (Baltimore: Johns Hopkins University Press, 1964), 14; Holley and Fisher, "History and Progress of Steam on Common Roads in the United States," 348–52; Levine, "History of the American Steam Car," 46–48.

16. See ch. 1.

17. *New York Herald*, July 6, 1839. See also *New York Post*, July 5, 1839.

18. Committee on the Explosion of the Moselle, *Report* (Cincinnati: Alexander Flash, 1838), 20–22; Glenn Weaver, *The Hartford Steam Boiler Inspection and Insurance Co.* (Hartford: privately printed, 1966), 3–5; John Ashcroft, *The Laws in Regard to the Inspection of Steam Boilers Passed by the States of New York and New Jersey* (New York: John Ashcroft, 1868), 52–57.

19. Weaver, *Hartford Steam Boiler Inspection and Insurance Co.*, passim, esp. 6; Jacob Harshman, *The Cause and Prevention of Steam Boiler Explosions* (Dayton: privately printed, 1855), 39–42; Franklin Institute Committee on the Explosion of

Steam Boilers, *Report* (Philadelphia: John C. Clark, 1836); John G. Burke, "Bursting Boilers and the Federal Power," in Melvin Krainzberg and William H. Davenport, eds., *Technology and Culture, An Anthology* (New York: Schocken Books, 1971), 105–106.

20. Levine, "History of the American Steam Car," 47–48; Davison, *History of Steam Road Vehicles*, 16; Holley and Fisher, "History and Progress of Steam on Common Roads in the United States," 352.

21. J. K. Fisher, "Railways and Other Roads," *Journal of the Franklin Institute*, Third Series, 24 (September 1852), 152–59.

22. Bailey, "The Other Revolution," 13; Davison, *History of Steam Road Vehicles*, 16; John Carteret, "The Genesis of the Automobile," *Automobile Magazine* 1 (October 1899), 30; John Bentley, *Oldtime Steam Cars* (Greenwich: Fawcett Books, 1953), 21; Levine, "History of the American Steam Car," 49–51.

23. Holley and Fisher, "History and Progress of Steam on Common Roads in the United States," 353, 359; Levine, "History of the American Steam Car," 19–20, 56–57; Bailey, "The Other Revolution," 33.

24. Holley and Fisher, "History and Progress of Steam on Common Roads in the United States," 353; Bailey, "The Other Revolution," 33.

25. Holley and Fisher, "History and Progress of Steam on Common Roads in the United States," 365; *New York Times*, August 31, September 27, October 4 and November 1, 1863. Anderson, *Story of the American Automobile* cites the *Scientific American* of November 24, 1866 for an endorsement of steam automobiles. For a short biography of Holley, see Committee on History and Heritage of American Civil Engineering, American Society of Civil Engineers, *A Biographical Dictionary of American Civil Engineers* (New York: American Society of Civil Engineers, 1972), 61–62.

26. Holley and Fisher, "History and Progress of Steam on Common Roads in the United States," 367.

27. The exchange between Fisher and C. A. Busted appeared in the *New York Times* on the dates cited in note 22 above.

28. J.K. Fisher, letter to the editor, *New York Times*, August 31, 1863.

29. ASCE History Committee, *Biographical Dictionary of American Civil Engineers*, 61–62; *Scientific American*, March 1863, as cited in Anderson, *Story of the American Automobile*, 32–35; Bentley, *Oldtime Steam Cars*, 21; Bailey, "The Other Revolution," 35–36.

30. Bailey, "The Other Revolution," 39–41; "H. A. House," *Dictionary of American Biography*, vol. 5; Lewis C. Strang, "America's First Automobile," *Automobile Magazine* 1 (November 1899), 133; Levine, "History of the American Steam Car," 59–60.

31. Bailey, "The Other Revolution," 43–44; Bentley, *Oldtime Steam Cars*, 21: Davison, *History of Steam Road Vehicles*, 22–23; Fletcher, *English and American Steam Carriages and Traction Engines*, 53.

32. *Wisconsin State Journal* (Madison), July 24, 1878; Bentley, *Oldtime Steam Cars*, 22; Bailey, "The Other Revolution," 41; Anderson, *The Story of the American Automobile*, 37; "How Motor Vehicles Stand Before the Law in New York State," *Horseless Age* 4 (April 26, 1899), 23; *Newburyport Daily News*, August 29, 1899.

33. *New York Times,* July 6, 1868; Bentley, *Oldtime Steam Cars,* 20–21; John F. Dillon, *Commentaries on the Law of Municipal Corporations* (4th ed., Boston: Little, Brown & Co.,1890), vol. 2, 812; Davison, *History of Steam Road Vehicles,* 1–2.

34. Charles C. McLaughlin, "The Stanley Steamer: A Study in Unsuccessful Innovation," in Hugh C. Aitken, ed. *Explorations in Enterprise* (Cambridge: Harvard University Press, 1965), 260; Statement of Robert U. Ayres, Resources for the Future, U.S. Congress, Senate Committee on Commerce and Subcommittee on Air and Water Pollution of the Committee on Public Works, 90th Congress, Second Session, *Joint Hearings on the Automobile Steam Engine and Other External Combustion Engine Alternatives to the Internal Combustion Engine,* U.S. Serial #90–82 (May 27 and 28, 1968), 8; Davison, *History of Steam Road Vehicles,* 1–2; Fletcher, *English and American Steam Carriages and Traction Engines,* 228. The Senate Committee hearings will hereafter be cited as *Muskie Committee Hearings.*

35. J. K. Fisher, "Letter to the Editor of the *New York Times,*" August 31, 1863; Davison, *History of Steam Road Vehicles,* 11, 20, 23.

36. Davison, *History of Steam Road Vehicles,* 219; "The Use of Steam Carriages on the Street Railways and Common Roads," *Engineering News* 3 (April 22, 1876), 131; McLaughlin, "The Stanley Steamer: A Study in Unsuccessful Innovation," 266; Bailey, "The Other Revolution," 44.

37. Hiram Percy Maxim, *Horseless Carriage Days* (New York: Dover, 1962 reprint of the original 1936 edition), 4; Allen Nevins and Frank Ernest Hill, *Ford, the Man, the Times, the Company* (3 vols., New York: Scribner's, 1954), I, 54; Charles E. Duryea, "The American Motor Car Industry," *Motor* 11 (March 1909), 34; Elwood Haynes, *The Complete Motorist* (privately printed pamphlet in the Library of the National Museum of History and Technology, 1914), 8; Levine, "History of the American Steam Car," 65. Bailey, "The Other Revolution," 46 cites *Scientific American* (May 21, 1892) on Olds's steam experiments.

38. Maxim, *Horseless Carriage Days,* 4. Maxim is best known as the inventor of the most efficient machine gun of World War I. Nevins and Hill, *Ford, the Man, the Times, the Company* I, 54. The claim deserves some skepticism. The 1893 World's Fair more likely led to his first experiments. Charles E. Duryea, "The American Motor Car Industry," *Motor* 11 (March 1909), 34.

39. Elwood Haynes, *The Complete Motorist* (privately printed pamphlet in the Library of the National Museum of History and Technology, 1914), 8. Levine, "History of the American Steam Car," 65; Beasley, *The Suppression of the Automobile,* 79, 89, 112. Many experimented with electric vehicles as well.

40. *New York Herald,* February 17, 1901, as cited in Editors of *Automobile Quarterly,* eds., *The American Car Since 1775,* 385; Levine, "History of the American Steam Car," 128–29; McLaughlin, "The Stanley Steamer: A Study in Unsuccessful Innovation," 266; *Muskie Committee Hearings,* 199; Ray Stannard Baker, "The Automobile in Common Use," *McClure's Magazine* 13 (July 1899), 205.

41. Beasley, *Suppression of the Automobile,* 129.

42. William Greenleaf, *Monopoly on Wheels: Henry Ford and the Selden Automobile Patent* (Detroit: Wayne State University Press, 1961), 15–20; Allen Nevins and Frank Ernest Hill, *Ford, The Man, The Times, The Company* (3 vols., New York:

Charles Scribner's Sons, 1954), 1, 369–70. The technology was still premature, since Karl Benz did not build the first operational i.c. car until 1886.

43. Ibid.

6. THE EMERGENCE OF THE INTERNAL COMBUSTION AUTOMOBILE: AN URBAN PHENOMENON

1. Pierre Bardou, Jean-Jacques Chanaron, Patrick Fridenson and James M. Laux, *The Automobile Revolution: The Impact of an Industry* (Chapel Hill: University of North Carolina Press, 1982), ch. 1. The Smithsonian Institution in Washington still displays the Silent Otto shown at the 1876 Centennial Exposition.

2. For example, see Sylvester Baxter, "Berlin: A Study of Municipal Government in Germany," *Bulletin of the Essex Institute* 21 (April, May, June, 1889, 55).

3. Bardou, et al., *The Automobile Revolution*, ch. 2; James J. Flink, *America Adopts The Automobile, 1895–1910* (Cambridge: MIT Press, 1970), 29–31. In recent years, of course, the front-engine, front-drive mode developed by Alex Issoginis and the rear-engine, rear drive mode developed by Ferdinand Porsche have been more common.

4. Bardou, et al., *Automobile Revolution*, ch. 2; William Plowden, *The Motor Car and Politics, 1896–1970* (London: The Bodley Head, 1971), *passim*; Kenneth Richardson, *The British Motor Car Industry, 1896–1939* (London: The MacMillan Press, 1979), *passim*. Britain lagged behind the other producers, despite the huge London market, probably because of poor roads and poor engineering training. The English just seemed to lack imagination. Parliamentary laughter greeted an assertion that cars might some day replace trolleys during the debate over repeal.

5. Ibid.

6. Eric Monkkonen, *America Becomes Urban: The Development of U.S. Cities and Towns, 1780–1980* (Berkeley: University of California Press, 1988), 293.

7. The original registration forms, unfortunately not tabulated, are in the Maryland state archives. Registration in Maryland was perpetual, but the system went into force only in May 1904. The 1905 figures include 1904 registrants and reflect all the car owners in the state. The 1909 data are only for cars newly acquired that year. Maryland refused to accept out-of-state registrations and constables vigorously prosecuted D.C. drivers in the spring of 1904, so most D.C. residents probably secured Maryland licenses. More of them registered cars in Maryland than residents of Baltimore, although Baltimore had nearly 200,000 more citizens. Residents of the rural tidewater counties accounted for 14% of the state's population in 1910, 10% of the cars owned in 1904 and 14% in 1909. Car ownership lagged well behind in rural central and western Maryland, where wealth was more evenly distributed. According to Flink, *America Adopts the Automobile*, 167, only 18 states had annual registration by 1910. I checked all the ones in the northeast and only Maryland and New Hampshire retained the original data.

8. *Report of the Secretary of State, New Hampshire, 1907–1911*. This report printed a list of all the car owners in the state and their addresses.

9. Flink, *America Adopts the Automobile*, 19–21: John B Rae, *American Automobile Manufacturers* (Philadelphia: Chilton, 1959), 5–8; John B. Rae, *The American Automobile* (Chicago: University of Chicago Press, 1965), 5–7; Nevins and Frank

Ernest Hill, *Ford, The Man, The Times, The Company* (3 vols., New York: Scribner's, 1954), 1, 125–31; Lawrence R. Gustin, *Billy Durant, Creator of General Motor* (Grand Rapids: William B. Eerdmans Publishing Co., 1971), 45–67; "A Gas-Propelled Carriage," *Scientific American* 60 (January 5, 1899), 9.

10. This account draws heavily from George S. May, *A Most Unique Machine: The Michigan Origins of the American Auto Industry* (Grand Rapids: Eerdsman, 1975). May's account supplants the other histories of the early automobile, by digging out these references to the Columbian Exposition from manuscript sources, rather than relying on the self-serving accounts of the American automotive pioneers, none of whom mentioned European influences or the Fair in their memoirs.

11. *New York Times*, September 22, 1895.

12. May, *A Most Unique Machine*, 25–32.

13. *New York Times*, August 25, 1895; November 16, 1895.

14. Gustin, *Billy Durant*, 91; Rae, *American Automobile Manufacturers*, 13.

15. Sylvester Baxter, "Berlin" 55; Charles Duryea, "The American Motor Car Industry," *Motor* 11 (March, 1909), 128; William Plowden, *The Motor Car and Politics 1896–1970* (London: The Bodley Head, Ltd., 1971), 21–24; James J. Flink, *America Adopts the Automobile*, 12–15; Allen Nevins, *Ford*, 1, 125–31; Oliver McKee, "The Horse or the Motor," *Lippincott's Monthly Magazine* 57 (March 1896), 379; Robert Lew Seymour, "The Horse and His Competitors," *The Chatauquan* 22 (November, 1895), 196–99; John B. Rae, *American Automobile Manufacturers*, 5–8, 13; John B. Rae, *The Road and Car In American Life* (Cambridge: M.I.T. Press, 1971), ch. 1.

16. John B. Rae, *The Road and Car in American Life* (Cambridge: M.I.T. Press, 1971), Ch. 1

17. Sylvester Baxter, "The Automobile in Local Transit," *Automobile Magazine* 1 (February, 1900), 503. See also "The Motor Car in England," *Scientific American* 75 (December 12, 1896), 423.

18. R. H. Thurston, "The Automobile in Business," *Horseless Age*, 7 (February 6, 1901), 39.

19. "The Possibilities of Mechanically-Propelled Vehicles for Common Roads," *Engineering News* 35 (March 5, 1896), 153.

20. As quoted in L. Scott Bailey, "The Other Revolution," in Editors of *Automobile Quarterly, The American Car Since 1775* (New York: L. Scott Bailey, 1971), 77.

21. Rae, *The American Automobile Manufacturers*, 68–70.

22. Nevins, *Ford*, 1: 172–75, 200; Gustin, *Durant*, 36; Flink, *America Adopts the Automobile*, 29; Rae, *American Automobile Manufacturers*, 8–40.

23. Glenn A. Niemeyer, *The Automotive Career of Ransom E. Olds* (East Lansing: Michigan State University Business Studies, 1963), 25; Elwood Haynes, *The Complete Motorist* (Privately printed pamphlet in the Library of the National Museum of History and Technology, 1914), 10; Hiram Percy Maxim, "Automobiles," *American Manufacturer and Iron World*, 70 (April 3, 1902), 373–75; John Hammond Moore, "South Carolina's Wonderful Anderson Car," *Smithsonian Journal of History* 1 (Summer 1966), 63–66; Baker, "The Automobile in Popular Use," 207.

24. For a survey of the recent literature on urbanization and innovation, see Kenneth L. Sokoloff and B. Zorina, "Democratization of Innovation During Early Industrialization: Evidence from the U.S., 1790–1840," in National Bureau of Ec-

onomic Research, *Working Papers,* #10 (December, 1989); Lawrence Brown, *Innovation Diffusion: A New Perspective* (London: Methuen, 1981), 1–21. Torstern Hägerstrand, *Innovation Diffusion as a Spatial Process* (Chicago: University of Chicago Press, 1987), 115–26 has done a geographical study with mathematical rigor to trace the spread of car registrations in a Swedish region, which finds a similar spread of the automobile outward from cities in Sweden.

25. Charles W. Boas, "Locational Patterns of American Automobile Assembly Plants 1895–1959," *Economic Geography* 37 (July 1961), 218–30. For a more detailed description of this process and supporting data, see Clay McShane, "American Cities and the Coming of the Automobile, 1870–1910" (Ph. D. Dissertation, University of Wisconsin—Madison, 1975), 176.

26. Haynes, *The Complete Motorist,* 12.

27. Bardou, et al., *The Automobile Revolution,* chs. 4 and 6; Laux, *In First Gear,* 101–20; Richardson, *The British Motor Car Industry,* 70–88.

28. William Baxter, Jr., "The Evolution and Present Status of the Automobile," *Popular Science Monthly* 57 (August 1900), 412.

29. Horace E. Parker, "Opinions of Anti-Speed Organizations," *Horseless Age* 10 (November 5, 1902), 497.

30. Don M. Berkebile, "The Motor Wagon Experiments of W. T. Harris," *Antique Automobile* 33 (September 10, 1969), 31–39; "The Motor Car in 1896," *Engineering Magazine* (February 1897), 857.

31. Henry C. Moore, *Omnibuses and Cabs, Their Origin and History* (London: Chapman & Hall, 1902), 119.

32. In a last-ditch attempt to display the possibilities of their fading technology, the brothers became actively involved in racing, especially attempts on the land speed record. Racing was a commercial, as well as personal disaster, because, when one of the Stanley brothers was killed while racing, it revived all the public fears about steamers.

33. Paul Barrett, *The Automobile and Urban Transit, The Formation of Public Policy in Chicago 1900–1930* (Philadelphia: Temple University Press, 1988); Scott Bottles, *Los Angeles and the Automobile* (Berkeley: University of California Press, 1987); Mark S. Foster, *From Streetcar to Superhighway, American City Planning and Urban Transportation, 1900–1940* (Philadelphia: Temple University Press, 1981).

34. Arnold Paul, *Conservative Crisis and the Rule of Law, Attitudes of Bar and Bench 1887–1895* (New York: Harper, 1967), 12–18.

35. "Risks Encountered on the Streets of Cities," *Scientific American* 60 (June 1, 1889), 343.

36. Charles Pratt, "A Sketch of American Bicycling and its Founder," *Outing* 17 (July, 1891), 344.

37. Ibid., 345–46; Charles Pratt, "The League of American Wheelmen and Legal Rights," *Outing* 7 (January, 1886), 454–56; John F. Dillon, *Commentaries on the Law of Municipal Corporations* (5th ed., Boston: Little, Brown, 1911), 1060.

38. In the Matter of Wm. M. Wright, S. Conant Foster and Henry H. Walker, 29 *Hun,* 259 (1882).

39. Norman L. Dunham, "The Bicycle in American History" (Ph.D. Diss., Harvard University, 1956), 280–86.

40. Burton Willis Potter, *The Road and Roadside* (Boston: Little, Brown, 1886),

42–58; George B. Clementson, *The Road Rights and Liabilities of Wheelmen* (Chicago: Callaghan & Co., 1895), vi, 93–94, 136–38.

41. 43 *Kan.* 671 (1892), as quoted in Clementson, *The Road Rights and Liabilities of Wheelmen*, 93–94.

42. John F. Dillon, *Municipal Corporations* (4th ed., Boston: Little, Brown & Co., 1890), 812; Dillon, *Municipal Corporations* (5th ed., 1911), 1086.

43. "Restrictions of Traffic on Highways," *Engineering Record* 41 (February 10, 1900), 122; Dillon, *Municipal Corporations* (5th ed., 1911), 1060; Xenophon P. Huddy, *The Law of the Automobile* (Albany: Matthew Bender & Co., 1906), 30.

44. Cary Goodman, *Choosing Sides: Playground and Street Life on the Lower East Side* (New York: Schocken, 1979), xiii.

45. "The Legal Status of the Motor Vehicle," *Horseless Age* 6 (May 9, 1900), 1612; Flink, *America Adopts the Automobile*, 178–79; "Editorial Comment," *Automobile Magazine* 1 (October, 1899), 81–93.

46. Chicago v. Banker, 112 *Ill. App.* 94, as cited in Huddy, *The Law of the Automobile*, 33.

47. H.C. Waite, "Automobiles in Our Cities," *Automobile Magazine* 3 (April, 1901), 356.

48. For three such predictions, respectively by a park planner, municipal engineer and political reformer, see Sylvester Baxter, "Parks and Boulevards in American Cities, Part II," *American Architect* 62 (October 22, 1898), 27; Thomas Conyngton, "Motor Carriages and Street Paving," *Municipal Engineering* 16 (April, 1899), 220–24; and Ray Stannard Baker, "The Automobile in Common Use," *McClure's Magazine* 12 (July, 1899), 195–208.

49. The Transportation of Goods in Towns and Cities," *Engineering News* 35 (May 14, 1896), 320. See also William Baxter, Jr., "The Evolution and Present Status of the Automobile," *Popular Science Monthly* 57 (August, 1900), 411–12.

50. Hiram Percy Maxim, *Horseless Carriage Days* (New York: Dover Publications, 1962 reprint of the original, 1936 edition), 5.

51. "The Transportation of Goods in Towns and Cities," 320–21. See also "The Possibilities of Mechanically-Propelled Vehicles," 153–54; McKee, "The Horse or the Motor," 379; Maxim, "Automobiles," 373–75.

52. Maxim, "Automobiles," 373–75; Sylvester Baxter, "The Automobile in Local Transit," *Automobile Magazine* 1 (February 1900), 501; "The Motor Car in England," 423; 'The Possibilities of Mechanically-Propelled Vehicles," 153.

53. John Hanna, "Evolution of Community Transportation," *Electric Railway Journal* 75 (September 15, 1931), 495; "Some Advantages of the Automobile," *Horseless Age* 10 (October 8, 1902), 377; McKee, "The Horse or the Motor," 380–82; Maxim, "Automobiles," 373–75.

54. "The Possibilities of Mechanically Propelled Vehicles," 153; Baxter, "The Auto in Local Transit," 503; "Some Advantages of the Automobile," *Horseless Age* 10 (October 8, 1902), 377.

55. "Some Advantages of Automobiles," 377; Harold Bolce, "The Horse vs. Health," *Appleton's Magazine* 11 (May, 1908), 532–38; S.M. Butler, "Speed Regulations for Automobiles," *Municipal Journal and Engineer* 12 (May, 1902), 202. For a complete discussion of the automobiles and street cleaning, see Joel Tarr, "Urban Pollution - Many Long Years Ago," *American Heritage* (October, 1971), 68–69.

56. Samuel P. Hays, *The Response to Industrialism: 1885–1900* (Chicago: University of Chicago Press, 1957), *passim,* esp. 99–104, 188–93; Robert H. Wiebe, *The Search for Order 1877–1920* (New York: Hill and Wang, 1967), *passim,* esp. 111–32; Robert Fishman, *Bourgeois Utopias: The Rise and Fall of Suburbia* (New York: Basic Books, 1987), 156.

57. James J. Flink, "Three Stages of American Automobile Consciousness," *American Quarterly* 24 (October, 1972), 455.

58. William E. Scarritt, "The Low Priced Automobile," *Munsey's Magazine* 29 (May, 1903), 179. "Effect on Land Values and the Distribution of Population," *Horseless Age* 1 (March, 1896), 1.

59. Frank Parsons, *The City for the People* (Philadelphia: C.F. Taylor, 1901), 7. Parsons wrote the reference to airplanes two years before the Wright Brothers' first flight. Italics mine.

60. Edward A. Bond, "The New York Highway Commission," *Municipal Journal and Engineer* 13 (November 1902), 212–13; "The Automobile as Vacation Agent," *Independent* 56 (February 6, 1904), 1259; Frederick Coburn, "The Five-Hundred Mile City," *The World Today* 11 (December 1906), 1251, 1255.

7. THE EPITOME OF POSSESSIONS: THE CAR IN POPULAR CULTURE

1. Henri Lefebvre, *Everyday Life in the Modern World,* tr. Sache Rabinowich, (New York: Harper, 1971), 1.

2. Advertisements before this date, if they featured drivers at all, usually showed chauffeurs. Most accident reports listed chauffeurs as drivers. Michael Ebner, *Creating Chicago's North Shore: A Suburban History* (Chicago: University of Chicago Press, 1988), 182 reports that the first resort owner on the North Shore to appeal to weekend automobilists advertised not only a garage, but also separate rooms for chauffeurs. "The Troubles and Pleasures of an Inexperienced Beginner with a Gasoline Automobile," *Horseless Age* 9 (January 27, 1902), 114 *et seq.;* Michael J. French, *The U.S. Tire Industry: A History* (Boston: Twayne Publishers, 1991), 18; *The Independent* 64 (1910), 571.

3. On changing automotive technology, See James J. Flink, *America Adopts the Automobile, 1895–1910* (Cambridge: MIT Press, 1970), *passim;* John Rae, *The American Automobile* (Chicago: University of Chicago Press, 1966), *passim,* esp. 58–61; Allen Nevins with the assistance of Frank Ernest Hill, *Ford, The Man, The Times, The Company* (Vol 1, New York: Scribner's, 1954), 58

4. Kathryn Hume, *How's The Road?* (San Francisco, 1928), 19. Theoretically, the Lincoln Highway, completed in 1925, allowed coast to coast travel on paved roads.

5. National Automobile Chamber of Commerce, *Motor Vehicle Facts and Figures,* 1931 (New York, 1931), 8.

6. Harlan P. Douglass, *The Suburban Trend* (New York: Johnson Reprints, 1970 reprint of the original 1925 edition), 114–15 and 154. Douglass claimed that suburbanites only used their cars to supplement trolleys for commuting at that date, with the significant exception of Los Angeles. One measure of the greater use of cars in LA is the fact that, by 1914, it had the highest auto fatality rate in the nation (*New York Times,* February 10, 1914).

7. Ralph C. Epstein, *The Automobile Industry* (New York: A. W. Shaw, 1928), 94.

8. *Oxford English Dictionary*. The *New York Times* used it first on June 12, 1899.

9. I am indebted to Michael Ebner for a provocative conversation that started me thinking about the issue of how the press covered automobility.

10. Macy's (*New York Times*, September 18, 1895) and Altman's (October 2, 1898) had owned two of the earliest autos in the city.

11. *New York Times*, May 31, 1896. The paper had carried a few articles about experimental cars over the previous five years, the first occurring on May 31, 1891.

12. Flink, *America Discovers the Automobile*, 36–37; *New York Times* July 11, 1899; James J. Flink, *The Car Culture* (Cambridge: The MIT Press, 1975), 17–19.

13. *New York Times*, May 31, 1896; September 7, 1900; October 7, 1901; September 1, 1904; October 22, 1905; and December 3, 1905.

14. *New York Times*, August 30, 1902; April 15, 1902; April 21, 1902; January 28, 1904; May 1; 1904; and January 8, 1944.

15. "Horseless Carriage Contest," *Cosmopolitan* 21 (September, 1896), 546; *Outing* 15 (June, 1902), 695. One reprint of the Gould photo is in Oliver Jensen, Joan Patterson Kerr, and Murray Belsky, ed., *American Album* (New York: *American Heritage* Publishing Co., 1968), 315. This source is typical of other textbooks and collections of historical photos have reprinted the photo as a symbol of robber baron conspicuous consumption. Both *Munsey's Magazine* and the *Times* reprinted the photo. John Jakes, *The American Small Town: Twentieth Century Place Images* (Hampden, CT: Archon Books, 1982), 49–50 discusses popular photography and cars.

16. *New York Times*, November 20, 1905; Peter J. Schmitt, *The Arcadian Myth in Urban America* (New York: Oxford University Press, 1969), 153, 161. Warren Belasco, *Americans on the Road: From Autocamp to Motel, 1900–1945* (Cambridge: MIT Press, 1979) does a masterful job of tracing the evolution of motor camping. Both reprint (Schmitt on the dust cover, Belasco on page 9) the 1902 photo of a lonely motorist at the rim of the Grand Canyon (see illustration 7.2). Schmitt notes that the Model T did make the conquest of nature possible for urban residents, at least in the summer months when drivers could use rural roads. Attendance at the eleven U.S. National Parks went from 69,000 in 1908 to 334,799 in 1915. More than 55,000 cars visited the parks that year. Kodak images of those trips abound.

17. *New York Times*, March 29, 1907.

18. Melvin G. Holli and Peter D'A. Jones, *Biographical Dictionary of American Mayors, 1820–1920* (New York, 1983); *New York Times*, January 12, 1913; Virginia Scharff, *Taking the Wheel: Women and the Coming of the Motor Age* (New York: The Free Press, 1991), 79–81; Theodore Roosevelt suffered nearly irremediable damage to his 1912 presidential campaign when a car accident knocked him out of commission for two weeks.

19. Milwaukee Chamber of Commerce, *Milwaukee Illustrated* (1912), n.p.; John W. Ripley, "The Art of Postcard Fakery," *Kansas Historical Quarterly* 38 (Summer, 1972), 129–31.

20. *New York Times*, January 7, 1917.

21. James E. Paster, "The Snapshot, The Automobile, and The Americans," in Jan Jennings, ed., *Roadside America: The Automobile in Design and Culture* (Ames: Iowa State University Press, 1990), 55–62.

22. C.H. Claudy, "Motor Emigrants," *Home and Garden* 24 (1913), July to December, 80.

23. *New York Times* July 7, 1911.

24. The quote is from John Henry Mueller, "The Automobile: A Sociological Study" (Ph.D. Dissertation, University of Chicago, 1928), 111.

25. Daniel Horowitz, *The Morality of Spending: Attitudes Towards the Consumer Society in America, 1875–1940* (Baltimore: Johns Hopkins University Press, 1985) 51–80 and 98–116 summarizes these moralistic views, especially prominent in the *Independent* and *Women's Home Companion*, which were on the decline. Elaine Taylor May, "Pressure To Provide: Class, Consumerism and Divorce in Urban America, 1880–1920," *Journal of Social History* 12 (Winter 1978), 180; *New York Times*, May 9, May 10, June 5, and September 13, 1910; Irving Bacheller, "Keeping Up With Lizzie," *Harper's* 121 (1910), 688.

26. Randy Roberts, *Papa Jack: Jack Johnson and the Era of White Hopes* (New York: Free Press, 1983), 119–25; *New York Times*, January 12, 1913.

27. Robert S. Lynd and Helen Merrill Lynd, *Middletown: A Study in Modern American Culture* (New York: Harcourt, Brace, 1926), 256.

28. Kathleen Smallgried, *More Than You Promise: A History of Studebaker* (New York: Harper, 1942), 195.

29. Bardou, et al., *The Automobile Revolution*, ch. 2.; Scharff, *Taking the Wheel*, 96; Rae, *American Automobile Manufacturers*, 61.

30. Mueller, "The Automobile: A Sociological Study," 111. Peter Roberts, *Any Color as Long as Its Black . . . , The First Fifty Years of Automobile Advertising* (New York: William Morrow and Co., 1976), 58–59; Marchand, *Advertising the American Dream*, 156.

31. Leo Levine, *Ford: The Dust and the Glory* (New York, 1968), 46–49, 141–42.

32. *New York Times*, October 13, 1907.

33. David B. Wise, *Illustrated Encyclopedia of the World's Automobiles*, (New York: A&W Publishers, 1979), *passim*.

34. Ibid., With the exception of the well-known Mercedes, these were all American makes, most of short duration. See Peter Marsh and Peter Collett, *Driving Passion: The Psychology of the Car* (London, 1986) 69, on Rolls-Royce.

35. Flink, *America Adopts the Automobile*, shows early "plain and simple" ads.

36. My graduate student, Mark Szmigel, systematically sampled advertising from *McClure's, Ladies Home Journal, Scientific American, Saturday Evening Post,* and *Munsey's*, all mass circulation magazines in an unpublished 1991 seminar paper, "The Dawn of a New Era: Automobile Advertisements in Popular Magazines." Roberts, *Any Color So Long As Its Black,* has the best printed collection of early car ads which I have seen. My analysis of advertising derives heavily from Roland Marchand's work for a later period, *Advertising the American Dream, Making Way for Modernity, 1920::1940* (Berkeley: University of California Press, 1985).

37. Roberts, *Any Color So Long As Its Black,* 55.

38. Roberts, *Any Color So Long As Its Black,* 34–35; Marchand, *Advertising the*

American Dream, 22. The classified advertising section, which began to appear regularly in the *Times* after January 2, 1918, also emphasized plain and simple advertising.

39. Roberts, *Any Color as Long as Its Black,* 51. Italics mine.

40. *Saturday Evening Post,* December 7, 1912, 55. Peerless used the same classical iconography in an ad which appeared on the back page of *Munsey's,* December, 1912. The ads in Roberts, *Any Color as Long as Its Black,* 49 show Pierce evolving from a generalized appeal to status to one focussing on the more "sporty" group.

41. Loren Baritz, *The Good Life: The Meaning of Success for the American Middle Class* (New York: Harper, 1990), 87.

42. Szmigel, "The Dawn of a New Era," 10–12. Only one ad in the mainstream magazine, a Cole ad in *Saturday Evening Post,* showed a woman driver. Marchand, *Advertising the American Dream,* 32–35 notes that ad agencies did not hire women until the 1920s.

43. *Scientific American* 102 (January 15, 1910), 82; *McClure's,* May 1912, 63; *Saturday Evening Post,* May 18, 1912, 21. The Interstate ad is cited in William Bruce Wheeler and Susan D. Becker, eds., *Discovering the American Past,* Vol. 2 (Boston: Houghton Mifflin Co. 1990, 2nd ed.), 77.

44. Wheeler and Becker, *Discovering the American Past,* 72.

45. *New York Times,* February 27, 1916; *Ladies Home Journal,* May, 1917, 36 and back cover.

46. *Saturday Evening Post,* May 5, 1917, 76; Marchand, *Advertising the American Dream,* 22.

47. Scharff, *Taking the Wheel* 35–50.

48. Robert Lacey, *Ford, The Men and the Machine* (New York: Ballantine Books, 1986), 159. The speculation about Ford's subconscious is mine.

49. "Use of Illuminated Girls," *Electrical World,* May 10, 1885, 2; Gwen Ifill, "We Flew by Instinct. . . . ," *Boston Herald-American Magazine,* May 11, 1980, has an interview with Jessie Carter, one of the first (1935) stewardesses.

50. *American Heritage* Albums, *Automobile Honeymoon* (Westport, CT.: Westport Communications Group, 1977), liner notes. E. L. Widmen, "The Automobile, Rock and Roll, and Democracy," in Jan Jennings, ed. *Roadside America: The Automobile in Design and Culture* (Ames: Iowa State University Press, 1990), 82 counts 105 songs for the same period.

51. Ibid.

52. Collett and Marsh, *Driving Passion,* 16; Widmen, "The Automobile, Rock and Roll, and Democracy," 82–83.

53. Julian Smith, "A Runaway Match: The Automobile in American Film, 1900–1920," in David L. Lewis and Lawrence Goldstein, eds. *The Automobile and American Culture* (Ann Arbor: University of Michigan Press, 1983), 179–182. Smith claims, perhaps too cutely, that films turned physical transport into emotional transport. Broadway also succumbed to the use of cars as a plot device. *Scientific American* reviewed *Beauty and the Beast* (March 1, 1902), claiming that it was the first stage show to use a car.

54. Ibid., 183.

55. Ibid., 184.

56. Ibid., 189.

57. David K. Vaughn, "The Automobile in American Juvenile Series Fiction, 1900–1940," in Jennings, ed. *Roadside America*, 74–77 summarizes this literature. Garis achieved his greatest success writing the Uncle Wiggily series. James Braden wrote the less successful Automobile Boys series (five volumes, 1908–13).

58. Clarence Young, *The Motor Boys, or Chums through Thick or Thin* (New York: Cupples and Leon, 1906), 6 and 221.

8. GENDER WARS

1. All writers on this subject owe an enormous debt to Virginia Scharff's superb *Taking the Wheel: Women and the Coming of the Motor Age* (New York: the Free Press, 1991). Some citations in this chapter are from Scharff's 1987 University of Arizona Ph.D dissertation, "Re-inventing the Wheel: American Women and the Automobile in the Early Car Culture."

2. These registrations, unfortunately untabulated, are in the Maryland State Archives. Registration was perpetual, but the 1905 data include all cars registered after the first state registration law went into effect in May 1904. The 1909 data only includes cars purchased that year. I determined gender by the first name of the registrant or driver. In just over 10 percent of the cases it was impossible to determine gender by name, either because the applicant used first and middle initials, rather than a first name; because names were androgynous (e.g. Dale, Jean, Leslie); or because I could not assign them a gender (e.g. Thelesphon, Dixi, Ceylon, Spharzie, Oley). Gender percentages are derived from the total of drivers whose gender is known. This likely inflates the proportion of woman drivers, since most of the excluded names involved individuals who indicated initials, usually, I assume, a male practice.

In the springs of 1904 and 1905 severe conflict existed between D.C. drivers and suburban Maryland constables. At that date most car owners were primarily interested in weekend drives in the country, so I believe that the data likely include almost all cars in the District. The 1909 District data seem less accurate. By that date hostilities had eased. Some owners may have been primarily interested in commuting. By then Washington car owners probably knew that the Maryland Secretary of State had told motorists to paint the registration number on their cars, a system easy to beat by just painting random numbers. Information on men is based on a one in four sample.

I checked the archives of the twelve states north of North Carolina and east of Ohio. Only Maryland and New Hampshire retained any records.

3. The lists (unfortunately without totals) contained all licensed drivers and individuals registering cars in 1907. In 1911 the report listed every car owner in the state, his or her make of car, and its horsepower. The Secretary collected the data in alphabetical order, by town. Registration data, necessary for taxes and enforced by a requirement that each car carry a license, was likely accurate. Comparative data are based on a one in four sample of male drivers.

Driver's licenses were available on application, requiring neither testing nor a minimum age. However, in a state where only one resident received a traffic ticket in 1906 and where only 19 of the 311 tickets issued in 1911 went to residents, it seems likely that some drivers just did not bother to get a license. Five percent of the women owners in 1906 did not hold driver's licenses. Presumably they employed chauffeurs. I also excluded nonresidents (mostly summer visitors) from the computations and from table 8.1. In 1906, three of the twenty-two nonresident drivers were women. I have excluded motorcyclists (192 in 1906), Chauffeurs (44 in 1906) and dealers (23 in 1906). There was no woman in any of these groups.

I determined gender in the same manner as for Maryland. See note 1.

4. The decline in the proportion of women registered may be artifacts of Maryland's peculiar nonresident registration system.

5. *New York Times,* February 4, 1917.

6. U.S. Department of Transportation, *Personal Travel in the U.S.* , Vol 1 (Washington, D.C. 1986), 34. In 1986 7% of U.S. adult men and 14% of U.S. adult women did not have driver's licenses. Women still tend to get licenses at later ages than men.

7. Charles Sanford, "Women's Place in American Car Culture," *Michigan Quarterly* 19 (Fall, 1980), 542.

8. The discussion of masculinity in this and succeeding paragraphs derives from Joe Dubbert, *A Man's Place: Masculinity in Transition* (Englewood Cliffs: Prentice-Hall, 1979); Peter Stearns, *Be A Man: Males in Modern Society* (New York: Holmes and Meier, 1979); and E. Anthony Rotundo, "Body and Soul: Changing Ideals of American Middle Class Manhood, 1770–1920," *Journal of Social History* 16 (Fall 1983), 23–38.

9. John Higham, "Reorientation of American Culture in the 1890s," in John Higham, ed., *Writing American History* (Bloomington: University of Indiana Press, 1970), 79.

10. Olivier Zunz, *Making America Corporate, 1870–1920* (Chicago: University of Chicago Press, 1990).

11. Rotundo, "Body and Soul," 32.

12. John R. Stilgoe, *Borderland: Origins of the American Suburb, 1820–1939* (New Haven: Yale University Press, 1988), 266–67.

13. *My Man and I* (New York, 1870), 74.

14. (New Brunswick: Rutgers University Press, 1990), 179–81. The new household division of labor was determined in part by the inability of new middle-income suburbanites to afford servants. Men seemed to participate more in household activities during the progressive era and then in the 1920s restrict themselves to these relatively limited activities, according to Marsh.

15. Mark C. Carnes, *Secret Ritual and Manhood in Victorian America* (New Haven: Yale University Press, 1989), 2–5; Dubbert, *A Man's Place,* 69. For example, see the *New York Times,* August 2, 1917 account of the lynching of Industrial Workers of the World leader Frank Little in Butte, Montana and the branding, tarring and feathering of socialist of Dr. Ben Reitman on May 15, 1912 outside of San Diego. On a cross-country trip, James Montgomery Flagg reported rural Klansmen in Missouri staging a motorcade in their new model Ts designed to intimidate their less well-off neighbors. *Boulevards All the Way—Well, Maybe: Being an Artist's Truthful Impression of the USA from New York to California and Return, By Motor* (New York: The Doran Co., 1925), 72.

16. Margaret Marsh, *Suburban Lives* (New Brunswick: Rutgers University

Press, 1990), 77–79; T. Jackson Lears, *No Place of Grace: Anti-Modernism and the Transformation of American Culture, 1880–1920* (New York), 1981, ch. 3.

17. Dubbert, *A Man's Place,* 9.

18. Ronald Edsforth, *Class Conflict and Cultural Consensus* (New Brunswick: Rutgers University Press, 1987), 16

19. Some of Lewis's women characters also use the car for escape in *Fill 'er Up* (New York: Grosset and Dunlop, 1919) and *Main Street* (New York: Harcourt Brace, 1923). Cars also played a small role as symbols of status and freedom in Booth Tarkington's popular 1916 novel, *Seventeen* (New York: Grosset and Dunlap).

20. Robert Penn Warren, *All the King's Men* (New York, 1946) as quoted in Charles Reagan Wilson and William Ferris, eds., *The Encyclopedia of Southern Culture* (Chapel Hill, 1989), 597.

21. John Updike, *Rabbit Redux* (New York: Knopf, 1971), as quoted in Cynthia Dettelbach, *In the Driver's Seat: The Automobile in American Literature and Popular Culture* (Westport, CT.: Greenwood Press, 1976), 46.

22. Jack Kerouac, *On the Road* (New York, 1957), as cited in ibid., 35.

23. William Faulkner, *The Town* (New York, 1961), quoted in ibid., 67.

24. January 3, 1900.

25. Cited in Virginia Scharff, "Re-inventing the Wheel," 64.

26. Alice Huyler Ramsey, *Veil, Duster and Tire Iron* (Covina, privately printed, 1961), 7.

27. *New York Times,* January 3, 1900, March 10, 1908, March 11, 1908.

28. *New York Times,* September 3, 1915.

29. C. T. Fish, "My Lady at the Wheel," *National Safety News* 7 (March, 1923), 25. This report contained reports from city officials on mortality rates, in one case back to 1913.

30. *New York Times,* April 14, 1912

31. Montgomery Rollins, "Women and Motor Cars," *Outlook* (August 7, 1909), 859–60.

32. *New York Times,* November 10, 1903; Ballard Campbell, "The Good Roads Movement in Wisconsin, 1890–1911," *Wisconsin Magazine of History* 49 (Summer, 1966), 284–87. Professor Campbell has kindly shared with me his notes for this essay, in which he traced the Milwaukee Auto Club members in the Milwaukee City Directory. See also Scharff, *Taking the Wheel,* 75.

33. Robert Sloss, "What a Woman Can Do With an Auto," *Outing* 56 (April, 1910), 67, 69.

34. Letitia Stockett, *America, First, Fast and Furious* (Baltimore: Normington, 1930), 258; Kathryn Hume, *How's the Road* (San Francisco: privately printed, 1928), 42; Mrs. Andrew Cuneo, "Why There Are So Few Women Drivers," *Country Life* 13 (March, 1908), 516; *New York Times,* March 5, 1916

35. H. C. Penman, "Motoring and Nerves," *Harper's Weekly* 62 (April 15, 1916), 413; Ibid., 3–4. Audrey Allison, although not a motorist, gave a detailed description of these problems in strange cities in *Adventures of a Book Agent* (Boston: Four Seas Co., 1925). The calculated rudeness of men in train stations, downtown streets, and hotels actually drove Allison, a clever, tough sales agent, to tears on several occasions.

36. Ramsey, *Veil, Duster and Tire Iron,* 11

37. *New York World*, June 14, 1902; Michael Teague, *Mrs. L: Conversations with Alice Roosevelt Longworth* (Garden City: Doubleday, 1981), 66–82.

38. L. T. Martin, "Where Women Runs Her Car," *Harper's Weekly* 55 (May 6, 1911), 12 as cited in Michael Berger, "Women Drivers!: The Emergence of Folklore and Stereotypic Opinions Concerning Feminine Automotive Behavior," *Women's Studies International Forum* 9 (1986), 261.

39. See Eric Partridge, *A Dictionary of Slang and Unconventional Usage* (Eighth edition, New York: Macmillan, 1984).

40. Scharff, "Re-inventing the Wheel," 59. Note the decline in D.C. registrations in Table 8.1 above

41. Robert Leinert, "Moving Backward," *Michigan Quarterly Review* 19 (Fall, 1980), 554; Lydia Simmons, "Not From the Back Seat," *Michigan Quarterly Review* 19 (Fall, 1980), 550; James West, *Plainville, USA* (New York: Columbia University Press, 1945), 47.

42. C. H. Claudy, "The Woman and Her Car," *Country Life in America* 23 (January 1913), 41.

43. Mrs. A Sherman Hancock, "Women at the Motor Wheel," *American Homes and Gardens* 10 (April 1913), 6.

44. See n. 1.

45. There may have been electrics in the District unregistered in Maryland. By 1909 it was clear that their limited cruising radius made them lousy touring cars.

46. F. G. Moorehead, "Women Drive to Fortune," *Illustrated World* 24 (November 1915), 334–37; Burr C. Cook, "Women as Auto Mechanics," *Illustrated World* 25 (June 1916), 503–4; *New York Times*, July 15, 1917; Scharff, *Taking the Wheel*, 106.

47. Edwin Wildman, "The City of the Automobile," *Munsey's Magazine* 22 (February 1900), 704–712.

48. E.g., Robert Bruce, "The Place of the Automobile," *Outing* 37 (October 1900), 65–69 featured four photos of socially prominent women in their cars.

49. *New York Times*, June 4, 1904.

50. Hilda Ward, "The Automobile in the Suburbs From a Woman's Point of View," *Suburban Life* 5 (November 1907), 269–271.

51. Ibid., 270–71. For other examples of this line of thought, see C. H. Claudy, "The Woman and Her Car," *Country Life in America* 23 (January, 1913), 41–42; Robert Bruce, "The Promise of the Automobile in Recreative Life," *Outing* 36 (January, 1900), 82–85 and "The Automobile as Vacation Agent," *The Independent* (June 2, 1904) 1256–60. Most of these focussed more on the use of cars by suburban men, especially for access to suburban golf courses.

52. *New York Times*, January 7, 1912.

53. Vol. 24 (1913), July to December.

54. Susan Strasser, *Never Done: A History of American Housework* (New York, 1982), *passim*; Joann Vanek, "Time Spent in Housework," *Scientific American* (November 1974), 16–20.

55. Mary Erin Cullen, "The Quiet Guardian of the Hearth Fire: Respectability and Social Control in Post-Victorian America" (unpublished seminar paper in the author's possession, 1991), 2–6; John F. Kasson, *Rudeness and Civility: Manners in Nineteenth Century Urban America* (New York: Hill and Wang, 1990), 124; Emily

Holt, *Encyclopedia of Etiquette* (New York: Doubleday, 1921), 362; Ramsey, *Veil, Duster and Tire Iron*, 3; Alice Roosevelt Longworth, *Crowded Hours* (New York: Scribner's, 1933), 66.

56. Mary E. Sherwood, *Manners and Social Uses* (New York: Harper and Brothers, Inc., 1918 edition), *passim.*; Marion Harland and Virginia DeWater, *Everyday Etiquette* (Indianapolis: Bobbs-Merrill, 1905), 221 and Holt, *Encyclopedia of Etiquette*, 359–62; *Boston American*, May 6, 1910; Ethel Watts Mumford, "Where is Your Daughter This Afternoon?" *Harper's Weekly* 68 (January 17, 1914), 28. Emily Post, *Etiquette in Society, in Business, in Politics and at Home* (New York: Funk and Wagnalls, 1922), 289, 614 was the first of the etiquette books to tolerate unchaperoned driving.

57. Scharff, "Re-inventing the Wheel," 10–1

58. Frances Thornton, quoted in the *New York Times*, April 12, 1914.

59. Kathryn Hume, *How's the Road?* (San Francisco: privately printed, 1928), 3–4.

60. Ellen K. Rothman, *Hearts and Hands: A History of Courtship in American* (New York: Basic Books, 1984); Beth L. Bailey, *From Front Porch to Back Seat: Courtship in Twentieth Century America* (Baltimore: Johns Hopkins University Press, 1988).

61. Kathy Peiss, *Cheap Amusements: Working Women and Leisure in Turn of the Century New York* (Philadelphia: Temple University Press, 1986), *passim.*

62. May 1, 1904. The allegations of prostitution were likely a commonplace reaction of the older generation to dating and the increased presence of young women in the streets.

63. John C. Burnham, "The Progressive Era Revolution in American Attitudes Towards Sex," *Journal of American History* 59 (March 1973), 885–908. Anxieties over a topic as taboo-laden as sex may not necessarily reflect real behavior changes. James R. McGovern, "The American Woman's Pre-World War I Freedom in Morals and Manners," *Journal of American History* 55 (September, 1968), 315–33; Alfred Kinsey, et al., *Sexual Behavior in the Human Female* (Philadelphia: W. B. Saunders, 1953), 336. Only 71 of his 8,000 women, nonrandom sample were born before 1900. This was about half the level of sexual activity of the generation that matured in the 1920s. Those who used cars for this purpose tended to have married younger than the rest of the sample. In most cases the male involved was their fiancee. Kinsey's data contained many methodological problems, so this information is less precise than it looks.

64. Other writers of juvenile fiction imitated Penrose with the shorter lived Automobile Girls (6 vols., 1910–1913) and Motor Maids (6 vols., 1910–1913) series.

65. Laura Dent Crane, *The Automobile Girls at Washington, or Checkmating the Plots of Foreign Spies* (Philadelphia: Henry Altemus Co., 1913), 8.

66. Ibid., 10 and 26.

67. Penrose, *The Motor Girls on Tour*, 1.

68. Margaret Penrose, *The Motor Girls in the Mountains or the Gypsy Girl's Secret* (Cleveland: Goldsmith Publishing Co., 1917), 30–31.

69. Laura Dent Crane, *The Automobile Girls Along the Hudson or Fighting Fire in Sleepy Hollow* (Philadelphia: Henry Altemus Co. 1916), 39.

70. Penrose, *The Motor Girls in the Mountains*, 4. Typically the chaperones

show up in the first few pages of the works, where a scanning mother might find them, then fade out of the plot.

71. Ibid., 10.

72. Laura Dent Crane, *The Automobile Girls At Washington*, 135–39.

73. Vaughn, "The Automobile in Juvenile Fiction," 75–77.

74. Penrose, *The Motor Girls on Tour*, 246.

75. *American Heritage* Albums, *Automobile Honeymoon* (Westport, Ct.: Westport Communications Group, 1977).

76. Scharff, "Re-inventing the Wheel," 30.

9. RED LIGHT, GREEN LIGHT

1. *New York Times*, September 14, 1899.

2. Ibid., July 11, 1899.

3. Ibid., December 3, 1905. This was probably something of an overestimate. John P. Fox, "Traffic Regulation in Detroit and Toronto" *American City* 13 (September, 1915), 175.

4. According to 1912 rates cited by New York City planner Nelson P. Lewis in "Planning of Streets and Street Systems," in Arthur Blanchard, ed. *American Highway Engineers Handbook* (New York: John Wiley and Sons, 1919, first ed.), 383. Comparable figures for other cities were: London, 6.19; Paris, 8.54; Chicago, 10.4; Berlin, 6.8.

5. *Annual Report of the City Engineer of the City of Minneapolis* (Minneapolis, 1906), 16–17, as cited in Eric Monkkonen, *America Becomes Urban: The Development of U.S. Cities and Towns, 1780–1980* (Berkeley: University of California Press, 1988), 172–74.

6. Paul Barrett, *The Automobile and Urban Transit: The Formation of Public Policy in Chicago, 1900–1930* (Philadelphia: Temple University Press, 1983) notes that Chicago's frequent grade crossings explained that city's high traffic fatality rate.

7. J. Michael Thomson, *Great Cities and Their Traffic* (London: Victor Gollancz Ltd., 1974), 234–43. Of cities for which data existed, Lagos had the highest traffic mortality rate.

8. *New York Times*, August 24, 1910, January 17, 1911; January 14, 1914. On Los Angeles, see "Causes of Fatal Accidents on Highways," *American City Magazine* 16 (March 1916), 187. This article was based on a graduate class paper by William Smith of the University of Southern California and presented to the Southern California Sociological Association.

9. Ibid., May 6, 1909. For a complete list of incidents, see *The New York Times Index*, 1901–1906.

10. *New York Times*, May 24–27, 1903. Anti-auto incidents did not occur only in New York. The *Times* reported on cases in other cities and historian Paul Barrett has described them in Chicago (Barrett, *The Automobile and Urban Transit*, 58).

11. Michael Berger, *The Devil Wagon in God's Country* (Hampden, Ct.: Archon Books, 1971), 58.

12. *New York Times*, June 22, 1905; July 20, 1904.

13. Michael Ebner, *Creating Chicago's North Shore: A Suburban History* (Chicago: University of Chicago Press, 1988), 173; *New York Times*, August 19, 1907.

Cooler heads prevailed and the federal authorities settled for a lawsuit. *Annual Report of the New Hampshire Secretary of State, 1911.*

14. *New York Times,* July 22, 1907 and July 2, 1908; Berger, *The Devil Wagon,* 97–101.

15. Horace E. Parker, "Opinions of Anti-Speed Organizations," *Horseless Age* 10 (November 5, 1902), 497.

16. *New York Times,* May 27, 1902.

17. March 26, 1902.

18. Parkhurst's mathematics left something to be desired.

19. *New York Times,* February 28, 1906. Seven years later, when he was President of the U.S., while out for a Sunday drive, Wilson's chauffeur would hit a delivery boy at the corner of 14th Street and Pennsylvania Ave. The President and the chauffeur took the boy to an emergency room and Wilson promised him a new bicycle (*New York Times,* October 15, 1913).

20. Xenophon P. Huddy, *The Law of Automobiles* (Albany: Matthew Bender & Co., 1906). See also M. C. Krarup, "The Causes of Automobile Accidents, a Presentation of the Principal New Factors Introduced Through Automobilism, and Affecting the Safety of Traffic on Highways," *Horseless Age* 10 (July 16, 1902), 57–89.

21. Ibid. The different rulings probably reflect different state constitutions, not just judicial whimsy.

22. Colonel Albert A. Pope, "Automobiles and Good Roads," *Munsey's Magazine* 29 (May, 1903), 168.

23. James Rood Doolittle, *The Romance of the Auto Industry* (New York: The Klebold Press, 1916), 441.

24. Ballard Campbell, "The Good Roads Movement in Wisconsin, 1890–1911," *Wisconsin Magazine of History,* 49 (Summer 1966), 273–93.

25. Ibid.; These data are from notes which Professor Campbell graciously shared with me and did not appear in the article. Surprisingly, the President of the Club was a Catholic priest, the Reverend F. J Szukalski.

26. *Milwaukee Sentinel,* April 28, 1907.

27. James J. Flink, *America Discovers the Automobile, 1895–1910* (Cambridge: MIT Press, 1970), 170–72

28. Flink, *America Discovers the Automobile,* 172; Joel W. Eastman, *Styling vs, Safety: The American Automobile Industry and the Development of Automotive Safety, 1900–1966* (Lanham, MD: University Press of America, 1964), x and 37.

29. *New York Times,* May 19, 1914 and February 16, 1916. State courts also refused, at first, to enjoin road races.

30. Flink, *America Discovers the Automobile,* 184. New York was not alone. Richard A. and Nancy L. Fraser, *A History of Maine Built Automobiles* (E. Poland, Maine: privately printed, 1991), 121 indicates that the Maine chapter of the Auto Club of America wrote and lobbied Maine's basic motor vehicle law.

31. *New York Times,* January 18, 1911; January 18, 1909.

32. Ibid., July 31, 1901; June 3, 1902.

33. Ibid., October 1 to October 9, 1904.

34. Ibid., October 12, 1904; March 31, 1906. The New York Marathon, begun in the 1980s, probably draws larger crowds.

35. Ibid., November 20, 1905 (editorial headline); June 19, 1907; June 14, 1905.

36. Ibid., July 18, 1907.

37. For example, see ibid., August 8, 1905.

38. Ibid., October 5; March 5, 1906; editorial, February 9, 1909.

39. Charles Zeublin, *American Municipal Progress* (New York: MacMillan, 1916), 142–43. Local precincts staffed the Broadway corners on an ad hoc basis.

40. William Phelps Eno, *The Science of Highway Traffic Regulation* (New York: Brentano's, 1920), *passim*; "William Phelps Eno," *National Cyclopedia of American Biography* (New York: James T. White & Co., 1965), Vol. 47, 613–14. Eno's bequest to Yale provided that the school must teach the rotary method of control. This may explain why more traffic rotaries were built in the northeast, especially New England, in the 1920s and 1930s. All the sources on the history of traffic engineering cite him as the author of the rules of the road. However, Francis Greene, New York's Police Commissioner claimed that one of his captains wrote the first set of rules after a trip to Europe ("Progress in New York Police Force," *Municipal Journal and Engineer* 14 (April 4, 1906), 316–17). It is possible that Eno, a major publicity hound, took credit for someone else's work.

41. The discussion of these rules in this and succeeding paragraphs derives from the *New York Times,* November 8 to December 5, 1903 and "Rules of the Road in New York, *Municipal Journal and Engineer* 16 (January, 1904), 31–32. State courts threw the speed limit out.

42. "Automobile Regulations in Cities," *Municipal Journal and Engineer* 15 (December, 1903), 255; "Street Traffic Regulations," *Municipal Journal and Engineer* 20 (January, 1906), 22; Flink, *America Discovers the Automobile,* 187; Barrett, *The Automobile and Urban Transit,* 138.

43. *New York Times,* May 15, 1905 *et seq.* Eno claimed credit for inventing the islands, but the San Francisco Merchants Association had built one in 1903. See "An 'Isle of Safety' in San Francisco," *Municipal Journal and Engineer* 14 (April 1903), 187.

44. Goodrich, "Traffic Engineering Reminiscences," *Institute of Traffic Engineers Proceedings* 21 (1946), 107.

45. Barrett, *The Automobile and Urban Transit,* 62–64. The transit trade press complained bitterly about the resulting delays and loss of riders.

46. On changing traffic behavior, see the *New York Times,* December 9, 1906; October 9, 1908; December 5, 1909; and January 2, 1910. For the derivation of jaywalking see Mitford A. Matthews, ed., *Dictionary of Americanisms* (Chicago: University of Chicago Press, 1951).

47. F. E. Rankin, "Automobile Accidents in Detroit," *National Safety Council Proceedings* 5 (1916), 238.

48. Mark S. Foster, *From Streetcar to Superhighway: American City Planners and Urban Transportation, 1900–1940* (Philadelphia: Temple University Press, 1981), 110; "Flurry of Speed Legislation," *Horseless Age* 9 (January 15, 1902), 65. Flink, *America Discovers the Automobile,* 195 cites one example.

49. *New York Times,* May 7, 1905; June 19,1907; August 7, 1908; May 7, 1909; Woods, "Keeping City Traffic Moving," 632.

50. Edward H. Bennett and William E. Parsons, *Plan of St. Paul* (St. Paul: City Planning Board, 1922), 30–34.

51. As cited by Barrett, *The Automobile and Urban Transit in Chicago,* 140.

52. *New York Times,* January 7, 1917.

53. William Holden, "Traffic Census Results and Methods: St. Louis," *Engineering News—Record* 53 (November 2, 1916), 834 and Walter Wilson Crosby, "Preliminary Investigations," in Arthur H. Blanchard, ed. *American Highway Engineers Handbook* (1st ed., New York: John Wiley & Sons, 1919), 171–75. The quality of road, population density of the area, and methodology were ill-defined and different for all three studies. Clearly, suburbs were becoming automobilized, but it is hard to put an exact value on this.

54. *New York Times,* August 16, 1916.

55. April 7, 1912.

56. Michael Ebner, *Creating Chicago's North Shore: A Suburban History* (Chicago: University of Chicago Press, 1988), 226

57. National Automobile Chamber of Commerce, *Automobile Facts and Figures,* 1922, 16; "Motor Buses in New York City," *Engineering Magazine* 34 (October 1907), 195–96.

58. Harry Perry, "Taxicab Operators and Builders in America," *Commercial Vehicle* 3 (February 1908), 36–38; Courtlandt Nicoll, " New York Cab Situation," *National Municipal Review* 11 (January 1903), 99–103," Roy Payne, "Franchises for Taxicab Companies," *National Association of Taxicab Owners Proceedings* 15 (1925), 50–60. It is striking that the taxi industry concentrated on the single-rider luxury trade to the point that nobody ever thought of putting in multiple meters for multiple riders.

59. W. R. Metz, "Cost of Upkeep of Horse-Drawn Vehicles Against Electric Vehicles," *A.S.M.E. Proceedings* (1913), 129–38. By that date driving skills were so widespread that chauffeurs were paid at the same rate, $2.40 a day, as teamsters. *New York Times,* April 7, 1912.

60. Stephen D. Thatton, "The Disappearing Car Truck," *Harper's Weekly* 57 (January 11, 1915), 27; Graham Romeyn Taylor, *Satellite Cities* (New York: D. Appleton & Co., 1915), 99–100.

61. F. Van Z. Lane, "Relation of the Motor Bus to Urban Development," *American City Magazine* 10 (May 1914), 462–66.

62. *Dictionary of Americanisms.*

63. Edward Hungerford, *The Personality of American Cities* (New York: West, McBride & Co., 1913), 13, 90, 171, 190, 206. Likely the ban on cheap cars failed.

64. Robert H. Whitten, "Unchoking Our Congested Streets," *American City Magazine* 23 (October 1920), 353.

65. Hungerford, *Personality of American Cities,* 22, 43.

66. *New York Times,* January 17, 1917, *American City Magazine* 17 (May 1917), 165

67. George Ethelbert Walsh, "Traffic Congestion in New York," *Cassier's Magazine* 31 (June 1908), 151–52.

68. Newark City Plan Commission, *Comprehensive Plan of Newark* (1915), 2, 33, 44. The Commission's secretary, Harlan Bartholomew, later a well-known traffic engineer, probably wrote the report. In the same two years auto registration was up 113% in Newark and truck registration 20%.

69. Barrett, *The Automobile and Urban Transit in Chicago,* 30. In 1911 Chicago

police did make an attempt, doomed by recalcitrant teamsters, to keep wagons off the trolley tracks.

70. Howard L. Preston, *Automobile Age Atlanta: The Making of a Southern Metropolis*, 1900–1935 (Athens: University of Georgia Press, 1979), 48 and 140.

71. McClellan and Junkersfield, Inc. Engineers, *District of Columbia Traffic Survey* (District of Columbia, Public Utilities Commission, 1925), 181.

72. Ross Eckert and George W. Hilton, "The Jitneys," *Journal of Law and Economics*, 15 (October 1972), 294. Unless noted otherwise, the following materials on jitneys derive from that source. The *Dictionary of Americanisms* lists other possible derivations.

73. Clyde L. King, "The Jitney Bus," *American City Magazine* 12 (June, 1915), 481; Robert M. Fogelson, *The Fragmented Metropolis: Los Angeles*, 1850–1930 (Cambridge: Harvard University Press, 1967), 167–68; Preston, *Automobile Age Atlanta*, 48.

74. Interview with New York cabbie Peter L. McShane. Illegal jitneys are evidently making a comeback today in New York's outer boroughs.

75. Chicago Municipal Reference Library, *Rates of Fares in Public Motor Vehicles in Large Cities* (Chicago, 1913); Preston, *Auto Age Atlanta*, 56.

76. Scott Bottles, *Los Angeles and the Auto* (Berkeley: University of California Press, 1987), 76.

77. W. A. House, "Analysis of Ordinances Governing the Operation of Jitneys in the Various Cities of the U.S. and Canada," (New York: American Electric Railway Association, 1915); Henry C. Spurr, *Motor Vehicle Transportation* (Rochester: Public Utilities Reports, Inc., 1922) acknowledged that court rulings were unfair to jitneys.

78. Richard N. Farmer, "What Ever Happened to the Jitney?" *Traffic Quarterly* 19 (April 1965); Blaine Brownell, "A Symbol of Modernity: Attitudes Towards the Automobile in Southern Cities in the 1920s," *American Quarterly*, 24 (March 1972), 36–37. There were segregated taxi companies in some cities, which served blacks whom regular cabs refused to pick up. See, for example, "Color Line Taxi Does Well in Cincinnati," *National Taxicab and Motor Bus Journal* (December 1925), 35.

79. "The Parking Problem," *Automobile* 35 (December 21, 1916); George E. Walsh, "Traffic Congestion In New York," *Cassier's Magazine* 31 (June 1908), 151–52.

80. Miller McClintock, *Street Traffic Control* (New York: McGraw-Hill, 1925), 187; Edward Mueller, "Aspects of the History of Traffic Signals," Unpublished paper in the library of the National Museum of American History, 1967), 7.

81. Zeublin, *American Municipal Progress*, 142.

82. *New York Times*, December 12, 1912; Barrett, *The Automobile and Urban Transit in Chicago*, 30; Bottles, *Los Angeles and The Auto*, 67–68; John P. Fox, "Traffic Regulation in Detroit and Toronto," *American City Magazine* 13 (September 1915), 177. Fox, who was the traffic expert for New York's Committee on a City Plan, acknowledged that the lead in traffic engineering had passed from New York to midwestern cities like Detroit.

83. *New York Times*, October 1, 1908. Eno, *Science of Highway Traffic Regulation*, 38–41; Goodrich, "Traffic Engineering Reminiscences," 105; John Gillespie,

"Street Traffic Zones and Signals," *American City Magazine* 15 (November, 1916), 542–46.

84. *New York Times*, January 14, 1916; Joseph Sabath, "What a Traffic Court Can Do," *American City Magazine* 17 (August, 1917), 126–29.

85. *New York Times*, May 19, 1914.

86. Barrett, *The Automobile and Urban Transit in Chicago*, has the best account of this process, 55–62.

87. *New York Times*, December 5, 12 and 21, 1912; Arno Dosch, "The Science of Street Traffic," *World's Work* 27 (February 1914), 401–402. Voluntarism could help a little. The Fifth Avenue Association claimed to have improved traffic flow by having its members receive deliveries in the morning.

88. Dana Frank, " 'Food Wins All Struggles': Seattle Labor and the Politicization of Consumption," *Radical History Review* 51 (Fall 1991), 69.

89. Frederick H. Elliott, "New Uniform Rules for Street Traffic," *American City Magazine* 14 (July 1916), 124–25

90. Dosch, "The Science of Street Traffic," 405–407. Improving traffic flow attracted so much additional travel that the bridge was jammed again by the early 1920s.

91. "Street Crossing Signals," *Municipal Journal and Engineer* 23 (December, 1902), 464; *New York Times*, March 10, 1914, March 14, 1914; Gordon Sessions, "Traffic Devices: Historical Aspects Thereof," (Washington D.C.: Institute of Traffic Engineers, 1971), 22; Goodrich, "Traffic Engineering Reminiscences," 105. The most imaginative variation on this theme involved giving a policeman a beach umbrella, divided into four red and green quadrants marked "stop" and "go." See the photo in the *Engineering News-Record* 54 (September 15, 1917), 469.

92. Nelson P. Lewis, *The Planning of the Modern City* (New York: John Wiley, 1916), 201 and 213; Mueller, "Traffic Devices," 8–9; Sessions, "Traffic Devices," *passim*; Lewis, *Planning the Modern City*, 201 Goodrich, "Traffic Engineering Reminiscences," 106.

93. For a photo of the first light, see Alfred Benesch, "Regulating Street Traffic in Cleveland," *American City Magazine* 13 (September, 1915) 182. Sessions, "Traffic Devices," claims priority for a 1912 light in Salt Lake City. The Salt Lake City light apparently had little impact elsewhere. I can find no mention of it in the engineering literature.

94. "An Italian's Advice to Italian Immigrants," *American Review of Reviews* 61 (July, 1917), 100.

95. Barrett, *The Automobile and Urban Transit in Chicago*, 156–69; Fogelson, *The Fragmented Metropolis*, 251.

10. THE MOTOR BOYS REBUILD CITIES

1. Quoted in Jon Teaford, *The Twentieth Century American City: Problem, Promise and Reality* (Baltimore: Johns Hopkins University Press, 1988), 41–42.

2. (Boston: Ticknor, 1887).

3. Stanley K. Schultz, *Constructing Urban Culture: American Cities and City Planning*, 1800–1920 (Philadelphia: Temple University Press, 1989), 22–23. Thomas could only publish his utopia in 1891, after the success of *Looking Backwards*.

Schultz cites Mary Griffith, *Three Hundred Years Hence* (1836) as predicting "curious vehicles that moved by some internal machinery."

4. Stanley K. Schultz, *Constructing Urban Culture*, 22–32 and Rebecca Read Shanor, *The City That Never Was: Two Hundred Years of Fantastic and Fascinating Plans That Might Have Changed the Face of New York City* (New York: Viking, 1988), *passim*. Schultz also describes a second set of utopias that involved self-sufficient rural or small town communes.

5. Bellamy, *Looking Backwards*, 39.

6. Ibid., 107–13, 151; Sylvester Baxter, "Parks and Boulevards in American Cities, Part II," *American Architect* 62 (October 22, 1898), 27.

7. Cynthia Zaitzevsky, *Frederick Law Olmsted and the Boston Park System* (Cambridge: Harvard University Press, 1982), 122. Baxter was a friend of Bellamy's who wrote the introduction to later editions of *Looking Backwards*.

8. On the utopian vision of Lloyd, George, and Bellamy, see John L. Thomas, "Utopians for an Urban Age: Henry George, Henry Demarest Lloyd and Edward Bellamy," *Perspectives in American History* 6 (1972), 135–63.

9. Clarence Stein, "Dinosaur Cities," *Survey* 54, 134–38. Chicago did start construction of Wacker Drive, a double-decker street suggested in the Burnham Plan, by 1916, virtually the only elevated roadway constructed before the late 1920s. See also *New York Times*, May 26, 1911, January 10, 1916, June 12, 1918; "Development of the City," *Municipal Journal and Engineer* (February, 1905), 56–62; "Regulation of Street Traffic," *American City Magazine* 13 (September 1915); "How to Prevent Congestion at Street Crossings," *Municipal Journal and Engineer* 16 (January, 1906), 33; Running highways through buildings presents problems of ventilation, vibration, weight support, and grade level, as well as cost.

10. Harland Bartholomew, *Comprehensive Plan of Newark* (Newark: City Plan Commission, 1915), 44; William Phelps Eno, *The Science of Highway Traffic Regulation* (New York: Brentano's, 1920), 61; Zane Miller, *Boss Cox's Cincinnati* (New York: Oxford University Press, 1968), 219; The Newark plan was one of the first city plans to devote major attention to cars.

11. Shanor, *The City That Never Was* outlines numerous plans. See p. 8 for this proposal. This estimate strikes me as being high. Tens of thousands is more like it. The only elements of this plan ever implemented were southern extensions of Sixth and Ninth Avenues.

12. Ibid., 8–9.

13. Ibid., 12 and 15.

14. Henry Hope Reed, *Central Park: A History and a Guide* (New York: Clarkson N. Potter, 1967), 42–43.

15. Roy Rosenzweig and Elizabeth Blackmar, *The Park and the People, A History of Central Park* (Ithaca: Cornell University Press, 1992), 415.

16. Thomas S. Hines, *Burnham of Chicago: Architect and Planner* (New York: Oxford University Press, 1974), 239–40. Obviously aesthetics also drove Burnham's vision. His city beautiful plans embodied concepts developed earlier for the 1893 World's Fair and the 1901 Washington Plan. Still, plans made after he became a car-owning suburbanite paid much more attention to suburban roads and radial boulevards.

17. Ibid., 351.

18. As quoted in Hines, *Burnham,* 325.

19. Le Corbusier, *The City of Tomorrow,* tr. Frederick Etchells, (Cambridge: MIT Press, 1971 reprint of the 1929 translation of the original, 1924 French edition), 3. Le Corbusier had a profound effect on American urban planning. Some critics have blamed his influence for the development of high-rise public housing, the "vertical slums" that dominated federal housing policy for many years in the mid-twentieth century.

20. Daniel Burnham and Edward Bennett, *Plan of Chicago* (Chicago: Commercial Club of Chicago, 1909), 17–18; Mark Foster, *From Streetcar to Superhighway: American City Planners and Urban Transportation, 1900–1940* (Philadelphia: Temple University Press, 1981), 4.

21. M. Christine Boyer, *Dreaming the Rational City: The Myth of American City Planning* (Cambridge: MIT Press, 1983), 50. Boyer argues that the new planners sought to impose an upper-class sense of order and hegemony on cities.

22. Interview with the author, July 1979.

23. Leonard Walleck, "The Myth of the Master Builder: Robert Moses, New York and the Dynamics of Metropolitan Growth Since World War II," *Journal of Urban History* 17 (August, 1991), 358. Bennett, however, suggested those boulevards not far from the paths of existing rural roads, which in turn had followed Indian paths.

24. This summary is based on my reading of twelve of the pre-1917 plans and summaries of thirteen others that appeared in the engineering or city management press. Herbert Croly, "What is Civic Art?" *Architectural Record* 16 (July 1904), 41–51. Stanley Schultz notes (*Constructing Urban Culture,* 211) that when the emphasis shifted to "The City Efficient" after 1910, the plans became more grounded in reality.

25. Burnham, *Plan of Chicago,* 30.

26. Ironically, they refused to implement the plan when an earthquake destroyed their city within a year of its completion, preferring business as usual under stress.

27. Owen R. Lovejoy, "Making Boston Over," *Survey* 22 (September 4, 1909), 765.

28. Burnham, *Plan of Chicago,* 89.

29. "Street Improvements in Old Cities," *Engineering Record* 16 (October 4, 1905), 420; Preston, *Auto Age Atlanta,* 111; Virgil Bogue, *Plan of Seattle* (Seattle: Seattle Municipal Plan Commission, 1911), 25; Shanor, *The City That Never Was,* 5.

30. Hines, *Burnham,* 331. There were overpasses over both, but at infrequent intervals.

31. Burnham, *Plan of Chicago,* illustrations CIX, CXII, CXV, CXVIII, and CXXVIII. The text has one brief mention of the possibility of putting separate lanes for trolleys on radial avenues, but twice complained that trolleys "seized" streets (pp. 84 and 89).

32. Foster, *From Streetcar to Superhighway,* 42; Hines, *Burnham of Chicago,* 320–24; Mel Scott, *American City Planning* (Berkeley: University of California Press, 1971) 107; Barrett, *The Automobile and Urban Transport,* 73; William Wilson,

The City Beautiful Movement (Baltimore: Johns Hopkins University Press, 1990), 294.

33. Burnham, *Plan of Chicago,* 36 and 42. He also describes them once in a footnote. He extended the planning area for 60 miles because that was the distance that a car could cover in two hours.

34. *Survey,* a periodical devoted to urban reform causes, reported on Boston's city plan in the same issue as Chicago's in Owen R. Lovejoy, "Making Boston Over," *Survey* 22 (September 4, 1909), 764–78. This plan focussed more on traffic issues, because of Boston's archaic colonial street system, waterfront freight congestion, and difficult railway terminal situation. Although its secretary, Sylvester Baxter, was an auto enthusiast, this plan (or at least the summary in the *Survey*) did not mention cars either.

35. William H. Wilson, *The City Beautiful Movement* (Baltimore: Johns Hopkins University Press, 1985), 226.

36. J. Stubben, "Practical and Aesthetic Principles for the Laying Out of Cities," *American Society of Civil Engineers Transactions* 29 (1893), 718–36; "St. Louis Boulevards in the Business District," *Journal of the Association of Engineering Societies* 13 (August 1894), 190; Roderick S. French, "Chevy Chase Village in the Context of the National Suburban Movement, 1870–1900," *Records of the Columbia Historical Society* 49 (1974), 300–29; John Brunner, "The Grant Boulevard, Pittsburgh," *Engineering Record* 45 (January 18, 1902), 55; "Street Traffic in London," *Engineering Record* 16 (August 5, 1905), 138; "Street Improvements in Old Cities," *Engineering Record* 16 (October 14, 1905), 420; "Planning Towns and Cities," *Municipal Journal and Engineer* 22 (March 6, 1907), 224–27; "City Planning and Replanning," *Engineering News* 58 (October 31, 1907).

37. "Goethals to Build Roads," *The Automobile* 26 (April 15, 1917), 683.

38. "Parkways and City Beauty," *Municipal Journal and Engineer* 23 (November 20, 1907), 589. The Concourse's location atop a ridge made these underpasses relatively inexpensive.

39. Andrew W. Crawford, "Proposed Philadelphia Parkways," *Municipal Journal and Engineer* 14 (May 1903), 211–18; Charles Zeublin, *American Municipal Progress* (New York: MacMillan, 1916), 334; Mel Scott, *American City Planning,* 60.

40. Wilson, *The City Beautiful Movement,* 294.

41. George Norton, "The Engineer and City Planning," *American Society of Civil Engineers Transactions* 86 (1923), 1333–37. Norton's ideas overstated this. They involved more than a little of the kind of historical myth-making that all professions engage in.

42. For one exception, see "Roads for Motor Vehicles," *Engineering Record* (January 19, 1907), 58, which predicted 100 mile an hour suburban roads.

43. Quoted in Howard L. Preston, *Automobile Age Atlanta: The Making of a Southern Metropolis, 1900–1935* (Athens: University of Georgia Press, 1979), 30.

44. George Tillson, "The Passing of Cobblestone," *American Society for Municipal Improvements Proceedings,* 10 (1903), 197. Tillson reported that Brooklyn alone employed nearly 2,000 workers to pave over its cobbles. See also "Roads for Motor Vehicles, *Engineering Record* 51 (January 9, 1907), 8; *New York Times,* Jan-

uary 3, 1906; Logan W. Page, "Automobile and Improved Roads," *Scientific American* 109, (September 16, 1913), 178–79; W. A. Howell, "Report of the Committee on Street Paving," *American Society for Municipal Improvements Proceedings* 30 (1920), 145–56; Allan Nevins, *Ford: The Times, The Man, The Company* (New York: Scribner's, 1954), 2, 381.

45. Raymond Parlin, "Preparing for Snowstorms," *American City Magazine* 12 (April, 1915), 21.

46. Frederick Reimer, "Highway Traffic," *American Society for Municipal Improvements Proceedings*, 25 (1915), 556–602.

47. "Report of the Committee on Traffic in Streets," *American Society for Municipal Improvements Proceedings* 21 (1914), 184–92.

48. Hugill, "Good Roads and the Auto," *Geographical Review* 72 (July 1982), 336–40; Blanchard, *American Highway Engineers Handbook* (New York: Wiley, 1919), *passim*.

49. Blanchard, *American Highway Engineer's Handbook*, *passim*; *New York Times*, January 2, 1910; December 12, 1912; April 28, 1918; Oscar Leser, "What the Great Fire Has Accomplished for Baltimore," *Municipal Engineering* 29 (November, 1905) 373; Paul Barrett, *The Automobile and Urban Transit: The Formation of Public Policy in Chicago, 1900–1930* (Philadelphia: Temple University Press, 1983), 71; Robert M. Fogelson, *The Fragmented Metropolis: Los Angeles, 1850–1930* (Cambridge: Harvard University Press, 1967), 251; William M. Kinsey, "Increased Radius of Curbs at Street Corners," *American City Magazine*, 11 (April 1911), 220; Lewis Mumford, *The Highway and The City* (New York: Harcourt, 1963), 178; Christine Meisner Rosen, *Great Fires and the Process of City Growth in America* (New York: Cambridge University Press, 1986), *passim*. Eno, *The Science of Highway Traffic Regulation*, 67 urged the removal of trees. Last year I had students in my history of the automobile course do photographic histories of the main street in their towns or neighborhoods. The students lived primarily in Boston neighborhoods or inner suburbs. In more than two-thirds of the cases, trees disappeared from the side of the road between 1900 and 1920. There might be other reasons for this, such as disease. Cynthia Zaitzevsky notes the destruction of the park strip along the Olmsted-designed Beacon Street in the Boston suburb of Brookline by the end of the 1920s in *Frederick Law Olmsted and the Boston Park System* (Cambridge: Harvard University Press, 1982), 113.

50. "Street Traffic Regulations," *Municipal Journal and Engineer* 23 (November 20, 1907), 577.

51. *New York Times*, March 27, 1913.

52. Shanor, *The City That Never Was*, 117.

53. Hugill, "Good Roads and the Automobile," *passim*; Bruce F. Seely, *Building the American Highway System: Engineers as Policy Makers* (Philadelphia: Temple University Press, 1987), 36. Congress created an Office of Public Roads in 1910 with a vestigial $50,000 budget and only funded the Federal Aid Highway Act of 1916 with a $5,000,000 budget. See Seely, *Building an American Highway System*, 41–44.

54. U.S. Department of Commerce, *A Quarter Century of Financing Municipal Highways, 1937–61* (Washington, D.C.: Government Printing Office, 1961), 3; Hug-

ill, "Good Roads and the Automobile," 339; John C. Burnham, "The Gasoline Tax and the Automobile Revolution," *Mississippi Valley Historical Review* 68 (December 1961), 435–69.

55. *New York Times*, January 31, 1916; February 3 and 7, 1908; Municipal Committee, Cleveland Chamber of Commerce, *Cleveland Pavements* (privately printed pamphlet), 10–12.

56. Theodore White, "The Use of Oil on Macadam Pavements," *Municipal Engineering*, 29 (October 1905) 270–73. For a discussion of road policy at the state level, see Don S. Kirschner, *City and Country: Rural Responses to Urbanization in the 1920s* (Westport, CT.: Greenwood, 1970), 183–200.

57. "Goethals to Build Roads," *The Automobilist* 36 (April 13, 1917), 681.

58. Hugill, "Good Roads and the Automobile," 332–34.

59. As quoted in the *New York Times*, January 12, 1913.

60. Burnham, *Plan of Chicago*, 36–41. Burnham acknowledged that most of the suburban road system he planned already existed.

61. Rock Creek Parkway ran through Washington's most fashionable neighborhoods to the Montgomery County, Maryland, suburbs. However, Congress did not fund completion of the road until the 1935. Isolated by park lands on both sides, this parkway had a more effective design. Evidently Kansas City and Washington were not alone. In 1917 the American Institute of Architects complained that cities were gutting parks to create or widen suburban radials. See William H. Wilson, *The City Beautiful Movement in Kansas City* (Columbia: University of Missouri Press, 1964), 128; Kansas City, Mo. Board of Park Commissioners, *Special Report for the Blue Valley Parkway* (Kansas City, 1912).

62. Fred J. Wagner, "Long Island's Motor Parkway," *House Beautiful* (August, 1914), xiv.

63. Robert Miller, "The Long Island Motor Parkway: Prelude to Robert Moses," in Joanne P. Kreig, ed., *Robert Moses: Single-Minded Genius* (Interlaken, N.Y.: Heart of the Lakes Publishing, 1989), 152–58. Vanderbilt unwisely chose a patented concrete system, which did not last long; so, the Woodward Avenue pavements built in Wayne County outside Detroit became the key technical precedent for concrete roads. The Parkway had limited value as a traffic mover, because it was only 23 feet wide, one lane in each direction. It never made much money because of this. In the 1920s motorists would not pay tolls to suffer the backups inevitable on such a narrow road. Vanderbilt could not condemn land, so his road followed a circuitous route. Robert Moses refused to buy the road from Vanderbilt in the 1930s, saying he would only take it as a gift. His Northern State Parkway parallelled the Vanderbilt and bankrupted it by 1938. Vanderbilt then gave the road to Nassau County, which turned it over to an electric company for a power line right of way. Like the steam cars of the mid-nineteenth century, the road was an example of premature innovation. The Dupont family built a similar private parkway in Delaware.

64. For Olmsted's original plan, see James J. R. Croes, *Report of the Landscape Architect and the Civil Engineer Upon the Laying Out of the Twenty-Third and Twenty-Fourth Wards* (New York, 1876). Gilmore Clark, the construction superin-

tendent for the Bronx River Parkway, reminisced about it in an essay "The Parkway Idea," in W. Brewster Snow, *The Highway and the Landscape* (New Brunswick: Rutgers University Press, 1959), 33–47.

65. Norman T. Newton, *Design on the Land: the Development of Landscape Architecture* (Cambridge: Harvard University Press, 1971), 598–600; "Beauties of Bronx River to be Restored," *New York Times*, September 22, 1912.

66. John Nolen and Henry V. Hubbard, *Parkways and Land Values* (Cambridge, MA., 1937), 72–110.

67. *New York Times*, February, 8 and 15, March 7, April 13, May 14, September 17 and December 30, 1922.

68. "News of the Municipalities," *Municipal Journal and Engineer* 23 (July 24, 1907), 110.

69. Jay Downer, "Parkways and Superhighways," *American Society for Municipal Improvements* 36 (1930), 49–52; Gilmore Clark, "Our Highway Problem," *American Magazine of Art* 25 (November, 1932), 285–90.

70. Leonard Walleck, "The Myth of the Master Builder: Robert Moses, New York and the Dynamics of Metropolitan Development Since World War II," *Journal of Urban History* 17 (August 1991), 339–62; Robert A. Caro, *The Power Broker, Robert Moses and the Fall of New York* (New York: Vintage, 1975), 168, 318; William A. Proctor, "Problems Involved in the Planning and Development of Through Traffic Highways," (M.A. Thesis, Stanford University, 1939), 222–31, 305. The Proctor thesis is still the best work on the evolution of American highway design between the two world wars.

71. Ironically, Olmsted designed Beacon Street, but the park strip was gutted twice, once in the 1890s for a trolley line, once in the 1920s to allow parking.

72. A few of the post-1915 plans suggested that residential streets in new suburban plats have only twenty foot widths, with the idea that narrowness would keep through traffic off them. This had some impact. Many 1920s subdivisions had streets narrower than their 1890s predecessors. See Louis A. Dumand, *A Brief List of Suggestions to Public Improvement Associations from the Committee on Downtown Streets of the Chicago Association of Commerce* (pamphlet at the Library of Congress, no date, c. 1915); Harland Bartholomew and Thomas Adams, "City Planning as Related to Public Safety," *National Safety Council Proceedings* (1918), 360.

73. Stoyan Tsanoff, "Children's Playgrounds," *Municipal Affairs* II (June, 1898), 294.

74. Cary Goodman, *Choosing Sides: Playground and Street Life on the Lower East Side* (New York: Schocken Books, 1979), *passim*.

75. Arthur Woods, "Keeping City Traffic Moving," *World's Work*, 31 (April, 1916), 632.

76. *New York Times*, August 7, 1908; *New York Times*, May 10, 1909; Thomas Adams and Harlan Bartholomew, "City Planning and Public Safety," *Engineering News-Record* (September 26, 1918); Seymour Toll, *Zoned American* (New York: Grossman, 1969), 123–55.

77. Charles Beard, *American City Government* (London: T. Fisher Unwin, 1913), 243–44, 334–38 and 372–76.

78. Delos Wilcox, *The American City: A Problem in Democracy* (New York: MacMillan, 1904), 28–31, 42–43, 136–37; Charles Zeublin, *American Municipal Progress* (New York: MacMillan, 1916), 21–54, 141–43, 336, 398.

79. Edith Abbott, *The Tenements of Chicago,* 1908–1935 (Chicago: University of Chicago Press, 1936), 478.

80. Frederick C. Howe, *The City the Hope of Democracy* (Seattle: Univerity of Washington Press, 1905; reprint, 1967), 203–205.

81. Edward Bennett, *Plan of Minneapolis* (Minneapolis: the Civic Commission, 1917), 108.

82. A. F. Weber, "Suburban Annexations," *North American Review* 166 (May 1898), 616. See also Adna Ferrin Weber, *The Growth of Cities in the Nineteenth Century* (Ithaca: Cornell University Press, 1967 reprint of the original 1899 edition), 458–75.

83. Richard Wade, "Urbanization" in C. Van Woodward, ed. *The Comparative Approach to American History* (New York: Basic Books Inc., 1968), 97–99.

84. Sinclair Lewis, *Babbitt* (New York, 1920), 11.

INDEX

Designer:	Dan Zedek
Text:	Fairfield Medium
Compositor:	Impressions, *a division of* Edwards Brothers
Printer:	Edwards Brothers
Binder:	Edwards Brothers